Revival

A PEOPLE SATURATED WITH GOD

Brian H. Edwards

DayOne

ISBN 978-1-84625-643-1

British Library Cataloguing in Publication Data available

Published by Day One Publications
Ryelands Road, Leominster, HR6 8NZ
Telephone 01568 613 740
Toll Free 888 329 6630 (North Americal)
email—sales@dayone.co.uk
web site—www.dayone.co.uk

Cover design by Kathryn Chedgzoy

Printed by 4edge Limited

This is a companion volume with
Praying for Revival

This book is dedicated to a generation of young preachers and pastors who may know little of the story of revival but who long for the presence of God in their ministry

'LORD, I have heard of your fame;
   I stand in awe of your deeds, O LORD.
Renew them in our day,
   in our time make them known;
   in wrath remember mercy'

(Habakkuk 3:2)

Contents

Foreword

I and many of my peers are the intended audience for this book. We have never experienced revival in the church and have been neglectful of the history of revival. We have even been suspicious of the subject because all too often we have encountered the twin failings of spurious revivalism or an obsession with revival that despairs of the value of the ordinary regular ministry of the church. However, we feel deeply the desperate spiritual state of our nation and our own inadequacy; we long for a more powerful work of God that will honour his name and see multitudes converted to Christ.

Brian Edwards has written a thrilling account of God's special work in revival over many centuries and in numerous places. He is a wise guide to interpreting these events, helpfully bringing together the common factors in genuine revivals, stressing the sovereignty of God in revival, and critiquing some of the excesses that may accompany it.

I would encourage everyone to read this book. It will challenge and inspire us to a renewed passion for God, prayer, holiness and urgent evangelism. It will also help us to maintain a correct biblical balance between the regular life and ministry of the church and the desire for God to do more. It will also stir our hearts to long for more of the felt presence of God.

Above all I pray that it will guard us against spiritual complacency or fatalism, and lead to a renewed hunger for a truly powerful gospel-centred work of God in our nation.

John Stevens

National Director,

The Fellowship of Independent Evangelical Churches

July 2019

1. Setting the scene

Howell Harris gave an account of the preaching of Daniel Rowland in Wales during March 1743: 'O such power as generally attends the labours of brother Rowland, in particular, is indeed uncommon and almost incredible until one sees it himself. Their singing and praying is indeed full of God! O how did my soul burn with sacred love when I was among them! They fall almost as dead by the power of the Word, and continue weeping for joy, having found the Messiah; some mourning under a sense of their vileness, and some in the pangs of the new birth! I am now in Pembrokeshire where Rowland has been preaching; he has been wonderfully attended with blessings in these borders also. The power at the conclusion of his sermons, was such that multitudes continued weeping and crying out for the Saviour and could not possibly forbear.'[1]

In 1858 John Girardeau was leading an evening service at his church in Charleston, North Carolina, when 'He received a sensation as if a bolt of electricity had struck his head and diffused itself through his whole body. For a little while he stood speechless under the strange physical feeling. Then he said: "The Holy Spirit has come; we will begin preaching tomorrow evening." He closed the service with a hymn, dismissed the congregation, and came down from the pulpit; but no one left the house. The whole congregation had quietly resumed its seat.... The Holy Spirit had not only come to him, He had also taken possession of the hearts of the people. Immediately Girardeau began exhorting them to accept the Gospel. They began to sob, softly, like the falling of rain; then, with deeper emotion, to weep bitterly, or to rejoice loudly, according to their

1 Evans, *Howell Harris Evangelist*, p.34.

circumstances. It was midnight before he could dismiss his congregation. A noted evangelist from the North, who was present, said, between his sobs, to an officer of the church: "I never saw it on this fashion." The meeting went on night and day for eight weeks.'[2]

During 1905 John Kemp, the pastor of Charlotte Chapel in Edinburgh, visited Wales and when he related the story of God's great work there to his own congregation, a movement of the Spirit began at the chapel. The following year a fresh wave of new life came to the church: 'It was at a late prayer meeting, held in the evening at 9.30, that the fire of God fell. There was nothing, humanly speaking, to account for what happened. Quite suddenly, upon one and another came an overwhelming sense of the reality and awesomeness of His presence and of eternal things. Life, death, and eternity seemed suddenly laid bare. Prayer and weeping began and gained in intensity every moment. As on the day of laying the foundation of the second temple, "the people could not discern the noise of the shouts of joy from the noise of the weeping of the people" (Ezra 3:13). One was overwhelmed before the sudden bursting of the bounds. Could it be real? We looked up and asked for clear directions, and all we knew of guidance was, "Do nothing." Friends who were gathered sang on their knees. Each seemed to sing, and each seemed to pray, oblivious of one another. Then the prayer broke out again, waves and waves of prayer; and the midnight hour was reached. The hours had passed like minutes. It is useless being a spectator looking on, or praying for it, in order to catch its spirit and breath. It is necessary to be in it, praying in it, part of it, caught by the same power, swept by the same wind. One who was present says: "I cannot tell you what Christ was to me last night. My heart was full to overflowing. If ever my Lord was near to me, it was last night.'[3]

A similar description is found of a church meeting in Malawi in 1910: 'An elder began to pray, confessing before all the sin of having cherished

2 Lacy, *Revivals in the Midst of the Years*, pp. 112–14.
3 Kemp, *Joseph W. Kemp*, pp. 32–33.

a spirit of revenge for an evil done him. Then another began to pray, and another and another, till two or three were praying together in a quiet voice, weeping and confessing, each one unconscious of the other. Suddenly there came the sound of "a rushing wind". It was the thrilling sound of two thousand five hundred people praying audibly, no man apparently conscious of the other. I could think of no better image to describe the noise than the rushing of wind through the trees. We were listening to the same sound as filled that upper room at Pentecost. Not noisy or discordant, it filled us with a great awe.'[4]

Duncan Campbell described a meeting in the Isle of Lewis, Scotland, during 1949: 'The lad rose to his feet and in his prayer made reference to the fourth chapter of Revelation, which he had been reading that morning: "O God, I seem to be gazing through the open door. I see the Lamb in the midst of the Throne, with the keys of death and of hell at his girdle." He began to sob; then lifting his eyes toward heaven, cried: "O God, there is power there, let it loose!" With the force of a hurricane the Spirit of God swept into the building and the floodgates of heaven opened. The church resembled a battlefield. On one side many were prostrated over the seats weeping and sighing; on the other side some were affected by throwing their arms in the air in a rigid posture. God had come.'[5]

Wales, North Carolina, Malawi, Scotland from 1743 to 1949—a common theme runs through each account. Here is something unusual and powerful; it is God at work, but not in his normal way. Here are outpourings of the Holy Spirit that cannot be dismissed by talk of culture, psychological pressure or empty enthusiasm. We are reading the serious yet exciting stories of God in revival when the only response possible is an awesome: 'God has come.'

---

4 Orr, *The Flaming Tongue*, p. 125.

5 Woolsey, *Duncan Campbell*, pp. 134–5.

2. Why this book?

A book may be judged by its intention. The intention of this book, and its companion volume *Praying for Revival*, is the creation of a sound biblical and historical understanding of revival, a heart-longing for God to come in our day, and serious prayer to this end. The Bible is only the framework here. A study of the biblical ground for believing in revival through the Old and New Testaments is covered in *Praying for Revival.*

In the mid twentieth century, prayer and talk amongst evangelicals on the subject of revival was commonplace. That is no longer true. A great deal of noise and excitement without much light, extinguished an understanding of true revival. A canny Highlander once expressed himself in prayer: 'Lord it must hae grieved yer hairt tae see sae much o' the steam blowin' oot thro' the whistle that should hae gang tae the piston.' On the other hand, there has been a sterile correctness in the assumption that all the church must do is preach the true gospel and the rest would follow. Over the past half century and more, for all our hard work as evangelical Christians, we have made little impact upon our nation—whichever side of the Atlantic we occupy.

Our 'free' nations have reached a low ebb spiritually and therefore morally. Christianity is despised and ridiculed. But there is nothing new about this. The eighteenth century was, if possible, worse. Joseph Carlyle described that century: 'Soul extinct, stomach well alive.' Writing in 1736, Bishop Joseph Butler lamented:

'It is come, I know not how, to be taken for granted, by many persons, that Christianity is not so much as a subject of inquiry; but that it is discovered to be fictitious. And accordingly they treat it, as if, in the present age, this were an agreed point among all people of discernment; and nothing remained, but to set it up as a principal subject of mirth and ridicule, as it were by way of reprisals, for its having so long interrupted the pleasures of the world.'[1]

Modernise the English and that would be a perfect description of the Western world in the twenty-first century.

Even where numbers are increasing, we have little cause for satisfaction. We are hardly reducing the multi-millions who are careless of God, and the spiritual life of our churches is revealed in the sparse attendance at our prayer meetings. The quality of our righteousness is rarely an embarrassment to the world. We have some large Sunday morning congregations dotted around the country where many sit gazing round the hundreds and conclude that Christianity is doing well. But let them slip out into the sunshine where the congregation will look far less impressive in the light of the crowded playing fields and the thousands of families crawling round the Motorway or Freeway, in search of their chosen exit to a day's happiness.

Another escape route has been to immerse ourselves in the social needs of the nation. Our care for issues of debt, poverty, homelessness, abortion, addiction, slavery and much else is to be commended, but the danger is that these things can keep us busily away from the real issue of seeking God. We can sit comfortably that evangelicals are—where they have always been—at the sharp end of social care; but how much evangelical social involvement is a cover for our failure to prepare a fallen society for the world to come?

Enter the world of marketing and management. Christian leaders are badgered by books and conferences that will help them to increase their leadership skills, their management control and the size of

1 Joseph Butler, *The Analogy of Religion, Natural and Revealed, to the Constitution and course of Nature*, London 1736, preface.

their churches. Not all of this is wrong—in fact it will almost always guarantee some degree of growth—but still we are avoiding the real issue: Where is God?

For all our excessive noise, extravagant claims and efficient administration, the world around us is hardly aware that we exist. God is not felt among his people. And often we don't care. Even some who do care have come to the despondent conclusion that nothing can change; these are days of hard work and small returns, and there we must let the matter rest.

The estimate that just three percent of the population in the UK are evangelical Christians is naively optimistic.[2] It is hard to discover the workshop, office, classroom, college, or street where three out of every hundred are evangelical Christians. If such a figure is accurate, then most evangelical Christians are unrecognizable during the week and keep out of the way of Christian fellowship on Sunday.

However, this book is not written to depress the discouraged. On the contrary, it is written for those who are honest enough, whatever their evangelical label, to admit that we are making little impact on our nation and that God is not seen and felt to be among us. When the psalmist realized this and faced reality, he decided upon a definite course of action; he looked back to what God had done in the past:

'I thought about the former days, the years of long ago;
I remembered my songs in the night.
My heart mused and my spirit enquired …
Then I thought, "To this I will appeal:
the years of the right hand of the Most High."
I will remember the deeds of the LORD;

2 By contrast, see page 237 for the figures for religion In England and Wales in the 1851 religious census.

yes, I will remember your miracles of long ago.
I will meditate on all your works
and consider all your mighty deeds'
(Psalm 77:5–6, 10–12).

With that biblical precedent, the plan of this book is simple. From Scripture and history it will introduce revival to those who may never have read much on the subject. This is not a classic analysis of revival. That has been ably done, from the many detailed accounts available, to the wide sweeps of John Gillies' *Historical Collections of Accounts of Revival* (1754) and William Sprague's *Lectures on Revivals of Religion* (1832). There are modern assessments by Edwin Orr, who stands unequalled in the vast treasure he has left us of what God has been doing in the world, the heart-cry of Martyn Lloyd-Jones in the book of his sermons on *Revival*, and the challenge of Arthur Wallis *In the Day of Thy Power*.

However, few Christians have read even one small book on the subject of revival, and that *must* be changed if God is to hear a cry for him to revive his people. Revival is contagious: the story of a revival there often excites people to long for it here. But a contagion does not spread without contact. This book will help the reader 'touch' the heart of true revival. It will be impossible to refer to all the accounts of revival in the history of the church—even if anyone knew them all. We must be content to be introduced to the broad canvas of revival, from the well-known and well-documented eighteenth century 'Awakening' to those little-known and more localized events that are none the less real.

> Revival is contagious: the story of a revival there often excites people to long for it here. But a contagion does not spread without contact

Revivals widely separated from each other historically, geographically and culturally have been chosen. The same revivals are referred to again and again to illustrate certain features common to them all.

An essential qualification

Nothing written in this study of revival is intended to decry, belittle or dismantle our present-day church planting, restoring, training and equipping. The days in which we live in the twenty-first century are hard for congregations in the free nations because of a brain-washed apathy and unbelief in society, and harder for congregations in repressive nations because of violent persecution. In each case it is right that we work diligently and efficiently to win people to Jesus Christ as Saviour and Lord and to grow churches through this. Our preaching, apologetics, and all else must continue. We thank God for the growth of many churches, the planting of new ones and the restoring of old ones. Without this essential qualification you will misjudge the purpose of this book.

The awesome presence of God is rarely experienced. We return home still out of touch with heaven

However, we are all aware that too often our Christian congregations show little response apart from appreciating a 'good sermon' when they hear one. Lives are generally not changed, sinners are rarely converted. Today, we sing our hymns and songs (old and new) with an accompanying band (good and bad) and sometimes 'enjoy' our worship, but the awesome presence of God is rarely experienced. We return home still out of touch with heaven.

In 1910, Jonathan Goforth, who was greatly used by God in revival across China, returned from the Missionary Conference in Edinburgh deeply saddened. Hundreds of mission leaders from all over the world had gathered and fine sermons had been preached but: 'Of the many who addressed that great missionary gathering, not more than three emphasised God the Holy Spirit as the one essential factor in world evangelisation … one could not help but conclude that the giving of the Gospel to lost mankind was largely a matter of better organization, better equipment, more men and women … The dethronement of the idol of ecclesiastical self-sufficiency was apparently too great a price to pay.'[3] Is this something for our evangelical churches to hear? Have we, as Duncan Campbell once wrote, 'been outmanoeuvred by the strategy of hell, because we have tried to meet the enemy on human levels by human strategy?'[4]

Is it that vital missing factor of the presence of God by his Holy Spirit in transforming power that we most urgently need? With that, all our preparation and programmes will be charged with a new dynamic leading to radically changed lives among Christians and unbelievers alike.

A brief history of revival

Unfortunately, the published accounts of revival rarely begin much before the eighteenth century. This gives a distorted view of the history of the church. A movement of God in the fourteenth century ran through to the seventeenth. Those three hundred years were the most dramatic in the history of Europe. They marked a widespread return to New Testament Christianity and the authority of Scripture which we refer to as the 'Reformation'. A reformation is only different from revival if it is imposed by the 'authorities', in which case it is not a 'people's movement'. The Reformation of the sixteenth century, and its prelude, was a people's movement.

Europe was stirred even before the Reformation. In the twelfth century, Peter Waldo of Lyons sent out his preachers across France, Flanders, Germany, Poland, Bohemia, Austria and Hungary. As a result of this

3 Goforth, *By My Spirit*, pp. 188–9.
4 Wallis, *In the Day of Thy Power*, Foreword.

gospel preaching, the Waldensians—a people in the Piedmont valleys whose history and faith precedes Waldo and reaches to apostolic days—spread at such a rate that they covered vast areas of the continent. Two by two the preachers travelled central and eastern Europe and then beyond, until hundreds of thousands shifted their allegiance from the formal and secular church of the day to Christ himself. So far-flung was the Waldensian movement that it is said the missionaries could travel from Cologne in Germany to Florence in Italy, a distance of nearly six hundred miles as the crow flies, and stay every night at the home of one of the brethren.[5] One historian has called the sending out of these 'Poor men of Lyons', 'the most remarkable missionary movement that has ever occurred'. By 1592, when Henry IV of France made a treaty with the churches in the Piedmont valleys, it was claimed that the Protestants outnumbered the Catholics in the proportion of one hundred to one. That must be called revival. But how many Christians today have heard of it?

In England at the end of the fourteenth century, John Wycliffe led a team of Bible translators. The resulting 'Poor Preachers', or Lollards, went throughout the country with their handwritten copies of the Bible in English. So successful were they that over a century later a chronicler was compelled to admit: 'They everywhere filled the kingdom; so that a man could scarcely meet two men on the road but one of them was a disciple of Wycliffe.' Allowing for some exaggeration, this complaint reveals a revival of true Christianity among the people.

The eager hands that received William Tyndale's printed New Testament in English in 1526 were part of a new wave of revival. Over the next ten years the Bible in English, at that time a book outlawed by the Catholic authorities, was smuggled across the country and distributed by the thousands. In 1537 even King Henry VIII, having filled his prisons with evangelicals, despaired of stemming the tide and gave the Bible his

5 Baird, *Protestantism in Italy & the Waldenses*, p.274.

royal licence. The following year he ordered 'the whole Bible of the largest volume in English' to be placed in every parish church in the land.

If we had more detailed records it might be found that the revival during the early part of the Reformation was even greater than the 'Great Awakening' three hundred years later. The contemporary records of the early Reformation period are almost entirely official documents and the writings of leaders. What we do not have is the account of the movement of the Spirit in the lives of tens of thousands of ordinary men and women. Few of these could write, and the age when everyone kept a diary was two hundred years away. For this reason, the heartbeat of revival is largely missing.

To think of the Reformation only as a reformation of theology is a great mistake. All over Europe God was stirring the people, and vast numbers were brought to a joyful salvation. Men like John Wycliffe, and later Hugh Latimer, in England, Jan Hus in Bohemia (Czechoslovakia), Gerhard Groote in Holland and Martin Luther in Germany were undoubtedly leaders of revival among the people. In the long history of the church, revival is not as rare as we may imagine, and the vantage-point of eternity will show that there has never been a time in the story of the church when, somewhere, God has not been powerfully at work by his Spirit in a supernormal way. However, because the detail is missing, most of our illustrations have to be confined to the past few centuries.

It is a mistake, therefore, to think of revival only terms of the well recorded events of the eighteenth to twentieth centuries. However, across Britain and North America, these centuries saw significant periods of an outpouring of the Spirit. What is known as the First Awakening began on both sides of the Atlantic in the early 1700s with Jonathan Edwards, George Whitefield and John Wesley, to name only three of scores. A Second Awakening commenced in the mid-nineteenth century, and the year 1859 is known as a revival year. However, this is misleading because throughout the first 30 years of the nineteenth century there were many revivals in localities across Britain and America; some of the most powerful evidences of the Spirit at work were in Cornwall early in the century where church growth was phenomenal. Perhaps the most influential revival in history commenced in Wales in 1904 and spread throughout the foreign mission field as we shall see later.

However, the story of revival is endless, and many have doubtless never been recorded. Of those that are on record, some were brief and local, yet vital in the life of the community. Examples of this are on Skye, Scotland (1812–14), at Mousehole in Cornwall (1818), Eden Valley in Cumbria among the Irish navvies (1860/61), Guernsey, a Channel Island (1881), Llanfairfechan Quarry in Wales (1904/05),and Elcho Island among the aboriginal people of Australia (1979).

In the early 1960s, revival was very much on the prayer agenda of evangelical Christians. However, this coincided with the growth of the Charismatic Movement and an understanding of true revival was lost in a mixture of spurious and genuine claims of renewal. Consequently, a whole generation, or more, are now strangers to the subject of revival, and therefore they cannot be expected to pray for it. If, at the close of this book, we are a little more knowledgeable about the subject, and a little wiser about what we are asking for, and what dangers we should be on guard against, then a small part of its purpose will have been served. On the other hand, if it awakens a dissatisfaction with where we are and creates a longing for God to come and be honoured in revival, then the intention will have been adequately fulfilled.

'Restore us again, O God our Saviour,
and put away your displeasure towards us.
Will you be angry with us for ever?
Will you prolong your anger through all generations?
Will you not revive us again,
that your people may rejoice in you?

Show us your unfailing love, O LORD,
and grant us your salvation'
(Psalm 85:4–7).

From chapter 4 on, one great story of revival in the Bible has been chosen and its themes illustrated by cameos from history. In this way we can admire both the detail and the panorama at once. In three main sections we will look at the events *before* revival, *during* revival, and the immediate and lasting results *after* revival. This book breaks no new ground; it reaps from the fields of others.

However, there is one significant limitation to any record of revival. A correspondent from the Khassi Hills in India in 1905 commented, 'The great things of the Revival cannot be recorded, men can only describe the commonplace events. It is necessary to come into touch with the Spirit's power in order to see and feel what the work is; many scenes are too holy, too sacred to be described, and yet God wants us to make known His power, and so glorify His name. Those who write, do so in the hope that even an imperfect account may be blessed by God to rouse the interest and expectations of men and get them to feel their need of, and to plead for, a similar blessing.'[6]

6 Jones, *India Awake*, p. 24.

3. What is revival?

Edwin Orr, one of the greatest authorities on the subject of revival, reported on two churches in a town in America both advertising revival meetings. One displayed a board: 'Revival here every Monday night.' The other promised, 'Revival here every night except Monday.' That humorously illustrates how loosely the word has been used.

For some, 'revival' is a synonym for 'mission' or 'campaign'. It is something a church arranges, and God may or may not bless. Others have confused 'revival' with words like 'renewal' and 'restoration'. Unless we are careful in our definitions, effective communication becomes impossible. Revival is something far bigger than missions or renewal. Revival swallows up all other words as the shark swallows the shrimp.

Almost as soon as we try to *define* the word revival, we find ourselves *describing* what a revival is. This at least shows that revival is not simply a theological concept for academics and historians to discuss. Revival is intensely practical; it always has huge results for the church. Duncan Campbell, who was himself involved in revival in the middle of the twentieth century, defined it as 'a community saturated with God.'[1] It is doubtful that we shall ever get closer to the heart of revival than that. He described revival as he witnessed it in the Western Isles of Scotland between 1949 and 1952:

'In writing of the movement, I would like first to state what I mean by revival as witnessed in the Hebrides ... The road and hill-side become sacred spots to many when the winds of God blow. Revival is a going of God among his people, and

1 Campbell, *The Price and Power of Revival*. On three occasions in this book he uses the phrase: 'saturated with God'.

an awareness of God laying hold of the community ... In a successful campaign we may see many brought to a saving knowledge of the truth, and the church or mission experience a time of quickening, but so far as the town or district is concerned no real change is visible; the world goes on its way ... but in revival the fear of God lays hold upon the community, moving men and women, who until then had no concern for spiritual things, to seek after God.'[2]

Charles Haddon Spurgeon experienced continuous revival in his church in London for many years in the middle of the nineteenth century and he was correct in his general conclusion that, as he explained in 1866 in his magazine *The Sword and the Trowel*: 'To be revived is a blessing which can only be enjoyed by those who have some degree of life. Those who have no spiritual life are not, and cannot be, in the strictest sense of the term subjects of a revival ... A true revival is to be looked for in the Church of God.'[3]

Similarly, preaching at the Keswick Convention in 1922, Douglas Brown, who was used in a revival the year before, maintained, 'Revival is a church word; it has to do with God's people. You cannot revive the world; the world is dead in trespasses and sins; you cannot revive a corpse. But you can revitalize where there is life...'[4]

Evan Roberts had made the same claim in Wales in 1904: 'My mission is first to the churches. When the churches are aroused to their duty, men of the world will be swept into the Kingdom. A whole church on its knees is irresistible.'[5] Rhys Bevan Jones, who preached in Wales throughout 1904, declared that if ever there was a slogan for revival it was this: 'Bend the church, and save the people.'[6]

2 Campbell, *The Lewis Awakening*, pp. 14–15.
3 Hayden, *Spurgeon on Revival*, p. 59.
4 Brown, *Revival Addresses*, p. 77.
5 Jones, *Rent Heavens*, p. 55.
6 As above, p. 56.

Whilst this is generally true, there are occasions when the Spirit has begun a powerful work in the unbelieving world first. The Acts of the Apostles is only one example of this. It is pointless to quibble over whether or not this is revival. If our fundamental definition is a people saturated with God, then it is no matter in what community it begins.

However, for our purpose, we can accept that true revival almost always begins with those who are believers in New Testament Christianity and, as Edwin Orr wisely reminds us, 'more particularly those who had enjoyed the New Testament experience of conversion and regeneration'.[7] Revival is therefore an evangelical experience; it is an 'evangelical awakening'. But it never remains tucked safely within the evangelical community. Sooner or later, to a greater or lesser extent, revival spills over. As an illustration that the Spirit is not tied to the church, Duncan Campbell described occasions on Lewis in the 1950s when: 'The *community becomes saturated with God*, so that many of those who find the Saviour come into saving relationship with Him before they come near any Church or place of meeting'.[8]

The hallmarks of revival

Revival is a sovereign work of God's Holy Spirit in an unusual awakening of spiritual life among God's people. This is accompanied by:

an awesome awareness of God
a deep conviction of sin
a longing for holiness of life
a renewed joy and love for the Father and the Son
a passion to reach the lost

It generally leads to a significant number of the lost coming to a true faith in Christ.

7 Orr, *The Eager Feet*, p. 142.
8 Campbell, 'The Price and Power of Revival'.

In this we have both the *definition* and the *description* of revival.

However, within the boundaries of these 'hallmarks' no two revivals are identical; one can be radically different from another. This is illustrated in nineteenth century America. The Cane Ridge revival of 1801 was a 'Camp Meeting'. These were always boisterous meetings, but this year was exceptional. It is described as a time of noise and confusion at which one observer noticed seven preachers addressing different sections of the crowd; hundreds were crying out in repentance and scores were falling down as if shot by cannon. By contrast, half a century later, the Prayer Revival that began in Fulton Street New York in 1857 continued well into the following years and was marked by no noise or confusion; the prayer meetings across the country were described as 'still, solemn, aweful'. These meetings simply 'rolled like a wave over the whole country' and, quietly and in calm order, an estimated one million came to Christ. What no one can doubt is that both revivals had a transforming impact on society.

Revival is something that *God* brings about. It is impossible for the church to create true revival. Though we may prepare and pray for it, revival is the work of the sovereign God; not primarily for the benefit of his people, but for his own honour and glory. Commenting upon Acts 2:1, 'When the day of Pentecost came,' Arthur Wallis claims: 'Every genuine revival is clearly stamped with the hallmark of divine sovereignty, and in no way is this more clearly seen than in the time factor. The moment for that first outpouring of the Spirit was not determined by the believers in the upper room but by God, who had foreshadowed it centuries before in those wonderful types of the Old Testament.'[9] For this reason, revival often takes God's people by surprise; God gives no prewarning. What happened in the time of Hezekiah in the Old Testament was 'done so quickly' (2 Chronicles 29:36), and the same was true 700 years later when, on the day of Pentecost, 'Suddenly a sound like the blowing of a violent

9 Wallis, *In the Day of Thy Power*, p.57.

wind came from heaven and filled the whole house...' (Acts 2:2). No matter how long people have been praying for it or expecting it, when it comes it is always a surprise.

When God came to the north of Korea in January 1907 it was on the Monday following a particularly formal and weary Sunday; the missionaries and national Christians longed for revival, but it hardly seemed that this would or could be the time.[10] At Broughshane, a village four miles from Ballymena in Northern Ireland, it was May 1859 when revival began, and the Presbyterian minister in the village, Archibald Robinson, records, 'We had been praying for and expecting some such precious blessing, but were taken by surprise, so sudden, powerful, and extraordinary were the manifestations of the Spirit's presence.'[11] When revival came to the Republic of Moldova in Eastern Europe in 1988, Christians had been praying and fasting for a month for freedom of faith and Christian prisoners to be released. One month later both happened as Gorbachev relaxed restrictions across the Soviet Union. But the Christians were not expecting revival which came 'suddenly and unexpectedly ... it all happened so spontaneously.'[12]

In one of his most impassioned sermons, Spurgeon was pleading for an expectation of revival: 'The old-stagers in our churches believe that things must grow, gently, by degrees; we must go step by step onward. Concentrated action and continued labour, they say, will ultimately bring success. But the marvel is, all God's works have been sudden. When Peter stood up to preach, it did not take six weeks to convert the three thousand...'[13]

In addition to this suddenness, meetings are lengthened, crowds gather, and sermons have to be preached; not because it is all arranged in advance,

---

10 Blair & Hunt, *The Korean Pentecost*, pp. 70–71.
11 Paisley, *The Fifty-Nine Revival*, p. 38.
12 Wise, *Celestial Fire*, pp. 61, 123.
13 *The Story of God's Mighty Acts*, a sermon preached by Spurgeon, 17 July 1859.

but because God is at work. People will arrive without warning for a meeting, moved by an unseen hand. Isaiah described such a time when God did 'awesome things that we did not expect, you came down and the mountains trembled before you' (Isaiah 64:3). In revival God takes over; it is his sovereign work. At Herrnhut in 1727, Count Nikolaus of Zinzendorf acknowledged, 'Hitherto we had been the leaders and helpers. Now the Holy Spirit himself took full control of everything and everybody.'[14] Revivals are never publicized in advance; they cannot be, because God chooses the time.

Surprisingly, there is little that is new in revival. All the elements we discover in revival, whether in the Bible or in the story of the church, are present in the normal life of the church. However, in revival they are heightened and intensified. There are phenomena in revival, as we will see, but these are few and should be considered incidental. The main difference between the normal life of the church and revival is that in revival the old things have new life. The church should always pray, preach and evangelize, Christians should always long for holiness. It ceases to be the church without these. What is new is the *way* the Christians pray and preach, seek after holiness and forgiveness and witness to their faith. In revival there is remarkable life and power that cannot be explained adequately in any human terms. Christians do everything at a different level in revival.

We cannot manufacture revival any more than a schoolboy can make a masterpiece by copying a Constable

We cannot manufacture revival any more than a schoolboy can make a masterpiece by copying a Constable. When a revival begins to fade, there is a temptation to stir up enthusiasm and keep it going; we try to relight

14 Davies, *The Moravian Revival*, p.7.

the fire ourselves. On the other hand, some are content to let the fire go out and settle down for the long wait before the next spontaneous ignition. Both are contrary to Scripture; revival is something God brings about, but we do have a part in that. Prayer is where our part begins.

The American evangelist in the nineteenth century, Charles Finney, firmly believed that revivals could be produced by following a set of rules.[15] He followed his own rules and was undoubtedly used by God and many lives were changed. Jonathan Goforth, used powerfully by God in China in the early twentieth century, followed Finney in believing that 'God's revival may be had when we will and where we will.'[16] That story by Edwin Orr of the two church notice-boards sums up the efforts of men. We may not agree with the theology of Finney and Goforth, but we cannot deny that God used them. Perhaps God is saying to the church today: 'You do not have, because you do not ask' (James 4:2). And we will never seriously ask for revival unless we know what it is.

Some things are essential if we are to demonstrate our seriousness for God. There are preparations that we can make, but we must be careful to distinguish between the things that are essential in our preparation for revival, and the things that almost always accompany revival. Lloyd-Jones made the same point when he referred to the characteristics of revival preparation: 'This is no time for singing, it is time for thinking, for preaching, for conviction. It is a time for proclaiming the message of God and his wrath upon evil, and all our foolish aberrations. The time for singing will come later. Let the great revival come, let the windows of heaven be opened, let us see men and women by the thousands brought into the Kingdom of God, and then it will be time to sing.'[17]

---

15 See the companion volume to this: *Praying for Revival*, for a critique of Charles Finney's theology of revival.

16 Goforth, *By My Spirit*, p. 180.

17 Lloyd-Jones, *Revival—Can we make it happen?*, p. 63.

Petrus Octavianus, from the Indonesian Missionary Fellowship, who was significantly used by God in the revival in Borneo in 1973, did not preach an easy message. It was claimed that he had no time for frills or gimmicks, and he made it clear that 'Revivals do not begin happily with everyone having a good time. They start with a broken and contrite heart.' One contemporary report reminded its readers that the church in Borneo did not need 'an upsurge of bright gatherings or an emotional binge, but repentance, confession and the forsaking of sin'.[18]

This subject is a serious one. It may be the most serious that any Christian could be reading about in these days. There is something that God can do which few of us have ever seen. We may have felt his touch and experienced a little of his presence, but there is more—much more. Nothing should fully satisfy us on earth until our community is 'saturated with God.'

18 Lees, *Drunk Before Dawn*, pp. 182–183,33.

4. Before revival

The state of the church and the nation

What happened in the time of King Hezekiah in Judah, seven hundred years before Pentecost, will be the biblical framework for this book. There can be no doubt that this was a powerful work of God's Spirit and it bears all the hallmarks of revival noted earlier.[1] Hezekiah's story is well told in three places in the Old Testament: 2 Kings 18–20; 2 Chronicles 29–32 and Isaiah 36–39. He is introduced as a young man of twenty-five around the year 716 BC. We know nothing about his earlier years except that his father was Ahaz and his mother was Abijah, but we do know the life of his father Ahaz, because it is well recorded for us. He was a godless man and so was the age in which he lived; this is clear from 2 Chronicles 28:1–4, 22–27. Hezekiah inherited this steady decline in the nation spiritually and morally. The temple was closed, true worship was ended and the greatest sins that could be committed by Judah were being committed, including the sacrifice of some of Hezekiah's brothers to the god Moloch. As a result, Judah had suffered humiliating defeats by Syria (Aram), Israel, Edom and the Philistines. The fortunes of Judah were desperately low. The prophet Isaiah was resident in Jerusalem, and he was strident in his condemnation:

---

1 Not all would agree that what happened in the time of Hezekiah can be described as revival. Erroll Hulse, for example, concluded 'What was accomplished under Hezekiah is surely better described as a reformation.' (*Give Him No Rest*, p. 61). However, as we will see, it bears all the hallmarks of revival. See also the twin volume to this, *Praying for Revival*, to appreciate the full work of the Holy Spirit in the Old Testament.

'Ah, sinful nation, a people loaded with guilt,
a brood of evildoers, children given to corruption!
They have forsaken the LORD;
they have spurned the Holy One of Israel
and turned their backs on him ...
From the sole of your foot to the top of your head
there is no soundness—
only wounds and bruises and open sores,
not cleansed or bandaged or soothed with oil.
Your country is desolate.'
(Isaiah 1:4,6,7).

To be accurate and consistent, when the Old Testament prophets preach against the nations, we should apply that to the unbelieving world; when they preach against Israel, it is to an apostate church, and when they preach against Judah it is to the chosen people who have become cold and disobedient. That is where it hurts.

In Isaiah 62 the prophet declares that he would go on preaching until the city (Jerusalem) that is indistinguishable from the surrounding nations becomes 'a crown of splendour in the LORD's hand' (v. 3) and her righteousness becomes so attractive that the nations long for it (v. 2), and until 'her righteousness shines out like the dawn, her salvation like a blazing torch' (v. 1). Although the prophet may have preached chapter 62 sometime after the revival years of Hezekiah, when a fresh revival was needed, certainly the same conditions were true in the time of the new king.

Outwardly there are many good things among evangelical churches today. A resurgence of strong biblical theology and some healthy inter-church relationships leading to cooperation in church planting and evangelism is good. Programmes to equip young men for the ministry and an army of faithful preachers and their small congregations maintaining a bold stand in the face of strong opposition or cold indifference is all encouraging.

However, our evangelical churches must recognize that Isaiah is preaching to us. Beneath our outward 'success' there is the rottenness of worldliness, carelessness, a lack of deep commitment and a triviality about holy things. Too many churches are divided and quarrelsome; too many leaders are proud of their reputations and hard work to build their own empires. Across the country, hundreds of small, elderly congregations are in 'survival mode' as any young people they had drift out into the mainstream of the world. Many Christians think and behave like the world and are afraid to act differently. We are making little impact in our society, and our churches are not growing vigorously by regular, life-changing conversions. What growth there is, is too often simply shuffling the pack as discontented or awkward Christians move from one church to another where they are welcomed without question. Revival is not when the churches exchange members, but when the Holy Spirit changes lives.

Revival is not when the churches exchange members, but when the Holy Spirit changes lives

Revival is needed not first because of the state of the world, but because of the state of the true church. Only when we realize this will we plead with God to send us revival. When God came to the Congo (Zaire) in 1953 it was two months before large numbers of people were being saved. But those two months were a painful time for the church.

Today we are good at analysing the nation around us. We can catalogue the sins of Edom and Moab, Syria and Assyria, Egypt and Babylon; we even know what is wrong with Israel, that apostate church that hardly knows what it believes and whose morality has sunk to the depths of the society around. But God's finger points at Judah. Isaiah was preaching in the days of Hezekiah's great-grandfather, grandfather and father, and

Hezekiah was listening when it came to his turn. He might have found it depressing as Isaiah tore the church apart, but the king soon realized that the prophet had not come to blow bubbles, but to burst them.

We fool ourselves into thinking that our churches shine like the dawn and blaze like a torch, whilst in reality many of them are in almost total eclipse. The world has effectively snuffed out our light. Our Lord never knocks timidly at the door of the unbeliever's life, but he does plead with his people: 'Come now, let us reason together' (Isaiah 1:18). 'Here I am! I stand at the door and knock' (Revelation 3:20) is never spoken to the soul dead in sin, but to the local church that is distastefully lukewarm and should be alive for God. Too many of our churches are like Laodicea.

In 1722, prior to the eighteenth century revivals, Daniel Defoe complained: 'No age since the founding and forming of the Christian church was ever like, in open atheism, blasphemies, and heresies, to the age we now live in.' Deism, with its coldly distant and unconcerned God riddled the Established Church in England. Across the Atlantic at the same time, Jonathan Edwards complained of 'a time of extraordinary dullness in religion' in his North American town of Northampton.[2] This, in spite of periodic revivals in New England between 1679 and 1718. More than two hundred years later, the Free Church Presbytery of the Isle of Lewis, off the west coast of Scotland, expressed its concern: 'not only in the chaotic conditions of international politics and domestic economics and morality, but also, and especially, in the lack of spiritual power from Gospel Ordinances.'[3]

Before God came down in power at Cambuslang and Kilsyth in Scotland in 1742, spiritual life was at a very low ebb. Two faithful ministers were preaching, William McCulloch at Cambuslang and James Robe at Kilsyth, but for years they had seen very little fruit for

2 Edwards, *A Narrative of Surprising Conversions*, p. 9.
3 Campbell, *The Lewis Awakening*, p. 11.

their hard work. Neither man was greatly gifted in public speaking, and McCulloch, 'whose voice was thin and weak and whose utterance was slow',[4] was nicknamed an 'ale-minister', because when it came to the sermon many in the congregation would leave to quench their thirst in the ale-house next door! Robe described conditions in the church as 'a formal round of professional duties ... and as to the multitude they were visibly profane.'[5]

Prior to the revival in Wales in 1859 the same problem existed: 'The means of grace had become more or less a formality, made unattractive to the world by the coldness even of its orthodoxy; sinful practices were rampant and carried on openly without any sense of shame; the church was spiritually "asleep", oblivious of its mission to the world, and satisfied with its lukewarmness. The prayer meetings were not burdened for the souls of the unconverted, and preaching was theoretical, oratorical and "popular" in the worst sense.'[6] In March 1860, David Charles, the Principal of Trevecca College, reflected on the years before revival came to Wales: 'Our congregations had been in a very listless mood for many years, and we had all at times felt somewhat discouraged at the small results of our labours for the salvation of souls; and frequently had we asked—"How long, Lord? Wilt Thou hide Thyself for ever? Lord, where are Thy former loving-kindnesses?"'[7]

At the Association meetings of the Calvinistic Methodist churches during the 1840s and '50s, the subjects for discussion reveal the state of the churches: 'The inefficiency of the ministry, and the low state of religion'; 'Worldliness in its relation to religion'; 'The ungodliness of the present generation'; 'The hardness of the times', and so on.[8]

4 Roberts, *Scotland Saw His Glory*, p. 128.
5 Dallimore, *George Whitefield*, vol. 2, p. 121.
6 Evans, *When He is Come*, p. 23.
7 Phillips, *The Welsh Revival*, pp. 142–3.
8 As above, p. 24.

Before we hurriedly move on, pause and review some of those descriptions:

'a time of extraordinary dullness in religion.'
'the lack of spiritual power from Gospel Ordinances.'
'a formal round of professional duties.'
'The means of grace had become more or less a formality, made unattractive to the world by the coldness even of its orthodoxy.'
'The prayer meetings were not burdened for the souls of the unconverted.'
'Our congregations had been in a very listless mood for many years, and we had all at times felt somewhat discouraged at the small results of our labours for the salvation of souls.'
'The inefficiency of the ministry, and the low state of religion.'

Honesty compels us to conclude that this is all too descriptive of our own day.

An alarming description of one church in the Assam district of India prior to the revival of 1905 led to urgent prayer by the missionaries: 'Nearly all the members, men and women, were given to drinking, some smoked ganja. They quarrelled, they fought, they lived immoral lives, and shielded each other so that the missionary would not find these things out. It was almost impossible to get them to attend more than one service on the Sabbath day, and the weekly service was very badly attended. The missionary often felt ready to give them up altogether, it seemed a hopeless church.'[9]

The problem with our nation is not the government, the media, the education system, or the economic conditions. It is not even the lifeless institutional religion that believes anything and nothing. The real challenge lies with the evangelical churches many of which are cold, complacent and unattractive to the watching world.

---

9 Jones, *India Awake*, p. 2.

'Agnosticism about all ultimates'

Impacting this evangelical scene, there can be little doubt that the accelerating rise of secular atheism and its aggressive attack on the Christian faith has led to a generation who have no sense of eternity in their mind (Ecclesiastes 3:11). The inevitable outcome is a society lost and hopeless. In a society that has everything it needs materially, it is a tragedy that half the hospital beds are taken up by mental health patients, suicide among young people is rising steadily, alcohol is responsible for over half of all violent crime and our city streets are no longer safe. At work, at home, and even at sport, we are not a happy people. In spite of the rapid growth of a belief in no God, atheism is a hard religion to follow because it runs contrary to that voice within us all that cries out to us that there is a God and an eternity and a judgement to come. C. S. Lewis criticized Rudyard Kipling and his age for lacking 'a doctrine of ends' and concluded: 'He has a reverent, pagan, agnosticism about all ultimates.'

But here is the tragedy and the indictment: People do not touch eternity in our meetings, they rarely hear of it in our conversation and they certainly do not see it as the priority of our lives. Of course, it glances off our gospel here and there, but we are not passionate about heaven and hell or the second coming of Christ, and we have lost a sense of accountability to God.

One thing revival does is to reawaken, in both Christians and the community around, a sense of the reality of eternal issues, even among those who may never be won for Christ. When Joseph Carlyle, the clergyman and orientalist, described the eighteenth century as 'Soul extinct, stomach well alive', how did that change? God sent a revival that swept across the nation until hundreds of thousands knew that God was real. When upwards of 20,000 people gathered on Kennington Common in London in the mid-eighteenth century, they had come to hear George Whitefield preach on eternity. In 1737 he described a church congregation:

'They were all attention, and heard like people hearing for eternity.'[10] This is exactly the same description that Alexander Webster used five years later during the revival at Cambuslang in Scotland: 'They hear as for eternity...'[11] When God comes in revival, whole communities are aware that there is a God and that eternal issues really matter. Not everyone will believe, but everyone will be made to think.

When Hezekiah came to the throne, he did not begin by analysing the disastrous effects of the rampaging Assyrian army; he called on the Levites to 'Consecrate yourselves now and consecrate the temple of the LORD' (2 Chronicles 29:5). He knew exactly where the problem of the nation really lay. If we start here, we have hope for revival. But we must start *now*. Whole books can be written analysing what is wrong with the church and the nation today, but there is hardly a need for this. We must simply admit that we are not an eternity-minded people. We live like the world we are supposed to be saving. Our priorities are world-related rather than heaven-directed; our treasure is on earth. Revival always begins by putting eternity back into the minds of the Christians, and only when the church takes eternity seriously can we expect the world to do so.

10 Dallimore, *George Whitefield*, vol. 1, p. 1148.
11 Above, vol. 2, p. 128.

Before revival

Those God uses

> Revival begins with those who in bad times remain good, in godless days remain Christian, in careless years remain constant and who hold eternity in their hearts

Revival begins with those who in bad times remain good, in godless days remain Christian, in careless years remain constant and who hold eternity in their hearts. It also requires those who care for the honour of God. Hezekiah cared. He was only twenty-five when he came to the throne, but clearly the state of affairs had been bothering him for a long time, and he made up his mind to do something.

God frequently uses particular men in revival; we need not be afraid of this because it is God's way. He is not only the God of the end but the means to that end, which is so often committed Christian leaders. This was always God's way in the Bible. At every major junction of Jewish Bible history God prepared particular men, and occasionally women, to lead his people. Jesus chose his disciples and sent them out to establish churches in the power of his Holy Spirit. The story of the first-century church is woven around the lives of men like Peter and John, Philip and Stephen, Paul and Silas, Barnabas and Mark. God has chosen, with few exceptions, to build his church by preparing particular men.

Some of the names in the story of revival are well known. Three hundred years ago, there were men like John and Charles Wesley, George Whitefield, Howell Harris and Daniel Rowland in Britain, Nikolaus of Zinzendorf in Saxony and Hans Hauge in Norway. Across the Atlantic, Jonathan Edwards in New England and David Brainerd among the North

American Indians. In the nineteenth century God used Charles Grandison Finney, Asahel Nettleton in America and later Jeremiah Lanphier and Dwight L. Moody. Back home in Britain, in 1859 he prepared Humphrey Jones and David Morgan in Wales, James McQuilkin in Ulster, Charles Haddon Spurgeon in England and, a little earlier, William Chalmers Burns, Robert Murray M'Cheyne and Brownlow North in Scotland. In the twentieth century he prepared Evan Roberts and Rhys Bevan Jones in Wales, Douglas Brown in England and Jock Troup and Duncan Campbell in Scotland. Further afield, John Sung in China, Bakht Singh in India and Petrus Octavianus in Borneo. All these, and many others, we shall meet as the story progresses. If it is generally God's method to use particular men in revival, we need to pray for God to give us such men today. We may not agree with every aspect of their theology; many would disassociate from Finney's theology of revival, but few can deny he was 'humble, holy, prayerful, and a blessing to all'.

Those whom God uses in leadership in revival are always men who have met with God in a powerfully personal way and have a burning passion for the glory of God and a life of holiness. When the Holy Spirit comes in power upon his people he creates a longing for right and pure living. Anything that claims to be a work of the Holy Spirit but does not bring about a desire to be holy must be suspect. The physical appearance of a man bears no significance for his leadership in revival. It was said of the apostle Paul: 'In person he is unimpressive and his speaking amounts to nothing' (2 Corinthians 10:10), yet he preached with 'a demonstration of the Spirit's power' (1 Corinthians 2:4).

When the Holy Spirit comes in power upon his people he creates a longing for right and pure living

Silas Told was converted through the powerful preaching of John Wesley and became one of Wesley's earliest teachers and prison visitors. He described his first sight of the five feet six-inch Wesley at a crowded meeting at five o'clock in the morning in London: 'I had a curiosity to see his person, which, when I beheld, I much despised. The enemy of souls suggested that he was some farmer's son, who, not able to support himself, was making a penny in this low manner.'[1] David Brainerd, who travelled hundreds of miles in wild and dangerous frontier territory to preach to the North American Indians in the 1740s, was a sickly tuberculosis sufferer. Similarly, the first sight Rajamani had of Bakht Singh, the leader of the revival in South India in the early 1940s, was very disappointing. He was expecting a strong, smart and well-dressed converted Sikh; instead: 'Here was a lean, unimpressive young man with neither moustache nor beard, and not dressed up like a great preacher in tie and collar and shoes either, but barefoot and simply clad. I felt sure that, just as I had been disappointed in so many preachers before, so I would now be disappointed in this man also.'[2]

The men whom God has used in revival have come from no stereotyped background. At Herrnhut in Saxony the two men who worked together in a revival that fell on the community in 1727 were a rich and well-educated count, Zinzendorf, and a modest carpenter, Christian David. The Wesley brothers and George Whitefield were university educated men when God used them in the eighteenth century. Billy Bray, the Cornish miner, and Jock Troup the Scottish barrel maker, had little education. William Carvosso, who was powerfully used by God across Cornwall as a lay Evangelist after 1771, could barely read or write until the age of sixty-five. On the other hand, John Sung was a brilliant scientist when he joined the Bethel Band in China.

When God poured out his Spirit at Pentecost, you could hardly have found a more mixed group of men. The two most widely used men in the book of Acts were a fisherman and a university graduate.

---

1 Told, *The Life of Silas Told*, p. 6.
2 Rajamani & Kinnear, *Monsoon Daybreak*, p. 59.

Hezekiah instructed the priests and the Levites who should have been instructing him.

Although Evan Roberts became a significant leader during the 1904–5 revival in Wales, this was not apparent at first. Early in 1904 one local newspaper contrasted what was happening in Wales with the work of God in the eighteenth century. Canon Wynne Jones addressed the Montgomeryshire Clerical Association on the revival and the paper commented, 'There was the peculiarity about the movement that, unlike the great revival in John Wesley's day, it did not appear to have any visible head to direct and organize it. Evan Roberts himself was represented as too unassuming to claim anything like leadership…'[3]

Whilst we may admire and honour those God has used in revival, we must beware of falling into the danger of giving some particular authority to their practices, preferences or principles, as if the fact that God used them validates all they did. The Arminian-Calvinism squabble between Wesley and Whitefield is well known. Rhys Bevan Jones maintained a very different approach from Evan Roberts, laying far greater emphasis upon preaching, and yet both were greatly used by God in Wales in 1904. William Haslam was surprised, when preaching in Scotland, to hear the rustling of the pages of Bibles as the congregation followed his references carefully; he was not used to this in Cornwall and actually discouraged it by not giving full references; he felt it hindered the flow of the sermon. On the other hand, Bakht Singh in India urged the people to bring a Bible and even made them display their copies for all to see. William Haslam and Duncan Campbell had little problem with women preaching during revival times, whilst for others this was unthinkable. During the 1830s, Finney, modelled what became widely accepted as the definition of

3 Harris, *Extracts From the Welsh Press*, p. 2.

revival in North America. Finney turned the means that he employed into a methodology for all to copy.[4]

We shall never settle these issues on the basis of whether or not God used such practices. Scripture is to be our guide. There is sufficient diversity between revivals to warn us that when men become our authority, however great and godly they may be, we are in danger. A leader may gain his reputation by denominational progression, academic excellence, force of character, organizing ability or a capacity for sheer hard work. However, someone has commented that what the church needs today is heaven-anointed men, not human-appointed machines.

Revival will rarely begin only by the faithfulness of a few good and godly men; there will almost always be others who join in the longing and praying and preparing for revival. God stirs a few here and there to pray until, as is sometimes the case, thousands or tens of thousands are assaulting heaven with the insistent demand that God should come among his people.

Revival will rarely begin only by the faithfulness of a few good and godly men; there will almost always be others who join in the longing and praying and preparing for revival

In 1857 Jeremiah Calvin Lanphier, the New York city missionary, was so troubled by his 'noisy, busy, restless, worldly city' that he sent out an advertisement for a one hour noon-day prayer meeting to be held on Wednesdays in the Old Dutch Church at the corner of Fulton Street in downtown New York. After half an hour, one man joined him and five more by 1.00 p.m. Two weeks later there were twenty. Within six months

4 *Finney's Lectures on Theology*, Eerdmans 1953. The lectures were originally given to the students at Oberlin College in America in 1846. It was hugely influential and a quarter of a million were sold. The first publication in England was in 1851. See *Praying for Revival* for a discussion of Finney's method.

10,000 businessmen were praying for revival; by the end of the year there were one hundred and fifty prayer meetings in New York and Brooklyn and they soon spread right across the land. Within two years it is estimated that one million converts were added to the churches.[5] Although God used Lanphier for the initial vision of concerted prayer, for what was arguably the most fruitful and widespread revival ever experienced in America, a unique feature of this revival was that there was no single leader; laymen, many almost unknown, led prayer meetings that saw hundreds converted.

James Alexander, a cautious Presbyterian minister and observer of revival in America, who had despaired at the revivalism of Charles Finney with all its manipulation and extravagance, wrote to a friend in March 1858 commending Lanphier's revival of prayer: 'The uptown prayer meetings are very sober and edifying. I am told the general tendency in all is to increased decorum. The openness of thousands to doctrine, reproof etc. is undeniable. The publisher of Spurgeon's sermons says he has sold a hundred thousand ... There are meetings of great size, as free from irreverence as any you ever saw. I have never seen sacramental occasions, more tender and still than some meetings held daily in our part of the town.'[6]

In 1858, a minister of Aberdare in Wales wrote of the urgent need for revival and made suggestions as to how a revival might come. His suggestions included 'a pure ministry—apostolic preaching ... the awakening must start in the pulpit ... the church must be in full sympathy with the ministry.'[7] This last is a vital point. In emphasizing the importance of the leaders, it cannot be stressed too much that others must be in harmony with the leadership. Preparing for revival is not the work of the leaders alone. In 1856 Mrs Colville in Ulster influenced a

5 Prime, *The Power of Prayer*, pp. 8ff. First published in 1859, it is the best record of this outstanding revival.
6 Murray, *Revival and Revivalism*, p. 344.
7 Evans, *When He is Come*, p. 31.

young man towards Christ who, after his conversion, gathered a few friends for prayer; these prayer meetings led to the Ulster revival of 1859 and the conversion of an estimated 100,000 people. In understanding the way God used men like Dwight L. Moody in America or James McQuilkin in Ulster, we must never forget the contribution of hundreds of unknown prayer warriors and preachers. A description of some of these unknown men in Cornwall through the late seventeenth and early eighteenth century is humbling: 'They fulfilled punishing schedules, expected little if any pay, put up with violent opposition and failure to provide hospitality. They were expected to submit to a simple lifestyle, they were flexible, utterly committed, and dependent on "faith"'.[8]

8 Isaac, *A History of Evangelical Christianity In Cornwall*, p. 140.

Before revival

An experience of God

Hezekiah 'trusted in the LORD ... held fast to the LORD and did not cease to follow him' (2 Kings 18:5–6). The secret of Hezekiah's later ministry began here. Hezekiah's determination to 'make a covenant with the LORD' was no idle promise. It expressed something of his deep and personal relationship with God. He was constant. Even allowing for his later disobedience in the matter of the Babylonian envoys, 'The LORD was with him' (v. 7). The name Hezekiah means 'whom Jehovah strengthens'.

When the early disciples looked for a man to make up the place left by Judas Iscariot, they set the qualification as 'one of the men who have been with us the whole time the Lord Jesus went in and out among us, beginning from John's baptism to the time when Jesus was taken up from us. For one of these must become a witness with us of his resurrection' (Acts 1:21–22). This qualification was not only so that the new apostle would be a good apologist, having clear convictions about the life, death and resurrection of Christ, but so that he would be a man who had experienced the living and risen Christ. The purpose of Pentecost was not only to give power to the apostles' preaching, but to give reality to their experience. By the opening of Acts, the disciples had no doubt that Christ was risen from the dead, but still they needed a powerful experience of being 'filled with the Spirit' (Acts 2:4). God wanted to use men who were utterly convinced, both by their theology and their experience, that Christ was a living, powerful and personal Saviour.

Robert Murray M'Cheyne, greatly used by God in Dundee in 1839, had prayed from his heart, 'Lord, make me as holy as a saved sinner can be.'[1] The evidence of his sincerity in this prayer is seen in the fact that people would be moved to tears just by seeing M'Cheyne in the pulpit or walking down the corridor of the church. David Brainerd spent whole nights in prayer, so did Wesley and Whitefield, and this was before revival came. They were men who knew what they wanted and were determined to get it. In those whom God uses, there has always been personal revival, convincing them of the greatness and glory of God, before public revival.

David Brainerd made the following entry in his diary, dated 12 July 1739:

'As I was walking in a dark, thick grove, *unspeakable glory* seemed to open to the view and apprehension of my soul. I do not mean any external brightness, for I saw no such thing, nor do I intend any imagination of any body of light somewhere in the third heaven or anything of that nature, but it was a new inward apprehension or view that I had of God, such as I never had before, nor anything which had the least semblance of it. I stood still, wondered and admired. I knew that I never had seen before anything comparable to it for excellency and beauty, it was widely different from all the conceptions that ever I had of God or things Divine. I had no particular apprehension of any one Person in the Trinity, either the Father, the Son, or the Holy Ghost, but it appeared to be *Divine Glory*. My soul *rejoiced with joy unspeakable* to see such a God, such a glorious Divine Being, and I was inwardly pleased and satisfied that He should be *God over all* for ever and ever. My soul was so captivated and delighted with the excellency, loveliness, greatness, and other perfections of God, that I was even swallowed up in Him...'[2]

1 Bonar, *Memoirs and Remains*, pp. 151–7.
2 Page, *David Brainerd*, pp. 29–30.

Jonathan Edwards, who was like a father to Brainerd, describes similar experiences of his own. Writing of an occasion in 1737 when he rode to a wood in order to be alone to think and pray he concluded:

'I had a view that for me was extraordinary, of the glory of the Son of God as Mediator between God and man, and His wonderful, great, full, pure and sweet grace and love, and meek and gentle condescension. This grace that appeared so calm and sweet, appeared also great above the heavens. The person of Christ appeared ineffably excellent with an excellency great enough to swallow up all thought and conception—which continued, as near as I can judge, about an hour...'[3]

Four years before Brainerd's experience, Howell Harris, who was used in the Awakening across Wales, described how, on 18 June 1735, he met with God. It was so real that he referred to it often throughout his life:

'I felt suddenly my heart melting within me like wax before the fire with love to God my Saviour; and also felt not only love, peace, etc. but longing to be dissolved, and to be with Christ; then was a cry in my inmost soul, which I was totally unacquainted with before, "Abba Father! Abba Father!" I could not help calling God my Father, I knew that I was his child, and that He loved me, and heard me. My soul being filled and satiated, crying, "Tis enough, I am satisfied. Give me strength, and I will follow thee through fire and water." I could say I was happy indeed! There was in me a well of water, springing up to everlasting life, John 4:14. The love of God was shed abroad in my heart by the Holy Ghost, Romans 5:5.'[4]

---

3 Edwards, *Select Works*, p. 32.
4 Evans, *Howell Harris*, pp. 8–9.

On 10 October 1821 Charles G. Finney was praying alone in his office when: 'The Holy Spirit descended upon me in a manner that seemed to go through me body and soul.' Five years later Finney experienced a vision of Christ: 'I seemed drawn nearer and nearer to God—nearer and nearer to the Presence that filled me with such unutterable awe and trembling.'[5]

It is this deep and personal knowledge of God, captivating the whole soul with the glories of God's character, that is lacking among Christian leaders today. We hardly understand the language, let alone share the experience.

Before the outbreak of the China-Japan war in 1937, Dr John Sung travelled all through China and beyond into Java, Singapore, Malaysia, Burma and Thailand, and God used him powerfully in revival; but he had 'a profound spiritual experience which changed the direction of his life and led him to give himself and his rich talents to God for the salvation of his people'.[6]

At the time of his call to return to the work of an evangelist, Duncan Campbell experienced such an overwhelming sense of the love of God that he wondered if he could bear it. This, together with an awesome awareness of the reality of hell, left him no option but to obey the command of God.[7]

For others, personal revival came in a less dramatic way, sometimes over a period of time, even years, but always, step by step, they are led into a closer walk with God and a deeper understanding of God. This is not achieved through any set formula, and it has no doctrinal label that should be tied to it. God comes in a thousand different ways to his people. We shall always miss the mark when we long for another man's experience. Leaders in revivals have wanted God and holiness and have done everything in their power to gain both. Sometimes unusual things happened in their lives and ministry, but this was incidental. Sadly,

5 Rosell, *The memoirs of Charles G. Finney*, pp. xxxi–xxxii, p. 75.
6 Lyall, *God Reigns in China*, p. 33.
7 Woolsey, *Duncan Campbell*, p. 24.

when Humphrey Jones took to 'prophesying' in 1859, his ministry and leadership in the revival in Wales came to an end. The weakest part of Evan Roberts' ministry in Wales in 1904 was his encouragement of certain 'gifts' that occasionally spoiled his meetings.

A study of the lives of men God used in Bible times reveals the same. Time after time we can identify the experience of God that changed their life: Abraham at Mamre (Genesis 15), Jacob at Luz (Genesis 28), Moses in the Midian desert (Exodus 3), Joshua outside Jericho (Joshua 5), Gideon under the oak in Ophrah (Judges 6), Samuel in the tabernacle (1 Samuel 3), Isaiah in the temple (Isaiah 6), and so we could continue. Always the revelation of God in their lives convinced them of the Creator's holiness and sovereign power. No one is ever used in revival whose experience of God is no more than a coldly impersonal theology. Revival leaders are men with hearts on fire. It is as if God has invaded their lives in every part and taken them captive; they are men who love God, trust in him, hold fast to him and never cease to follow him. Their ministry is an all-consuming passion. And they fear above everything losing the sense of the presence of God. Most of the great men of revival had a strong hold on theology, but never at the expense of a vivid and life-changing relationship with God.

Spurgeon could claim that barely fifteen minutes went by without his turning his thoughts towards God. Preaching at the Keswick Convention in 1922, a year after revival in Lowestoft, Douglas Brown declared, 'Revival begins with a vision, and the vision begins with a new sense of Jesus Christ. Revival does not begin in a theology, but in a theophany. It begins in a revelation of Jesus Christ Himself and a sense of the nearness of the Master.'[8] There is a heart-beat in this somewhat loose wording of Douglas Brown. He did not deny the importance of theology, far from it, nor did he pretend by 'theophany' to have seen God; he was making the

8 Brown, *Revival addresses*, p. 8.

point strongly that revival begins with men who have a deep, firm and life-changing experience of God. Today, men who have few interests apart from God are considered out of touch and boring; perhaps these are the men God is looking for.

Yet these men were always concerned that God should have the honour for anything he chose to do through them. Deep experiences of God did not allow them to boast of themselves, any more than Paul did in the New Testament. The apostle experienced things he felt it unwise even to write down (2 Corinthians 12:4), and the only boasting he allowed was of those things that showed up his weakness.

In 1737 George Whitefield was on his way to Georgia when he prayed, 'God, give me a deep humility, a well-guided zeal, a burning love and a single eye, and then let men or devils do their worst!' Five years later he could still record in his diary: 'I spent most part of my time in secret prayer ... Pray that I may be very little in my own eyes, and not rob my dear Master of any part of his glory.'[9]

During the first two months of 1859, David Morgan did not preach beyond Cardiganshire, but a meeting at inappropriately named Devil's Bridge on New Year's Day was typical of what was to follow all over Wales that year. On the way home from the meeting, an old minister described both it and David Morgan's response: 'The evening service was terrible. So near was the revivalist to his God, that his face shone like that of an angel, so that none could gaze steadfastly at him. Many of the hearers swooned. On the way home I dared not break the silence for miles. Towards midnight I ventured to say, "Didn't we have blessed meetings, Mr Morgan?","Yes," he replied; and after a pause, added, "The Lord would give us great things, if He could only trust us." "What do you mean?" I asked. "If He could trust us not to steal the glory for ourselves."

9 Dallimore, *George Whitefield*, vol. 1, p. 140; vol. 2, p. 124.

Then the midnight air rang with his cry, at the top of his voice, "Not unto us, O LORD, not unto us, but unto Thy name give glory."'[10]

When three ministers of the United Free Church of Scotland visited the scenes of revival in Scotland in 1921, they reported: 'The men whose names come to the front would be the last to take credit. They are honest, earnest, modest young men, with a humble idea of their own ability.'[11] Those are the qualities that God is looking for in the men he will use in revival. This is a far cry from these days of self-assertive leadership training.

It was said of Asahel Nettleton, whom God used in revival in America in the early eighteenth century: 'This favoured servant of Christ came, with no trumpet sounded before him, in the meekness of his master, and the Lord was with him in very deed.'[12] If praise was directed towards him, or if he suspected too much confidence was placed in him, Nettleton would disappear from the scene, much to the annoyance of those waiting for his ministry. Douglas Brown described revival as 'the humbling of self before the ... majesty of that consciously present Jesus.'[13]

God brings revival not for the enjoyment of his people, but for the glory of his name

God brings revival not for the enjoyment of his people, but for the glory of his name; and he will not share that glory with men: 'Surely his salvation is near those who fear him, that his glory may dwell in our land' (Psalm 85:9). The moment men boast of their achievements the glory will depart. 2 Chronicles 32:25 is the most tragic later comment upon Hezekiah: 'But Hezekiah's heart was proud, and he did not respond to the kindness shown him; therefore the LORD's wrath was on him and on Judah and Jerusalem.' It was at this time he boastfully showed his

10 Evans, *When He is Come*, pp. 69–70.
11 Ritchie, *Floods Upon the Dry Ground*, p. 107.
12 Thornton, *God Sent Revival*, p. 71.
13 Brown, *Revival Addresses*, p. 9.

treasures and power to the Babylonian envoys, and the revival came to an end (2 Kings 20:12–13). The men God uses in revival have a firmer hold upon another world than upon this one, and their love for Christ far outweighs the treasure of men. Whatever faults there may be in their character, whatever frailty in their lives, a passion for Christ is dominant.

Perhaps Howell Harris expressed this as clearly as any when he wrote in his diary: 'I must have the Saviour, indeed, for he is my all; all that others have in the world, and in religion, and in themselves, I have in Thee; pleasures, riches, safety, honour, life, righteousness, holiness, wisdom, bliss, joy, gaiety, and happiness … And if a child longs for his father; a traveller for the end of his journey; a workman to finish his work; a prisoner for his liberty; an heir for the full possession of his estate; so, in all these respects, I can't help longing to go home.'[14]

God is looking for men and women who love him like that and whom he can therefore trust with revival.

14 Evans, Howell Harris, p. 65.

Before revival

Holiness of life

It is impossible to read the story of Hezekiah without being impressed with his longing for everything to be done in line with the holy character of God. The revival that swept through the nation and brought cleansing from the house of God outwards, had actually begun in the heart of the king. God looks for those who will be willing to surrender anything and everything so long as their life can be kept clean. This is an essential part of personal revival.

In encouraging his congregations in Wales in 1904 to prepare for revival, Evan Roberts would remind them that the Spirit would not come until the people were prepared: 'We must rid the churches of all bad feeling—all malice, envy, prejudice, and misunderstandings. Bow not in prayer until all offences have been forgiven: but if you feel you cannot forgive, bend to the dust, and ask for a forgiving spirit. You shall get it then.'[1]

The men God chiefly used in the Bible, and who stand as an example to us today, were men whose experience of God led them into a passionate desire to be holy. They were men with a sensitive conscience. Joseph learned holiness in the face of fierce temptation (Genesis 39:6–10), and, to the average Christian today, Daniel might seem to have been unnecessarily precise in his insistence upon keeping his distance from the contamination of Babylon (Daniel 1:8). But without exception those whom God uses in revival are men and women who fear God and sin, and nothing else. They take seriously the command: 'Be holy as I am holy, says the LORD.' Of course, there is a Pharisaic self-righteousness that is not holiness at

1 Evans, *The Welsh Revival of 1904*, p. 166.

all, but Christian leaders must strive for purity of mind and heart above everything. The New Testament is full of urgent commands and warnings concerning personal holiness:

'Be ... innocent as doves...' (Matthew 10:16)
'Be innocent about what is evil' (Romans 16:19).
'In regard to evil be infants' (1 Corinthians 14:20).
'Touch no unclean thing' (2 Corinthians 6:17).
"There must not even be a hint of ... it is shameful even to mention...' (Ephesians 5:3,12).
'Whatever is pure ... think about such things' (Philippians 4:8).
'Set your minds on things above...' (Colossians 3:2).
'Keep oneself from being polluted by the world' (James 1:27).
'Hating even the clothing stained by sinful flesh' (Jude 23).

As a child of four years, Zinzendorf prayed, 'Dear Saviour do thou be mine, and I will be thine.'[2] It was that spirit of total commitment that stayed with him and led to the outpouring of God's Spirit at Herrnhut in 1727. Wesley wrote to his father in 1734: 'Where I am most holy myself, there I could most promote holiness in others.'[3] This was four years before his conversion. But although he might later express himself more to the glory of God, yet the thrust of his concern was always the same.

David Brainerd recalls the time when he was among the Indians in North America and the night before a pagan festival he went to the woods to be alone with God. His experience during that night reveals the kind of men God can trust in revival:

2 Greenfield, *Power from on High*, p. 26.
3 Telford, *The Letters of Rev. John Wesley AM* Vol. 1, p. 173.

'All things here below vanished, and there appeared to be nothing of any considerable importance to me but holiness of heart and life, and the conversion of the heathen to God. All my cares, fears, and desires, which might be said to be of a worldly nature disappeared, and were, in my esteem, of little more importance than a puff of wind. I exceedingly longed that God would get to himself a name among the heathen, and I appealed to him, with the greatest freedom, that he knew I "preferred him above my chief joy."'[4]

The *North Wales Guardian* on 14 April 1905 reported the assessment of Evan Roberts made by the vicar of Rhosllanerchrugog (Rhos), Rev. Thomas Pritchard: 'He believes him to be true to the backbone and understands the man's nature thoroughly. Above all he is faithful to God and his conscience; he cannot be bought or bribed; his strength is his character sanctified by communion with the invisible.'[5] That was high praise by a wise and cautious leader.

Duncan Campbell describes his own experience of surrendering fully to Christ. He was shot from his horse and seriously wounded in one of the last cavalry charges of the Great War. While a Canadian trooper was carrying him on horseback to the casualty clearing station, Campbell reviewed his life and saw how empty it had been, even as a Christian. He prayed M'Cheyne's prayer: 'Lord, make me as holy as a saved sinner can be.' At that moment the Spirit seemed to come into his life in such power and he experienced the presence of God in such reality that he felt he was going straight to heaven. From then on, he was a man with eternity in his mind.[6]

After twenty-six years of apparently successful ministry in a large London Baptist Church, Douglas Brown became acutely aware that something was missing from his life: 'Christ laid his hand on a proud minister, and told him that he had not gone far enough, that there were

4 Page, *David Brainerd*, p. 57.
5 Harris, *Extracts from the Welsh Press*, p. 27.
6 Woolsey, *Duncan Campbell*, p. 51.

reservations in his surrender ... He nearly broke my heart while I was preaching.' Throughout November and December of 1920 an intense struggle went on; it carried on through to January of the following year. Then in February 1921 Douglas Brown was wrestling in prayer when he felt able to yield his life fully to God: 'Then something happened. I found myself in the loving embrace of Christ for ever and ever; and all power and all joy and all blessedness rolled in like a deluge ... God had waited four months for a man like me; and I said: "Lord Jesus, I know what you want; you want me to go into mission work. I love thee more than I dislike that."'[7] In the same month, whilst Douglas Brown was conducting a mission in Lowestoft in Suffolk, God began a revival that spread across East Anglia and up to the fishing ports of Scotland.

The men God uses in revival have a burning conviction that God will not hold back from giving 'good things' to his people and so they have a bold impertinence to ask and expect good things from him. But they are equally sure that these are only given to 'those whose walk is blameless' (Psalm 84:11). They know that sin will quench the Holy Spirit, and their passion for God is equalled only by their fear of offending him. These are not men who take God lightly. Their understanding of the holy character of their Creator is awesome in its scope.

Hezekiah prayed, 'O LORD Almighty, God of Israel, enthroned between the cherubim, you alone are God over all the kingdoms of the earth. You have made heaven and earth...' (Isaiah 37:16). Bold he could be, but not over-familiar. Hezekiah did not see God as a 'Big Daddy', but an awesome, holy, heaven-enthroned sovereign Creator. Like the psalmist, he knew that God could be angry 'against the prayers of your people' (Psalm 80:4). The prophet Isaiah had certainly warned him that if he did not put away evil and 'learn to do right' then God would not listen, 'even if you offer many prayers' (Isaiah 1:15–17).

7 Brown, *Revival Addresses*, pp. 80–83.

None of this implies that the men God uses are incapable of error. Hezekiah failed in the matter of the Babylonian envoys and he stripped the temple of its treasures in a futile attempt to pay off the Assyrians. The squabbles between Whitefield and Wesley and between Harris and Rowland over points of doctrine, hardly do justice to the men. Humphrey Jones returned from America determined to 'set Wales alight', and by God's hand he did, until his foolish 'prophesyings' later put him out of usefulness to God. Howell Harris could be intolerant and arrogant, and Evan Roberts could be headstrong and unwise. And so we could go on.

The fact that God uses a man at a particular time, and in a remarkable way, does not give authority or infallibility to all the man does or believes. A man may not be perfect, but he must be clean. Long before revival comes, those God uses have a great opinion of God and are touch-sensitive to sin.

A man may not be perfect, but he must be clean. Those God uses have a great opinion of God and are touch-sensitive to sin

Before revival

Obedience to the word of God

Not only are the leaders in revival men with a deep experience of God and a passion for holiness, but, as we should expect, they are obedient to the word of God. Hezekiah 'did what was right in the eyes of the LORD ... He held fast to the LORD and did not cease to follow him; he kept the commands the LORD had given Moses' (2 Chronicles 29:2; 2 Kings 18:6). How diligent Hezekiah was is seen in the book of Proverbs: 'These are more proverbs of Solomon, copied by the men of Hezekiah king of Judah' (Proverbs 25:1); in the next few verses the word 'king' is mentioned many times. The proverbs that caught Hezekiah's attention, and which he ordered to be copied out, were those that spoke of the life of a king. Hezekiah was concerned to know what God's word had to say to *him*. That is where revival begins.

All who have been used by God in spiritual revival were diligent in the study of Scripture and the application of the Scripture to their own lives. God uses men and women who submit to his authority. He does not trust revival to those who have little regard for his word. Revival never begins with the 'liberal' wing of the church. I am not aware of any exception to this. Revival is an *evangelical* awakening. A significant comment is made by an observer of the revival in China from 1927–39, himself a national. Gih Tsu-wen reported that the revival was hardest and slowest in those schools and institutions where 'modernism' was taught; the poison had to be taken out of their system before students could be converted.

Long before revival broke out under the preaching of George Whitefield, he records his own relationship to Scripture: 'I began to read the Holy Scriptures upon my knees, laying aside all other books and praying over, if possible, every line and word. This proved meat indeed and drink indeed to my soul. I daily received fresh light and power from above. I got more true knowledge from reading the Book of God in one month than I could *ever* have acquired from *all* the writings of men.'[1]

If God is to entrust the evangelical churches today with revival, perhaps we have to begin by examining how committed we really are to the clarity and authority of his word. If we allow our interpretation to be tarnished by the moralistic, scientific or political agenda then we have betrayed our trust. More even than this, it is obedience to his word that counts. Two hundred years after Hezekiah, God assessed the attitude of the people in Jerusalem: 'As for you, son of man, your countrymen are talking together about you by the walls and at the doors of the houses, saying to each other, "Come and hear the message that has come from the LORD." My people come to you, as they usually do, and sit before you to listen to your words, but they do not put them into practice. With their mouths they express devotion, but their hearts are greedy for unjust gain' (Ezekiel 33:30–31).

A. W. Tozer, the American pastor and author, commented, 'Christians don't tell lies; they sing them in their hymns.' It is a great tragedy that we come and listen to preaching, but we do not do what God tells us. The men God uses in revival were always those who did not merely pay lip-service to the authority of Scripture. They had a fear of being disobedient. A statement of the centrality of Scripture in the life of the church is presented as the first recorded words of the disciples in the assembled church in the Acts of the Apostles: 'Brothers, the Scripture had to be fulfilled' (1:16). This is no accident. The first action taken by the disciples that can properly be called church organization was the direct result of the application of Scripture. The Scriptures were used in preaching (2:17), in the prayer meeting (4:25) and in policy-making (15:15). The early Christians had no doubt at all that the Holy Spirit had

1 Dallimore, *George Whitefield*, vol. 1, p. 81.

spoken through the mouth of the prophets in the Old Testament and the words were to be accepted without question. Never, in the book of Acts, did the church call a council or conference to discuss the nature of biblical inspiration. For these Christians, what the Scripture said, God said, and there could be only one proper response from the church: 'Therefore it is necessary...' (1:21). Obedient action must follow.

If we long for revival, we must begin here. Jonathan Goforth was greatly used in China and elsewhere in revival from 1908 onwards. Looking back at those years he had this to say: 'We wish to affirm, too, that we can entertain no hope of a mighty, globe-encircling Holy Spirit revival without there being first a back-to-the-Bible movement.'[2] Goforth certainly practised what he believed, for in nineteen years he read through his Chinese New Testament fifty-five times.

The reason for this essential acceptance of Scripture is that in revival God uses his word to change and correct his people, and there is always a renewed love and acceptance of Scripture. God will not trust leadership into the hands of those who deny the very weapon he is going to use more effectively than any other. Mary Peckham was converted under the ministry of Duncan Campbell and she described his preaching: 'He seemed to go from Genesis to Revelation preaching the Word. He quoted so much and applied it to our hearts. We were confronted with what God said. This was his authority, and this was the strength of his preaching.' Another wrote, 'He spoke to the heart with tremendous authority and boldness, and he thundered forth the message with the utmost sincerity, quoting numerous biblical texts and passages as he went. You certainly knew where you stood before a holy God at the end of those meetings.'[3]

Martyn Lloyd-Jones experienced revival in his church in Aberavon during the 1930s. In 1931, 135 were added to the church by conversion. But

2 Goforth, *By My Spirit*, p. 185.
3 Peckham, *Sounds from Heaven*, pp. 84,101.

Lloyd-Jones was marked out during his time in Wales, and throughout his later ministry, as a preacher who took his authority exclusively from the Bible. During his ministry in London from 1938 until his retirement thirty years later he could hold between 1,500 and 2,000 at his evening congregation, and his preaching had as its greatest appeal a firm, uncompromising confidence in the authority of Scripture and the necessity of obedience to it.

In November 1854, eighty years before Lloyd-Jones arrived in London, Brownlow North was converted in Scotland. From a life of idle pleasure and godless indifference, once saved his powerful and urgent preaching stirred Scotland and Ulster by the revival year of 1859. For him, the Bible was his infallible guide to be believed and obeyed without question or hesitation. He wasted no time even to debate with those who denied Scripture; Brownlow North simply preached it. To enquirers he would advise, 'Go home and read your Bible,' and shortly before his final illness he declared to a friend: 'There is nothing for any of us but the Bible.'[4]

Spurgeon preached to in excess of six thousand people every Sunday night at the Metropolitan Tabernacle during the nineteenth century and his church experienced continuous revival for many years, with sixty new members each month being added to the membership. Spurgeon claimed no other authority than the word of God and when he saw the Bible being downgraded by those in positions of church leadership, he exposed their actions fearlessly. The personal attacks that his courage attracted almost certainly shortened his life.

Lloyd-Jones, North and Spurgeon were not exceptional. Peter Waldo in the twelfth century, John Wycliffe in the fourteenth, Tyndale and Luther in the sixteenth, Edwards, Whitefield and Wesley in the eighteenth, and a host of others, were fully committed to the authority of the Bible. And they were equally committed to obedience to it. They did not preach what they did not believe, and they did not believe what they did not obey.

4 Moody Stuart, *Brownlow North*, pp. 129, 213.

Before revival

Courageous determination

It required great courage and self-discipline to go for that which Hezekiah most longed for: 'Now I intend to make a covenant with the LORD, the God of Israel, so that his fierce anger will turn away from us' (2 Chronicles 29:10).That is the kind of man God will hear. Whatever else others might do, Hezekiah would allow nothing to deflect him from this great purpose. Humanly speaking, he took a great risk in setting out to transform the nation; they might not want it or be ready for it. Assassination was not unknown to the kings of Israel and Judah. If revival came, it would not mean an easy ride; hard work and holiness are never divorced, but Hezekiah was determined.

God rarely uses in revival leadership those who are afraid of hard work and suffering because he would not be able to trust them with the commitment that revival demands. The apostle Paul listed in his letter to the Corinthians his hard work and suffering for the gospel (2 Corinthians 11:23–28).

Whitefield was not afraid of hard work. He preached at his Tabernacle in London every day (except Saturday) at 6.00 a.m. and 6.00 p.m. In addition, he preached three or four times each Sunday and on many more occasions throughout the week, at weddings, funerals and home meetings. He also kept up a wide correspondence. He spoke of being 'continually hurried and [I] scarce have time to eat bread.'

To preach to the North American Indians, David Brainerd travelled through 3,000 miles of dangerous frontier territory, mostly alone and whilst suffering from tuberculosis. God blessed him with revival. John Wesley travelled 5,000 miles each year on horseback and preached, on average, three sermons a day; he wrote more than 250 books, edited over 450 publications and could quote from the Greek New Testament as easily as from his English version.

God came to Ethiopia in such power when the missionaries were expelled that the church grew from forty-eight to 10,000 between 1937 and 1943. We are told, 'The leaders were and are common, ordinary men with an uncommon, extraordinary faith in Christ.'[1] They were men willing to suffer repeated imprisonment, flogging and many cruelties, and yet stand firm to the gospel. God prepared courageous men, ready and willing to give up everything in order to be available to God. It is this 'extraordinary faith in Christ' that marks out leaders in revival.

They were also determined men. Before the 1904 revival in Wales, Evan Roberts was challenged by a church elder never to miss the fellowship meeting: 'Remember to be faithful,' the elder warned him. 'What if the Spirit descended and you [are] absent? Remember Thomas! What a loss he had!' Roberts tells us that from that moment he determined: 'I will have the Spirit. And through all weather, and in spite of difficulties, I went to the meetings ... Prayer meetings Monday evening at the chapel; prayer meeting Tuesday evening at Pisgah (Sunday School branch); Church meeting Wednesday evening; Band of Hope Thursday; Bible class Friday evening. I could sit up all night to read or talk about revivals. It was the Spirit that moved me to think about revivals.'[2] Roberts was determined to get revival from God and he saw no cost and no discipline as being too great in order to achieve that.

When God came to Lewis off the west coast of Scotland in 1949, a local minister, James Murray MacKay, had prayed with his church officers for four months that God would pour out his Spirit in revival. They were determined to keep on until God heard them. The men God uses in revival

---

1 Davies, *Fire on the Mountains*, p.245.
2 Evans, *The Welsh Revival of 1904*, p.64.

are those who are wholly committed to him, passionately longing for God, and determined never to give up until God has his way with them. They may not be gifted in the eyes of the world, but they have a gift from God that may have no name in Scripture and therefore is little spoken about today—a gift of diligent and courageous determination.

Where are the men with courage and determination to lead the church forward and never to give up the vision of what God can do? 'Revival', claimed Douglas Brown, 'begins with a vision.'[3] Anything will distract us from the determined search for revival. Sometimes it is the fear of being misunderstood, or that our fellow-leaders will not share the vision, or that the church will not follow. Therefore, a passing acknowledgement of the need for revival is followed by a rush into better structures and better management, more hectic activity and harder work. We will adopt anything rather than make a serious covenant with the Lord to give neither him nor ourselves any rest until he comes.

3 Brown, *Revival Addresses*, p.8.

Before revival

Bold and urgent prayer

You cannot read far into the story of a revival without discovering that not only is prayer part of the inevitable result of an outpouring of the Spirit, but, from a human standpoint, it is also the single most significant cause. 'In the first month of the first year of his reign, [Hezekiah] opened the doors of the temple of the LORD and repaired them' (2 Chronicles 29:3). The fact that this was the first recorded action of his reign shows that he made it a priority. Opening the doors of the temple was his way of re-establishing his relationship with God, and that of the people, because the Ark of God was in the Holy of Holies in the temple, and it was there that the high priest brought the prayers of the nation before God. Hezekiah started here because he was aware that this was the root of the people's trouble: 'Our fathers were unfaithful; they did evil in the eyes of the LORD our God and forsook him. They turned their faces away from the LORD's dwelling-place and turned their backs on him' (v. 6). That was their sin—prayerlessness. What Hezekiah did in that action of reopening the temple was to bring himself back into a true and prayerful relationship with God.

> Those God uses in revival are never flippant and careless before God, but they are bold

The courageous determination in the life of those God uses in revival is seen also in their boldness in prayer. They are never flippant and careless before God, nor are they over-familiar or presumptuous—but they are bold. The confidence and insistence of Hezekiah with God is seen in his prayer when Sennacherib, King of Assyria, threatened the city. Hezekiah was aware of the sovereign power of God, and on this ground he took his stand; he expected God to act, and even demanded it:

'O LORD, God of Israel, enthroned between the cherubim, you alone are God over all the kingdoms of the earth. You have made heaven and earth. Give ear, O LORD, and hear; open your eyes, O LORD, and see; listen to the words Sennacherib has sent to insult the living God ... Now, O LORD our God, deliver us from his hand, so that all kingdoms on earth may know that you alone, O LORD, are God' (2 Kings 19:15–16,19). He had determined '...to make a covenant with the LORD, the God of Israel, so that his fierce anger will turn away from us' (2 Chronicles 29:10).

One of the most powerful prayers recorded in the Bible comes from Daniel, who confessed his sin without reservation (Daniel 9:1–16) and then boldly urged God to respond:

'Now, our God, hear the prayers and petitions of your servant. For your sake, O Lord, look with favour on your desolate sanctuary. Give ear, O God, and hear; open your eyes and see the desolation of the city that bears your name. We do not make requests of you because we are righteous, but because of your great mercy. O Lord, listen! O Lord, forgive! O Lord hear and act! For your sake, O my God, do not delay, because your city and your people bear your Name' (Daniel 9:17–19).

All the ingredients of great and confident praying are found in that cry of Daniel: an honest confession of sin and a total lack of confidence in himself are contrasted with Daniel's conviction that God must respond to defend his name and honour.

Even more daring is the prayer of Asaph who challenged God: 'How long will the enemy mock you, O God? Will the foe revile your name forever? Why do you hold back your hand, your right hand? Take it from the folds of your garment and destroy them!' (Psalm 74:10,11). An accurate equivalent in today's language would be: 'Stop dithering and take your hands out of your pockets and do something!'

A similar pattern is found in the story of the young church in the book of Acts. In spite of fierce opposition, the Christians expected their Sovereign Lord to act for them: 'You spoke by the Holy Spirit through the mouth of your servant David: "Why do the nations rage and the peoples plot in vain?"... Now, Lord, consider their threats and enable your servants to speak your word with great boldness. Stretch out your hand to heal and perform miraculous signs and wonders through the name of your holy servant Jesus' (Acts 4:25, 29–30). For the early church, prayer was not an option but a necessity. They were 'devoted' to it (Acts 2:42), and the definite article, '*the* prayer', in the Greek of Acts 1:14; 2:42 and 6:4 implies a commitment to corporate prayer. They were sufficiently bold to tell God what they expected from him.

Those whom God uses in revival are men and women of prayer. That is their great priority. This is true of a community also. Our fundamental problem today may be a simple one: 'You do not have because you do not ask.' And when we do ask it is half-hearted and insincere, 'because you ask with wrong motives' (James 4:2–3). We want revival to improve our reputation, vindicate our theology, add to our denomination, or just to encourage or excite us. We want revival for our benefit, not for God's honour. God frequently brings his people to the point of desperation before he sends revival; only then will they learn that, 'Without me you can do nothing.'

William Bramwell was determined that God must and will come. A powerful Wesleyan preacher towards the end of the eighteenth century and the first twenty years of the nineteenth, Bramwell was on the Dewsbury preaching circuit and longing for God to come in revival. He had been praying fervently for this when God gave him the assurance that the revival, which actually broke out in 1792, would come. Here is his own description: 'As I was praying in my room, I received an answer from God in a particular way, and had the revival discovered to me in its manner and effects. I had no more doubt. All my grief was gone; I could say, "The Lord will come; I know he will come, and that suddenly."'[1] Duncan Campbell maintained: 'Desire for revival is one thing; confident anticipation that our desire will be fulfilled is another.'[2]

In 1739 David Brainerd wrestled with God all night for his North American Indians:

> 'I exceedingly longed that God would get to Himself a name among the heathen ... Indeed, I had no notion of joy for this world. I cared not where or how I lived, or what hardships I went through, so that I could but gain souls to Christ. I continued in this frame all evening and all the night. When I was asleep I dreamt of these things, and when I waked (as I frequently did), the first thing I thought of was this great work of pleading for God against Satan.'[3]

The next morning he returned to his Indians with 'a strong hope that God would bear the burdens and come down and do some marvellous work among the heathen'. The following day their wild dancing was transformed first into repentance for sin and then joy in salvation.

John Wesley records a meeting in Fetter Lane when, with his brother Charles and George Whitefield: 'About three in the morning, as we were continuing instant in prayer, the power of God came mightily upon us, insomuch that many cried out for exceeding joy, and many fell to the ground.'[4] George Whitefield drew up a list in his diary of those actions by which he would judge himself each day. There were fifteen items, and

1 Paul Cook in Westminster Conference papers, *Preaching and Revival*, p. 94.
2 Woolsey, *Duncan Campbell*, p. 113.
3 Page, *David Brainerd*, p. 58.
4 Wesley's *Journal*, New Year's Day 1739.

the first three concerned his prayer life.[5] Whitefield's diary shows that his 'stated hours of prayer' were in the morning, at midday and at night. And he kept to these times, as a minimum, with strict discipline.

Jonathan Edwards argued that it is through intimacy with heaven that men are made great blessings in the world. In his carefully disciplined prayer life he gave his congregation in Northampton, New England, an example of this. Nearly a century after Edwards first saw revival in New England, Daniel Baker was greatly used by God on the same continent. After his settlement as pastor of the Independent Church in Savannah in 1828 he spent a day 'in fasting, humiliation, and prayer'. The site he chose for this was a brick tomb in a Negro cemetery, but it became a Bethel. His cold congregation was revived, his ministry was transformed and, until his death in 1857, Baker saw the continuous hand of God on his ministry with hundreds converted.

The constant prayer of Billy Bray in Cornwall was: 'Souls I must have, and souls I will have.' Whitefield prayed, 'O Lord, give me souls or take my soul.' It is said of David Morgan that for ten years before 1858 he never prayed in public without praying for revival.[6] In 1904 Joseph Jenkins in Cardiganshire in Wales prayed for the careless young people of his church, sometimes praying until he lost all sense of time. Jenkins had read Andrew Murray's *With Christ in the School of Prayer* and he was convicted of not discharging his duty as a minister. He set himself to pray as never before, until God came down.

Across Wales, many had been praying for revival from the turn of the century.[7] Commenting upon that revival in Wales in 1904, R. B. Jones looked back to the latter years of the previous century. From 1897 many younger ministers were meeting together to pray for revival: 'This fellowship intensified their hunger, bringing it at last to a pitch near to

5 Dallimore, *George Whitefield*, vol. 1, pp. 80–81.
6 Evans, *When He is Come*, p. 25.
7 Evans, *The Welsh Revival of 1904*, pp. 45–48, 57.

desperation.'[8] One minister recalled that on a Saturday evening when his sermon preparation was finished, he spent time in prayer and 'There would come upon him such a power as would crush [him] to tears and agonizing praying.'

Almost every Christian leader today laments a lack of personal prayer, but very few are determined to do much about it. We are not sufficiently concerned to make a radical alteration in our diaries and get down to the 'unproductive' and unnoticed battle of assaulting heaven. Many would prefer to be compared with Hezekiah rather than his father Ahaz, but it was the latter who' shut the doors of the LORD's temple', and in our lack of prayer we have done just that. When Hezekiah received news of a national emergency, he went immediately to God (2 Kings 19:14–19); faced with our weakness today we too often tackle the problem ourselves.

Prayer in the churches

However, prayer cannot be left only to the leaders. Churches must pray also. Joel 2:15–17 is a significant passage for us to come to terms with:

'Blow the trumpet in Zion,
   declare a holy fast,
   call a sacred assembly.
Gather the people, consecrate the assembly;
bring together the elders, gather the children,
   those nursing at the breast.
Let the bridegroom leave his room
   and the bride her chamber.
Let the priests, who minister before the LORD,
   weep between the temple porch and the altar.
Let them say, 'Spare your people, O LORD.

8 Jones, *Rent Heavens*.

Do not make your inheritance an object of scorn,
a byword among the nations.
Why should they say among the peoples,
"Where is their God?"'

Here is a community of the people of God called to pray for revival, and it clearly involved a radical alteration of their regular programme. The first hint of revival is frequently a stirring in the life of prayer in the church. However, it is often the example of the leaders that brings about this burden for prayer. Hezekiah set the example for the people by his own commitment to God in prayer.

Count Nikolaus Ludwig of Zinzendorf and Pottendorf was the leader of a Moravian community of around three hundred that settled on his estate in Saxony. They were a disparate and dispirited group, constantly arguing over theology and trivia. God began to work among them on 12 May 1727 and a spirit of prayer continued. On 16 July 1727, 'The Count poured forth his soul in a heart-affecting prayer, accompanied with a flood of tears; this prayer produced an extraordinary effect, and was the beginning of the subsequent operations of the life-giving and energetic Spirit of God ... a number of Brethren covenanted together of their own accord, engaging to meet often on the Hutberg [a mountain in Saxony], to pour out their hearts in prayers and hymns, and to be subject one to the other in love.' Zinzendorf, with a dozen or so brethren, spent a whole night in prayer. At their communion service on Wednesday 13 August 1727 the Spirit of God came down in such a way that: 'The whole place represented truly a visible tabernacle of God among men, and there was nothing to be seen and heard but joy and gladness.'[9] This was the beginning of the Moravian revival that within a few years sent missionaries across the world.

9 *The Memorial Days of the renewed Church of the Brethren*, pp. 102, 95.

The revival that came to England in 1859, and particularly to the preaching of Charles Haddon Spurgeon, can be traced back six years to the prayers of his London congregation. Spurgeon himself commented:

'When I came to New Park Street Chapel it was but a mere handful of people to whom I first preached, yet I could never forget how earnestly they prayed. Sometimes they seemed to plead as though they could really see the Angel of the Covenant present with them, and as if they must have a blessing from him. More than once we were all so awe-struck with the solemnity of the meeting that we sat silent for some moments while the Lord's Power appeared to overshadow us; and all I could do on such occasions was to pronounce the benediction, and say "Dear friends, we have had the Spirit of God here very manifestly tonight; let us go home and take care not to lose His gracious influence." Then down came the blessing; the house was filled with hearers, and many souls were saved.' [10]

In a powerful sermon preached in Surrey Music Hall on Sunday morning 17 July 1859 Spurgeon urged his people to prayer for the lost: 'Have we not tried to preach without trying to pray? ... O dear friends! Let us agonise in prayer, and it shall come to pass that this Music Hall shall witness the sighs and groans of the penitent and the songs of the converted.' [11] Spurgeon's own life of disciplined prayer was an example to them all.

The same pattern is found before the 1859 revival in Ulster. James McQuilkin had been converted by the witness of an English lady in 1856 at his home town of Ballymena, and before long he had led three friends to Christ. The four of them agreed to meet every week for prayer and Bible Study. They chose the old schoolhouse near Kells, and during the winter of 1857–58 each of them gathered an armful of peat and made his way to

10 Hayden, *Spurgeon on Revival*, p. 14.
11 Spurgeon, *Revival year Sermons*, p. 32.

the schoolhouse every Friday evening. The peat fire warmed their bodies and their prayers called down fire from heaven. Two more joined them, including an old man named Marshall, but it was not until New Year's Day 1858 that they saw their first conversion. By the end of that year the prayer meeting had grown to fifty. They prayed 'for an outpouring of the Holy Spirit upon ourselves and upon the surrounding country. This was the one great object and burden of our prayers. We held right to the one thing and did not run off to anything else.' The prayer group was ridiculed for praying in this way 'but we kept right on praying until the power came'. It did come, and by the close of the following year 100,000 people had been converted in Ulster.[12]

It has always been this urgency and determination about prayer that is key to revival. More than a hundred years ago Brownlow North, who was greatly used in revival both in Scotland and Ireland, complained to the General Assembly of the Presbyterian Church of Scotland: 'I believe there is one thing for which God is very angry with our land, and for which His Holy Spirit is so little among us, that is, the neglect of united prayer, the appointed means of bringing down the Holy Spirit.'[13]

Thomas Phillips reported in detail on the revival across Wales in 1859 and concluded, 'Prayer meetings have been the principal means with us of awakening the churches.'[14] William Griffiths of Llanharan urged his people to pray and reported,

> 'When the stated Sabbath arrived, we were blessed with remarkable earnestness at the throne of grace for the descent of the Holy Spirit to revive the church and convert the world. Ever since that memorable Sabbath, the prayer meetings presented a new aspect—they gradually increased in warmth and number during

12 Paisley, *The Fifty-Nine Revival*, p. 17.
13 Greenfield, *Power From on High*, p. 68.
14 Phillips, *The Welsh Revival*, pp. 122, 48–51.

the following months. This continued to February (1859) ... when it pleased Jehovah to pour down His Spirit from on high, as on the day of Pentecost.'[15]

A meeting of the Congregational Churches of Monmouthshire on 14 June had urged upon the churches the need for prayer for revival: 'The Conference unanimously recommended ... that the first Sabbath of next August should be set aside to hold prayer meetings throughout all the churches of Monmouthshire, and as many other counties of Wales as will see fit to join us in this important matter.' The Baptists had encouraged the same, and all over the country pastors took up the challenge. Among many, William Jenkins of Brynmawr found his congregation praying 'as I have never heard them pray before. A new burden seemed to press on their hearts.'[16]

In Japan, in 1883, a week of prayer for revival was followed by a great outpouring, and during the next seven years church membership rose from 5,000 to 30,000. Early in 1900 the churches set themselves to pray for a work of God, and a call went out for prayer that 'the Spirit of the Lord [would] prepare the way for a meeting of Pentecostal power'. Prayer meetings were held with as many as 800 gathering at one time. A year later missionaries were speaking of a 'Pentecost in Japan'.

Reporting on the revival in Shillong in the Khassi Hills of India in 1905 one eyewitness commented: 'There are many who ask "How did the revival begin?" To this we can only answer that "The wind bloweth where it wants"; but we know for a certainty that many people have been praying for a revival, praying, hungering, thirsting for it.' In Wales Christians were praying that the Lord in his mercy would not withhold the blessings from Khassia, and in Khassia a very earnest spirit of expectation prevailed.[17]

15 Evans, *When He is Come*, p. 37.
16 Evans, *When He is Come*, pp. 36–38.
17 Jones, *India Awake*, p. 64.

Nearly forty years later in India the Spirit of God came to Madras when the Christians began to spend whole nights in prayer. One, who had never prayed like this before, described how he felt at the close of his first night of prayer: 'I thought about an hour must have passed but to my amazement I saw that it was nearly daybreak.'[18]

Jonathan Goforth, working in China at the time of revival in 1908, wrote of the great impression that the prayer life of missionaries in Korea made upon him:

'Mr [William] Swallen of Pyongyang told me how that the missionaries of his station, both Methodists and Presbyterians, upon hearing of the great Revival in the Khassia Hills of India, had decided to pray every day at the noon hour until a similar blessing was poured out upon them. "After we had prayed for about a month," said Mr Swallen, "a brother proposed that we stop the prayer meeting, saying, 'We have been praying now for a month, and nothing unusual has come of it. We are spending a lot of time. I don't think we are justified. Let us go on with our work as usual, and each pray at home as he finds it convenient.' The proposal seemed plausible. The majority of us, however, decided that, instead of discontinuing the prayer meeting, we would give more time to prayer, not less. With that in view, we changed the hour from noon to four o'clock; we were then free to pray until supper-time, if we wished. We kept to it, until at last, after months of waiting, the answer came."'[19]

Joseph Kemp described the prayer that preceded successive waves of revival at Charlotte Chapel, Edinburgh, in 1905 and 1906:

'The meetings became marked by a deeper outgoing of the soul to God in prayer than ever; and a passionately expressed desire for the salvation of men was a

18 Rajamani & Kinnear, *Monsoon Daybreak*, p. 61.
19 Goforth, *By My Spirit*, p. 29.

dominant feature. Towards the close of 1906 there were indications that the Lord was about to move in our midst once more. The attendances at the 7 a.m. prayer meetings on Lord's Days increased, and the meetings were marked by a deepening spirit of prayer. This was followed up by the same prayer spirit in the week-night meetings.'[20]

Before God began the revival that swept across Borneo in the 1970s, he had been preparing the ground by giving the missionaries a burden to pray. One missionary comments, 'At the Field Conference in 1970 and over the following years, God began to work in the missionary team. There are frequent mentions of an increased urgency in prayer for revival…' The turning-point came when a group of Bornean students spent the whole night in prayer and fellowship. In June 1972 the missionaries held a houseparty for the students and this led to an even greater desire for prayer. Two students began to pray each evening at 9.30 p.m; gradually the group grew and then divided into two groups until a great wave of student prayer was reaching God for revival in Borneo.[21]

In 1921 even the *Yarmouth and Gorleston Times* for 10 November acknowledged: 'God has become very near and the secret of it all can be summed up in one word—prayer.'[22] For two years before revival commenced in Lowestoft in February 1921, the ministers of London Road Baptist Church and Christ Church covenanted with their people to pray, and eighty or more met regularly on Mondays and Saturdays: 'What prayer meetings we used to have' recalled one lady.[23] Jackie Richie reminds us that this revival was preceded by a time of spiritual decline:

20 Kemp, *Joseph W. Kemp*, p. 32.
21 Lees, *Drunk Before Dawn*, p. 178.
22 Ritchie, *Floods Upon the Dry Ground*, p. 106.
23 Griffin, *A Forgotten Revival*, p. 113.

'Yet, in the mending lofts, on the boats and along the quays there were those who had a hunger for God. Days and nights were spent in prayer before the Throne of Grace. God had moved upon the hearts of these people who had little education and whose material means were limited, but who were "far-ben" with Him ... These men "whose hearts the Lord had touched", had received a vision and were willing to wait upon God until the vision became a reality.'[24]

Revival came to Lewis in 1949 as groups of Christians, here and there throughout the island, set themselves to pray. Peggy and Christine Smith prayed, alone in their cottage. Peggy was eighty-four and blind; Christine was eighty-two and crippled with arthritis. They prayed until they knew that God was going to send revival. But these were only two of many. For months James Murray MacKay and his church leaders prayed for an outpouring of God's Spirit.[25]

Methodism in the nineteenth century knew about the importance of prayer both to call down and maintain revival. Whenever they detected a decline in the revival, they renewed their effort in prayer. The work of God in revival throughout various parts of England in the nineteenth century, and in America at the same period, may be traced to the Baptist 'Call to Prayer' in 1784, which was taken up elsewhere in Europe, and the 'Union for Prayer' in 1785 and the American 'Concert of Prayer' from 1795.[26]

When God came to Redruth in Cornwall in 1814 there had been a series of special prayer meetings early in February of that year. In 1901 in Melbourne, Australia, 2,000 'home prayer circles' for an outpouring of God's Spirit resulted in the city being 'moved from end to end by the mighty movings of the Spirit of God'. These 'home prayer circles' caught

24 Ritchie, p. 14.

25 Woolsey, *Duncan Campbell*, pp. 113–114. See also *Praying for Revival* 'I was there' for the account of Duncan Campbell.

26 See for example Orr, *The Eager Feet*, p. 148.

on in England and elsewhere by 1902, and it is partly to these that the revivals in various parts of the world from 1904–1907 owe their origin. There is an account of revival that came to a church in Wales in 1903, a year before the general movement of God there: Four young men, all less than eighteen years old, had gone to the mountains every night for months to pray for their church. When the secret was discovered the church was so moved that they all turned to prayer and 'In an incredibly short time the whole neighbourhood was ablaze with divine fire.'[27]

Prayer for revival should never be self-centred. If we long for the glory of God then we will be ready to invest prayer time that others too will receive the Spirit of God in revival. Following a conference in the Philippines in 1975, two hundred participants returned to their home countries determined to raise prayer for China, then in the grip of Mao Zedong. In Britain, for example, the 'China—Too Hard for God?' campaign led to many committing themselves to pray for that great nation. What has been happening in China can only be understood in terms of revival. Since the first Protestant missionary, Robert Robinson, entered China in 1807, Fenggang Yang, of Purdue University's Center on Religion and Chinese Society, estimates that there are between 93 million and 115 million Protestants in China, with fewer than 30 million attending officially registered churches; and the church is growing at ten percent each year.[28] Across the world thousands of Christians have never ceased to pray for China since the last missionaries were expelled in 1948 when there were less than one million Christians in the country.[29]

Almost 250 years earlier, Asahel Nettleton in America knew the importance of communities praying for each other. At Milton he urged the Christians to pray for revival but then added, 'Whether you do or not,

---

27 Jones, *Rent Heavens*, pp. 31–32.
28 On-line: The Council of Foreign Relations, October 2018.
29 Lyall, *God Reigns in China*, pp. 160,167.

it is possible there may be one, for Christians in other places have agreed to pray for you'!'[30]

Prayer for revival must surely be one kind of preparation that is never wrong; it is essentially God-centred and not man-centred. It tells God we are trusting in him. Commenting upon Zechariah 12:10, 'I will pour out on the house of David and the inhabitants of Jerusalem a spirit of grace and supplication...' the Puritan Matthew Henry wrote, 'When God intends great mercy for his people, the first thing he does is to set them a-praying.' Similarly, John Wesley was convinced that 'God does nothing but in answer to prayer.' Arthur Pierson, who for many years edited 'The Missionary Review', made the same claim: 'From the day of Pentecost, there has been not one great spiritual awakening in any land which has not begun in a union of prayer, though only among two or three; no such outward, upward movement has continued after such prayer meetings have declined.'[31]

A minister in Caernarvonshire, prior to 1859, speaks for many since: 'It came to the mind of the Lord's people in this place to hold a meeting for prayer once a week; and the particular subject of the prayers was to plead that God would also visit them in the influences of His Spirit, as comforter and convicter. This meeting was quite popular for a while; but somehow or other it gradually diminished, until the attendance at the gatherings was very low.'[32] Fortunately it was the news of revival in Cardiganshire, much closer than America, that revitalized the prayer meeting and 'The dawn finally broke in the young people's Sunday night prayer meeting.' But this gradual diminishing of our determined prayer is a mark of our lack of urgency and longing for revival.

A greatly increased interest in the prayer meeting is not only evidence of revival, it is also evidence that revival may be on the way. The ready response of the priests to Hezekiah's order to reopen the temple was not in

30 Thornton, *God Sent Revival*, p. 60.
31 Greenfield, *Power from on High*, p. 68.
32 Evans, *When He is Come*, p. 38.

itself the revival, but it was the early rain that promised a harvest shortly to follow. God waits to see whether those who say they are concerned for the state of the church and the nation are serious enough to pray on. His promise for ever stands: 'If my people, who are called by my name, will humble themselves and pray and seek my face and turn from their wicked ways, then will I hear from heaven and will forgive their sin and will heal their land. Now my eyes will be open and my ears attentive to the prayers offered in this place' (2 Chronicles 7:14–15). Hezekiah knew that condition and was determined to fulfil it.

Commenting on the prayer that preceded the revival in Shotts in 1630, one writer remarked that while God sometimes works without his people, he never refuses to work with them.[33]

Is he waiting for his church today?

---

33 *Narratives of Revivals of Religion*, p. 12.

Before revival

Responding to accounts of revival

Hezekiah was interested in the life of King David because he lived 'just as his father David had done' (2 Chronicles 29:2). Presumably this is how he found those proverbs written by David's son, Solomon (Proverbs 25). Hezekiah inherited the rich stories of God's care for his people in the past and he could say with the psalmist: 'We have heard with our ears, O God; our fathers have told us what you did in their days, in days long ago...' (Psalm 44:1).

When David felt hounded and hard-pressed, with a thirsty soul that was unsatisfied even after praying, he set his mind upon what God had done and that gave him hope in God: 'I remember the days of long ago; I meditate on all your works and consider what your hands have done' (Psalm 143:5).

When Asaph felt neglected or rejected by God, and when he was tempted to doubt God's love, he knew what his response should be: 'Then I thought, "To this I will appeal: the years of the right hand of the Most High." I will remember the deeds of the LORD; yes, I will remember your miracles of long ago. I will meditate on all your works and consider all your mighty deeds' (Psalm 77:10–12).

Most Christians today are disinterested in what God has done in the past.

> Most Christians today are disinterested in what God has done in the past

In 1839, William Chalmers Burns told the congregation at Kilsyth in Scotland about revival in the churchyard at Shotts in 1630, when five hundred were converted during one sermon by John Livingstone. As Burns retold the story, he felt himself so deeply moved that he pleaded with the people from this godless town to respond at once. They did, and revival came to Kilsyth. In August of the same year Burns was preaching at St Peter's in Dundee in the absence of the minister, Murray M'Cheyne, who was in Israel. For some time M'Cheyne had made it a habit to use the Thursday evening meeting not only for prayer and Bible study, but also for 'reading accounts of Missions, Revivals of Religion etc.'. When Burns related what was happening at Kilsyth the people were prepared, and revival came to Dundee as well.[1]

During 1858 God was moving powerfully across America, and there can be no doubt that it was this work of revival that inflamed the minds of many in Britain for a similar outpouring of the Spirit here. The General Assembly of the Presbyterian Church of Ireland, meeting in Dublin in 1858, agreed to send two of its leaders, William Gibson and William McClure, to witness the revival in America at first hand; they returned with enthusiastic reports which they shared in meetings and in a book, resulting in a longing for God to do the same in Ulster.

Meanwhile, reports of the same work in America were being received in Wales. William Jenkins, the minister of the Congregational Church at Brynmawr, was typical of many ministers at this time:

> 'Ever since the news of the outpouring of the Spirit upon the American churches reached our country, I longed and prayed that the Lord would, in his infinite mercy, visit poor Wales. I immediately brought the subject before the church and earnestly exhorted them to "seek the Lord" ... I related every fact and incident I could glean ... in order to produce in the minds of my people the desire of a similar visitation ... Some of [our aged members] ... prayed as I have never heard them pray before. A new burden seemed to press on their hearts ... There were

1 Orr, *The Eager Feet*, p. 148.

no less than eighty-five added to the church in about six months after those prayer meetings. This was in the year 1858.'[2]

Those prayer meetings for revival stopped after a while but restarted when the people heard of the revival in Cardiganshire under David Morgan's preaching. They were given further incentive when news of the revival in Ireland reached them. A young preacher called Humphrey Jones arrived back in his native Wales from America in 1858 determined to set Wales ablaze with revival. Scotland was affected both by news from America and also from Ireland. Prayer meetings for revival began in Edinburgh, Glasgow and Aberdeen and when revival began in Aberdeen in 1859 it was commonplace for people to be converted in the prayer meetings for revival.

Asahel Nettleton was preaching in America during the first half of the nineteenth century and his biographer notes that the spiritual awakenings were contagious and spread from one congregation to another. Often when a pastor and his parishioners heard about a revival in a nearby town or parish they went to see for themselves and frequently caught the flame and carried it back to their own vicinity. The revival at Wethersfield, just south of Hartford, is an example. Jacob Brace was the pastor of a church in Newington, to the east of Wethersfield. The people in this town 'heard with awe' of what was going on in their sister church, and they occasionally visited there to observe for themselves. They did not want to be 'passed by'.[3]

There can be little doubt that the Welsh revival of 1904 was one of the most influential revivals ever. In 1905 the pastor at Charlotte Chapel in Edinburgh was persuaded by his church officers to go to Bournemouth for a rest. Joseph Kemp stayed there for only a day or two because the

2 Evans, *When He is Come*, pp. 37–38.
3 Thornton, *God Sent Revival*, pp. 119–120.

sight of so many invalids made him feel worse! He had heard of the revival in Wales and determined to go there instead. Years later he reflected on that visit: 'I spent two weeks watching, experiencing, drinking in, having my own heart searched, comparing my methods with those of the Holy Ghost; and then I returned to my people in Edinburgh to tell what I had seen ...' His wife took up the story of that introduction of revival to Charlotte Chapel:

'The evening he returned from Wales was memorable. A large meeting was in full swing when he walked down the aisle of the chapel. The people listened eagerly as he told of his visit and its effect upon his own soul. After telling the story he tested the meeting, asking if there was a man willing to be saved. About five seats from the front a man rose, saying, "I want you to pray for me." This man was the first of hundreds who were saved during the revival in Charlotte Chapel. The people were now on the tiptoe of expectancy for a revival. A Conference on January 22, 1906, addressed by several workers who had visited Wales, lasted from 3.30p.m. until midnight. From that day it was felt that the fire of God had fallen; and as far as Charlotte Chapel was concerned, God had answered prayer and reviving had come.'[4]

As 'observers' and missionaries returned to their fields of service from furlough in Wales, the effect of this powerful work in Wales spread to virtually every continent of the world. The Calvinistic Methodist Church of Wales had a number of missionaries working in India in the Khassi and Jaintia Hills in Assam. In 1905 revival came there in a power and intensity that equalled that in the homeland. A missionary describes how the first news of revival in Wales began to affect the missionaries in Assam: 'When we read of the wonderful work of the Spirit in Wales, our desire for a spiritual Revival in India was fanned into flame. Every week when

4 Kemp, *Joseph Kemp*, pp.29–30.

the mail arrived bringing fresh news, the desire became more intense, and almost unknown to ourselves we began to pray for the Spirit, and to expect a real Revival.'[5]

Similarly, in Madagascar Thomas Rowlands, from Trefgarn in Pembrokeshire, learned of the revival in Wales and this stirred up a longing in many: 'If for Wales, why not for Madagascar?' On 5 May 1904 revival came and soon Rowlands' wife was writing in her diary: 'I think it must have been like the first Pentecost ... Never in our missionary career have we had such joy and gladness.'[6] In America the Welsh churches longed for the same spirit of revival and received it. It spread across the border into Mexico. In France the French Home Office was sufficiently concerned about revival there to order an enquiry into the effects this 'religious excitement' might have upon those suffering from 'nervous instability'. Sweden, Denmark, Germany, Belgium, Hungary and Bulgaria were all touched in 1905 by revival traceable to Wales. Africa, Australia, New Zealand, China, Korea and, as we have seen, India were all blessed by the revival fire from tiny Wales. Edwin Orr, reflecting on this spread of revival from Wales comments simply: 'The story of the Welsh Revival is astounding.'[7]

Revival in the Manchuria district of China in 1908 was a great-grandchild of Wales. A longing for revival among the national Christians and missionaries in Manchuria was quickened by Jonathan Goforth's description of revival in Korea the year before; that revival in Korea was itself sparked by missionaries in Pyongyang, the capital of North Korea, hearing of the work of the Spirit in the Khassi Hills of India. The revival in India in 1905 was the product of Wales.

What is not appreciated is that the 1904 revival in Wales was itself stimulated by the news of revival in Melbourne, Australia two years earlier

5 Jones, *India Awake*, p. l.
6 Orr, *The Flaming Tongue*, p. 115 and article in *Evangelical Times*, Sept 1986.
7 Orr, *Evangelical Awakenings*, p. 14.

under the preaching of two American missionaries, Reuben Torrey and Charles Alexander. And this was preceded by some 1700 prayer meetings for revival. In 1904 Torrey and Alexander were conducting a mission in Wales.[8]

This revival contagion cannot be explained in terms of human psychology. Christians could attend meetings and, as for example in Korea, 'return to their homes ... taking the Pentecostal fire with them'.[9]

> Revival contagion cannot be explained in terms of human psychology

Similarly, in 1921, when the Scottish fishermen were converted in Yarmouth and returned to their fishing ports in Scotland: 'It was like moving from one revival fire into another.'[10] In the Congo in 1953 a letter sent from one missionary to another describing the revival hundreds of miles away was like a spark that began an awakening there also.

As Hezekiah was influenced by the life of King David, so the lives of men greatly used by God have had an equally contagious effect in the story of revival. Many have been stirred to long for God in revival by reading the life of David Brainerd—including John Wesley, who recommended that all his Methodist preachers should read the life of Brainerd. James McQuilkin was moved to pray for the power of God in Ulster after reading the story of George Müller of Bristol, and Rajamani in Madras was greatly challenged by the lives of C. T. Studd and Hudson Taylor.

Most of those whom God uses in revival have themselves been made aware of what God has done in the past. This is not true of all, because there are times when God comes to a part of his church that has no knowledge of such things. But that is not so with us. We have a rich history of God at work among his people in revival and we are foolish not to take

---

8 Davies, R. E., *I Will Pour Out My Spirit*, p. 175.
9 Blair & Hunt, *The Korean Pentecost*, p. 75.
10 Ritchie, *Floods Upon the Dry Ground*, p. 54.

advantage of learning all we can about past revivals so that we are responsive to God's possibilities for us. We need to understand what God has done and expand our faith for what God can do. Perhaps he waits for us to be responsive to what he has done in the past.

> We need to understand what God has done and expand our faith for what God can do

'Like cold water to a weary soul is good news from a distant land' (Proverbs 25:25).

5. During revival

Here again is our definition and description of revival: 'Revival is a sovereign work of God's Holy Spirit in an unusual awakening of spiritual life among God's people. This is accompanied by an awesome awareness of God, a deep conviction of sin, a longing for holiness of life, a renewed joy and love for the Father and the Son, and a passion to reach the lost. It generally leads to a significant number of the lost coming to a true faith in Christ.'

The presence of God

It is not possible to read of a genuine spiritual revival in the history of the Christian church without discovering such phrases as: 'The felt presence of God' or 'the awesome presence of God.' When Duncan Campbell described revival as 'a community saturated with God', he did so from personal experience. He knew what it was to feel the awesome presence of God which is undoubtedly a hallmark of revival. Writing of revival, Spurgeon commented, 'By his coming, salvation is brought near, and glory, even the glory of the presence of the Lord, tabernacles among men.'[1]

We may *believe* the promises of God that he is always present when Christians meet together. However, revival is altogether different. God is *felt* to be there, and even the unbeliever is compelled to admit, 'God is really among you' (1 Corinthians 14:25). In revival the presence of God becomes a tangible, felt experience.

1 Spurgeon on Psalm 85:9 in *The Treasury of David*.

The presence of God was familiar to many of the greatest leaders in the Old Testament and the phrase 'the face of God', which is well translated 'the presence of God', occurs often. Moses refused to consider a forward march unless God kept his promise. For Moses, it was one great hallmark of their worship and activity that distinguished the Israelites from the surrounding nations. This 'felt' presence of God was convincing evidence that these people were in favour with the Sovereign Lord: 'Then Moses said to him, "If your Presence does not go with us, do not send us up from here. How will anyone know that you are pleased with me and with your people unless you go with us? What else will distinguish me and your people from all the other people on the face of the earth?"' (Exodus 33:14–16). It was the presence of God that so filled Solomon's Temple that the priests could no longer remain there (1 Kings 8:10–11).

On Wednesday, 13 August 1727, when God came among the small community of exiles at Herrnhut on the estate of Count Nikolaus of Zinzendorf in Saxony, he records, 'A sense of the nearness of Christ was given to us all at the same moment ... what the Lord did for Herrnhut, from that time till the winter of the same year, is inexpressible. The whole place appeared like a visible tabernacle of God with men.'[2] One report of the revival in Cambuslang in 1742 speaks of the 'gracious and sensible [felt] presence of God'.[3] In 1839 in Dundee M'Cheyne expressed the same experience like this: 'The private meetings for prayer have spread a sweet influence over the whole place.'[4]

A prayer meeting attended by thousands in Wales in 1859 left one man aware only of God. He walked away in silent awe. A friend stopped him, and commented, 'What a glorious sight that was, when the thousands were engaged in silent prayer at Mr Morgan's request! Did you ever see anything like it, Mr John?' He answered solemnly, 'I didn't see one of

2 Davies, *The Moravian Revival*, p.7.
3 Dallimore, *George Whitefield*, vol.2, p.128.
4 Bonar, *Memoirs and Remains*, p.94.

them: I saw *no one but God*. I am going home. How terrible is this place! It is too terrible for me. My flesh is too weak to bear this weight of glory…'[5]

Rhys Bevan Jones commented on the years 1904–5 in Wales: 'A sense of the Lord's presence was everywhere. It pervaded, nay it created, the spiritual atmosphere, It mattered not where one went, the consciousness of the reality and nearness of God followed.' He described a scene at Amlwch, Anglesey during one of the most powerful meetings he ever experienced in Wales in 1904: 'The whole place at that moment was so awful with the glory of God—one uses the word "awful" deliberately; the holy presence of God was so manifested that the speaker himself was overwhelmed; the pulpit where he stood was so filled with the light of God that he had to withdraw! There; let us leave it at that. Words cannot but mock such an experience.'[6]

Frequently, such expressions are recorded as: 'The house was often so full of the divine presence that ungodly men trembled terror-stricken…'[7] People could feel the presence of God even at a distance from a town. In 1905, far away in Australia, God was at work; at meetings in Bowden Methodist Church the congregations were reluctant to leave and 'Manifestations of the Divine Presence and power were marked and felt by all present.'[8] In 1906 Joseph Kemp described the coming of the Spirit to Charlotte Chapel in Edinburgh: 'Quite suddenly, upon one and another came an overwhelming sense of the reality and awesomeness of His presence and of eternal things.'[9] In January 1907, when God came among his people in North Korea a missionary records: 'Each felt as he entered the church that the room was full of God's presence … That night in Pyongyang … [there was] a sense of God's nearness impossible

5 Evans, *When He is Come*, p. 90.
6 Jones, *Rent Heavens*, pp. 43–44.
7 Evans, *When He is Come*, p. 55.
8 Orr, *The Flaming Tongue*, p. 111.
9 Kemp, *Joseph W. Kemp*, p. 32.

of description.'[10] In Shantung, China, in 1908 'the presence of God seemed completely to fill the building' and the people could hardly even pray.[11] When revival came among the Zulus in Mapumulo, KwaZulu Natal in 1966, Erlo Stegen wrote, 'Everybody was conscious of the presence of God without anybody saying a word. All I could do was to bow down and worship the God of Heaven.'[12]

Among the fishing ports on the east coast of England in 1921, tough, burly fishermen were giving testimony to how God had dealt with them: 'As these recently converted people got up and told how and when they were saved, the atmosphere was charged with the presence of God.' It is recorded that in Yarmouth that year, 'The entire town was in the grip of the presence of God.' So evident was this that even the *Yarmouth & Gorleston Times* for 10 November reported: 'God has become very near.'[13] Phrases such as: 'An awesome awareness of God', 'the powerful presence of God' and 'a sense of God's presence in the town' are used to describe the 'atmosphere' at that time.[14]

In 1949 Duncan Campbell was at Arnol on the island of Lewis, off the west coast of Scotland. When God came down, the community became 'alive with an awareness of God.' Elsewhere in the Western Isles, a man came to the home of a minister in great concern for his spiritual welfare. The minister asked, 'What touched you? I haven't seen you at any of the services.' The man replied, 'No, I haven't been to church, but this revival is in the air. I can't get away from the Spirit.'[15] Duncan Campbell commented, 'Perhaps the most outstanding feature in this part of Harris was the awe-inspiring sense of the presence of God….'[16] Others at this

10 Blair & Hunt, *Korean Pentecost*, p. 71.
11 Goforth, *By My Spirit*, p. 156.
12 Stegen, *Revival among the Zulus*, p. 62.
13 Ritchie, *Floods Upon the Dry Ground*, pp. 54, 106.
14 Griffin, *A Forgotten Revival*, p. 117.
15 Woolsey, *Duncan Campbell*, p. 122.
16 Campbell, *The Lewis Awakening*, p. 24.

time have commented, 'You could sense and feel the presence of God everywhere', and again 'God was everywhere, in the very atmosphere. Whether they were godly or godless, people knew that God was there.'[17]

When Liviu Olah was inducted to the pastorate of the Baptist Church in Oradea in 1974, Romania was under the vicious leadership of the communist regime of Ceausescu. Liviu's preaching was powerfully effective and 'The presence of God was so real that some spoke of divine power in the very air they breathed.'[18]

This 'presence of God' defies human explanation, but Duncan Campbell claimed, 'I have no hesitation in saying that this awareness of God is the crying need of the church today.'[19] It cannot be made up for by the counterfeit of religious sobriety or enthusiastic wildness. It is altogether different from anything the church normally experiences. It is this sense of God's presence that compels a reverent awe of God: '"Should you not fear me?" declares the LORD, "Should you not tremble in my presence?"' (Jeremiah 5:22).

Solemn respect for God

A significant aspect of worship in the time of Hezekiah was a holy seriousness and respect for God. There were some noisy scenes in their worship, but their attitude to God is revealed in the phrases: 'The whole assembly bowed in worship ... When the offerings were finished, the king and everyone present with him knelt down and worshipped' (2 Chronicles 29:28–29). The choir and the band are no necessary barrier to revival; nor are they necessary evidence of it.

When Whitefield took part in the preaching and communion service at Cambuslang in 1742 one report claims, 'The thing most remarkable, was the spiritual glory of this solemnity...,' and Alexander Webster of

17 Peckham, *Sounds from Heaven*, pp. 90–91.
18 Birnie, *'Just call me Paul'*, p. 57.
19 Peckham, *Sounds from Heaven*, p. 29.

> No one takes revival lightly; there is joy, but not jollity. A holy seriousness is a hallmark of true revival

Edinburgh described the 'solemn, profound reverence [that] overspread every countenance' during the services at Cambuslang.[20] Revival came to Carloway on the Isle of Lewis between 1934 and the beginning of World War II, and an elder in the Free Church recalls, 'The churches were full, and the solemnity at these services was awe-inspiring…'[21] And so we could continue. No one takes revival lightly; there is joy, but not jollity. A holy seriousness is a hallmark of true revival. 'Solemnity' appears to be another key word in describing revival meetings.

In 1839 Murray M'Cheyne wrote of the revival in Dundee: 'It pleased God … to bring an awfully [dreadfully] solemn sense of divine things over the minds of men … There is far more solemnity in the house of God.' An awful [dreadful] and breathless stillness pervaded the assembly: 'each hearer bent forward in the posture of rapt attention'.[22] Under Asahel Nettleton, it was said, 'There seems to have been an increasing solemnity while the work continued.'[23] This affected the whole community. From Ulster during 1859 it was reported, 'During the service there were indications of an unusual solemnity, the most intense earnestness being depicted on every countenance…'[24] A contemporary newspaper claimed that the most striking feature of the revival in Wales in the same year was 'a pervading and overwhelming solemnity…'[25] In Wales in 1905 at some prayer meetings even the speakers felt bound to silence: 'There was a mysterious silence as though all knew that Someone was on the

---

20 Dallimore, *George Whitefield*, vol. 2, p. 128.
21 Macaulay, *The Burning Bush in Carloway*, p. 33.
22 Bonar, *Memoirs and Remains*, pp. 499, 500.
23 Thornton, *God Sent Revival*, pp. 67–68.
24 Paisley, *The Fifty-Nine Revival*, p. 23.
25 Evans, *When He is Come*, p. 90.

threshold … Each soul was enjoying a glad fellowship—face to face with God Himself so that all that is of man disappeared leaving only Light and Unfearing Awe. We, poor sinners, in the midst of the flame of His presence possessed by fear without fright, awe without anguish, humility without servility.'[26]

Joy and singing

Singing has always been part of the worship of God. From the moment of creation, the morning stars and the angels themselves have worshipped God in song (Job 38:7). The Israelites sang when God set them free from slavery in Egypt (Exodus 15) and when God brought his people back from their exile in Babylon (Psalm 126:2). David 'sang to the LORD' when God rescued him from his enemies (2 Samuel 22); he then established a choir for the temple worship. Psalm after psalm encourages us to sing out our worship of God and this was David's own natural response to God's personal deliverance (Psalm 40:3). It was in this long tradition of choral worship that Hezekiah encouraged his priests and Levites to 'praise the LORD with the words of David and of Asaph' (2 Chronicles 29:29–30). This privilege followed into the New Covenant (Ephesians 5:19; Colossians 3:16).

Singing is the natural response to the great joy that inevitably accompanies revival. The young church of Pentecost was found praising God 'with glad and sincere hearts' (Acts 2:46–47), and even prison could not silence their hymn-singing (Acts 16:25). It is these two things, singing and joy, that are found together in the time of Hezekiah:

'They sang praises with gladness' (2 Chronicles 29:30).
'All the people rejoiced at what God had brought about' (29:36).
They 'celebrated for seven days with rejoicing' (30:21).

---

26 Jones, *The King's Champions*, p.67.

'For another seven days they celebrated joyfully' (30:23).
'There was great joy in Jerusalem' (30:26).

Revival will always affect our worship, not necessarily by introducing new things but by bringing new life into what we do. When the Spirit of revival came to the Isle of Lewis in the middle of the last century, the churches still sang their metrical psalms slowly and without accompaniment, but there was a new life and reality in the old ways.

Possibly more than anywhere else in our evangelical church life there has been a revolution in worship. For richer or for poorer, where we are today is radically different from where we were before the middle of the twentieth century. Much of this change has been of huge value to Christian worship. However, the introduction of music groups ('the band') and new lyrics and tunes have been a mixed benefit. On the one hand we can enjoy some theologically strong and poetically rich hymns and songs that are as good as the best written from the eighteenth century; excellent new tunes and sensitive music groups have added to our spiritual enjoyment of worship. On the other hand, many contemporary lyrics are careless and self-centred accompanied by sloppy tunes performed by loud and insensitive bands. Too often this leads to a superficial, excitable, congregation simply enjoying themselves rather than enjoying God.

Culture and temperament each play their part in revival. When the Spirit came to Wales in 1859, there were frequent outbursts of praising at the preaching services; sometimes the preachers were interrupted and not able to continue because the praising was so great. Although Joseph Kemp commented from Edinburgh in 1905, 'The confusion never gets confused',[27] occasionally it does.

A strong and deep sense of the presence of God and conviction of sin are always present in revival; equally it is followed by expressions of

27 Kemp, *Joseph W. Kemp*, p. 34.

unbounded joy. Joseph Benson, during his preaching tour in Cornwall in June 1794, commented on his visit to St Just: 'Almost all the inhabitants seem convinced for their souls' lost state, accompanied with great distress of mind; and when they obtain mercy, the transition is sudden, from the depth of misery to a state of unspeakable joy, that I'm sure if an infidel saw it he must be convinced that it is the Lord's doing.'[28] In a simple letter to his friends in England, an elder in the church of Bario in Borneo revealed this change from tears of sorrow to songs of joy. He was writing on 7 November 1973, shortly after revival had come to the church there: 'The services are so different from what I have ever experienced before. When the Holy Spirit comes down upon the congregation, people begin to cry out in loud wailing ... After the sin problems have been dealt with by the Lord and forgiveness granted, then the service goes on with loud singing of praises while tears of joy are still flowing down.'[29]

Jonathan Edwards wrote of revival in Northampton, New England:

> 'This work of God ... soon made a glorious alteration in the town: so that in the spring and summer following 1735, the town seemed to be full of the presence of God: it was never so full of love, nor of joy, and yet so full of distress, as it was then. There were remarkable tokens of God's presence in almost every house. It was a time of joy in families on account of salvation being brought unto them; parents rejoicing over their children as new born, and husbands over their wives, and wives over their husbands ... God's day was a delight...'[30]

When God came to Cambuslang in 1742, the phrase 'joy unspeakable and full of glory' is found often in the records.[31] It was the only way that the writers could adequately express what God was doing in the lives of so

28 Isaac, *A History of Evangelical Christianity In Cornwall*, p. 111.
29 Lees, *Drunk Before Dawn*, p. 191.
30 Edwards, *A Narrative of Surprising Conversions*, p. 14.
31 Dallimore, *George Whitefield*, vol. 2, p. 131.

many. The revival that came to Beddgelert in Wales in 1817 was noted for its expression of gratitude to God: 'The outbursts of the joy of salvation [were] more powerful than were seen in some previous revivals.'[32] During one mission under R.B. Jones at Llanerchymedd in Wales there was so much singing and shouting for joy that one local wag announced, 'Look, there's the devil's funeral going by.'[33]

In faraway Assam, in north-eastern India, the effect of the 1904 awakening in Wales was carried back with a missionary, John Roberts, who had returned from furlough in Wales. The scene that at first shocked the Presbyterian missionaries was that of the rejoicing Khassi tribesmen, converted from head-hunting. When their conviction of sin gave way to unfettered rejoicing:

'In a united presbytery meeting of fifteen hundred folk, the singing overwhelmed the preaching, many of the awakened people dancing with joy, their arms outstretched, their faces radiant. Missionaries were astounded to see principal men and leading elders jump for joy. At first some missionaries disapproved, changing their minds as the revival transformed the Christians and won hundreds of non-Christians to the fellowship.'[34]

Merely to imitate this kind of behaviour will never produce a revival. But when such a spontaneous explosion of joy is genuine, there will be the accompanying sense of the presence of God. However, it is just as much part of revival when the response is quietly controlled. David Brainerd was working among the North American Indians when revival came; these were a people who were used to high excitement in their pagan religious ceremonies, and whom we might therefore expect to be extravagant in revival. In fact, Brainerd noted an absence of undue excitement in the

32 Evans, *When He is Come*, p. 14.
33 Jones, *The King's Champions*, p. 71.
34 Orr, *The Flaming Tongue*, p. 134.

meetings, and commented that often 'When their hearts have been glad they could not help crying.'[35] M'Cheyne particularly noted the same in Scotland, though deep emotion was certainly there. And it was said of a revival in Connecticut in 1799 that the people convicted were 'by no means noisy or boisterous'.

Sometimes the leaders themselves have a significant influence on the degree of excitement. There were more emotionally extravagant responses under the preaching of Wesley, who approved of them, than under the preaching of Whitefield, who disapproved. Similarly, the Welsh revival of 1904 under the leadership of Evan Roberts was noted for its noisy emotion, whereas a revival in Rhos at the same time under R. B. Jones was quietly controlled. Revival in Norway a year later, under Albert Lunde, lacked many of the marks of the Welsh revival but was none the less real. The American camp meetings, later copied by the Primitive Methodists in England, were often exuberant to a fault. However, we can never limit God in revival; the more we learn of his ways, the less we can be sure of what he will do.

We can never limit God in revival; the more we learn of his ways, the less we can be sure of what he will do

Singing almost always forms a significant part of a true spiritual revival; it is the natural overflow of the emotion of joy in forgiveness. Often the singing was the Psalms of David, 'sometimes set to none too good a metre', as someone has remarked. But the Spirit in revival did not seem to trouble with bad metre. Jonathan Edwards commented:

'Our public praises were then greatly enlivened; God was then served in our psalmody, in some measure, in the beauty of holiness ... There has been scarce any part of divine worship, wherein good men amongst us have had ... their

35 Page, *David Brainerd*, p. 106.

hearts so lifted up in the ways of God, as in singing his praises ... They [sang] with unusual elevation of heart and voice, which made the duty pleasant indeed.'[36]

In 1839 M'Cheyne noted that the psalm-singing in Dundee was 'so tender and affecting, as if the people felt that they were praising a present God'.[37] In Ulster, in 1859, 'The singing of the psalms was a perfect outburst of melodious sound.'[38] However, when a new wave of revival came to America under the ministry of Nettleton less than a century later it brought with it a new vogue of singing, and the result was a new hymnbook, *Village Hymns*. When God came to the Herrnhut community in Saxony in 1727 Count Zinzendorf wrote some excellent hymns for his people.

Revival and hymnody

The eighteenth century revival in England was accompanied by a fashion of 'modern' hymns. Philip Doddridge and Isaac Watts had both prepared the way, preceded in the seventeenth century by men like William Burton, Richard Baxter, Matthew Henry, John Mason and John Bunyan. The badly metred and poorly sung psalms were giving way to something a little more 'swift and jocund', though not to everyone's liking. Isaac Watts had published *Hymns and Spiritual Songs* and *Divine Songs for Children* by 1715, and these were followed by *Divine and Moral Songs*. The revival under Whitefield and Wesley gave a strong boost to hymn-writing. John Newton, the converted slave ship captain now preaching at Olney in Buckinghamshire, together with his friend and poet William Cowper, published *Olney Hymns* in 1779. John Wesley wrote and translated a number of hymns, but it was his brother Charles whose output was phenomenal: he is estimated to have written as many as 6,000 hymns.

36 Edwards, *A Narrative of Surprising Conversions*, p. 14.
37 Bonar, *Memoirs and Remains*, p. 116.
38 Paisley, *The Fifty-Nine Revival*, p. 23.

Singing formed such a major part of the worship of the early Methodist societies that John Wesley compiled some rules for Methodist singers.[39]

Howell Harris described the revival meetings in Wales during March 1743, particularly when Daniel Rowland was preaching; he commented upon the felt power of God and especially noted, 'Their singing and praying is indeed full of God.' Rhys Bevan Jones commented on the singing in Wales in 1904 that it was 'truly magnificent and stirring'—and that from the land of song. One witness, quoted by Rhys Jones, described the singing in this way: 'No need for an organ. The assembly is its own organ as a thousand sorrowing or rejoicing hearts found expression in the sacred psalmody of their native hills.'[40] The stirring words of William Williams', 'Here is love, vast as the ocean…', and its equally stirring tune, were sung all over the world and became the love song of the 1904 revival.[41] The now familiar 'Just as I am, without one plea…' was composed by Charlotte Elliott in 1836 and twenty-three years later was probably the most popular of the hymns sung in the revival.

When Joseph Kemp, the pastor of Charlotte Chapel in Edinburgh, reported to his own congregation after his visit to Wales in 1905, it was evidently the singing that impressed him greatly:

'In Wales I saw the people had learned to sing in a way which to me was new. I never heard such singing as theirs. They sang such old familiar hymns as "When I survey the wondrous Cross," and "There is a fountain filled with Blood," and "I need Thee, Oh, I need Thee." They needed no organist or choir or leader. Their singing was natural. The Holy Ghost was in their singing as much as in any other exercise. They had the New Song. People tell us our religion is joyless. Well, if

39 'Directions for Singing' published in *Select Hymns: with Tunes Annext* designed chiefly for the use of the people called Methodists. (1761).

40 Jones, *Rent Heavens*, pp. 49–50.

41 Composed by William Williams in his native Welsh and first published in 1847. Translated early in the twentieth century by William Edwards.

the saints of the Living God have no joy, who has? Jesus Christ has given us to see that joy is one of the qualities He imparts to the saints of God. The world knows nothing of it ...When a revival from God visits a congregation it brings with it joy.'[42]

5 March 1905 was the day the Holy Spirit revived the church in the village of Nongspung in the Khassi Hills of India. During the opening hymn of the Sunday Service: 'The people sang and sang, forgetting everything until one old man cried out asking someone to explain the hymn, which was done by one of the Christians, then the people began to sing it again, until the whole place was full of weeping tears of joy that they had such a wonderful Saviour.'[43]

On Lewis in 1949, groups of converts, unwilling to go home, would gather on the roadside or sea-shore singing praises to God and sharing together what God had done for them. One night in Ness the crowd was so great that they spilled out of the house into a field and sang 'until it seemed the angels were joining with them'.[44] Singing caught hold of the fishermen around the east coast of England in 1921: 'On the Denes [dunes] where most of the curing yards were, and across the river at Gorleston in the yards there, the songs of Zion were sung. Far out at sea as the boats lay at their nets, the singing of men who were redeemed wafted over the waves.'[45] Up in Fraserburgh Jock Troup saw scores of Scottish fishermen converted in services that were 'characterized by joyful singing'.

In 1973 in Borneo it is recorded: 'Somehow the singing was different. There was something beautiful, sweet and real about it all.'[46] And in Indonesia at about the same time, one eyewitness comments, 'Nothing I

42 Kemp, *Joseph W. Kemp*, pp.29–30.
43 Jones, *India Awake*, pp.21–22.
44 Woolsey, *Duncan Campbell*, p.124.
45 Ritchie, *Floods Upon the Dry Ground*, p.32.
46 Lees, *Drunk Before Dawn*, p.193.

have heard before compares with the singing I was enabled to hear in the actual revival centre on Timor. The wealth of songs in the revival churches is indeed amazing.'[47] Festo Kivengere confesses that before his conversion in the Uganda revival that began in the 1930s he was annoyed at the Christians singing everywhere, and found it offensive that the women should be singing Christian hymns as they filled their water-pots. Madras in the 1940s was filled with such joy as the Christians worshipped God and sang almost everywhere that one Hindu remarked, 'It looks as though Sermai Pattana has become a Christian city.'[48]

It is clear, therefore, that singing from the heart, which is vital, living, God-directed singing, is a natural overflow of the joy experienced in true revival. But there is no one kind of singing that God blesses in revival; he takes what the church normally uses and fills it with his Spirit. When revival came to Scotland and Ulster, only metrical psalms were sung, and without any instrument to accompany. In England, Charles Haddon Spurgeon led his congregation at the Metropolitan Tabernacle in hymns as well as psalms, but for him the organ was 'the devil's whistle' and it found no place at the Tabernacle.[49] Elsewhere psalms and hymns or hymns without psalms or hymns and songs and psalms were all sung, with or without accompaniment. There is no 'right' kind of singing in revival. It is how we sing that is different. David loved singing, whether alone on the hills or among the great congregation, but when God came and rescued him he described his singing as 'a new song' (Psalm 40:3), and the returning exiles described their singing as 'songs of joy' (Psalm 126:2). In revival, singing is the best we have in 'normal times', made better by the Holy Spirit.

---

47 Koch, *The Revival in Indonesia*, p. 260.
48 Rajamani & Kinnear, *Monsoon Daybreak*, p. 69.
49 In 1866 Spurgeon produced *Our Own Hymn Book*, for the Tabernacle. It contained 1060 items with special emphasis on hymns 'suitable for revivals, prayer-meetings, and earnest addresses to sinners.'

Longing for worship

Hezekiah 'opened the doors of the temple of the LORD' (2 Chronicles 29:3). Sooner or later revival always prompts a rush for the house of God. People who have not attended church in years now long to be there. No one talks of the unbeliever feeling a stranger in the place of worship; you can hardly keep them away from it—unless they are afraid of being converted.

In 1839 when M'Cheyne returned from Israel to his church in Dundee he reported, 'There was not a seat in the church unoccupied, the passages were completely filled, and the stairs up to the pulpit were crowded, on the one side with the aged, on the other with eagerly-listening children.' And for over four months, 'It was found desirable to have public worship almost every night.'[50]

A little over a century later, Martyn Lloyd-Jones was minister in Aberavon in Wales when God came in revival to the church. The description there in 1931 is typical of revival. It was the 'eagerness with which the congregations gathered' that impressed one observer:

'On a Sunday evening the building would start to fill as much as an hour before the 6.30 hour of service, with sometimes not a seat remaining empty by 6 p.m. The Monday and Wednesday meetings had both to be removed to the church itself on account of the numbers attending. Shopkeepers would arrive straight from their business without an evening meal. Night-shift workers, due to report for work at 8.30 p.m., would come in their working clothes, preferring to miss part of the meeting rather than the whole.'[51]

The same happened on the Isle of Lewis in 1949. At the close of meetings others arrived; people could not be kept away from wherever the Spirit

50 Bonar, *Memoirs and Remains*, p. 116.
51 Murray, *The First Forty Years*, p. 220.

was working. There was an irresistible power on Lewis, so that when the congregation moved out of the church and began to go home they were met by the people of the town wanting to know where God could be found.[52] In Borneo, in 1973, whole villages seemed to be going up to the place of worship.[53]

The first thing that happened when the Spirit of God began to move in the time of Hezekiah was that the doors of the temple were opened and people began to worship God again. Revival brings a love for worship and the lengthening of services. 2 Chronicles 30:23 describes this: 'The whole assembly then agreed to celebrate the festival seven more days; so for another seven days they celebrated joyfully.' These people had celebrated the festival of the Passover for a whole week. When they came to the end of the seven days there was a spontaneous decision to repeat it; this may be unprecedented in the Old Testament. In revival people long to be in the presence of God and to stay there. It is not planned that way, but God seems to contract time.

This happened at Cambuslang in 1742. Unusually for the church in Scotland, who normally celebrated communion on only a few occasions in the year, the session decided that in view of the great blessing of God during the revival they would arrange another service within a month. A minister reported on a revival in 1832 in Rhode Island, New England: 'Ordinarily ministers of New England preached twice on the Sabbath day and once in the evening of a week. Of late however the number of services have been much increased.' What he meant was three times at least on Sunday and many times during the week. In 1839 at St Peter's, Dundee the services occasionally went on until midnight because the people refused to leave. Just prior to this, at Kilsyth, William Chalmers Burns preached in a time of revival and on 22 September more than 12,000 people poured

52 Woolsey, *Duncan Campbell*, p. 117.
53 Lees, *Drunk Before Dawn*, p. 194.

into the town and the Sunday services continued throughout the day and concluded at daybreak on Monday.

A concise comment from Wales in 1859 summed up village after village and town after town: 'The chapel was full; the streets were empty.'[54] In 1904, Joseph Jenkins of the Calvinistic Methodist Church in New Quay, Wales, recorded in his diary: 'The revival goes on. I cannot leave the building ... until twelve and even one o'clock in the morning—I have closed the service several times and yet it would break out again quite beyond the control of human power.'[55] On 8 November 1904, at the Baptist Church in Rhos, the minister began what was planned to be a ten-day mission. The closing service of the mission commenced at ten o'clock in the morning and went through to ten o'clock in the evening. At this point the town of Rhos was 'ablaze' with a revival that lasted well into the following year.[56]

The 1859 revival in Ulster witnessed many scenes of meetings continuing long after the normal time for a service to close: 'The usual time for dismissal came, but they were heedless about the hour of the night. The day brightened in the heavens, the morning star was succeeded by the rising sun, but they still remained exhorting, praying, and praising the Lord. They did not leave the spot till five o'clock in the morning.'[57] The fishermen's revival in 1921 at Lowestoft on England's east coast also saw meetings continuing until the early hours of the morning: 'Whenever work was finished, meetings were held. Often due to bad weather the boats would tie up and many would gather together at all hours in different places. Meetings would often go on until three o'clock in the morning.'[58]

---

54 Phillips, *The Welsh Revival*, p. 59.
55 Evans, *The Welsh Revival of 1904*, p. 59.
56 As above, p. 117.
57 Paisley, *The Fifty-Nine Revival*, pp. 61–62.
58 Ritchie, *Floods Upon the Dry Ground*, p. 32.

During the early part of the Second World War meetings in Madras would sometimes last until ten or eleven at night, with three-hour sermons: 'But still they kept attending. It was unbelievable. No man could have brought it about; only God could create such a hunger for His Word.' [59]

In 1949 in Lewis, there was such a hunger to hear the word of God that when the services finished in the small hours of the morning the people assembled again a short distance away in the police station where many found the Saviour. At Barvas and Lochs the churches were crowded, with services continuing until three o'clock in the morning. Work was largely put aside, as young and old were made to face eternal realities.[60]

However, revival does not normally mean that work is neglected. More often the people find that the Spirit is invigorating, and long meetings into the night plus a full day's work go side by side. In the Welsh coal pits in 1904 men who had been at prayer meetings until the early hours rarely failed to report for work on time in the morning.

One of the longest meetings in revival on record took place at Tuckingmill in Cornwall. The year was 1814 and revival had spread from Redruth like a prairie fire. A service began in the Methodist chapel on Sunday, 27 February and the Holy Spirit was present in such power that the meeting could not be closed until the following Friday morning. People came and went, but the meeting continued. During the course of that week it was claimed that 2,000 people had professed Christ.

The following report from Ulster in 1859 is possibly the best summary of this love for worship in times of revival, which ignores the normal length of services and the need for rest:

'In this town [Ballymena] at present, at public worship on Sabbath, the churches are thronged—pews, alleys, and vestibules. The open-air services, whether in

59 Rajamani & Kinnear, *Monsoon Daybreak*, p. 68.
60 Campbell, *The Lewis Awakening*, p. 18.

town or country, on any evening of the week, are attended by thousands; and these services though so numerous are often not far distant from each other. Our congregational weekly prayer meeting was attended by some fifty persons ordinarily. During the three months past, whether held four times or seven times a week, it is attended by more than twenty times that number. The difficulty used to be to get the people into the church, but the difficulty now is to get them out of it. One night and morning we had three services. The first of these was three hours and a half. I pronounced the benediction intending to dismiss the people, but no, they kept possession, only a very few left. After some half hour we engaged in prayer and praise again. I pronounced the benediction, intending to dismiss the people, but no, they still kept possession, only a few left.'[61]

That minister left the meeting at two o'clock in the morning and commented, 'Many remained.'

It would be untrue to suggest that in revival no meeting ends at the stated time or that all services continue for many hours. However, things once considered dull and tedious become alive and meaningful in such a way that they cannot be left alone. Prayer, preaching and worship become the most enjoyable activities in life for both young and old. People cannot wait to get to the prayer meeting; it becomes the high point of the day. Today we have a carelessness in our churches, where many will not attend more than one service in a week. In revival the churches are overcrowded with people who only attend once—not because the congregation will not turn out for the evening, but because they will not go home in the morning.

Duncan Campbell commented, 'In revival time doesn't matter.' In more than one revival the claim was made that 'Clocks have gone out of fashion.'[62]

---

61 Paisley, *The Fifty-Nine Revival*, p. 184.
62 For example, Jones, *Rent Heavens*, p. 51.

During revival

A revival of Christ-centred preaching

Hezekiah was a man who relentlessly 'follow[ed] the word of the LORD' (2 Chronicles 29:15), and everything done in the revival was 'as prescribed in the Law of Moses' (30:16; 31:3, 21). Disobedience was to do anything 'contrary to what was written' (30:18). The willingness of the people to submit to the authority of God's word through the leaders is clear: 'The hand of God was on the people to give them unity of mind to carry out what the king and his officials had ordered, following the word of the LORD' (30:12). The immediate result of Pentecost was a sermon, and from there on the apostles saw themselves as 'heralds' of the good news (Romans 10:15; 1 Corinthians 1:21; 2:4). All whom God uses in exceptional times of spiritual power, both within the Bible and since, are men and women who trust God's word and place it at the centre of their belief and practice; they test everything by it. An evangelical theology of Scripture is the baseline of revival. Revival is an evangelical experience.

When Peter Waldo was converted to Christ around the year 1170, and discovered the clarity and authority of Scripture, he spread the good news by sending out preachers two by two, and the Waldensian movement reached out across Europe. Two hundred years later John Wycliffe was sending out his 'Poor Preachers', equipped only with the newly translated and hand-copied English Bible. A revival commenced which prepared the ground for the Reformation a century later. Hugh Latimer was an outstanding preacher during the Reformation, and wherever he preached, hundreds flocked to hear him. When Latimer preached before the young King Edward in 1548 courtiers crowded into the royal garden to hear him, and when he preached at St Margaret's in Westminster, the people crammed into the church until the pews cracked! The preaching of John Knox in Scotland transformed the religious inertia of that country. A century later, the Puritan ministers placed preaching above all their other public duties.

Writing of the revival in 1839 in Dundee, M'Cheyne claimed to have discovered nothing 'peculiar or different' in the work of the ministers: 'They have preached, so far as I can judge, nothing but the pure gospel of the grace of God. They have done this fully, clearly, solemnly; with discrimination, urgency, and affection. None of them read their sermons. They all, I think, seek the *immediate* conversion of the people, and they believe that, under a living gospel ministry, success is more or less the rule, and want of success the exception.'[1]

Commenting upon the revival in India in 1905, one missionary unknowingly summarized the place of Scripture in all true revivals: 'At the present time, perhaps, nothing may be found to be so appropriate as the supreme importance of the Bible, the whole Bible, and fundamentally, nothing but the Bible.'[2] Thirty-five years later in India, Bakht Singh invited his congregations to display their Bibles by raising them above their heads—and they were told to feel ashamed if they had not brought one; a van-load of Bibles was sold and 'People in Madras began to read the Bible as never before.'[3] If Scripture is at the heart of revival, it is hardly surprising that powerful preaching is at the heart of most revivals also.

> Preaching in revival times is not always graceful, polished, or eloquent, but it is always powerful

1 Bonar, *Memoirs and Remains*, p. 503.
2 Jones, *India Awake*, p. 18.
3 Rajamani & Kinnear, *Monsoon Daybreak*, p. 66.

Preaching in revival times is not always graceful, polished, or eloquent, but it is always powerful. By this word 'powerful', is not meant only that it changes lives, but that the sermons are felt by the congregation. The preaching of Asahel Nettleton in America from the 1830s onwards was described as 'vigorous and bold ... it was warm, pungent and awakening'. He was never 'graceful' as a preacher, but his plain, outspoken and serious ministry gripped the hearts and minds of his listeners. His biographer comments simply: 'His hearers tended to forget about the speaker and become engrossed in his message ... [the sermons] were eminently scriptural and plain, and made men feel that *they* were the men addressed, and not their neighbours.'[4] By contrast, George Whitefield was dramatic: frequently acting out a law court, donning the judge's black cap for the death penalty, and shedding tears. Even his natural squint did not detract from his theatrical preaching.

When Paul came to Corinth some considered that his eloquence, or lack of it, 'amount[ed] to nothing' (2 Corinthians 10:10), but both his message and his preaching were 'with a demonstration of the Spirit's power' (1 Corinthians 2:4); that was revival preaching. In revival, congregations do not discuss a man's style or eloquence, they do not even debate the content; they are moved to action. Revival preaching has a power and an authority that brings the word of God like a hammer to the heart and conscience; those who preach direct their words, not only to the mind, but to the heart. They demand a heart response to Jesus and not simply a head response to truth. They are always passionately opposed to cold, sterile orthodoxy.

One commentator on the eighteenth century Awakening rightly claims that 'the uninhibited and compelling urge to preach the Gospel' was a basic characteristic of all the personalities involved, whatever other gifts they might have:

---

4 Thornton, *God Sent Revival*, pp.68, 107.

'Both [Howell] Harris and [John] Wesley had keen organizing ability, both William Williams and Charles Wesley had unsurpassed genius to write hymns, [George] Whitefield's compassionate heart and breadth of vision well-nigh encircled the globe, and [Daniel] Rowland's communion seasons were heavenly, but each felt deeply the absolute priority and unique authority of preaching in the power of the Holy Spirit.'[5]

Preaching in revival is not dry theory, but a living and powerful force. Thomas Nelson, a Primitive Methodist preacher, left a record for his preaching at Sunderland collieries in 1823:

'On some occasions (for want of time to wash themselves), the colliers are constrained to come black to the preaching or else miss the sermon. And when the Lord warms their hearts with his dying love, and they feel Him precious in His word, the large and silent tears rolling conspicuously down their black cheeks, and leaving the white streaks behind, conspicuously portray what their hearts feel.'[6]

The same has been well reported of Whitefield and Wesley of the Colliers at Kingswood near Bristol.[7] Whitefield frequently describes the scene and the effect of his preaching in his diary. Here are just two glimpses taken almost at random. The first is at Kingswood on Sunday, 25 February 1739, and the second is later in the same year at Olney in Buckinghamshire:

'At four [in the afternoon] I hastened to Kingswood. At a moderate computation, there were about ten thousand people to hear me. The trees and hedges were full. All was hush when I began; the sun shone bright, and God enabled me to preach for an hour with great power, and so loudly, that all, I was told, could hear me

5 Evans, *Howell Harris*, p. 14.
6 Kendall, *The Origin and History of the Primitive Methodists*, Vol. 2 p. 203.
7 For example, Whitefield's *Journals* for 17, 20 February & 2 April 1739.

… The fire is kindled in the country; and, I know, all the devils in hell shall not be able to quench it.'

'Though it rained all the time, yet the people stood very attentive and patient. All, I really believe, *felt*, as well as *heard* the Word, and one was so pricked to the heart, and convinced of sin, that I scarce ever saw the like instance. The Word of God is quick and powerful, sharper than a two-edged sword.'[8]

Jonathan Edwards, who in the early days of his ministry slavishly followed his copious notes often barely looking at the congregation, commented that the congregations of New England in 1733 were 'eager to drink in the words of the minister as they came from his mouth'; and he noticed the changed attitude towards the sermon by those who were converted: 'Persons after their conversion often speak of religious things as seeming new to them; that preaching is a new thing; that it seems to them they never heard preaching before…'[9] To an extent, that is true whenever someone is converted, but in revival it is intensified. When William McCulloch reported on the revival at Cambuslang in Scotland that took place in 1742, and at which Whitefield was one of the preachers, he listed the number of sermons before the communion service: 'Four on the Fast day, four on Saturday, on Sabbath I cannot well tell how many, and five on Monday.'

The men who preach in revival are always unafraid and urgent, and the description of Duncan Campbell as a preacher shows how seriously they took their task:

'There was nothing complicated about Duncan's preaching. It was fearless and uncompromising. He exposed sin in its ugliness and dwelt at length on the consequences of living and dying without Christ. With a penetrating gaze

8 Whitefield's *Journals*, pp. 223, 274.
9 Edwards, *A Narrative of Surprising Conversions*, p. 14.

on the congregation, and perspiration streaming down his face, he set before men and women the way of life and the way of death. It was a solemn thought to him that the eternity of his hearers might turn upon his faithfulness. He was standing before his fellow men in Christ's stead and could be neither perfunctory nor formal. His words were not just a repetition of accumulated ideas, but the expression of his whole being. He gave the impression of preaching with his entire personality, not merely with his voice.'[10]

When revival came to Beddgelert in Wales in 1817: 'One of the outstanding characteristics was that the preaching of the gospel had a prominent, indeed a predominant place in it ... It was preaching which had the leading part in this revival.'[11] In 1859 the wind of the Spirit was blowing powerfully through many parts of Britain, and especially in Wales. Prayer was given new life and thousands poured into the early morning prayer meetings. However, nothing was allowed to interfere with the preaching—not even the times of prayer. David Morgan insisted upon the centrality of the preaching and in this way many extremes and excesses were avoided. Ministers were busy preaching throughout the Principality during 1859, and although there were exceptional men, like David Morgan himself, hundreds of ministers were used to feed the flame of revival.[12]

It is this emphasis on preaching and teaching that established young converts in their faith and ensured that so few turned back. Assessing the moral results of the 1859 revival in Wales, Thomas Phillips wrote a year later:

'On every occasion care is taken to instruct the people in the true and unchangeable principles of religion. They are cautioned against resting in a mere outward

10 Woolsey, *Duncan Campbell*, p. 127.
11 Evans, *When He is Come*, p. 15.
12 As above, p. 110.

profession. They are told that excitement is not conversion, that an awakening of the conscience to a sense of guilt and danger does not always result in a change of heart. It is strongly and constantly urged that whatever hope or confidence they may have in their own minds as to their having "passed from death unto life" it is a mistake, a delusion, unless it is accompanied by hatred to sin and a renunciation of it in every shape and form; love to holiness, and the practical discharge of every moral duty. They are told that the Bible is to be the standard of religious feeling, as it is of religious faith. In short, they are admonished to seek a thorough change of heart, and to furnish evidence thereof in holiness of life.'[13]

Rhys Bevan Jones admits that this was not so much the case in the 1904 revival. Certainly there was 'an intense hunger for the Word, and the awakened ones could not tolerate anything but the Word', but frequently the ministers felt unable to preach: 'Indeed, to cease preaching, at that time, seemed to many the natural thing to do.'[14] This was undoubtedly one of the weaknesses of the 1904 revival in Wales. Though thousands were saved, and the fire of revival in Wales spread all over the world, its failure to survive long, the number of those who fell away and the excesses that occasionally arose, were in large measure due to the fact that in many areas preaching was neglected. However, if this was a failure of Evan Roberts, it was certainly not that of R. B. Jones, who reasserted the importance of preaching and seems to have deliberately 'distanced' himself from Roberts' methods. Jones concluded thirty years later that this lack of preaching in the later ministry of Evan Roberts was a vital loss:

'Indeed, it is not too much to say that, when the human leader could no longer speak his characteristic, vital message, his work entered upon a new phase. The

13 Phillips, *The Welsh Revival*, pp. 81–82.
14 Jones, *Rent Heavens*, p. 53.

Word of God is not only pure but also purifying. Its giving forth, whether in reading, preaching, or teaching, has a vital effect upon a meeting's atmosphere and success; it lays an effectual check upon any elements therein that may be carnal. Others of the revival's leaders ... did not give up preaching and teaching the Word.'[15]

Robert Murray M'Cheyne commented upon the attention of the people to the word of God in 1839: 'I have observed at such times an awful and breathless stillness pervading the assembly; each hearer bent forward in the posture of rapt attention.'[16]

Of those days in Madras in the 1940s, one who was a leader through it all comments: 'I tell you, God's Word came alive to us then.' The evidence of this is clearly seen in the description of an evening in October 1940, during the monsoon season:

'The skies were dark and threatening and we thought it would be necessary to go inside: but a very large crowd had gathered, far more than the church could accommodate, and after prayer brother Bakht Singh decided we should carry on in the open. Suddenly it began to rain very heavily. He urged the people not to stir, but just to protect their Bibles by putting them under their clothes. He himself continued to preach with his Bible wide open. People just sat on the ground in the pouring rain with rivulets of water running beneath them. Though soaked to the skin they went on listening to God's saving Word. Only after a long time did it stop. There were mothers with babies in their arms, yet no one stirred until the meeting was over, and no one was anxious for it to conclude early. For a wind of God was blowing through Madras and the showers that watered our hearts were showers of blessing.'[17]

15 As above, p. 55.
16 Bonar, *Memoirs and Remains*, p. 501.
17 Rajamani & Kinnear, *Monsoon Daybreak*, p. 68.

Shortly before this, at Carloway on the Isle of Lewis in Scotland, a revival between 1934 and the outbreak of war was noted for 'the eager attention with which young and old listened to the preaching of the Word'.[18] A record of revival in Borneo in the 1970s comments, 'Their readiness to submit themselves to the Word was awesome.' And the evidence of this commitment is noted by the fact that three years after the revival, a missionary visited the Kelabit Highlands for a Bible-teaching tour and one of the first Kelabits to become a Christian in the revival followed him from village to village to get more teaching.[19]

Where Bible preaching is neglected in revival, however 'spiritual' the reason, dangerous excess and error will be lurking. Preaching was central in the New Testament, and the church in any age dare not depart from that example. James Alexander, an astute observer of revival in America in 1835 commented sadly: 'The Gospel is not attractive enough for people now-a-days. Ministers must bait their trap with something else. The old-fashioned topics are seldom heard.'[20]

A timely challenge for the twenty-first century?

Christ at the centre

> It is a revival of preaching in which Christ is at the heart for the heart

Revival is not only a revival of bold and warm-hearted preaching that is loved by the people and effective in their lives, it is also a revival of preaching in which Christ is at the heart for the heart. 2 Chronicles 29–30 are two chapters concerned with what took place in the temple when Hezekiah had cleared out the rubbish. Three major sacrifices were re-established: the sin offering, the burnt offering and the Passover. These were reminders to the people of sin and the offer of forgiveness. The people had been taking

18 Macaulay, *The Burning Bush in Carloway*, p. 32
19 Lees, *Drunk Before Dawn*, pp. 109, 198.
20 Murray, *Revival and Revivalism*, p. 337.

sin lightly, therefore, when God's Spirit came it was inevitable that the sacrifice of blood should become central once again. The Old Testament sacrifices were gospel sermons; it was the way God continually reminded his people of the enormity of their sin and the cost of reconciliation and the coming Messiah.

The constant emphasis on the blood of Christ in the New Testament as the way of salvation—for example Romans 5:9; Ephesians 1:7; Colossians 1:20—has never been popular. However, the sermons of the apostles were full of Christ. They recounted the historical facts of the gospel and declared that he had been 'killed, murdered, put to death, crucified, condemned, raised to life'. All this was because of who he was. Christ was 'glorified by God, the holy and righteous one, the author of life, Prince and Saviour, the Righteous One, Son of Man, Judge of the living and dead'. This was all at the heart of the New Testament message. And even though the Jews were offended at it, the apostles did not avoid the issue of the cross and the blood of Christ (Acts 2:36; 1 Corinthians 2:2). Paul wrote to the Corinthians: 'I resolved to know nothing while I was with you except Jesus Christ and him crucified' (1 Corinthians 2:2).

In revival Jesus Christ, and the blood of the cross particularly, are central to the preaching. Perhaps this is why many records of revival refer to the special blessings experienced at communion services when the gospel is preached both from the Scriptures and through the bread and wine.

It was at a communion service in the churchyard of the Kirk O'Shotts Parish Church on Monday 21 June 1630 that John Livingston preached a two-and-a-half-hour sermon after which it is recorded that five hundred people were converted. At Cambuslang in 1742 the presence of God was so real at the communion service held on 11 July that it was agreed, untypically for the Scottish Presbyterians, that they must celebrate it again. They arranged another service for 15 August and this was attended by some 20,000 people. Though only a few thousand were allowed to participate, hundreds were converted.[21] This was a reflection of 2 Chronicles 30:23 where 'the whole people agreed to celebrate the festival seven more days'. There are references to times of great spiritual blessing at communion services in revivals as far apart, historically and geographically, as the churchyard at Shotts in 1630 and Madras in 1940. In eighteenth century Wales, Howell Harris gave great prominence to this service, which he called 'the Royal Feast'. One writer has concluded that the root of the Methodist revival lay in the Lord's Supper.[22] Revival began at Herrnhut in 1727 whilst the community was at communion.[23]

In the eighteenth century Whitefield and Wesley found that the preaching of the cross was hated, just as it is hated now. Joseph Kemp returned from a visit to Wales in 1905 and reported to his congregation at Charlotte Chapel in Edinburgh that the dominating note of the Welsh revival was 'redemption through the Blood'.[24] We may assess the genuineness of the work of the Spirit by how central the blood of Christ is to the preaching and the worship.

There are times when, in revival preaching as in any faithful preaching, the law of God must be thundered. But always the message will come back to the cross. Duncan Campbell was often criticized for declaring the wrath of God night after night, but he saw this only as a prelude to the gospel. Those who listened to him could almost see his face glow with light when he turned to the great theme of the love of Christ and God's welcome to returning sinners; his after-meetings were designed especially for those seeking salvation, and these occasions were full of Christ.

Hezekiah began by reminding the people of past unfaithfulness and the 'dread and horror' when the 'anger of the LORD has fallen on Judah and

21 Robe, *When the Wind Blows*, pp. 157–161.
22 Evans, *Howell Harris*, p. 5.
23 Davies, *The Moravian Revival*, p. 6.
24 Kemp, *Joseph W. Kemp*, p. 30.

Jerusalem' (2 Chronicles 29:8–9). But once having fixed this backdrop in place, he offered forgiveness and reconciliation in the sacrifice.

David Brainerd commented that he saw the greatest effect of his preaching among the Susquehanna Indians of North America in the 1740s: 'When I insisted upon the compassions of a dying Saviour, the plentiful provisions of the Gospels, and the free offers of Divine grace to needy distressed sinners'.[25] When Jonathan Edwards wrote of the revival in Northampton, New England, in 1733 he described the centrality of Christ and the cross in the lives of the people:

'In all companies, on other days, or whatever occasions persons met together, Christ was to be heard of, and seen in the midst of them. Our young people, when they met, were wont to spend the time in talking of the excellency and dying love of Jesus Christ, the glory of the way of salvation, the wonderful, free, and sovereign grace of God, his glorious work in the conversion of a soul and the truth and certainty of the great things of God's word...'[26]

Whitefield travelled to Scotland in 1742, and he arrived at Cambuslang to find that God was already at work in revival and hundreds had been converted. One who was present at that time reported on the response of the crowds to the preaching of the gospel: 'During the time of divine worship, solemn, profound, reverence overspread every countenance, Many cry out in the bitterness of their soul. Some ... from the stoutest man to the tenderest child, shake and tremble and a few fall down as dead. Nor does this happen only when men of warm address alarm them with the terrors of the law, but when the most deliberate preacher speaks of redeeming love ... Talk of a precious Saviour, and all seem to breathe after him.'[27] In this revival at Cambuslang in 1742, there is no doubt that

25 Page, *David Brainerd*, p. 105.
26 Edwards, *A Narrative of Surprising Conversions*, p. 14.
27 Dallimore, *George Whitefield*, vol. 2, p. 128.

it was the loveliness of Christ and the benefits of his cross that formed the central part of the preaching.

In one of Count Zinzendorf's letters he described the kind of preaching that was typical of the Moravian revival in 1727:

'Our method in proclaiming salvation is this: To point out to every heart the loving Lamb, who died for us, and although He was the Son of God, offered Himself for our sins ... as his Mediator between God and man, his throne of grace, his example, his brother, his preacher of the law, his comforter, his confessor, his Saviour, in short, his all in all; by the preaching of His blood, and of His love unto death, even the death of the cross; never, either in the discourse or in the argument, to digress even for a quarter of an hour from the loving Lamb; to name no virtue except in Him, and from Him and on His account; to preach no commandment except faith in Him; no other justification but that He atoned for us; no other sanctification but the privilege to sin no more; no other happiness but to be near Him, to think of Him and do His pleasure; no other self-denial but to be deprived of Him and His blessing; no other calamity but to displease him; no other life but in Him.'[28]

Christ-centred preaching will lead inevitably to a Christ-centred people who love God's word and read it in a new light. During the eighteenth century Awakening in New England, Jonathan Edwards remarked on the new attitude to Scripture among the people: '[They] often speak of religious things as seeming new to them; that ... the Bible is a new book: they find new chapters, new psalms, new histories, because they see them in a new light...' And speaking of one convert who had been listening to the gospel for nearly seventy years, Edwards continued, 'Reading in the New Testament concerning Christ's sufferings for sinners, she seemed to

28 Greenfield, *Power from on High*, p. 49.

be astonished at what she read, as what was real and very wonderful, but quite new to her…'[29]

Powerful preaching is a hallmark of true revival. It is God's greatest and most effective weapon. In times of spiritual decline the church will resort to all kinds of antics to gain a crowd and stir enthusiasm, some of which will undoubtedly prove successful and a few of which will win souls, but revival shows where God's real interest lies. In a day when powerful preaching is rare, and even good preaching is scarce, it is inevitable that it will be dismissed. We must cry to God for such an awakening that will put preaching back in the centre of our worship and evangelism, and Christ back in the centre of our sermons.

God is not pleased when the sermons go over the heads or out of the mind; he has always intended the sermon to change thoughts and inflame hearts. In revival it always does.

29 Edwards, *A Narrative of Surprising Conversions*, p.44.

During revival

Urgency and eternity

We are told that from 'a cold start' it can take four years before someone, unfamiliar with the church, will make a commitment to Christ. 2 Chronicles 29:36 is a good description of revival because: 'Hezekiah and all the people rejoiced at what God had brought about for his people, because it was done so quickly.' It happened suddenly and unexpectedly. When God comes down, few go home to think; they face up to God's claim upon their lives there and then. Whatever God says, they determine that they will do immediately. In revival, the minds of people are concentrated upon things of eternity and there is an awareness that nothing matters so much as getting right with God. There is an immediacy and an intensity about revival that are absent in the normal life of the church. When God's Spirit comes down, he contracts time.

> When God comes down, few go home to think; they face up to God's claim upon their lives there and then

When the couriers were sent throughout Israel and Judah, they went with all speed and nothing could stop them from delivering their message (2 Chronicles 30:6). With the activity of Assyria in the land, Hezekiah must have known that the future for Israel was bleak. Hundreds of thousands had been deported into exile and more would follow (2 Kings 18:9–12). Therefore, this was their last chance to respond to the gospel before disaster overtook them. In revival, those who are chosen by God cannot wait to get right with God and Christians cannot wait to reach out with the gospel. It was 'in the first month of the first year of his reign'

(2 Chronicles 29:3) that Hezekiah began his great work. He could hardly have started sooner.

This sense of urgency is confirmed in the words of Jonathan Edwards when he was writing of the outpouring of the Spirit of God in 1733 in Northampton, New England:

'God has also seemed to have gone out of his usual way in the quickness of his work and the swift progress the Spirit has made in his operations on the hearts of many. It is wonderful that persons should be so suddenly yet so greatly changed. Many have been taken from a loose and careless way of living and seized with strong convictions of their guilt and misery, and in a very little time all things have passed away, and all things have become new.'[1]

Elsewhere Edwards remarks on this 'quickness' by declaring, 'There was as much done in a day or two as, at ordinary times, with all endeavours that men can use, and with such a blessing as we commonly have, is done in a year.'[2]

In America, Asahel Nettleton had been preaching on the subject of repentance in the town of Nassau in 1819. He describes his own sense of urgency in the meeting as he preached, and the response of the congregation: 'Never more expecting to meet my anxious hearers in this world, I urged them, by all the solemnities of the judgement, not to pass the threshold of the meeting house that night with impenitent hearts. They seemed to hear as for their lives.'[3]

Similarly, M'Cheyne described the preaching at Dundee in 1839 and claimed that in their sermons the ministers all sought 'the immediate conversion of the people'.[4] David Brainerd preached to the Susquehanna

1 Edwards, *A Narrative of Surprising Conversions*, pp.20–21.
2 As above, p.21.
3 Thornton, *God Sent Revival*, p.97.
4 Bonar, *Memoirs and Remains*, p.503.

Indians about the merits of Christ, and his willingness to save them and, Brainerd concludes, 'Therefore [I] pressed them to come without delay.'[5] When God worked powerfully at Charlotte Chapel in Edinburgh in 1905, Joseph Kemp recorded: 'There was nothing, humanly speaking, to account for what happened. Quite suddenly, upon one and another came an overwhelming sense of the reality and awfulness of His presence and of eternal things. Life, death, and eternity seemed suddenly laid bare.'[6]

An amusing story from the life of David Morgan during the 1859 revival in Wales illustrates the urgency in the appeal of preachers during times of spiritual awakening. Morgan had been criticized by some who thought that he did not give people sufficient time to think through the implications of their response to the gospel. The minister at Blaenannerch took him to task: '"What is this that I hear about you, David, my boy?" said John Jones. "What have you heard?", asked David Morgan guardedly. "What have I heard? What means this lugging of people into church fellowship without giving them time to sit down and consider and count the cost before they build?" "What time ought a sinner to get to consider, Mr Jones?" "More than you give them, by all accounts." "You are criticizing my method; what is your idea of a reasonable period for considering this great question?" Accepting the challenge John Jones retorted, "A month is not too much at least." David Morgan saw that his enemy was delivered into his hand, and replied, "Well! Well! God's Spirit says Today; the devil says, Tomorrow; but the old evangelist of Blaenannerch says, A month hence will do."'[7]

Our sympathies may well lie with the old evangelist of Blaenannerch, but the speed with which God works and the unexpectedness of it is found regularly in accounts of revival. When the Spirit of God came down at Redruth in Cornwall in 1814 the church was on occasions 'spontaneously

---

5 Page, *David Brainerd*, p.85.
6 Kemp, *Joseph W. Kemp*, p.32.
7 Evans, *When He is Come*, p.71.

crowded by seekers'. The same thing happened in Lewis and elsewhere; people were drawn irresistibly to where the Spirit was at work. No one advertises meetings a long way in advance during revival; no posters are put up or leaflets distributed. The Spirit is his own advertising agency. Few are left indifferent to what is happening; even those who are not converted are aware of God's presence, and many are alarmed at being close to the revival for fear of getting converted. When God came to Rhos in North Wales in 1904, a feared fighter of the town fled to the mountains to escape the revival, and God met him there.

The Spirit is his own advertising agency. Few are left indifferent to what is happening

Even when revival is 'in the air' and might be expected, it is often overwhelming in its suddenness. In Broughshane in Ulster in the year 1859, the people had been expecting revival; it was all around them. But they admitted they were 'taken by surprise, so sudden, so powerful, and extraordinary were the manifestations of the Spirit's presence ... I should say about one thousand people were suddenly, sensibly, and powerfully impressed and awakened.'[8]

It is this element of surprise that makes revival so uncomfortable for those who prefer their Christianity to be neatly ordered. The Spirit is unpredictable; this does not mean that he works in ways contrary to his character or holiness, or in defiance of his own revelation in Scripture, but he certainly works to an unexpected schedule.

The contracting of time makes life harder for the leaders. More sermons are preached, more counselling is done and generally more effort put in during revival. Whitefield and Wesley often preached themselves to near exhaustion, and the New England pastor Jonathan Edwards speaks of thirty converts a week for five or six weeks, all in need of pastoral care.

8 Paisley, *The Fifty-Nine Revival*, pp. 38–39.

He adds that extra meetings were commonplace.[9] But there is also an unusual enlivening in revival. Christians are able to preach and pray for longer without appearing to be tired. People will stay up late at their meetings, then go off to work the next day, and again stay up late at praise and prayer. 'There was life in the air,' was how one man explained it who had himself been involved in revival. Another has described how time and tiredness vanish; as meetings continue, sometimes all night, sleep becomes 'impossible or undesirable; it seemed a waste of time in such an atmosphere'. The Spirit giving life becomes a reality in many senses.

Time and tiredness vanish; as meetings continue, sometimes all night, sleep becomes 'impossible or undesirable'

This immediacy is evident in the story of the church in Acts. On the Day of Pentecost the crowd interrupted the sermon of Peter with the cry: 'What shall we do?' (Acts 2:37) and Peter demanded an instant response. Every sermon in Acts calls for the obedience of faith—at once. Paul reminded the men of Athens that God commands an immediate response: 'but now' (Acts 17:30). Whilst it is true that people did go away to think and debate further (Acts 17:32), the apostles never once encouraged people to do so; they preached for an immediate response. It was said of Wales in 1904 that you knew revival was on the way when you heard the 'Oh' of desperation and urgency in the prayers of the Christians.

Eternal realities

In 1859 when God swept Ulster with revival, the October meeting at the Maze racecourse attracted less than five hundred race-goers instead of the usual 10,000. Clearly some people were being made to think seriously

9 Edwards, *A Narrative of Surprising Conversions*, p. 21.

about eternity. Here is a description given by a minister in Comber, a small town in County Down, nine miles from Belfast:

'The whole town and neighbourhood were roused. Many did not retire to rest the first night at all, and for several days great numbers were unable to attend their usual vocations, but gave themselves almost unceasingly to the study of the Scriptures, singing and prayer: and for the first month, with about three exceptions, I did not get to bed till morning, such was the anxiety of the people for pastoral instruction and consolation.'[10]

In Wales in 1904, whole towns were stirred, and everybody was talking about God and eternity. The *North Wales Guardian* for 20 January 1905 carried the following reports:

'In consequence of the revival the annual eisteddfod arranged to be held on Friday Jan 27th at Llansantffraid near Oswestry has been postponed. The secretaries who have widely advertised the postponement, discovered that the usual eisteddfod enthusiasts were devoting themselves to the revival gatherings, and that choirs have been unable to obtain accommodation for practice. At a Football Association meeting at Chirk, when the draw for a charity cup was made, it was deemed useless to fix a match at Rhos, as the Black Park Club secretary announced that in a recent match—Rhos v. Black Park—the gate receipts only amounted to 9 shillings.'[11]

It was not that people considered either the eisteddfod or football as sinful, but their minds and lives were gripped with something far more important. In revival God puts eternity back into men's minds, not just as individuals, but as whole communities. Another newspaper in Wales

10 Paisley, *The Fifty-Nine Revival*, p. 11.
11 Harris, *Extracts from the Welsh Press*, p. 8.

reported 'a pervading and overwhelming solemnity, convincing even the most stoical that eternal realities had come into intimate contact with the men and women present'.[12]

Duncan Campbell recalls the same on the Isle of Lewis in 1949: 'News of what was happening in Barvas spread faster than the speed of gossip ... Within a matter of days the whole neighbourhood was powerfully awakened to eternal realities. Work was largely set aside as people became concerned about their own salvation, or the salvation of friends and neighbours: In homes, barns and loom-sheds, by the roadside or the peatstack, men could be found calling upon God.'[13]

12 Evans, *When He is Come*, p. 90.
13 Woolsey, *Duncan Campbell*, p. 119.

During revival

Conviction of sin and a holy life

Holiness can never be separated from revival. The question to be asked of any spiritual experience, either in an individual or a congregation, is: 'Are they a holy people who fear only God and sin, and who allow God's word to rule their lives?' Neither loud excitement nor sombre quietness, not even love and gifts, are any necessary evidence of revival. But a deep conviction of sin and biblical holiness are. God prefers light to heat, and holiness to happiness. Someone has described revival as the top blowing off. It is, but not before the bottom has fallen out.

In 2 Chronicles 29 not only did the Levites 'consecrate themselves' (v. 15) but they and the priests 'went into the sanctuary of the LORD to purify it' (vv. 15–16). That was furthest from the eyes of men and nearest to the eyes of God. In revival, especially, the 'secrets of a man's heart will be laid bare' (1 Corinthians 14:25). Holiness begins with an alarm at the sin lurking in the dark comers of life. The Levites dealt with 'everything unclean', and they threw all the rubbish into the valley of Kidron—the city's landfill dump. A deep conviction of past sin and neglect came over the leaders: 'The priests and the Levites were ashamed and consecrated themselves' (30:15). The past haunted them because they had tolerated the worship of Baal and Asherah and the cruel child-sacrifice (28:2–3).

In 'normal' times Christians hold on to those things that revival will snatch away from them. In Korea and Borneo even Christian leaders held on to their fetishes and charms, but the revival made them so ashamed that these things were publicly confessed. From 1935, a wave of conviction of sin spread across many churches in Rwanda: 'Convicted men and women would tremble violently, and even fall to the ground, being unable to kneel any longer; this was accompanied by remorse and weeping until peace of mind came.' Open confession of sins became common and this was certainly against the African culture of personal pride. Even a murderer owned up to his crime committed many years before.[1] Of this revival in Rwanda it was claimed: 'Missionaries and Africans found that the moral and spiritual "greys" to which they had become accustomed, became "black and white" under the blazing light of God's Holy Spirit.'[2]

This desire to be holy becomes a burning passion: 'They began the consecration on the first day of the first month, and by the eighth day of the month they reached the portico of the LORD. For eight more days they consecrated the temple of the LORD itself, finishing in the sixteenth day of the first month' (2 Chronicles 29:17). Here was a sixteen-day spring-clean until everything unclean was removed from the temple. The priests began at the centre and a week later they came to the vestibule and then they started all over again. They never gave up on their warfare against the unholy rubbish that had accumulated in the temple, until they could report to Hezekiah: 'We have purified the entire temple of the LORD, the altar of burnt offering with all its utensils, and the table for setting out the consecrated bread, with all its articles. We have prepared and consecrated all the articles that King Ahaz removed in his unfaithfulness while he was king. They are now in front of the LORD's altar' (vv. 18–19).

Revival is always a revival of holiness which begins with a terrible conviction of sin. It is often the form that this conviction of sin takes that troubles those who read of revival. Sometimes the experience is crushing. People weep uncontrollably, and worse. But there is no revival without tears of conviction and sorrow. In January 1907 God was moving

1 Osborn, *Revival—a precious heritage*, pp. 22, 46–48.
2 Osborn, p. 74.

in a powerful way in North Korea, and a Western missionary recalled one scene:

'As the prayer continued, a spirit of heaviness and sorrow for sin came down upon the audience. Over on one side, someone began to weep, and in a moment the whole audience was weeping. Man after man would rise, confess his sins, break down and weep, and then throw himself to the floor and beat the floor with his fists in perfect agony of conviction. My own cook tried to make a confession, broke down in the midst of it, and cried to me across the room "Pastor, tell me, is there any hope for me, can I be forgiven?" and then he threw himself to the floor and wept and wept, and almost screamed in agony ... Sometimes after a confession, the whole audience would break out in audible prayer, and the effect of that audience of hundreds of men praying together in audible prayer was something indescribable. Again, after another confession, they would break out in uncontrollable weeping, and we would all weep, we could not help it. And so the meeting went on until two o'clock a.m., with confession and weeping and praying...'

He went on to describe a meeting a few nights later when many Christians were brought to a deep conviction of sin: 'My last glimpse of the audience is photographed indelibly on my brain. Some threw themselves full length on the floor, hundreds stood with arms outstretched toward heaven. Every man forgot every other. Each was face to face with God. I can hear yet that fearful sound of hundreds of men pleading with God for life, for mercy. The cry went out over the city till the heathen were in consternation.'[3]

Scenes like these are typical of every recorded revival. There is no revival without deep, uncomfortable and humbling conviction of sin. It is

3 Blair & Hunt, *The Korean Pentecost*, pp. 72–73.

this terrible conviction of sin that led the Congolese Christians, during the revival in 1953, to sing a chorus of their own making:

'Receive salvation today,
This is the hour of judgement.'

The missionaries wanted to change the words to 'This is the hour of mercy,' but were pointed to Malachi 3:2–3. God had come as 'a refiner's fire'.

Revival in China in 1906 was 'marked by a wholly unusual conviction of sin'.[4] In 1921, in the revival that began in the East Anglian fishing ports of Lowestoft and Great Yarmouth, strong fishermen were literally thrown to the floor under conviction, until one eyewitness reported, 'The ground around me was like a battlefield with souls crying to God for mercy.'[5]

In 1949, on the Isle of Lewis off the west coast of Scotland, Duncan Campbell witnessed similar scenes of conviction over personal sin:

'The awful [dreadful] presence of God brought a wave of conviction of sin that caused even mature Christians to feel their sinfulness, bringing groans of distress and prayers of repentance from the unconverted. Strong men were bowed under the weight of sin and cries for mercy were mingled with shouts of joy from others who had passed into life.'[6]

Groups of people could be found by the roadside pleading to God for forgiveness. For some, the conviction of sin was so intense that they collapsed in the pews. In his reports, Duncan Campbell continually referred to the fact that 'conviction and distress of soul was very evident'.[7]

4 Orr, *Evangelical Awakenings in Eastern Asia*, p. 35.
5 Ritchie, *Floods upon the Dry Ground*, p. 30.
6 Woolsey, *Duncan Campbell*, p. 118.
7 Peckham, *Sounds from Heaven*, p. 89.

In the first half of the nineteenth century God used the ministry of Asahel Nettleton in revival for over thirty years, and during his preaching scenes of deep conviction were commonplace. One observer described a meeting at Calway near Saratoga Springs in the summer of 1819:

'This evening will never be forgotten. The scene is beyond description. Did you ever witness two hundred sinners, with one accord in one place, weeping for their sins? Until you have seen this, you have no adequate conceptions of the solemn scene. I felt as though I was standing on the verge of the eternal world; while the floor under my feet was shaken by the trembling of anxious souls in view of a judgement to come. The solemnity was still heightened, when every knee was bent at the throne of grace, and the intervening silence of the voice of prayer was interrupted only by the sighs and sobs of anxious souls. I have no time to relate interesting particulars. I only add that some of the most stout, hard-hearted, heaven-daring rebels have been in the most awful distress.'[8]

The same terrible conviction of sin was experienced in the previous century under the preaching of David Brainerd among the Susquehanna Indians in North America:

'I stood amazed at the influence which seized the audience almost universally and could compare it to nothing more aptly than the irresistible force of a mighty torrent or swelling deluge, that with its insupportable weight and pressure bears down and sweeps before it whatever is in its way. Almost all persons of all ages were bowed down with concern together, and scarce one was able to withstand the shock of this surprising operation. Old men and women who had been drunken wretches for many years, and some little children, not more than six or seven years of age, appeared in distress for their souls, as well as persons of middle age. And it was apparent these children (some of them at least) were not

8 Thornton, *God Sent Revival*, pp. 91–92.

merely frightened with seeing the general concern, but were made sensible of their danger, the badness of their hearts, and their misery without Christ, as some of them expressed it. The most stubborn hearts were now obliged to bow.'[9]

In October 1791 there was a powerful work of God in Bala, North Wales. It began during the preaching of Thomas Charles one Sunday evening, and by ten o'clock that night, 'There was nothing to be heard from one end of town to the other but the cries and groans of the people in distress of soul.'[10]

At Cambuslang in 1742, Dr John Hamilton of Glasgow observed, 'I found a good many persons under the deepest exercise of soul, crying out most bitterly of their lost and miserable state, by reason of sin; of their unbelief, in despising Christ and the offers of the gospel; of the hardness of their heart; and of their gross carelessness and indifference about religion ... not so much ... from fear of punishment as from a sense of the dishonour done to God.'[11] Men and women suffered such agony and distress over their sin that some would faint or cry out under the burden. One of the ministers, James Robe, freely admits that at first he did not approve of this and tried to stop it, even asking that these people should be carried away from the scene. However, he later admitted that this was wrong because always such suffering led eventually to a great peace and joy in forgiveness.[12]

When God came to Cornwall in 1814, the people spoke of the 'penitential pain' when men and women were in great distress over their sin. At Tuckingmill a meeting lasted from Sunday until Friday, with people coming and going all the time. This 'penitential pain' was extreme in some cases: 'Hundreds were crying for mercy at once. Some remained in great

---

9 Page, *David Brainerd*, pp. 80–82.
10 Paul Cook in Westminster Conference papers *Preaching and Revival*, p. 93.
11 Dallimore, *George Whitefield*, vol. 2, p. 123.
12 Robe, *When the Wind Blows*, pp. 108ff.

distress of soul for one hour, some for two, some six, some nine, twelve and some for fifteen hours before the Lord spoke peace to their souls—then they would rise, extend their arms, and proclaim the wonderful works of God…'[13]

So universal is this work of conviction in revival that Jonathan Edwards puts it at the top of his list in describing how the sinner is converted: 'Persons are first awakened with a sense of their miserable condition by nature [and] the danger they are in of perishing eternally.' In coming to this position, Edwards admits that 'Persons are sometimes brought to the borders of despair, and it looks as black as midnight to them a little before the day dawns in their souls. Some few instances there have been, of persons who have had such a sense of God's wrath for sin, that they have been overborne; and made to cry out under an astonishing sense of their guilt, wondering that God suffers such guilty wretches to live upon the earth…'[14]

If we shy away from such extreme convictions of sin, we need only turn to King David who knew the physical pain of a tortured conscience:

'O LORD, do not rebuke me in your anger
  or discipline me in your wrath.
For your arrows have pierced me,
  and your hand has come down upon me.
Because of your wrath there is no health in my body;
  my bones have no soundness because of my sin.
My guilt has overwhelmed me
  like a burden too heavy to bear …
My heart pounds, my strength fails me;
  even the light has gone from my eyes …
I am like a deaf man, who cannot hear,

13 Carvosso, *The Life of William Carvosso*, p. 48.
14 Edwards, *A Narrative of Surprising Conversions*, p. 25.

like a mute, who cannot open his mouth;
I have become like a man who does not hear,
whose mouth can offer no reply …
I confess my iniquity;
I am troubled by my sin'
(Psalm 38:1–4,10,13–14,18).

Does this explain the vivid language of Acts 2:37 '…cut to the heart'? And is this what happened to Saul of Tarsus outside Damascus?

Open confession of sins

Not infrequently this deep conviction leads to open and public confession. In Korea it was commonplace for times of confession, where wrong relationships were put right, to follow conviction of sin:

'Sometimes a man would get up and make only a partial confession of his wrongdoing, holding back the part he was really ashamed of; but the next night would find him back, pale and tortured, ready to rise at the first opportunity and confess his double sin in hiding his great sin the night before. Once the Spirit convicted a man, he seemed to get no rest day or night till he had unburdened his heart to the church and done what he could to repair the injury.'[15]

When God came to Borneo in the 1970s a headmaster and professing Christian stood before his school and confessed his sin of holding on to some of his most powerful charms.[16]

There are dangers in the public confession of sins, but the Spirit does not seek our permission. William Williams, who preached powerfully during the Welsh revival of the mid-nineteenth century, set out wise advice

15 Blair & Hunt, *The Korean Pentecost*, p. 77.
16 Lees, *Drunk Before Dawn*, p. 189.

for the handling of the 'Experience Meetings' in which new Christians were encouraged to confess sin. He listed what was unhelpful to mention as well as what would benefit everyone present.[17]

In the time of Jonathan Goforth in China in 1908, many missionaries warned their people not to confess particular sins publicly; however, it made no difference to those under conviction—including leaders—who confessed to lying, stealing and adultery.[18] The revival that swept across much of East Africa in the 1930s and '40s led to 'a wave of conviction and repentance' which included public confession of particular sins. This was certainly against the culture of both Africans and Western missionaries and caused some controversy.[19] In Moldova, when the Spirit of God came in power from 1968, one eyewitness reports: 'There is frequent reference here to "the repentance of the repentant ones" and self-examination on the part of believers to acknowledge and renounce known sin. I have been in many meetings where, after the preaching or after a Bible study, conviction of sin is such that the whole congregation will be on their knees crying out to God for forgiveness.'[20]

The remarkable events at Wheaton College, Illinois in March 1995 saw the student body broken in repentance and many came forward to confess particular sins openly. Their testimony was often supported by bringing their secret items so that 'within a few hours, five large plastic bags were filled with a range of items including books, magazines, videos, CDs, alcohol, and tobacco.' Whatever concerns we may have over explicit public confession, a large part of the student body was transformed, lives were changed, and many offered themselves for full-time Christian service. This work of the Spirit spread to other colleges and seminaries across the States. The faculty wanted nothing more than that the revival would be

17 Williams, *The Experience Meeting*, pp. 50–62.
18 Goforth, *By My Spirit*, p. 153.
19 Osborn, *Revival—a precious heritage*, pp. 16, 83–87.
20 Maureen Wise, author of *Celestial Fire*, in personal correspondence.

a 'prelude to lives of holiness, love, mission and service'. Wheaton had experienced a similar revival in 1950 when one prayer meeting continued unbroken for thirty-nine hours.[21]

This deep and painful conviction of sin is an inevitable part of true revival. Our tinted view of revival as a time of glory and joy and swelling numbers is only part of the story. Before the glory and the joy, there is pain; and that begins with the people of God. There are tears and godly sorrow. There are wrongs to put right, secret things, furthest from the eyes of men, to be dealt with. There are bad relationships, hidden for years, to be repaired openly. If we are not prepared for this, we would be wise not to pray for revival. Revival is not intended for the enjoyment of the church, but for its cleansing. When God came to the Congo in 1953, it was two months before the unbelieving world was touched; but those were a painful two months for the church, with missionaries, pastors, elders and evangelists confessing their sin.

Erlo Stegen, whom God used among the Zulus in Natal, insisted, 'The first characteristic of a revival is the overwhelming consciousness of the reality, greatness and holiness of God, and together with this, the powerful conviction of sin by the Holy Spirit. This is the most striking feature of the revival among the Zulus and the strongest evidence of its validity.'[22] All notable leaders in revivals would agree with this. In revival no one in the church takes sin lightly. God turns his anger into mercy but still he makes people 'feel' their sin.

We have an unholy church today because Christians do not feel sin or fear it. The God who punished the sins of Achan and of Nadab and Abihu, Uzzah and Ananias and Saphira is still as holy now as he was then. Isaiah's response to the presence of God was, 'Woe to me! ... I am ruined! For I am a man of unclean lips, and I live among a people of unclean lips, and my

21 Tears of Revival, pp. 19, 25, 31, 39.
22 Visser, *Revival and Conviction of Sin*, p. 249.

eyes have seen the King, the LORD Almighty' (Isaiah 6:3). An illustration of this is clearly seen in the experience at Baria in Borneo in 1973. One national Christian, Taman Ngau, records the time when the entire village seemed to be going to the church: 'There in the church we found the Lord. The whole place was full of the Spirit of the Lord. Young people were praying and worshipping. Some of them were confessing their sins and we began confessing too. We didn't realize we had sinned before, but we saw how filthy we were in the presence of a holy God.'[23]

Holiness of life

Confession is only the beginning. Duncan Campbell repeatedly declared that true revival is a revival of holiness and that holiness is more desirable than happiness. One man, converted under the preaching of Campbell, claimed that his conversion cost him $10,000; he had to return to America and work for a year 'to make restitution for things I had done as a sinner'. Two hundred years earlier, Jonathan Edwards commented that one effect of revival is to bring sinners 'immediately to quit their sinful practices'. Shortly after 1861, William Booth conducted evangelistic missions across Cornwall. He himself claimed that many of the agents of the mines were willing to allow the men to leave their work and attend the missions, only too glad that they should be converted: 'Whether saved or not themselves, they know that Christianity will bring about a reformation of character only too desirable in many instances.'[24]

> Revival does not persuade the world that the Christian faith is *fun*, but that it is *essential*

One reason why the world does not take Christianity seriously is because Christians don't. Revival does not persuade the world that the Christian faith is *fun*, but that it is *essential*.

23 Lees, *Drunk Before Dawn*, p. 194.
24 Isaac, *A History of Evangelical Christianity In Cornwall*, p. 257.

The first work of the Spirit is not to tell us that we can be happy, but that we must be holy—because God is.

We saw earlier the kind of leaders God uses in revival. They were men who trembled at sin and whose conscience was sensitive to the approach of sin; they were men who did not try to justify lazy, careless habits, but who lived disciplined and determined lives. They fear nothing but God and sin. Revival is always a revival of holiness, and the vessels God uses must be holy. A man may be extreme or even unwise in his leadership, but if he crosses the boundary into sin then God will set him on one side. Humphrey Jones was greatly used in Wales in 1859 until his pride robbed God of the glory, and then his effective ministry was ended.

As the leaders, so the people; there is no honour to God in an unholy people. When we look at the fruits of revival we shall see how great a reformation any revival brings to society. But the reason for deep conviction is so that the people will feel their sin and hate it. The deeper the pile-driving, the higher the building can rise. When revival comes to a society, priorities are focused on what pleases God. Families are reunited, relationships put right, cheap entertainment is abandoned, crime is reduced, betting shops are abandoned and even sports are set on one side. Instead, work output increases, and honesty is the norm. Wales became known as 'the land of the white gloves' referring to the fact that magistrates on circuit were presented with a pair of white gloves because there were no cases to be heard.

The first convert when revival came to the Zulus in KwaZulu–Natal in 1966 was a woman steeped in the power of witchcraft. She felt compelled to come to the Christians and pleaded to be delivered from her evil spirits. After much prayer the spirits were dispelled, and she found peace with Jesus. Erlo Stegen comments on the immediate transformation in her life: 'She looked like a saint who had been living in the presence of our Lord and Master for many years.'[25]

---

25 Stegen, *Revival among the Zulus*, pp. 62–63.

Revival in Oradea, Romania, in the 1970s was marked by an emphasis on 'faithful adherence to standards of holy living in the lives of believers ... Believers were concerned that their lives should clearly show the distinctiveness of behaviour which knowing and following Christ produced.' This was noted by friends and colleagues who frequently asked why their life had been so dramatically changed. Even the communist authorities noticed this.[26]

How many of us are ready for revival? Have we shown God we want it? There is a preparation that must begin now, and a concern to be holy will show God that we care. We will be saying to God, 'Lord, I long for revival, and this is how much I long: I want to be as holy as a saved sinner can be.' And if there is still no revival, we shall at least have done our duty and God asks us to do no more than that. The outcome is his, the preparation is ours.

'The LORD will indeed give what is good,
and our land will yield its harvest.
Righteousness goes before him
and prepares the way for his steps'
(Psalm 85:12–13).

26 Birnie, *'Just call me Paul'*, pp. 60–61.

During revival

Earnest prayer

In the first month of the first year of his reign, [Hezekiah] opened the doors of the temple of the LORD and repaired them (2 Chronicles 29:3). That is not merely a statement about a piece of ecclesiastical carpentry, it is possibly the most significant statement in this entire account of revival. Hezekiah began at the temple because by reopening the house of the LORD he was making it a priority that the people should come into the presence of God. Unless they came to God in his way, through the proper sacrifices offered in the temple, there could be no access to their Creator. When the Hebrews entered the temple to worship that was their approach to God in prayer. Without this initial action by the king, the statement of 2 Chronicles 30:27 would be impossible: 'The priests and the Levites stood to bless the people, and God heard them, for their prayer reached heaven, his holy dwelling-place.'

There are two periods of prayer implied here. The first was just *before the work of revival began* and the second was *during the revival itself.* All revival begins and continues in the prayer meeting. Before revival the prayer meeting is not always attended by many; sometimes only by a few, but someone is always praying. Then, when revival comes the prayer meeting is the first to benefit. Prayer has been called 'the great fruit of revival'.[1] The meeting that is so neglected by the church becomes the focal point of the life of the Christian community; Christians who have avoided a prayer meeting for years are now longing for the next occasion to call to God. Prayer is no longer a burden, though it may be a battle.

1 Evans, *When He is Come*, p 109.

When God began to move through the ministry of Whitefield he recorded, 'Sometimes whole nights were spent in prayer. Often we have been filled as with new wine. And often have we [been] overwhelmed with the Divine presence and crying out, "Will God indeed dwell with men upon earth? How dreadful is this place! This is none other than the house of God and the gate of Heaven!"'[2]

Murray M'Cheyne commented on the number of prayer meetings he found in his parish in Dundee when he returned from Israel in 1839: 'I found thirty-nine such meetings held recently in connection with the congregation, and five of these were conducted and attended entirely by little children. At present [March 1841, two years after the beginning of the revival] I believe the number of these meetings is not much diminished.'[3] M'Cheyne described these prayer meetings, at which: 'Serious men covered their faces to pray that the arrows of the King of Zion might be sent home with power to the hearts of sinners,' and many were 'bathed in tears'. The effect of such meetings was to 'spread a sweet influence over the place'.

One result of the revival in Ulster in 1859 was the rapid growth of prayer meetings. In the Connor district alone, 100 weekly prayer meetings commenced. During this revival in Ulster prayer meetings could be found everywhere, even in graveyards and gravel pits. In Ballymena the large Presbyterian Church in Wellington Street could be 'crowded in all its parts by a prayer meeting' and this on Saturday, the weekly market day, when at normal times 'a dozen persons could scarcely have been convened for such a purpose'.

An eyewitness has left a vivid account of one of these prayer meetings. It could be multiplied many times all over Ulster during that eventful year:

2 Dallimore, *George Whitefield*, vol. 1 p. 221.
3 Bonar, *Memoirs and Remains*, p. 498.

'For some time before the appointed hour, many of the younger converts assemble to sing together some favourite hymns. A little later the people pour in rapidly and soon every seat is occupied, men of business sitting beside their workers, all in their usual attire. A large proportion is made up of the scholars and of the lower classes, who were specially visited during the awakening. Some seem very anxious and all are solemn. On the faces of the recent converts there is such a beaming gladness that even a stranger can tell their story at a look ... The prayer which follows bears greatly on the three classes of worshippers, the converted, the anxious and the unawakened, and contains earnest pleadings for the Spirit's presence for the spread of the revival work...'[4]

One of the marks of the 1904 revival in Wales was the meetings for prayer and perhaps one of the most moving descriptions came from a reporter on the *Western Mail* of the prayer meetings deep underground in the coal pits:

'The workmen on the night shift had gone down half an hour earlier than the usual time so as not to interfere with the operations of the pit. Seventy yards from the bottom of the shaft, in the stables, we came to the prayer meeting. One of the workmen was reading the 6th chapter of Matthew to about eighty comrades. He stood erect amongst the group, reading in a dim, fantastic light that danced with the swinging lamps and vanished softly into surrounding darkness. A number of lamps were attached to a heavy post closely wedged to support the roof, and around the impressive figure the colliers grouped themselves ... Earnest men, all of them; faces that bore the scars of the underground toiler, downcast eyes that seemed to be "the homes of silent prayer"; strong frames that quivered with a new emotion.'[5]

4 Paisley, *The Fifty-Nine Revival*, p. 33.
5 Evans, *The Welsh Revival of 1904*, p. 126.

A similar scene, though this time among a fishing community on the east coast in 1921, describes a Sunday prayer meeting at Cairnbulg in Scotland:

'Every Sunday morning from 6.30 to 9.30 a.m. there was a prayer meeting. It was held in a net loft above a wash-house close by the sea and known as "Mary Clarke's Joe's loftie". Heat came from a small fire and light from a paraffin lamp, but the fellowship was sweet. Ages ranged from 16 years to 60 years and the spirit of prayer was tremendous. One man who was there told me how these folks "grasped hold of the horns of the altar binding the powers of evil in the name of Jesus".'[6]

Prior to the revival that swept across North America from September 1857 not a quarter of church members attended a prayer meeting regularly.[7] The revival commenced with a single prayer meeting and the hundreds of prayer meetings that followed were led by laymen and were orderly and calm, with a clear pattern at which people handed up notes requesting prayer for loved ones, colleagues or themselves. Thousands were converted in the prayer meetings. The same happened in Wales a few years later; some of the worst characters were converted simply by hearing the prayers of young converts: 'Their prayers are like live coals upon the consciences of their hearers.'[8]

Sometimes a burden of prayer has so overwhelmed a congregation that everyone prayed at once. There are reports of this in revivals in Korea, Borneo, India, even Wales, and elsewhere. In Korea in 1907 the missionaries felt a tension as if everyone longed to pray. Dr Lee said simply: 'If it helps you all to pray together, then pray in that way.' The reporter continued, 'Then a tide began to sweep through the church. There was no confusion; it was a single harmony of prayer, as if the voices

6 Ritchie, *Floods upon the Dry Ground*, p. 54.
7 Prime. *The Power of Prayer*, p. 39.
8 Phillips, *The Welsh Revival*, p. 57.

of all the praying congregation merged together to form a single cry to God. There was not the slightest disorder. The Holy Ghost welded them all together into one. As on the day of the first Whitsun, all souls were tuned to the same note, and unity of the Spirit held sway.'[9]

Joseph Kemp described similar prayer meetings a year earlier in Scotland at Charlotte Chapel. During the revival there most of the converts were born in the prayer meetings, which though 'held by invisible hands', were 'usually of a tumultuous sort': 'One does not readily take in the meaning of simultaneous praying, in a meeting of from 100 to 200 people, full to overflowing of a strong desire to pour out their hearts before the Lord. How could there possibly be time for each to pray separately? After all, what need is there to wait? His ear finds no difficulty in dealing with the simultaneous prayer of a revival meeting.'[10]

This simultaneous praying is not a necessary mark of revival. In reviewing similar forms of prayer around the world, the reporter from Korea comments wisely: 'There is a great difference between communal prayer inspired by the Holy Ghost, and communal prayer that merely represents a fading tradition harking back to some great event in the past. In general, traditions lack the wonderful harmony of the Holy Ghost.'

In revival, timid tongues are released to join in prayer. In 1938 a missionary visited the Lun Bawang people in Borneo. God had revived the tribes-people in the absence of missionaries and it was the times of prayer that particularly impressed him: 'At home, prayer is so often laboured. Young Christians have to be urged to pray in front of others. Not so in the isolated jungles of Borneo. With no direct teacher other than the Holy Spirit, these people pour out spontaneous full-hearted prayer.'[11]

When the Spirit of God came powerfully among the Moravian Community at Herrnhut in Saxony, in August 1727, adults covenanted to

9 Blair & Hunt, *The Korean Pentecost*, p. 15.
10 Kemp, *Joseph W. Kemp*, p. 34.
11 Lees, *Drunk Before Dawn*, p. 63.

cover each of the twenty-four hours in prayer, and by the end of the month the children were holding their own prayer meetings, spending many hours in 'praying, singing and weeping'. In 1905 in the Assam district of India there were occasions when work actually stopped as people came to the church at all hours of the day and night to pray; though instances of prayer interfering with work are not common. During the 1859 revival in England a Christian newspaper reported on the growth of prayer meetings in London. In August a prayer meeting was started at the Crosby Hall and within a month 100 people were meeting. By October there were six daily prayer meetings in the metropolis and by the end of the year the paper reported 120.

In revival, prayer becomes a delight and joy. And, as in so many aspects of revival, the form of the meetings may vary considerably. The vast prayer meetings attended by 18,000 people in Wales in 1859 were led by men specifically chosen to stand in a cart and pray whilst the great crowd added their 'Amen' or prayed silently. On the other hand, as we have noted, prayer meetings are reported across the world where the whole congregation prayed simultaneously like the waves crashing in unison against the shore. This may be reflected in Acts 4:24: 'They raised their voices together in prayer to God.' There is no kind of prayer labelled 'revival'. As with singing in revival, when the Spirit of God comes, he takes up the church's corporate prayer and breathes new life and zeal into it.

In revival, prayer becomes a delight and joy

At the start of the revival in Moldova, the membership of Jesus the Saviour Church in the capital city, Chişinău, was only twenty-five. During the 1990s they were baptising two hundred converts a year and Pastor Anatol described the prayer meetings at Chişinău: 'The awakening in our church started among the young people. We started with nights of prayer. Hundreds of young people were praying for their country. There was such a spirit of prayer.'[12] One visitor, well acquainted with this time of revival wrote, 'Torrents of fervent, believing prayers full of praise to God come pouring out—always full of thankfulness and praise ... Those converted in the revival are still full of zeal and sacrificial service and boldness to speak of the Saviour to anybody and to everybody. It is often as if the fear of man has been completely removed such is their boldness in witnessing and in preaching.'[13]

When Jonathan Goforth arrived in one district of Manchuria, China, in 1908 he was warned that the people were just like their 'hard-headed Presbyterians from the north of Ireland' and that no man prayed unless he was asked, and women, never. At his first preaching service, Goforth reported a flood of open prayer that continued until even the schoolchildren were taking part. People were so eager to pray that one had to begin before the one preceding ended in order to 'get started'.[14]

There is hardly a more powerful description of the part that prayer plays, both before and during revival, than that given by Joseph Kemp. Revival had come to Charlotte Chapel in Edinburgh in 1905 and two years later the church was still in the full experience of it. The members had prayed urgently for revival when their pastor returned from Wales in 1905, and when it came, even that insistent prayer was transformed:

'What can I report about our Prayer Meetings? Did ever anyone see such meetings? They used to begin at seven o'clock on Sunday mornings, but that was felt to be far too late in the day for the great business that had to be transacted before the Throne of the Heavenly Grace! The meetings now begin at six o'clock and go on for almost seven days a week, with occasional intervals to attend to business, household duties, and bodily sustenance! Some of you who are strangers may smile—many of us did—but we don't now. It is that continuous, persevering,

12 Wise, *Celestial Fire*, p. 111.
13 Maureen Wise, author of *Celestial Fire*, in personal correspondence.
14 Goforth, *By My Spirit*, pp. 44–45.

God-honouring weekly campaign of prayer that has moved the mighty hand of God to pour upon this favoured people the blessings of His grace in such rich abundance; and if ever you should be asked the secret of this church's great spiritual prosperity, you can tell them of the prayer meetings, and especially of the gatherings of God's people—forty to sixty strong—in the Upper Vestry every Sunday morning at six or seven o'clock—summer and winter, wet day and fine—to pray. Yes, that is the secret—the secret of our church's success and prosperity.'[15]

---

15 Kemp, *Joseph W. Kemp*, pp. 42–43.

During revival

A passion for the lost

An inevitable result of revival is found in 2 Chronicles 30:1–12: 'Hezekiah sent word to all Israel and Judah and also wrote letters to Ephraim and Manasseh, inviting them to come to the temple of the LORD in Jerusalem and celebrate the Passover to the LORD, the God of Israel ... They decided to send a proclamation throughout Israel, from Beersheba to Dan, calling the people to come to Jerusalem and celebrate the Passover to the LORD, the God of Israel ... At the king's command, couriers went throughout Israel and Judah with letters from the king and from his officials ... The couriers went from town to town in Ephraim and Manasseh, as far as Zebulun...'

> Much of our evangelism today is an effort; Christians have to be driven to it, and preachers are like pumps trying to get a large body of water out of a deep pit

Here was a great overflow of evangelism by Hezekiah and his people. Much of our evangelism today is an effort; Christians have to be driven to it, and preachers are like pumps trying to get a large body of water out of a deep pit. When a call is given for a door-to-door team, few turn up; when it is announced that there will be an outreach in the market, only a handful follow. When revival comes everybody turns up; everyone will be in the market. There is no effort in an overflow. Hezekiah and the people were so thrilled with their new relationship with God, and so grateful for all that it meant, that it was only natural they should want to share it with others. Evangelism comes naturally to a grateful heart.

For two hundred years Israel and Judah, the north and south, had been bitterly divided. By the time of Hezekiah, there had been eighteen bad kings in Israel, but in the year 722 BC, just six years before Hezekiah came to power, Assyria conquered Israel and, after plundering the land, deported nearly thirty thousand inhabitants. In their place Assyria settled thousands of foreigners who had been exiled from their own occupied lands. Therefore, the tribes of the north were a defeated people and, adopting the religions of their new settlers, they had also become an apostate people.

The proclamation was to be sent throughout Israel from 'Beersheba to Dan'. That is from the extreme south and north of the land. The entire nation was to receive the invitation to return to the LORD. There had been nothing like this for two hundred years. It was a brave thing to do in a land teeming with foreign settlers and Assyrian governors. Knowing the uncertainty of the times, it would have been all too easy for Hezekiah to forget the north and look only to secure his own borders. Hezekiah was aware of the dangers, but there was an urgency about the sending of the couriers. They were thorough and went 'from town to town' (v. 10). The reference in the same verse 'as far as Zebulun' was a mark of particular mercy since this tribe had felt the full force of the Assyrian invasion. 'Ephraim and Manasseh' were settled on the east side of the Jordan, furthest from Israel or Judah, and deeper into regions beyond.

Always when the church of Christ is revived by the Holy Spirit, evangelism and mission are the natural and inevitable outflow. One of the most remarkable missionary movements in the history of the church is one of the least known. The Waldensians in the Italian Piedmont Valley spread across Europe and, in spite of cruel and relentless persecution from the Roman Catholic church, by the sixteenth century they outnumbered Catholics in the Valley by 100:1.[1] Similarly, the 'Lollards', sent out by

1 Baird, *Protestantism in Italy*, p. 272.

John Wycliffe and his team in the fourteenth century with the English Bible in their hands, led so many to faith that it appeared to some that a man could scarcely meet two men on the road but one of them was a disciple of Wycliffe. There is no better way of explaining the spread of the Reformation except through evangelism with the word of God, and there is no better way of accounting for such evangelistic zeal than by the word 'revival'.

In revival, evangelism is not ordinary evangelism but a desperate concern, a passion, for those who have never yet received the invitation to return. Revival makes eternal issues a reality to both Christian and unbeliever. Without Christ, men and women are destined for hell. That means nothing to most people today because our spiritual awareness has been numbed by a secular mind-set and atheist propaganda. In revival, both evangelist and hearers feel the horror of hell and the reality of eternal issues. They feel also the glories of heaven. Eternity that is ordinarily remote, becomes real and vital. No great preacher in times of revival doubted the terrors of hell or the desperate danger of those without Christ. Some experienced visions of the lost in hell, and all of them were urgent to turn men and women away from the road to eternal punishment.

In 1743 David Brainerd began his missionary work among the Indians of North America at the forks of the Delaware River. He was himself the product of revival and he had a longing to reach the Indians. Brainerd recognized that to the eyes of reason: 'Everything that respects the conversion of the heathen is a dark midnight.' Brainerd was well spoken of by the presbytery and had received offers of attractive pastoral charges, but he had a passion for the Indians. There were times when he was caught up into heaven almost out of himself, pleading for the Indians. No one else cared much about them. This was dangerous North American frontier territory because their land and livelihood was being swept away from the Indians by the white settlers. On one occasion when he had been praying in the woods:

'All things here below vanished and there appeared to be nothing of any importance to me but holiness of heart and *the conversion of the heathen to God* ... When I was asleep, I dreamt of these things and when I waked, as I frequently did, the first thing I thought of was this great work of pleading for God against Satan.'[2]

This courageous 'Puritan' missionary, weakened by tuberculosis, set out on a journey of four hundred and twenty miles in hazardous and uncharted territory to the Susquehanna Indians. There, revival broke out—because one man had a passion for the lost.

Evan Roberts describes the spiritual experience he had before God used him so powerfully in the 1904 revival in Wales. The Spirit of God broke him into obedience until he was willing to do anything; then he was overwhelmed by the love of God. What followed sums up what many have felt in times of revival:

'Then the fearful bending of the judgement day came to my mind, and I was filled with compassion for those who must bend at the judgement, and I wept. Following that, the salvation of the human soul was solemnly impressed upon me. I felt ablaze with a desire to go through the length and breadth of Wales to tell of the Saviour; and had it been possible, I was willing to pay God for doing so.'[3]

During the previous century, Howell Harris had declared to his brother: 'Yet shall I be more satisfied when I am an instrument to bring one soul to the knowledge of God than if I got £1,000.'[4] In a less sophisticated way, a half-deaf, wizened old Penan tribeswoman in Borneo expressed the same thing when, having found Christ and the assurance of salvation, she hurried off 'to tell the ones in the jungle about this.'

2 Page, *David Brainerd*, p. 57.
3 Evans, *The Welsh Revival of 1904*, p. 70.
4 Evans, *Howell Harris*, p. 11.

Duncan Campbell's biographer described the evangelist's terrifying vision of the reality of hell: 'He seemed to be in a trance gazing into caverns of death, witnessing the agonies of hell. With horror he saw thousands from the Highlands and Islands of Scotland drifting to their doom, and heard a voice calling: "Go to them, go to them."'[5]

In the days of Hezekiah the message was very simple: 'Return to the LORD ... that he may return to you' (2 Chronicles 30:6). Hezekiah was not concerned to add to the number of his citizens and the growth of his kingdom. His concern was a call to repentance and reconciliation to God. It is quite clear from the prayer this king urgently offered to God later when Assyria turned its attention in his direction, that Hezekiah held a firm theology of the sovereignty of God: 'O LORD, God of Israel, enthroned between the cherubim, you alone are God over all the kingdoms of the earth. You have made heaven and earth...' (2 Kings 19:15). But this did not lull him into the belief that he could simply wait for the north to return to the LORD. He sent out evangelists. In revival the church discovers just how many elect live in their area. His couriers were similarly committed. The people had a 'unity of mind to carry out what the king and his officials had ordered, following the word of the LORD' (2 Chronicles 30:12). Their unity was on the basis of their good news and the desperate need of the people. The invitation was to come to the Passover sacrifice and worship at the altar in Jerusalem (30:8). Evangelism is an urgent call to come and be reconciled to God through the blood of the sacrifice.

In revival the church discovers just how many elect live in their area

These evangelists were confident in their message: 'If you return to the LORD, you will be shown compassion ... for the LORD your God is gracious and compassionate ... He will not turn his face from you if you

5 Woolsey, *Duncan Campbell*, p.98.

return to him' (30:9). All who are involved in revival are utterly convinced that there is no other gospel and that God is faithful to his promises. Commenting on the work of God in Dundee in 1839, Robert Murray M'Cheyne referred to the expectations of the ministers: 'They all, I think, seek the immediate conversion of the people, and they believe that, under a living gospel ministry, success is more or less the rule, and want of success the exception.'[6]

We have already referred to the courage of these evangelists. Israel was virtually swallowed up in the Assyrian Empire and Zebulun was hardly part of Israel; it was one of the frontier posts of the Assyrians. This was a missionary thrust for the regions beyond. These men were brave and visionary evangelists, not simply messenger boys. It was a large and dangerous area to cover and the Passover was getting close. They were in enemy-occupied territory and the jibes of unbelieving Israelites were the very least they could expect.

The outflow of revival has always been a courageous evangelism

The outflow of revival has always been a courageous evangelism. It is easy to scorn the early pioneer missionary with an image of the pith helmet, Bible in hand, and a train of native porters. But we ought to be careful that we do not touch God's anointed. Africa is littered with the graves of those pioneer missionaries. They went out knowing that a high proportion of them would never return. They went because they felt compelled by God to go.

The Moravian missionary work, which was a direct result of the revival among the community at Herrnhut in 1727, is legendary. Within five years, their first two missionaries travelled to the island of St Thomas in the Caribbean, infamous for its degraded way of life and the treatment of the

6 Bonar, *Memoirs and Remains*, p. 503.

slaves.[7] Eventually the Moravians gained an estimated thirteen thousand converts in the West Indies. Over the next sixty years their evangelists travelled to almost every country in Europe and covered vast areas of North and South America, Asia and Africa. Half a century before William Carey went to India the Moravians had spread the gospel in places barely known. They reached as far as Greenland, which so impressed England's national poet William Cowper that he described their work: '[They] plant successfully sweet Sharon's rose on icy plains and in eternal snows.' It has been claimed that the Moravians achieved more in twenty years than the entire evangelical church had done in two centuries. William Carey and John Newton are among many who acknowledge the challenge of these Moravian missionaries to their own lives, and the Methodist evangelist John Wesley was converted through the witness of Moravians.

Reflecting on the revival in Kilsyth in 1839, William Burns included the following as third on his list of benefits of revival: 'There is a close connection betwixt Missionary work and revivals. Our newly organized Missionary Society, in January this year [1839], has been marked by several people as an era. No church can be in a lively state when nothing is done for the heathen.'[8]

In a year of revival, 1859, David Livingstone made an appeal to the university students which led directly to the Universities Mission to Central Africa. In North America Dwight Moody arranged a meeting in 1886 which resulted in the Student Volunteer Movement, with its slogan: 'The evangelization of the world in this generation.' This movement sadly took a wrong doctrinal direction later, but its early goals were good. At the turn of the nineteenth century there were fourteen thousand Protestant missionaries around the world; by 1925, following the revivals of 1904–05, this figure had doubled. Geographically the world was opening. In 1800

7 *The Memorial Days of the Renewed Church of the Brethren*, p. 140.
8 *Narratives of Revivals of Religion, Kilsyth*, p. 12.

one third of the globe was unknown to Europeans, whereas a century later almost every country was known and open to missionaries. God was preparing the world by faster and easier travel just as he had prepared the Roman Empire for the first-century Christian missionaries. But the expansion of missionary activity cannot be explained solely in terms of colonialism and the steam engine; the greatest thrust behind world-wide evangelism in the nineteenth and early twentieth centuries was undoubtedly revival.

The greatest thrust behind world-wide evangelism in the nineteenth and early twentieth centuries was undoubtedly revival

Revival brings a personal passion for the lost. Among the benefits of the awakening in Ulster in this same year, 1859, one historian records 'a forward movement in philanthropic and missionary enterprise' which included the 'China and Zenana Missions'. During the 1904 revival in Wales the challenge was laid down that the genuineness of the work would be seen in its missionary results. R.B. Jones had no doubt, from his own experience, that, judged on this ground, the fruit of the revival stood the test. He traced missionaries from 1904 carrying revival to India, Madagascar, Africa, Poland, South America, Japan and many more places. Rhys Jones concludes, 'The records of all the Missionary Societies could bear eloquent testimony to the practical, lasting result of the Spirit's work in those days.'[9]

Great names from the eighteenth and nineteenth centuries were products of revival: William Carey went to India, Henry Martyn to India and Persia, Adoniram Judson to Burma, and Hudson Taylor to China. Far back in the dark period of the twelfth century God had moved in the life of Peter Waldo of Lyons and the revival that followed sent out

9 Jones, *Rent Heavens*, pp. 82–83.

hundreds of Waldensian preachers all across Europe. The same was true two centuries later when John Wycliffe gave England its first English Bible. A little over a century after Wycliffe, the radical reformers of Zurich (incorrectly known by history and their opponents as Anabaptists), set out to evangelize Europe; missionaries went out in small groups until, in spite of persecution from both Reformers and Catholics, their evangelistic zeal had captured the lives of scores of thousands.

Evangelism in revival is a spontaneous 'people movement'. In 1958 a missionary in Borneo asked permission from the government's District Officer to enter a particular area with the gospel. The disgruntled official replied, 'In fact you have already occupied the area.' The missionaries had not been there at all, but the Tagal tribes-people who had been converted simply gossiped Christ. This was exactly the response of the first-century Christians who evangelized wherever they went (Acts 8:4). When God came to the Kelabit Highlands in Borneo in 1973 even schoolchildren went out in evangelistic teams during their school holidays.[10]

> Evangelism in revival is a spontaneous 'people movement'

Commenting on the effects of the revival in the Khassi Hills in India in 1905, one writer concluded, '...and above all, an intense passion for souls and untiring efforts made to bring outsiders to the Saviour'.[11] During the revival in Madras men came straight from their offices to the church to collect a pile of Gospels and then they would go out, two by two, on their 'Tapping-the-Door Campaign'. Their aim was to introduce the Scriptures to every house in the city and each evening they walked miles to bring the gospel to these homes. A year later, in 1944, 'Gospel Raids' were started when, for several days at a time, a large group of Christians would visit

10 Lees, *Drunk Before Dawn*, pp. 148,192.
11 Jones, *India Awake*, p. 18.

distant towns and villages with the good news. One visit took them three hundred miles from Madras, and occupied them for three weeks. In 1947 the teams entered the slum areas of their city with the gospel. They could not offer financial help or food but had with them only the message of salvation; and many were led to Christ.[12]

Similarly, Festo Kivengere reports that in Uganda God 'kept sending us out. We went, whether we were invited or not, on foot, an assorted "ad hoc" team spilling over into neighbouring valleys, usually leaving "Jesus people" behind when we came back home. Ordinary folk, bound together in a true love-fellowship, can be a powerhouse for evangelism.'[13] The same thing was happening all over East Africa, from Rwanda to Burundi and Tanganyika.

When revival began in 1907 in Pyongyang, now the capital of North Korea, students from the theological seminary were involved and, together with others caught up in the Spirit's fire, they set themselves the task of spreading the gospel through the whole of Korea within a year. They determined to penetrate areas where no missionary had ever been and, as an aid to their witness, one million copies of Mark's Gospel were printed—and three quarters were sold in the first year. Many went abroad as missionaries, and wherever Korean settlements were found, these gospel couriers settled also. Some went to Siberia, some to remote islands and others to China. The 'Movement of the Millions', reaching out to China's vast population, was born in the Korean revival. Some of the best young men from the seminary were sent out in this wave of evangelism.[14]

When the north of China experienced revival in 1906, two things particularly marked it as a movement from God: 'a wholly unusual conviction of sin and great anxiety for the conversion of friends and

12 Rajamani & Kinnear, *Monsoon Daybreak*, pp. 102, 105–107.
13 Kivengere, *Revolutionary Love*, p. 41.
14 Morod, *The Korean Revival*, pp. 19–20.

neighbours.'[15] A missionary involved in the revival in the Shantung province of China in 1932 observed, 'Everywhere I went, the Christians had a zeal to search out the lost and win them to Christ ... Little children, old men and women, people of all ages where lives had been changed, thus witnessed.'

Following the collapse of communism late in the twentieth century, a period of revival swept across Moldova in Eastern Europe. At a time of civil war and great economic distress, Christians without work, food or heating in the winter, would be at a prayer meeting, Bible study or out evangelising every evening of the week. One pastor summed up his own experience of evangelism at this time:

> 'The period from 1990 to 2000 was a very special time. Often, I would walk six kilometres to church to preach the Gospel and would talk to everyone along the way about the Lord. On the main street, Stefan Cel Mare, in about 1995, as soon as you started preaching a crowd would gather. Everyone wanted to listen. They were starving to hear the Word of God.'[16]

When revival came to Romania under the communist regime in the 1970s: 'The zeal and commitment of the young believers was real and profound. On Saturday mornings in Oradea the railway station and bus stations would be crowded with groups of young believers setting off for the outlying villages to spend the day witnessing and sharing the Gospel with lost men, women and young people. They followed up their witness by regular prayer meetings in homes, watering the seed they had sown, often with tears.'[17]

Evangelism across mainland China throughout the 1990s can only be described as an explosion. In Zhejiang Province, as one example of many,

---

15 Quoted by Orr, *Evangelical Awakenings in Eastern Asia*, p.35.
16 Wise, *Celestial Fire*, pp.126, 63.
17 Birnie, *'Just call me Paul'*, p.61.

teams of young men went off in pairs all over China and their churches set up 24-hour prayer chain for them. The evangelists returned after two months and this conservative evangelical group estimated that over 10,000 people had come to faith.[18]

When the Holy Spirit came down at Pentecost Peter demonstrated the same courage. The man who had denied his Saviour and then locked himself indoors through fear of the Jews and the Romans, was now preaching in the open air. His business was to do what God was telling him; he had to preach. It was a burning fire.

Today we must go on preaching and evangelizing because that is God's way. But we must plead for revival when eternity becomes a vital reality. Evangelists from revival do not go out to bring a little Christian culture or morality, but to convert men and women to Christ.

18 Lambert, *China's Millions*, pp. 163–165.

During revival

Children and youth

Revival never by-passes young people, not even young children. When Hezekiah sent his evangelists throughout the northern territories, the promise of blessing included the children: 'If you return to the LORD, then your brothers and your children will be shown compassion by their captors and will come back to this land, for the LORD your God is gracious and compassionate…' (2 Chronicles 30:9). Shortly after, the prophet Isaiah promised a time of revival among the people which certainly included the next generation:

'I will pour water on the thirsty land,
   and streams on the dry ground;
I will pour out my Spirit on your offspring,
   and my blessing on your descendants.
They will spring up like grass in a meadow,
   like poplar trees by flowing streams.
One will say, "I belong to the LORD";
   another will call himself by the name of Jacob;
still another will write on his hand, "The LORD's",
   and will take the name Israel'
(Isaiah 44:3–5).

The form of these words has no necessary reference to children or young people; they may simply refer to the next generation when it is grown to adulthood. However, God's concern for children is found throughout the Bible. In Deuteronomy 6:4–9 parents are given specific instructions concerning their responsibility towards children. The word of God must be impressed on them and talked about with them. When Jerusalem was rebuilt at the return from exile, a grand dedication ceremony included Ezra reading the law of God to 'men and women and all who were able to understand', from daybreak until noon. Later, 'all who [were] able to understand' entered into a binding covenant to obey the LORD (Nehemiah 8:3; 10:28). When the prophet Joel urged the leaders to call a solemn assembly and bring the people to repentance, the children, even those still at their mother's breast, were included (Joel 2:15–16). During his earthly ministry, Jesus invited children to be brought to him: 'And he took the children in his arms, put his hands on them and blessed them' (Mark 10:16). On the Day of Pentecost the gospel was offered 'for you and your children' (Acts 2:39), and we have no need to take that as a vague reference to future generations.

Today, Christians generally have a low spiritual expectation for our children

Today, Christians generally have a low spiritual expectation for our children. It is rare to see children, or even teenagers, in our weekly prayer meeting; we never hear our children pray because we do not pray with them ourselves, and if they asked to come to a prayer meeting most parents would suggest that it is not really for them. We do not expect our children to enjoy the Bible. Because of our own coldness of heart, we would be astounded if our children wanted to go out and witness for Christ. Our children reflect us; they are what we are. One generation creates the environment that either stifles or invigorates the spiritual growth of the next.

One generation creates the environment that either stifles or invigorates the spiritual growth of the next

Jesus reserved some of his most solemn warnings to those who cause children to be offended at the gospel: 'If anyone causes one of these little ones who believe in me to sin, it would be better for him to have a large millstone hung around his neck and to be drowned in the depths of the sea' (Matthew 18:6). This is not only what Christ thinks about parents in an unbelieving world, it is also his judgement on Christian parents who stifle the spiritual growth of their children by their own coldness.

In Madras in 1949 the Sunday School teachers were so concerned for their children that they got up at 4.00 a.m. to pray for them. It is not surprising that revival soon followed among the children.[1] Jonathan Edwards complained, in 1733, that the young people especially, were careless and disinterested in listening to what God had to say through their parents or through the ministers of the gospel. But when the Spirit of God came in revival: 'The young people declared themselves convinced by what they heard from the pulpit and were willing of themselves to comply with the counsel that had been given; and it was immediately, and I suppose, almost universally, complied with.'[2]

Towards the end of 1741, George Whitefield had noted in his diary that many small children sat on the pulpit steps while he preached in the open air; they were listening to the preaching and handing up to him notes from the crowd. What impressed Whitefield was the fact that these children often received the eggs and filth that were thrown at him, and yet they appeared to be unconcerned for their own welfare. In an age when children were little noted, this is a significant entry in the diary of one of England's greatest preachers.[3] Following the preaching of Whitefield at Lyme in Connecticut, a minister in the town, Jonathan Parsons, wrote of his young people who had been careless before. He said they were so changed that, 'Whenever they fell into companies, the great salvation was the subject of their conversation.'[4]

---

1 Rajamani & Kinnear, *Monsoon Daybreak*, p. 120.
2 Edwards, *A Narrative of Surprising Conversions*, p. 10.
3 Dallimore, *George Whitefield*, vol. 2, p. 118.
4 Dallimore, *George Whitefield*, vol. 2, pp. 180–181.

When Asahel Nettleton arrived in Boston in the spring of 1819, large numbers of teenagers were converted: 'The volatile youth could no longer resist the influences of the Holy Spirit, but in deep solemnity were daily enquiring what they should do to be saved. Vain amusements were entirely suspended. Scenes of pleasure were forsaken and the trifles of time were lost in the awful [dreadful] concerns of eternity.'[5]

God came down among the Susquehanna Indians of North America in the 1840s and David Brainerd recorded in his diary:

'Old men and women who had been drunken wretches for many years, and some little children, not more than six or seven years of age, appeared in distress for their souls ... And it was apparent that these children (some of them at least) were not merely frightened with seeing the general concern, but were made sensible of their danger, the badness of their hearts, and their misery without Christ, as some of them expressed it.'[6]

The revival in Aberystwyth in 1805 began in the Sunday School and Thomas Charles described the 'powerful awakenings among the young people and children ... Hundreds of children, from eight years old and upwards, might be seen in the congregation, hearing the word with all the attention of the most devout Christian and bathed in tears.'[7]

In a letter dated 26 March 1841, M'Cheyne reviewed the revival which had taken place two years previously in Dundee and noted,

'The ministers ... believing that children are lost, and may through grace be saved, have, therefore, spoken to children as freely as to grown persons; and God has so greatly honoured their labours, that many children, from ten years old and upwards, have given full evidence of their being born again. I am not aware of

5 Thornton, *God Sent Revival*, p. 87.
6 Page, *David Brainerd*, pp. 81–82.
7 Evans, *When He is Come*, p. 13.

any meetings that have been held peculiarly for children, with the exception of the Sabbath-schools, the children's prayer meetings, and a sermon to children on the Monday evening after the Communion. It was commonly at the public meetings, in the house of God, that children were impressed; often in their own little meetings, when no minister was present.'[8]

At Berry Street Presbyterian Church in Belfast in 1859, three hundred children attended a midday children's meeting and a third of them found peace in Christ.[9] Joseph Jenkins, the Calvinistic Methodist minister at New Quay in Cardiganshire, Wales, described how God's Spirit came in 1859 first to the young people's after-meeting, when about sixty were present. He wrote of 'an overpowering sense of God's presence' that morning and it affected the whole church.

Amy Carmichael described how a new awakening came among the Tamils in Dohnavur in 1906: 'It was at the close of the morning service (22nd October) that the break came. The one who was speaking, was obliged to stop, overwhelmed by a sudden realization of the inner force of things. It was impossible even to pray. One of the older lads in the boys' school began to try to pray, but he broke down, then another, then all together, the older lads chiefly at first. Soon many among the younger ones began to cry bitterly and pray for forgiveness. It spread to the women.'

Amy Carmichael found it hard to recall all the details of that eventful day:

'It was so startling and so aweful—I can use no other word—that details escaped me. Soon [many] were on the floor, crying to God, each boy and girl, man and woman, oblivious of all others. The sound was like the sound of waves or strong wind in the trees ... For the next fortnight, life was apportioned for us much as it

8 Bonar, *Memoirs and Remains*, p. 504.
9 Paisley, *The Fifty-Nine Revival*, p. 68.

was for the apostles when they gave themselves continually to prayer and to the ministry of the word. Everything else had to stand aside. At first the movement was almost entirely among convert boys, schoolboys, our own children and workers, and some younger members of the congregation.'[10]

Seven months later she reported: 'Nearly all our children were out and out converted.'

In 1973 in Borneo, even 'little children' were brought to tears of repentance when God came down at the Vacation Bible School at Bario.[11] The amazing work of God in China, during the 1960s and '70s especially, has drawn millions of young people to Christ. In Swatow, north of Canton, where the church suffered so severely in the 'Cultural Revolution' of 1966, membership grew to five hundred, of whom eighty per cent were young people. A ninety-year-old pastor, who had been permanently disabled by the Red Guard, told visitors to China that he was caring for over 5,000 baptized Christians, of whom a large number were young people. In 1981, in one small conference in Kaifeng, eighteen young people were commissioned as local preachers.[12]

Children at prayer

In many instances, it is the children and youth who are most sincerely longing and praying for revival, and amongst whom it begins. References to the part played in revival by children and teenagers are abundant. Two years before the revivals at Kilsyth and Cambuslang in 1742, the minister at Kilsyth, James Robe, discovered that sixteen children in a nearby

In many instances, it is the children and youth who are most sincerely longing and praying for revival, and amongst whom it begins

10 Orr, *The Flaming Tongue*, pp. 18–19.
11 Lees, *Drunk Before Dawn*, pp. 195–196.
12 Lyall, *God Reigns in China*, pp. 170–171,184.

town were meeting together in a barn to pray, and in his own parish: 'Several young girls ... from ten to sixteen years of age, had been observed meeting together for prayer in an outhouse they had access to.' All this 'made deep impressions both upon young and old'. It is hardly surprising that when revival came, many children, some only eight years old, were brought to salvation.

When God visited the Moravian community in Saxony in 1727, it owed its origin in part to Count Ludwig of Zinzendorf praying desperately for his class of nine young girls between nine and fourteen years, who showed no evidence of spiritual life. However, 'No sooner had the fire of the love of Jesus been fully kindled in the Congregation there than the hearts of the children caught the flame' and immediately 'The children of both sexes felt a most powerful impulse to prayer, and it was impossible to listen to their infant supplications without being deeply moved and affected.' The report comments that a meeting of the children 'took place in the evening of the 26th of August, and on the 29th, from the hours of ten o'clock at night until one the following morning a truly affecting scene was witnessed, for the girls from Herrnhut and Berthelsdorf spent these hours in praying, singing and weeping. The boys were at the same time engaged in earnest prayer in another place. The spirit of prayer and supplication at that time poured out upon the children was so powerful and efficacious that it is impossible to give an adequate description of it in words.'[13]

A few years after this, in Northampton, New England, Jonathan Edwards witnessed the same thing. He found that the largest number of children converted in revival were between the ages of ten and fourteen and, writing nearly ten years after the event, the ever-cautious Edwards recorded, 'In the summer and autumn, the children in various parts of the town had religious meetings by themselves, for prayer, sometimes joined with fasting; wherein many of them seemed to be greatly and

13 *The Memorial Days of the Renewed Church of the Brethren*, pp. 130–134.

properly affected, and I hope some of them savingly wrought upon ... Now we had the most wonderful work among children that ever was in Northampton.'[14]

In 1742 God moved in the parish of Baldernock in Scotland, and children in the local school were particularly moved. The schoolmaster, James Forsyth, wrote of a young people's prayer meeting in his school, through which many were converted, 'None of them were above thirteen years of age—a few of them were so young as eight or nine.'[15]

Before the revival in Beddgelert in Wales in 1817, a spirit of prayer was noted not only among the church members, but among the children as well.[16] In 1859 across Wales, children were often used by God to bring the fire of revival into the adult community and some of the most powerful effects of the Spirit were felt in the children's prayer meetings. One minister in Aberaeron reported on 16 May: 'The youth of our congregations are nearly all the subjects of deep religious impressions. Many of them seem as if filled with the Spirit of prayer. Very young people, yea, children from ten to fourteen years of age, gather together to hold prayer meetings, and pray very fervently...' One minister compared the children to steam tugs sent out by the Spirit to draw the larger vessels into port![17] At Fishguard in the same year the first evidence of revival came through the prayer of young children.

There are many records of children at prayer during the '59 revival in Ireland and some claim that it was after children prayed that the revival began. Young school children held prayer meetings in the playground and by the roadside. Many led their own friends to the Saviour. Rev. Henry Montgomery recounts a children's prayer meeting during which a young girl asked God for salvation while a boy was praying; he turned to his

14 Edwards, *A Narrative of Surprising Conversions*, p. 151.
15 *Narratives of Revivals of Religion*, p. 2.
16 Evans, *When He is Come*, p. 15.
17 As above, p. 104.

friend and commented: 'God sooner far hears us wee fellows than He does big men.'[18]

The same thing happened in 1904 in Wales. Children met frequently for prayer, even using their playtime at school for that purpose. They held meetings in their own homes, and in barns, even in empty pigsties. The records are full of children taking part in the meetings. The *North Wales Guardian* for 27 January 1905 reported on meetings in Dolgellau which included reference to a 'Sunday afternoon children's prayer meeting' when 'Several very young children took part, and at the conclusion a short service was held in the public square.'

About the same time in India a missionary commented upon the children in the prayer meetings during the revival in the Khassi Hills: 'Two boys prayed afterwards, and one prayer in particular was very beautiful. I never knew what a child's prayer could be before.'[19] In the same year God moved among the congregation at Charlotte Chapel in Edinburgh and the pastor, Joseph Kemp, recording the many conversions in the Sunday School, commented, 'So keen were the children that they started prayer meetings of their own, and a sympathetic leader was appointed to guide them.'[20]

During the 1859 revival in Ulster, great gatherings were held in the Botanic Gardens in Belfast; numbers were so large that the crowds broke into smaller groups which included prayer meetings composed entirely of young people. One observer reported, 'In many parts of the gardens groups of boys and girls, some of them ragged, who had evidently belonged to the outcast classes, and were recently converted, prayed in language most affecting and impressive.' When the revival came to Belfast, Berry Street Presbyterian Church was the first to experience its power and in

18 *The Children in '59*, a New Year's address given to young people by Rev Henry Montgomery in Belfast 1909.
19 Jones, *India awake*, p.34.
20 Kemp, *Joseph W. Kemp*, p.31.

that church a midday children's meeting was attended by three hundred children, of whom a third found peace in Christ. At Coleraine the large school of the Irish Society was swept by the Spirit, and almost the entire school, both boys and girls, came under conviction of sin.[21]

It was the same at Mynydd Llandygai in Caernarvonshire: 'The dawn finally broke in the young people's prayer meeting where, under the influence of the Spirit, some prayed for deliverance, others wept bitterly, and others praised God for having at last visited His people. This went on for some hours and proved to be the first-fruits of a mighty awakening which soon spread to neighbouring churches.'[22]

In 1903 and 1904 in Denmark, 'a landslide' of young people began to fill the prayer meetings. In 1904 at Fransch Hoek in South Africa a Young People's Society heard of the work of the Spirit elsewhere and a prayer meeting of forty-two was soon attended by six hundred.[23] Mary Peckham reported on her experience as a teenager on Lewis in the time of Duncan Campbell. She records the groups of young people waking the minister late at night asking for 'a meeting' at which they could hear the word preached and pray. When young Donald MacPhail began his prayer with, 'Father', that very word reduced Mary to tears.[24] Scores of young people were not only converted at this time but were eager for the Bible teaching—and they prayed.

In October 1973 revival broke out among the students of the Junior Secondary School at Bario in Borneo. Two boys began to pray together and gradually the whole school was drawn in until the headmaster himself, opposed to the work of the Spirit at first, was brought to repentance.[25]

---

21 Paisley, The Fifty-Nine Revival, pp. 60, 68, 92–93.
22 Evans, *When He is Come*, pp. 38–39.
23 Orr, *The Flaming Tongue*, pp. 54, 119.
24 Peckham, *Sounds From Heaven*, p. 149.
25 Lees, *Drunk Before Dawn*, pp. 185–189.

Children and young people, when drawn into revival, have the same prayer and evangelistic passion that adults have. When God came to the Khassi Hills in India in 1905 a missionary reported home:

'The young people now begin to feel that it is their duty to speak to others. In one place where a very large market is held, about forty children went to the chapel to pray at noon, others soon joined them, and the Spirit of God was among them. Some went out of the meeting to speak to the people in the market and a great crowd from the Bazaar ran to the chapel and filled it, and the service which the children held with them was a very powerful one. When these returned to their work others took their place and thus it went on for hours. One writes, "At 10 o'clock at night we only seemed to be just beginning and I do not know when our meeting came to an end, but it was sometime in the morning." These children's meetings are becoming more general.'[26]

In Korea in 1907 even young children would run up to people on the street and plead with them to accept Christ as their Saviour. In Wales children prayed urgently and boldly for their parents. A young Christian at Rhosesmor was heard to pray: 'My father is ungodly; I am afraid to go home because of his swearing. Oh come and save him, Lord! Thou hast knocked at his door many times; compel him to open, and if he refuses, take the door off its hinges, Lord!' And when children were converted, 'They instantly crave permission to have family prayer, and thus divine worship is established in nearly every family in the country.'[27]

Perhaps of all the blessings revealed among children in revival is their awareness of the reality of God. On 22 October 1905 at Dohnavur in India one little girl expressed her understanding of the revival as the time 'Jesus came to Dohnavur'.

---

26 Jones, *India Awake*, p. 159.
27 Evans, *When He is Come*, p. 104.

R. B. Jones related a conversation between two children at Rhos in North Wales at the time of the 1904 revival:

'Do you know what has happened at Rhos?'
'No, I don't, except that Sunday comes every day now.'
'Don't you know?'
'No, I don't.'
'Why, Jesus Christ has come to live in Rhos now.'[28]

28 Jones, *Rent Heavens*, p. 42.

During revival

Error, excess and the unusual

Revivals can be very upsetting. In revival God has adequate scope for variety. When Spurgeon referred to revival as a time of 'glorious disorder', he did not mean everything is out of hand and 'wild', but God does not limit himself to the normal pattern of church life or even a mould stamped as 'revival'. No one comes to the subject of revival without prejudices and preferences. We know the kind of experiences and behaviour we would like to see or expect to see when the Holy Spirit is powerfully at work, and it is tempting to choose those examples that fit *our* pattern, and to ignore the rest.

It is a fact that most of the revivals recorded in history have had little of the phenomena recorded by a few. Typically, one observer of the Asbury College revival in 1970 commented, 'There were no awe-inspiring sounds, no mysterious winds, and no visible flames of fire. But perhaps it was the nearest thing to Pentecost America has experienced in this century.'[1] Jonathan Edwards wrote from experience when he commented, 'I have seen so much of the power of God in a more excellent way, as to convince me that God can easily do without phenomena.'[2]

However, God is no man's servant and his Spirit moves where and how he wants. In revival God has used ignorant and theologically careless preachers, as well as men of great learning and precision; he has used some who encourage 'wild' responses and some who expect order and discipline. Whatever our experience, preference, or evangelical doctrinal emphasis,

1 Duewell, *Revival Fire*, p.351.

2 Murray, *Jonathan Edwards, A new biography*, p. 243. From *The Works of Jonathan Edwards*, (Vol. 2, p. 275) Banner of Truth, orig. 1834.

if we dig over the ground we will find a revival somewhere to support our cause.

> Revival does not need a defence, it needs to be experienced

Revival can be criticised for the outrageous events found here and there. However, revival does not need a defence, it needs to be experienced. We dare not 'demolish' a revival simply because some aspects of it are not to our personal liking, doctrinal convictions, or denominational traditions. Some things are wrong because they are contrary to Scripture, other things are excessive, and some may be threatening because they are unusual. The fact that God may bless our failures and errors does not justify them. Occasionally it is hard to make a judgement because too much time separates us from the event, and we have insufficient evidence. However, for those who love to be thrilled by the unusual and the spectacular, there will be no true revival as long as they are seeking those things. Revival comes when Christians are longing for God, and God alone.

There are theological differences within the evangelical spectrum among those who are used in revival. Whitefield and Wesley could not both be right in their, at times bitter, controversy over election and free-will. Similarly, whilst we may rejoice in the experience and admire the courage of William Haslam of Baldhu in Cornwall, at times he allowed more unbridled Cornish emotion and noise than was always good for the honour of the gospel. When he acknowledged that between 1851 and 1854 his people had come to enjoy 'the gift of salvation more than the Giver himself', he was wrong to teach a separate experience of sanctification to make up for the deficiency.

Commenting on some of the problems encountered during the revival in Borneo during 1973, an elder statesman in Sarawak wrote,

'In any revival there are usually two opposite reactions or attitudes of people, including the Christians. Some people totally reject all that takes place and miss out on the fresh blessings and deeper things of God, and even miss out on salvation completely. On the other hand, others blindly accept everything without discerning, and are deceived by Satan or are misled by the flesh and are in danger of straying away from the truth. While we know it is the genuine work of the Holy Spirit, we must also remember that Satan is very active in time of revival doing his counterfeit work and trying to deceive. There is also the human element such as emotionalism and hypocrisy.'[3]

Those are wise words. Revival is a time of intense spiritual activity on both sides of the divide. If God is at work in power, so is the devil, who delights to counterfeit the good and holy work of the Creator. It is impossible to read of revival without, sooner or later, stumbling across some unusual, perhaps bizarre or even frightening events. Everything from visions to faintings, from prophesying to shrieking, has been recorded in the story of revival. It is the presence of these things that have led some to dismiss revival altogether as a dangerous hypnosis or an irrelevant side-show. True revival is neither, but it is hardly surprising that at times of great spiritual awakenings some will allow their emotion or their imagination to overtake a sound mind governed by the word of God.

There is an example of this in the time of Hezekiah: 'Although most of the many people who came from Ephraim, Manasseh, Issachar and Zebulun had not purified themselves, yet they ate the Passover, contrary to what was written. But Hezekiah prayed for them, saying, "May the LORD, who is good, pardon everyone who sets his heart on seeking God—the LORD, the God of his fathers—even if he is not clean according to the rules of the sanctuary." And the LORD heard Hezekiah and healed the people' (2 Chronicles 30:18–20). These people from the north were new converts to the covenant. God knew their hearts were sincere and they were not knowingly ignoring the ceremonial instructions, they were simply not aware of them.

---

3 Lees, *Drunk Before Dawn*, p. 197.

By its nature, revival brings in a large number of new converts in a short time, and it is not easy for them all to be taught the truth about God. New converts will watch what is happening and sometimes take it upon themselves to help forward the work of God. Some are inclined to believe that the more excessive their behaviour, the more authentic it must be. It is at this point that some of the errors and excesses creep in. Writing of revival at Kilsyth and Cambuslang in 1742, James Robe admitted to the presence of 'imprudences, irregularities, and exceptional things', but, he says, these were condemned and opposed by the leaders, though sadly the enemies of revival exaggerated them to disgrace the work.[4]

We must never be intimidated into assuming that where there is a genuine work of the Holy Spirit, everything that happens must be right, or that even if certain things are wrong we ought not to criticize them for fear of touching holy things. Sprague has left a wise comment on this from his wide understanding of revival: 'You may be assured that the cause of revivals is far more likely to suffer by an attempt on the part of its friends to pass off everything for gold, than by giving to that which is really dross its proper name.'[5]

Physical responses

One of the most common experiences in revival has been the physical effects of a deep conviction of sin. It was present in the ministry of John Wesley. During his meetings people would tremble, fall to the ground and faint. Others would cry out and scream. One illustration of many is taken from Wesley's own diary for the year 1739 during his ministry in Bristol. An incident that was very likely a genuine physical torment brought about by a deep conviction of sin and the opposition of Satan:

4 Robe, *When the Wind Blows*, p. 138.
5 Sprague, *Lectures on Revivals*, p. 221.

'May 2nd. John Haydon ... a man of regular life and conversation ... changed colour, fell off his chair, and began screaming terribly, and beating himself against the ground ... Two or three men were holding him as best they could. He immediately fixed his eyes upon me, and cried, "Aye, this is he who I said was a deceiver of the people; but God has overtaken me. I said it was all a delusion; but this is no delusion." He then roared out, "O thou devil! Thou cursed devil! Yea thou legion of devils! Thou canst not stay!" He then beat himself against the ground again, his breast heaving at the same time as in the pangs of death, and great drops of sweat trickling down his face ... We all betook ourselves to prayer. His pangs ceased, and both body and soul were set at liberty.'[6]

However, not all were genuine. Initially, Wesley did not discourage physical responses. Similar things happened under Edwards' and Whitefield's preaching in America. At first Jonathan Edwards accepted this but later cautioned Whitefield against it; it led directly to Edward's treatise on *Religious Affections*. These men came to see that such outbursts were no certain sign of a genuine work of the Holy Spirit. Whitefield then warned Wesley of the dangers and Wesley later realized how easily a show of this kind could be put on. Unhelpful physical responses in eighteenth century Wales led to accusations that the Methodists were 'jumpers' and 'stark mad'.[7]

At Kilsyth and Cambuslang the ministers noted that some, particularly among the girls and others who were for various reasons impressionable, cried out, fainted or threw fits. James Robe, one of the leaders, was not impressed and commented that 'The spirit of sal-ammoniac or hartshorn put to their noses was useful to revive them.'[8]

After a period of serious spiritual decline in America the Spirit of God moved across Kentucky, North and South Carolina and Western

6 Dallimore, *George Whitefield*, vol. 1, p. 322.
7 Jones, *The Fire Divine*, p. 89.
8 Robe, *When the Wind Blows*, p. 111.

Pennsylvania from 1799 to 1802. Many of the 'camp meetings': 'Seemed as in bedlam with emotionalized men and women weeping, groaning, shouting, jerking and dancing, or falling into trances and torpors. Such frenzies detracted from the revival in the eyes of many, especially the more conservative Presbyterians and Baptists, and were discredited among the better informed among the settlers.'[9] The genuineness of this time of revival cannot be doubted, but some of the responses were clearly exaggerated, unnecessary and harmful.

Much of the 'jerking' in this revival, during which the head twitched violently from side to side, was clearly psychological and had nothing to do with true religion. Many afflicted with it scorned the faith and had no interest at all in salvation. One careful documentation concluded, though not entirely accurately: 'John Wesley looked upon these physical agitations as proofs of the divine presence. Charles Wesley suspected and discouraged them. Whitefield was incredulous. Edwards put in an apology for them. But very few ministers favoured them.'[10] When Hugh Bourne and William ('Billy') Clowes in England heard of these camp meetings in Kentucky, they organized the same. The first was on 31 May 1807 at Mow-hill (Mow Cop) on the Cheshire-Staffordshire border. At times, four preachers would be preaching at the same time to various sections of the large crowd. Three years later the Primitive Methodist—whose story should be far better known in the subject of revival—were formed. Although they were a fast-growing and exuberant group who 'loved a good shout', Billy records in his journal: 'I have since been convinced that religion does not consist in bodily movements, whether shouting, jumping, falling or standing, but in the exercise of faith—in the soul taking hold of God and realizing a *present salvation.*'[11]

---

9 Lacy, *Revivals in the Midst of the Years*, pp. 74–75.
10 Fish, *Handbook of Revivals*, p. 19.
11 Clowes, *The Journal of William Clowes*, p. 46.

Not only did these excesses divide churches and whole denominations, but the more extreme elements drew off into fragmented groups such as the Stonites (after Barton Stone who denied the Trinity among much else) which slid into the sect known as the Shakers, a self-explanatory title. The extravagance of these Kentucky 'camp' meetings, and by 1812 there were an estimated four hundred annually across the United States, significantly changed the whole understanding of revival in the American scene.

In an in-depth analysis of the cause and course of these meetings, Iain Murray has provided an excellent assessment for us to learn from today.[12] In the aftermath of the American Revolutionary War (1775–1783) a spirit of independence, the populism of democracy, and an intolerance with the old conservative order, led to a lack of strong leadership. This, together with the rise of Arminianism, aided by the launch of *The Arminian Magazine* in 1789, led to the belief that revivals can be planned and maintained by techniques. It was fertile ground for the 'revivalism' of Charles Finney three decades later.[13] The 'falling exercise' led to the 'altar call' which were counted (literally) as evidence of conversion. Men wanted to carry a genuine revival forward and manipulated the crowds until, as one commentator noted, 'Hysteria became the chaff.'

However, we must not discount some physical responses as part of genuine spiritual revival. Asahel Nettleton, preaching in America in the first half of the nineteenth century, came across some who experienced 'horror of mind' which was so severe that they had to be taken away from the meeting until they found peace with God.[14] In Ulster during the 1859 revival they were known as the 'strikings-down' and one illustration will cover many. At Berry Street Presbyterian Church a strong, powerful man

12 Murray, *Revival and Revivalism*, pp. 163–190. For anyone troubled by this subject, this chapter is essential reading.

13 For an assessment of Finney's theology and method see the companion volume to this, *Praying for Revival*, ch. 1, and Murray, *Revival and Revivalism*, pp. 228–252.

14 Thornton, *God Sent Revival*, p. 60.

set up a loud and bitter cry in the meeting and fell down. He was carried outside thought to be unconscious; his response to an enquiry was: 'Yes, awfully conscious.' The sheer horror of his sin had thrown him to the ground; this was a regular church-goer who was convicted of formalism and self-deception.[15]

The 'phenomenon' of a physical response to the conviction of sin and the presence of God has been reported as far distant as Korea and India in times of revival. These physical responses have probably been the most debated part of the history of revivals; generally, the response to them depends upon whether the commentator is for or against the revival in the first place. An interesting example of this is found in the columns of the *Wrexham Advertiser* during 1859. On 16 July the paper carried a report from Rev. W. McIlwaine of St George's Church, Belfast, He took great exception to the physical responses in Ulster during that year and described them in the most alarming way possible:

'After a good deal of actual examination, I have to state I believe that there is a dangerous physical malady abroad and that its seat is in the nervous system. It affects poor young girls who are working in factories all day with very insufficient food, and these girls I have seen myself suffering under the complaints I shall mention. I have seen them in hysteria. I have known it to end in epilepsy. I have seen them in catalepsy. I have known it to result in many cases in madness. ... Now dear brethren let me affectionately appeal to you as men, as brethren, and citizens. What do you think of the men, who call themselves ministers of Christ that will collect these young creatures in a crowded congregation, night after night, and speak to them as the old divine of whom I have been reading? Every fibre of their feelings is wrought up to excitement, and when they fall into a swoon, not a drop of water is given them, and yet these men will insist that this is the working of the Spirit of God. I have no words to express my abhorrence of

15 Paisley, *The Fifty-Nine Revival*, p. 165.

such conduct as this. I tell you it is unworthy of any man, not to say a Christian minister ... I have seen whole roomfuls of these poor factory girls taken by it again and again, and one of these poor creatures told me she had suffered from it sixteen times. I ask you, were there sixteen convictions? They were sixteen epileptic fits.'

On 20 August the same paper carried a report of a lecture delivered by Rev. J. G. Short, who had recently spent some time in Ulster. Clearly Mr Short saw things differently:

'I will now speak to you of the physical manifestations by which this awakening has been so largely characterized. Many have looked upon these with wonder, and perplexity, and doubt. On this side of the channel they are commonly regarded as the results of mere animal excitement. This is a mistake. No one on the spot will ever dream of putting them down to such a cause. I never saw meetings more free from all display of mere feeling. A stranger going to any of these religious gatherings that now fill evening after evening, almost all the Protestant places of worship in Ulster, would feel at once there is no rant here, no effort to get up any artificial feeling. An unwonted solemnity and earnestness of feeling shows itself in the faces of the people—but attempts to create any mere excitement there are none ... in a short time, perhaps half a dozen or more will be found prostrate in the pews unable either to sit or stand. I have seen a considerable number of these "stricken" cases. I have seen strong men, as if smitten by an invisible hand, fall down nervous and helpless, as I was near to them. ... In every one of these "stricken" cases they cry for Jesus, and such a cry. I have heard many utter such words as "sweet Jesus", "lovely Jesus", in a very low tone of voice, but with a depth and tenderness of feeling that could not be described. ... The Saviour seemed as if visibly revealed, and as his love filled their souls, their faces looked as if they were literally transformed ... I am quite sure, that with rare exceptions there is no consistent way of explaining them, except by confessing that they are the work of God.'

These two reports deserve quoting at length, because they clearly reveal the different responses to the same phenomena. Perhaps Mr McLlwaine chose only to observe the extreme cases. However, these physical experiences in revival are too common and too widespread to be dismissed either as all human or satanic in origin. Even the cautious Scotsman Robert M'Cheyne reported from Dundee in 1839: 'I have seen persons so overcome [with love for Christ], that they could not walk or stand alone.'[16]

The whole of Psalm 38 should be read by any who doubt that physical effects cannot result from a deep conviction of sin. Here is part of that Psalm of King David:

'Your hand has come down upon me. Because of your wrath there is no health in my body; my bones have no soundness because of my sin. My guilt has overwhelmed me like a burden too heavy to bear. My wounds fester and are loathsome because of my sinful folly. I am bowed down and brought very low; all day long I go about mourning. My back is filled with searing pain; there is no health in my body. I am feeble and utterly crushed; I groan in anguish of heart. All my longings lie open before you, O LORD: my sighing is not hidden from you. My heart pounds, my strength fails me; even the light has gone from my eyes.'

When confronted by the risen Lord in all his glory, the apostle John 'fell at his feet as though dead' (Revelation 1:17). Similarly, Saul of Tarsus crashed into the dust outside Damascus and was blind for three days (Acts 9:4). We have a small view of God if we do not expect that when someone sees themselves in the light of God's holiness there will never be an intense reaction. What must be noted is that in true revival such a terrible experience of conviction is always followed by as great a joy in forgiveness. This physical reaction is not present in every revival and

16 Bonar, *Memoirs and Remains*, p. 501.

should never be prayed for as a sign of reality. To imitate such effects is a dangerous delusion. Wesley himself came to realize this and became less concerned whether or not they accompanied his meetings. There is a contagious psychology about phenomena like this: the more people expect them the more they will appear, but that proves nothing apart from the frailty of the human mind.

A valuable corrective comes from the experience of Duncan Campbell in 1949. There were times under his preaching when people were thrown to the ground in physical prostration. Campbell observed that where people were looking for such physical manifestations, they got them. And when they were not interested in such evidence, God said, 'Well, you don't need them,' and they did not have them. Campbell himself admitted there was a certain psychological aspect to it. One day a man came to the evangelist and told him that he was praying for this physical prostration in order to be satisfied with Christ. Campbell gave him a wise answer: 'You need only what makes you conscious you are a sinner. That is all.' The man was indignant: 'I am surprised that a man like you should give me that kind of advice. I want this special experience.' Campbell says the next time he saw this man he was being taken into a mental institution between two warders. When the evangelist saw him again some years later the man came to Campbell and admitted, 'Duncan Campbell, I am a wiser man today.'[17]

We might agree with the Rev. J. G. Short, who at the close of his lecture on the physical responses of people in the revival in Ulster commented, 'I have heard some say: "We do not like these bodily prostrations—we like all beside." I do not think it is seemly to say to God what it is we like in his work, and what we dislike. Is God to give account of his doings?'[18]

Occasionally the coming of God's Spirit is felt among God's people just as it was in Acts 4:31: 'After they prayed, the place where they were

17 Woolsey, *Duncan Campbell*, pp. 108–109.
18 *Wrexham Advertiser*, 20 August 1859.

meeting was shaken. And they were all filled with the Holy Spirit and spoke the word of God boldly.' An example of this happened at Arnol on the Isle of Lewis in the 1940s. Towards the close of a prayer meeting in the home of an elder, the local blacksmith was asked to pray. His prayer turned to the promises of God and to his own thirst for God and concluded, 'O God, your honour is at stake, and I now challenge you to fulfil your covenant engagement and do what you have promised to do.' At that moment the house shook and 'Dishes rattled in the sideboard, as wave after wave of Divine power swept through the house.' When this group of praying people closed the prayer meeting and went outside, they found 'the community alive with an awareness of God'.[19] We cannot explain this—we do not need to; it is simply an example of the powerful presence of God in revival prayer meetings.

Emotion, commotion and laughter

Revivals are times of strong emotion and it is a rare thing for this not to express itself. The cold insistence that all that is required for salvation is a mental assent to the truths of the gospel—an old error planted by Robert Sandeman in the eighteenth century[20]—is today equalled by those who imply that preaching is little more than a careful exegesis of Scripture. If we are safe only in firmly controlled order, revival will prove a terrifying experience. It is strange that those who object to the expression of emotion in religion are not averse to high emotion in the stadium. An awesome sense of the reality of God's presence, a deep conviction of personal sin, and an unbounded joy with total forgiveness, cannot help express itself. Methodism was born in revival and insisted upon a heart experience of God and not merely an intellectual acceptance of truth. This was the

---

19 Woolsey, *Duncan Campbell*, p. 133. A similar experience is recorded in Peckham, *Sounds from Heaven*, p. 162.

20 Known as Sandemanianism. For a careful analysis see Lloyd-Jones, *The Puritans: Their Origins and Successors*, pp. 170–190.

main reason for the Welsh 'Experience Meeting' where converts were encouraged to share their heart and their new spiritual life.[21]

Inevitably there are dangers, and some will allow their emotions to run wild. The American 'Camp Meetings' of the early nineteenth century are well known for their high emotion and commotion. At the Cane Ridge Camp in Kentucky in August 1801, people fell into trances, sang, danced and ran about wildly and experienced so-called 'Holy Spirit laughter'. Francis Asbury wrote to a friend: 'The people report they bark and snatch and make strong noises'[22] Unfortunately, Asbury and the Camp Meetings wanted noise and extravagance to prove that the 'revival' was of God. The fact that God only once used a donkey to speak like a man (Numbers 22:28–30) and it is never recorded that he would allow a man to descend to the voice of an animal, is evidence sufficient that many of these extreme responses were, at best, merely human and bore no resemblance to the work of the Holy Spirit. This is why William Williams of Pantycelyn, who lived during times of revival in eighteenth century Wales and who has been described as a Welsh Charles Wesley and Jonathan Edwards, set out seven important regulations for the 'Experience Meetings' in Wales. However, in general, as Joseph Kemp expressed it, 'The confusion never gets confused.'[23]

The degree of excitement and emotion in revival frequently depends upon the leaders and upon cultural characteristics, and this needs to be understood by leaders. A revival in Norway in 1905, which came directly from the Spirit's fire in Wales the year previously, was never charged with sensationalism, although this charge was often levelled against the work in Wales. The wise and careful vicar at Rhos in North Wales, the Rev. Thomas Pritchard, defended Wales against the charge of mere emotionalism by

---

21 See Williams, *The Experience Meeting*.

22 Frances Asbury, 'Letter to George Roberts' 18 August 1803, in *Journal and Letters of Francis Asbury*, 3:269.

23 As above, p. 34.

Emotion will always be part of revival, but commotion need not be

reminding people: 'Sneers are made at our Celtic temperament, but God gave it, and God can use it for the glory of His Name.'[24] The same contrast can be seen by a comparison of revivals in Wales and Scotland. Emotion will always be part of revival, but commotion need not be.

When Billy Bray, the converted Cornish miner, visited the church of William Haslam in Baldhu during 1853, revival was already in progress. Billy was known for his eccentric behaviour, and the congregation at Baldhu was known for its excessive noise in worship. It was inevitable that Billy would stir up the people and before long, comments Haslam: 'The people got what they called "happy" and shouted and praised God vociferously.' Haslam, who encouraged the people to respond in worship, tried in vain to bring them to order and only after some time could he quieten them down. William Haslam was sufficiently wise and discerning to comment, 'The power of God was great, though the demonstrations were very human.' Old William Aitken, a neighbouring minister and a strong friend of revival, came over and preached a sermon 'on the difference between emotion and principle.'[25]

William Williams has left a balanced defence and critique of phenomena in revival. He wisely concluded that whilst physical response will always be present when the emotions are stirred, this must not be from 'the excitement of emotionalism, but from a real knowledge and enjoyment of God.'[26] Billy Clowes a founder of the Primitive Methodists—known for their enthusiastic and loud worship whose praying could be heard a mile away—came to the same conclusion: '...religion does not consist in bodily movements, whether shouting, jumping, falling or standing, but

24 *North Wales Guardian*, 27 January 1905.
25 Haslam, *From Death Into Life*, p. 142.
26 Davies, *The Beddgelert Revival*, p. 132. Eryl Davies has given a helpful summary of Williams.

in the exercise of faith—in the soul taking hold of God and realizing a *present salvation.*'

Occasionally William Williams did not always meet his own conditions. Commenting on some of the meetings under William Williams and others, John Wesley wrote disapprovingly in his diary: 'It is common ... after the preaching is over, for anyone that has a mind to give out a verse of an hymn. This they sing over and over with all their might, perhaps above thirty, yea, forty times. Meanwhile the bodies of two or three, sometimes ten or twelve, are violently agitated, and they leap up and down, in all manner of postures, frequently for hours together.' Wesley generously but decisively responded, 'They are honest, upright men, who really feel the love of God in their hearts. But they have little experience, either of the ways of God or the devices of Satan who takes advantage of their simplicity in order to wear them out and to bring a discredit on the work of God.'[27] When he came across 'uncontrolled laughter' Wesley had no hesitation in attributing it to 'the working of the devil.'[28]

For all the Primitive Methodists' love of a 'good shout', Billy Clowes strongly disapproved of laughing in the meetings. Confronted with this phenomena on Thursday, 6 October 1725, he reproved the congregation, and commented in his journal, '...in my opinion, to laugh in the worship of God could not be the most excellent way; that strangers coming in, and witnessing such proceedings, would certainly conclude that the worshippers were very light and trifling; and that, for a preacher to laugh before his congregation, could not be tolerated.' Billy added that people came to be instructed and that preaching was a grave and serious matter; if people felt happy during the preaching, they should praise God as the psalmist did: 'Bless the LORD, O my soul, and all that is within me, bless his holy name.'[29]

27 Wesley's *Journal* for 27 August 1763.
28 Wesley's *Journal* for 21 May 1740.
29 Clowes, *Journal*, pp. 254–255.

Joseph Kemp described the effects of the revival at Charlotte Chapel in Edinburgh in 1905. The church was well and wisely led and yet when the flood came, 'There were irregularities, no doubt; some commotion, yes. There was that which shot itself through all prescribed forms and shattered all conventionality. But such a movement with all its irregularities is to be preferred far above the dull, dreary, monotonous decorum of many churches.'[30]

When William Haslam moved to Buckenham in Norfolk in 1863 he left behind the 'wild' scenes of Cornish praise in revival where the 'wrastlings in prayer' would embarrass his fellow churchmen. Someone had told him that the people of Norfolk were like turnips: 'They would not cry out, even though they were thrust through and through with the sword; and like turnip lanterns they would never take fire.' Haslam found this to be true, and though his preaching led to powerful times of revival, so that for seven years he preached to more than 1,000 each week in the Norwich Lecture Hall, the commotions of Cornwall were rare things in Norfolk.

Years later William Haslam answered the question which was often put to him, why he allowed such noise in his revival meetings:

'I lived amongst a people who were accustomed to outward demonstrations; and by descending to them in their ways I was enabled to lead many of them to higher things, and to teach them to rest not so much on their feelings, as on the facts and truth revealed in the Word of God. But theorize as we would, it was just a question, in many cases, of no work, or of decided manifestation. We could not help people being stricken down, neither could they help it themselves; often the most unlikely persons were overcome and became excited, and persons naturally quiet and retiring proved the most noisy and demonstrative. However, it was our joy to see permanent results afterwards, which more than reconciled us for any

30 Kemp, *Joseph W. Kemp*, pp.30–31.

amount of inconvenience we had felt at the time ... Most undeniable it is that many trying things happen in the excitement of a storm.'[31]

One thing is certain, noise and commotion are neither necessary to revival nor evidence of it. 3,000 miles away from Norfolk in East Anglia in 1863, a revival in Norfolk, Connecticut in 1798 was, 'by no means noisy or boisterous'—even though more than 150 professed conversion in the town. Similarly, in the same year at Granville in Massachusetts there were no 'outcries under conviction ... nor rants of joy after receiving comfort'. A year later at Lenox, in the same state, the movement of God was free from any extravagance of gesture or outcry.[32]

In December 1859, when revival had spread from Wales to North Shields, the *Newcastle Chronicle* commented, 'It is only candid to say that whatever may have been the case elsewhere, there has been no rant or nonsense here. The fact that Mr Alderman Mease and other prudent persons have taken a most active part being a guarantee for order and decorum. Dr and Mrs Palmer have also grown more cautious and hushed down anything approaching violent excitement.'

It is well understood that the Welsh revival under Evan Roberts in the south, unlike the careful and wise leaders in the north, was weak at this very point of commotion. There were 'moments of complete disorder ... While the speakers remained strangely detached' and emotional pressures were put upon the people: 'it's hardly surprising that many of the "converts" quickly relapsed—leaving only a remnant of really born-again people.'[33] Any who opposed this disorder were frequently accused of being in the bonds of Satan.

31 Haslam, *From Death Into Life*, pp. 68–69.
32 Orr, *The Eager Feet*, p. 54.
33 Jones, *The King's Champions*, p. 59.

Women preachers

Just as God has used women on the mission-field for 150 years, so they have been used in revival. During 1905 1,200 people crowded into the Calvinistic Methodist Chapel in Coedpoeth and hundreds more had to be turned away. According to the *North Wales Guardian* of Friday 31 March: 'The principal speakers were the evangelists Miss Davies [Maude Davies] and Miss Evans [Florrie Evans] of Newquay, who have worked with Mr Evan Roberts. They sang, prayed, and addressed the audience in English and Welsh alternatively.' On this occasion the expected minister had been prevented from attending 'owing to indisposition'. In the same edition, meetings at Rossett were reported, in which 'Mrs March, a well-known Liverpool lady ... gave an interesting address.' The young ladies Davies and Evans spoke at many meetings, first in conjunction with Evan Roberts in the south and later, as reported above, they travelled through North Wales also.

William Haslam's wife and Geraldine Hooper from Bath both assisted Haslam in his work in the West Country and in East Anglia. Haslam described the influence of Miss Hooper when she came to the rectory at Buckenham in Norfolk in 1863:

'When it was known that she would speak at the barn meeting in the evening, the people came out in crowds, and the place was filled in every comer. Her address was like kindling a fresh fire, and a very bright and warm one it was. The people became wild with admiration, and their eagerness to hear her was intense. Her fame spread so rapidly that the Norwich papers took up the subject. The editor of one of these papers began a series of tirades against Buckenham and the work. Week by week fierce and long articles were published, which of course did not stamp out the fire, but rather added fuel to it.'[34]

---

34 Haslam, *Yet Not I*, p. 163.

The role of women as preachers during times of revival is not common, but it is reported in various parts of the world. A Norwegian Evangelical Lutheran missionary, Marie Monsen, exercised an effective ministry in the Shantung province of China during the revival that commenced in 1932. Marie Monsen's testimony, messages and constant question to missionaries and nationals alike: 'Are you born again?' led the revival to be called 'the Born-again Revival'.

That people are converted through the preaching of women in revival is without question; what is questionable is whether they *ought* to be preaching and whether God's use of them justifies their actions. A rector's wife wrote to William Haslam to say that she and her husband had been praying for a revival in Norfolk for years but she added, 'If this is a revival, it has come in such a way that I cannot thank God for it.' This lady urged Haslam to submit the issue to the bishop, adding, 'Let us leave the question of women's preaching to his grave decision.' Haslam had no intention of doing so, but there was a higher judgement than the bishop's and a clearer one for both William Haslam and the rector's wife; on this, as on every subject, Scripture must be our guide, whatever men or women may think. One thing is certain, and that is that we are unwise to dismiss a revival simply because there are some aspects that conflict with our understanding of Scripture.

Physical healing and raising the dead

With few exceptions physical healing rarely plays a large part in revivals. They are almost unknown during the eighteenth century Awakening. Evan Roberts held healing meetings in 1904, and three years later in Korea some churches held a prayer meeting for healing once a month.[35] John Sung of the Bethel Band, who was so greatly used in China and elsewhere, deliberately kept himself at a distance from the 'spiritual gifts'

35 Morod, *The Korean Revival*, p. 36.

movement and Jonathan Goforth in China in 1908 commented on some cases of physical healing even though he admitted it was not part of his preaching.[36] And this has been true of many God has used in revival. Petrus Octavianus was greatly used by God in the Borneo revival in 1973; there were healings claimed from his ministry and he 'usually gave a fairly low-key opportunity at the end of a meeting for prayer for physical healing', but physical healing formed a very small part of the results claimed for the revival.[37] Today, parts of the Christian church major on physical healing under the mistaken belief that this is a necessary evidence of an outpouring of the Holy Spirit. It is a matter of historical fact that in the times of God's greatest work in the story of the post-apostolic church, physical healing is not generally present.

However, events accompanying revival in Indonesia during the 1960s and among the Zulus of Natal from 1966 have included documented accounts of healing and even raising the dead.[38] It has often proved hard to authenticate many claims, but to accept without reserve the astonishing miracles in the Bible and yet dismiss them arbitrarily when reported today betrays our Western scepticism.

The place of healing in the Korean revival earlier in the twentieth century is revealed by one of the missionaries in an interesting comment when the churches held prayer meetings for healing:

'Before I attended this prayer meeting for the sick, it had been in my mind to tell the congregation assembled there that a man's salvation is more important than his cure. I intended to say to them: "Preach the Word! Forgiveness of sins is greater than healing of the body." I did not carry out my intention. What we in the West present as good theology, applying to biblical times, is actually carried out in practice today by these simple, devout people. As I have already mentioned, out

36 Goforth, *By My Spirit*, p. 146.
37 Lees, *Drunk Before Dawn*, p. 183.
38 Koch, *The Revival in Indonesia*, pp. 136–142 and *God among the Zulus*, pp. 170–172.

of thirty prayer meetings there was only one for the sick, the rest being devoted to the worship of God and intercessions of every kind.'[39]

The following report comes from Madras during the years of World War II. It is typical of the attitude of leaders even where God has given healing in revival:

'There were wonderful answers to prayer. The sick were prayed for and some were healed. A leper one day asked leave to give a five-minute testimony at a meeting. The week before, he had sat huddled in a blanket in the comer of the church with two leprous sores on his leg. Long treatment had failed to heal him and he had been given up as hopeless. Then he asked to be anointed and prayed for, and there-upon had been completely restored with no trace of his disease. But the emphasis was never on healing the body but always on bringing sinners to repentance and faith. The preaching brought a constant challenge to our hearts for it set high standards of life. "As he which hath called you is holy, so be ye holy in all manner of conversation; because it is written, be ye holy; for I am holy" (1 Peter 1:15–16). God sought in us hearts devoted to Him alone.'[40]

When revival came to the Shantung province of China in 1932 some remarkable instances of healing are recorded, but Dr Charles Culpepper, a missionary in China at the time, sets these in perspective: 'However, throughout the district, healing was not stressed. The emphasis was on repentance and confession of sin. The proof of the reality of the revival was seen in transformed lives ... the revival ... reminded me of the work in Samaria in apostolic days. Through the key of prayer of faith for sickness, doors were opened for the gospel.'[41]

---

39 Morod, *The Korean Revival*, p. 39.
40 Rajamani & Kinnear, *Monsoon Daybreak*, pp. 69–70.
41 Culpepper, *The Shantung Revival*, p. 64.

In his full treatment of revival in mainland China, Tony Lambert allows only twelve pages for 'signs and wonders'.[42] He makes no mention of speaking in tongues but does deal with healing. His comments are valuable. Undoubtedly there are instances of miraculous healing that have been carefully verified. When Zhao Su'e was dying with widespread cancer in October 1989, she was in a military hospital in Taixing. At the age of twenty-one she was given a one percent chance of survival. A Christian witnessed to her, Zhao Su'e believed and the cancer receded. Her parents and siblings came to Christ also. She knew of only ten Christians in Taixing but an old building was reopened, a church established and five years later there were known to be more than 5,000 Christians in Taixing County and almost every village in the county had Christian meetings. Fully healed, Zhao Su'e continued to be active in local church work.

Whilst Tony Lambert was able to cite other similar accounts, he wisely warned that 'some frankly incredible stories', wild and unverified, have come out of China. The Buddhist culture of shamans and spirits led to many untaught Christians following a dangerous mixture of the false with the true. The Christians in China never hold public 'healing meetings' and are wisely able to discern and pray for deliverance from spirit possession.

Tongues, visions, dreams and prophecy

Some issues that become significant for the churches when they are living without revival are insignificant when revival comes. The explanation is that in revival there are far more urgent and important matters to occupy the Christians. One example is that of 'speaking in tongues'. It is not necessary for us to discuss what this gift is, or even what part it should or should not play in the churches today, but as a matter of fact: 'tongues' rarely accompany revival.

42 Lambert, *China's Millions*, pp. 109–120.

During the eighteenth century Awakening under the preaching of men like Edwards, Whitefield and Wesley, tongues were virtually unknown; Edwards did not believe in the continuance of this gift. Yet, as we have seen, there were in Wesley's meetings some strange and excessive emotional experiences. One eyewitness of the Korean revival in 1907, who was convinced that 'All the spiritual gifts mentioned in the New Testament are to be recognized', specifically noted, 'The "gift of tongues" was not part of this revival.'[43] 'Tongues' were exercised a little during the revival in Borneo in 1973, but sadly they caused a division that took more than a year to heal.[44] Evan Roberts, whose leadership in the 1904 revival in Wales bore many characteristics of Pentecostal worship, actually discouraged 'tongues'; this was not because he did not believe in the gift, but because he did not consider the church ready to discern the true from the false.

The well-publicised outbreak of tongues-speaking in the old Methodist Church building in Azusa Street in Los Angeles in April 1906 is noted as the commencement of the modern Pentecostal movement. The meetings there continued for three years and the phenomena was gradually exported across the world. People came from all over to witness the tongues phenomenon. Significantly it was tongues that was exported, not always revival. Christians were often excited and their spiritual life enhanced, but the hallmarks of true revival were mostly absent, and the tongues-speaking caused many divisions among the churches. It led to the formation of the Assemblies of God and the International Church of the Foursquare Gospel. This 'foursquare gospel'—Christ as Saviour and Healer, the baptism of the Holy Spirit, speaking in tongues, and the Second Coming—laid emphasis on the phenomena. This is always a sign of a weakened or distracted 'revival'.

---

43 Morod, *The Korean Revival*, p. 20.
44 Lees, *Drunk Before Dawn*, p. 196.

Kurt Koch, whose reports on the revival in Indonesia during the 1960s have been open to the charge of being extravagant and misleading, is for this very reason interesting on the subject of 'tongues'. When he spoke to the leaders of revival on Timor, Indonesia, Koch asked them what part 'speaking in tongues' had played in the revival and he received this reply:

'Within a space of about two and a half years some 200,000 natives have become Christians. We have at the same time experienced thousands of cases of healing, together with many other miracles of faith, and yet we know of only one single instance of a person speaking in tongues, and even then the person doesn't use his gift in public.'[45]

Kurt Koch devoted four pages to the subject of tongues in his account of the revival among the Zulus. He outlined many cases of this phenomena from the trivial to the demonic and concluded that almost all were 'carnal confusion'.[46]

Reports of visions and dreams in revival are not common. In 1921 Jock Troup saw a vision of a man at Fraserburgh calling on God to send the evangelist to that town. On the strength of this, Troup left the work he was doing at Yarmouth and went to Fraserburgh. Soon after he arrived he went to the town square where a crowd gathered and he started to preach. Because of the intense cold Jock Troup suggested they find a church in which they could continue the meeting. They went to the Baptist church and were met by the minister and his elders who had just concluded a special meeting at which it had been decided to send an invitation to Jock Troup to come and conduct an evangelistic mission. Amongst the group of elders Jock recognized the face of the man in his vision.[47] Fraserburgh

45 Koch, *The Revival in Indonesia*, p. 265.
46 Koch, *God among the Zulus*, pp. 192–195.
47 Ritchie, *Floods Upon the Dry Ground*, pp. 57–60.

was the scene of some of the greatest work of God under the preaching of Jock Troup.

The *North Wales Guardian* for 20 January 1905 reported the following dream related to one of its correspondents during the Welsh revival: 'The coachman of a gentleman well known in Anglesey dreamed that his master came forward in a revival meeting and said, "I have come forward to show that I am not ashamed to confess Christ." He mentioned the dream to several persons next day, and that evening was astonished to see his master step forward at the revival meeting and say, "I have come forward to show that I am not ashamed to confess Christ." The incident created a profound sensation, especially amongst those to whom the coachman had previously related his dream. My informant, a Methodist minister, assures me he has personally verified the statements made above.'

During the revival at Baldhu in Cornwall between 1851 and 1854, William Haslam records, 'Every week, almost every day, we heard of some remarkable dream or striking vision.' He went on to relate a number of these, recognizing that some people would dismiss them as mere superstition. The examples he gives come from his own first-hand knowledge, and there is no reason to doubt. Some of these dreams or visions were direct prophetic warnings to individuals which were fulfilled. Interestingly, they were given within the geographical area touched by revival and rarely strayed beyond.[48]

Heavenly singing

At Beddgelert in Wales during 1817 and 1818 'singing of a myriad voices' was heard by many people and at different times and became a feature of this revival. Small groups, including those who were adamant that such things were not possible, all became convinced of this 'heavenly

48 Haslam, *From Death Into Life*, pp. 88 ff.

singing' which was described by one present as: 'the sound of a thousand myriad, myriad sweet voices singing ... a harmony of the most excellent kind ... [which] left men rooted to the ground, overwhelming them completely.' Some who heard this were described as the most trustworthy and responsible members of the churches. These people saw nothing and could not decipher words and they heard no known tune, but all claimed that it was the sweetest and most glorious singing they had ever heard—and that in the land of song![49]

The same experience is reported from India when God came to the Khassi Hills in 1905. A group of Christians were on their way to the presbytery at Pariong and they stopped frequently on the road to pray. At one place, 'Some of them heard beautiful singing that no man could describe.' At first they thought it was another party on the road, but there was no one around.[50] Others during this revival claimed to see angels. In the Khassi Hills at this time visions were common, 'But they all tend to bring men to see their sin and to see Christ as their Saviour.'[51]

As one might expect from the Western Islands of Scotland, little emphasis was made on phenomena in revival during the 1940s and 1950s. However, there are well-attested examples of groups of people hearing 'beautiful singing' and wonderful music and visions and dreams foretelling events that were fulfilled. Alexander Macleod, an elder in the Free Church of Scotland at Point on the Isle of Lewis, left on record two occasions when, in 1957, he and others heard heavenly singing: 'We could not understand the words but it was like the singing of a congregation, but singing as I have never heard singing! I will never forget it as long as I live! It was awesome! ... We were filled with amazement.' When the minister joined them and heard their account he responded, 'This is nothing but

49 Davies, *The Beddgelert Revival*, pp. 76–79.
50 Jones, *India Awake*, p. 22.
51 As above, p. 33.

the singing of the Angels, singing and seeing Christ exalted and sinners repenting of their sins.'[52]

There is no reason for us to be suspicious of these claims; they are paralleled in Scripture (Luke 2:13–14), and the outcome in revival is always to draw people closer to Christ. Inevitably there were 'spurious signs and prophecies', but the Khassi Christians soon learnt to sift the wheat from the chaff.

Error and the extreme

Almost all whom God has used in revival are quick to point out that these unusual things are merely incidental to the work of God. One writer in *The Life of Faith* for January 1905 concluded, 'It is possible to be occupied too exclusively with the mere incidents of the movement—deeply impressive, thrilling, and important as they are.' R. B. Jones commented that the sensational provides 'copy' for the journalist, but the more vital things are of little interest to him.[53] Those who, in the late twentieth century, claimed as evidence for the Spirit the head banging, strange noises and the like, Jim Packer referred to as 'restless existentialists.'[54]

Almost all whom God has used in revival are quick to point out that these unusual things are merely incidental to the work of God

Humphrey Jones is a sad example of taking over from God. His revival ministry came to an end after his claim to special revelations. The weakest part of the ministry of Evan Roberts was the freedom he gave to the meetings and the lack of preaching in them. Men like R. B. Jones were aware of the need for the converts to be taught from the word of God and

52 Peckham, *Sounds of Heaven*, pp. 104–107, 167.
53 Jones, *Rent Heavens*, p. 40.
54 Packer, *A Quest for Godliness*, (Crossway 1990), p. 30.

it was their ministry that saved the 1904 revival in Wales from greater losses once the fire had passed.

A godly and wise pastor in Kenya, Heshbon Mwangi, commented that in virtually every year of revival in that country from 1970 Satan launched an attack upon the church through extreme emphasis on phenomena: visions, dreams, false prophecies, and false emotional responses.[55]

The danger of revival excitement getting into the wrong hands is clearly seen from the sad episode of James Davenport in the eighteenth century. Davenport was mentally unbalanced, but he gave the appearance of being a very spiritual man, and when Whitefield first met him in 1740, he too accepted this assessment. Davenport threw himself enthusiastically into the revival but saw himself as a great reformer with a special relationship to God. Soon he was claiming direct revelations and demanding that ministers should give account to him, denouncing those who refused. In 1741 even the students at Yale, including the godly David Brainerd, were for a while taken in by him; by 1743 he had a considerable following. A year later, Davenport came to his senses and published a full apology for his behaviour. But the damage had been done, and this kind of extremism always provides fuel for the fires of the opponents to revival.

John Wesley had similar problems with George Bell, an ex-corporal of the Life Guards who led away a number of the Methodists by claiming that he had achieved perfection. He believed he had authority to represent God in London, had the power to heal the blind and raise the dead and, finally, knew that the end of the world was imminent. Bell's following was never large for he was clearly a fool, but again the cause of revival was hurt by men like this.

A leader in the Shantung revival in China in 1932 admitted there were 'excesses and extravagances' because Satan is always present to destroy the work of God 'first by ridicule and second by duplicating it'. Tony

55 Bewes, *Under the Thorn Tree*, pp.90–91.

Lambert records the number of cults that have penetrated China on the back of true revival, including eight cult groups that are indigenous to China. Watchman Nee, the godly pastor who was martyred in 1972, led the biblically based 'Little Flock'. However, his second in command, Witness Lee, drew away an offshoot known as the 'Shouters'. This fast-growing group has brought discredit to gospel truth by his extreme views; many of his followers considering Witness Nee a new Messiah. The rapid growth of the church in China has meant that in many areas strong biblical teaching is lacking and this allows error to gather momentum. In one province in 1994 there were fewer than forty registered pastors and only twenty-four Elders to cover more than 2,000 Three-Self Movement churches and meeting points.[56]

For a time in Angola, the extreme prophetic Toko Movement—boasting dreams, visions, tongues etc—caused a sad compromise to the work of God in that country. When a group of their leaders met with leaders from Uganda and Rwanda in 1952, they were told, 'We have seen all these things in the early days of revival in Rwanda and Uganda, but God has shown us how Satan uses these things to spoil revival.'[57]

Almost every revival on record has been infiltrated by excess or error that has brought discredit to the genuine, fuelled the critics, and stifled the freedom of the Spirit. However, error, phenomena, or unusual things, make up a very small part of the history of revival. Revival itself is unusual, and the great work of conviction, conversion and the creation of a holy life put everything else in the shade. When Duncan Campbell was asked for an explanation of supernatural manifestations, he replied that the main reason was assurance: God granted them to encourage weak and trembling faith to grasp the promises of life.[58] Campbell never encouraged such things, but he did not despise what God allowed. Considering that

---

56 Lambert, *China's Millions*, pp. 121–130, 92.
57 Osborn, *Revival—a precious heritage*, p. 113.
58 Woolsey, *Duncan Campbell*, pp. 108–109.

in revival men's minds are more in touch with eternity and more sensitive to the Holy Spirit, it is not so much surprising that these phenomena exist, but that there are not more of them.

An encouragement from the well taught pastors in many of our evangelical churches today is that they should be sufficiently grounded in Scripture and good theology to be discerning in revival. The downside is an over scrupulous commitment to the nuances of their theology. We must never forget that as the wind blows where it wills, so does the Spirit. Since the Spirit will never act contrary to his revelation in Scripture, that must always be a controlling guide.

Whenever the focus in a 'revival' is on the phenomena, that will soon spoil any work of God

Whenever the focus in a 'revival' is on the phenomena, whether it is tongues, prophecies, visions, healings, faintings or whatever, it will produce a great weakness that will soon spoil any work of God. Jonathan Edwards warned ministers not to introduce things that are 'new and strange', and George Whitefield learned by his own failed prophecy the danger of 'mistaking fancy for faith, and imagination for revelation.'[59]

59 Iain Murray, *Jonathan Edwards* (Banner of Truth 1987), p. 242.

During revival

Opposition

Great though the numbers of converted may be in revival, there are almost always more left outside the Kingdom of God than are brought in. Revival will often harden men and women and create opposition against the gospel. Normally, the unbelieving world can simply ignore the church and all that it stands for; its message seems to have little significance for daily life. In revival God becomes a serious threat. People are aware of eternal issues, and the presence of God and the power of the gospel is disturbing. Thousands are affected, and even influenced by revival, who never experience salvation. In Rhos in 1904 strong men were afraid to go to work in case they got converted, and once at work they were afraid to come home again for the same reason. Because people feel threatened, they will lash out in opposition and ridicule.

Revival dismissed or ridiculed

When Hezekiah sent his couriers to the north with the invitation to come and worship in Jerusalem: 'many people' responded. But not all accepted the call; there was a strong opposition: 'The couriers went from town to town in Ephraim and Manasseh, as far as Zebulun, but the people scorned and ridiculed them' (2 Chronicles 30:10). Paul met the same response seven hundred years later, and Athens is just one example where 'some of them sneered' (Acts 17:32).

In 1745 David Brainerd was among the North American Indians at Susquehanna and he described the transformation among the Indians of all ages when the Spirit came in revival: 'I stood amazed at the influence which seized the audience almost universally ... The most stubborn hearts were now obliged to bow.' He then recorded that the white settlers were almost universally unmoved: 'There being a multitude of white persons present I made an address to them at the close of my discourse to the Indians, but I could not so much as keep them orderly, for scores of them kept walking and gazing about and behaved more indecently than any Indians I ever addressed. And a view of their abusive conduct so sunk my spirits that I could scarce go on with my work.'[1]

Murray M'Cheyne recognized the same contrast in Dundee in 1839. The work of the Spirit in that town was so real and widespread that, 'The effects that have been produced upon the community are very marked. It seems now to be allowed, even by the most ungodly, that there is such a thing as conversion. Men cannot any longer deny it.' M'Cheyne went on to describe the change in the town with a greater awareness of the importance of the Sabbath, and of the danger of sin. But, he adds, 'Multitudes of those who live within the sound of the Sabbath bell continue to live on in sin and misery.'[2] Following Cambuslang in 1742 the ministers noted that some of those who scoffed, or professed and then fell away, went further into sin than before.

We cannot dismiss this in cultural terms because in the time of Brainerd, God was working in revival in other parts of America amongst the white settlers. The renowned lexicographer, Dr Samuel Johnson, went to many of the revival meetings addressed by George Whitefield in the eighteenth century and he greatly admired the evangelist. David Garrick, certainly the most popular stage actor in London at the time, heard Whitefield preach and longed that he could say, 'Oh!' like Whitefield could say it. But these two men have left no record of a vital spiritual change resulting. In excess of 20,000 people would listen to Whitefield on Kennington Common, but not all were converted. Many came to scoff, went away scoffing and died scoffing.

---

1 Page, *David Brainerd*, pp.80–81,87.
2 Bonar, *Memoirs and Remains*, p.500.

Some, of course, are more open to be persuaded. Jonathan Edwards remarked that when news spread of the work of God in Northampton, New England, in the 1730s, 'Many scoffed at and ridiculed it; and some compared what we call conversion, to certain distempers. But it was very observable of many, who occasionally came amongst us from abroad with disregardful hearts, that what they saw here cured them of such a temper of mind.' Edwards went on to remark that many who came to scoff went away converted.[3]

Friendly fire

Sadly, opposition often comes from those who should be supportive. Hezekiah's evangelists were ridiculed by those who outwardly professed to worship the same God. The apostles in the early church were first opposed by the Jews, who could read the story of God's plan of salvation in their own Hebrew Scriptures. The Jews were offended by the miracles and envious of the success of the gospel, so 'They were filled with jealousy and talked abusively against what Paul was saying' (Acts 13:45). Some of the most vigorous opposition to revival has come from the professing church.

When God moved among a group of Christians in Madras in 1940 the churches at first were supportive until they realized that the man God was using was Bakht Singh. Suddenly the ministers' conference came to a decision: 'We in the Indian Ministers' Conference have met and passed a resolution never again to make any place available to this Punjabi preacher. Our objection is that he is not an ordained minister, and therefore had no right to baptize anyone.'[4] Every church was closed to Bakht Singh.

The revival that accompanied Evan Roberts was denounced by a Congregational minister, Peter Price, as 'a sham ... a mockery, a blasphemous travesty of the real thing'. What made this all the more sad

3 Edwards, *A Narrative of Surprising Conversions*, p. 15.
4 Rajamani & Kinnear, *Monsoon Daybreak*, pp. 76–77.

was the fact that Price's own church at Dowlais had been blessed with revival and the addition of hundreds of converts a few months previously in 1904. Price clearly objected to Roberts' style and had good cause to be concerned for some of the excesses that accompanied him. Unfortunately, Price overplayed his opposition and could not recognise the hand of God. Dr Forbes Winslow, a psychiatrist, was even more extreme: 'I would have men like Evan Roberts locked up as common felons, and their meetings prohibited like those of socialists and anarchists as being dangerous to the public.' Even though four doctors had signed a certificate of Roberts' physical and mental health, it was jibes like this, and the cruel attack by Peter Price, that almost broke the evangelist and by the spring of 1906 he began to retire from public life.[5]

The same had been the experience of Jock Troup in Fraserburgh in 1921. When the Baptist Church proved too small for the revival meetings an application was made for the use of other buildings, but it was refused on the ground that the preacher was not an ordained minister.[6] The work in Lowestoft in that year was dismissed by the President of the Baptist Union, Dr J. C. Carlile, as 'an emotional wave' produced by a 'hypnotic preacher'. The Lowestoft ministers from all denominations responded: 'The results are of the most tangible and convincing kind and must carry conviction to the most sceptical observer. Christian ministers, and workers from other towns who have come to witness for themselves what has been taking place in this district, have not hesitated to declare, "This is the Lord's doing; it is marvellous in our eyes!"'[7] They added that many came to 'scoff and to question, but they stayed to pray.'

Sadly, because of the long and sad history of disunity among evangelical congregations in Scotland, and in spite of the evident presence of God under the preaching of Duncan Campbell and others across the Western

5 Evans, *The Welsh Revival of 1904*, pp. 131–138.
6 Ritchie, *Floods Upon the Dry Ground*, p. 58.
7 Griffin, *A Forgotten Revival*, p. 107 quoting from *The Christian*, 26 May 1921.

Isles of Scotland from 1949 to 1953, the Free Presbyterian Church and Free Church of Scotland strongly opposed the revival, closed their churches to Campbell, discouraged their people from attending the meetings, and in some cases even arranged alternative meetings. It is recorded, 'No Free Church minister ever attended even one of the meetings of the 1949 revival ... And all, bar one, criticised it.' Some even suggested the devil sent Duncan Campbell to the islands to create havoc in the churches. The reasons were that Campbell belonged to the Church of Scotland, a denomination mixed with both liberals and evangelicals, he was not a trained theologian, and did not preach a concise Calvinism expected of him. However, Duncan Campbell was passionate about the sovereignty of God, and he preached law, judgement, hell and holiness—Christ was the centre of his preaching. It is to his credit that in his reports Duncan Campbell names no ministers or churches even when he records on 26 April 1950: 'The most bitter opposition.' Two weeks later he could add 'opposition has vanished. The whole district is moved.' He once referred to Brethren and Pentecostals 'causing confusion'.[8]

Whitefield in England went through a similar experience two hundred years earlier. His greatest opposition came from the Church of England authorities and he was refused permission to preach in their buildings. It was this very opposition that forced him into field preaching. When Whitefield preached in America he experienced the same and recorded in his diary: 'Five churches have already been denied me, and some clergy, if possible, would oblige me to depart out of these coasts.'[9] Frequently, his diary reveals the opposition he received from clergymen in sermons and pamphlets and personal abuse. Dr Joseph Trapp was one of the most eminent Anglican clergymen in London and he wrote and preached powerfully against Whitefield. Trapp's chief concern was the

8 Peckham, *Sounds from Heaven*, pp. 117–123, 151,171.
9 Dallimore, *George Whitefield*, vol. 1, p. 219.

shame and reproach of preaching and praying in the open air. On one occasion Whitefield and John Wesley sat up until one in the morning 'in conference with two clergymen of the Church of England, and some other strong opposers of the doctrine of the New Birth.' Whitefield concluded in his diary with a weary understatement: 'I am fully convinced there is a fundamental difference between us and them.'[10]

Perhaps the most tragic of all evidences of 'friendly fire' was the serious disagreement between Wesley and Whitefield themselves. John Wesley hated the Calvinism represented by Whitefield, believing that it must stifle evangelism and holiness. When Wesley refused even to discuss the issues with Whitefield, the latter published a rebuff to Wesley's Arminian theology. For all the huge areas of agreement the two men had, this ongoing dispute brought discredit on the evangelical revival. At times the squabbles became vitriolic.

In the 1740s the Erskine brothers in Scotland dismissed Whitefield over their differences on ecclesiology as 'a poor, vainglorious, self-seeking, puffed up creature.' For her part, Lady Selina, the Countess of Huntingdon, not only encouraged a new and bitter pamphlet war against Wesley and his Methodists, but dismissed Wesley for his free-will theology, as 'a papists unmasked, a heretic, an apostate.'[11]

Perhaps we should not be too hard on them. In an age before libel laws, even Christians were less delicate than they are now. Hardly less tragic was the rift between Howell Harris, who had been so powerfully used in England and Wales earlier in the eighteenth century, and Daniel Rowland another powerful preacher in revival. Their disagreement on whether we can properly speak of God the Father suffering and dying led to the withdrawal of Harris from the Welsh Calvinistic Methodists.[12] One historian concludes, 'Inevitably therefore, that work suffered a serious

10 As above, vol. 1, pp. 226–227.
11 Jones, *The Fire Divine*, pp. 73–75, 96.
12 Harris's view is known as Patripassianism, the suffering of the Father.

eclipse without the guidance of a man of [Harris's] calibre. For twelve long years Harris and Rowland went their separate ways, and Welsh Calvinistic Methodism went into temporary decline.'[13] Happily, they were fully reconciled before the death of Harris in July 1773. Commenting on mistakes in American revivals at this time, Iain Murray observes, 'Good and harm can be done by the same men, at the same time, even in a revival.'[14]

However, these tragic divisions were not typical of revivals. Certainly in America in the 1770s, men of different church persuasions shared the same pulpit and it did not matter who was being blessed with revival so long as God was honoured.[15] In England, the irenic spirit of clergymen like John Newton who experienced revival in Olney and frequently met with the Baptists and Independents in and around his parish, was an example to all. Fortunately, he was not alone.

Opposing revival because it does not fit our personal preference or ecclesiastic dogma is illustrated by the opposition of William Hamilton, a Presbyterian minister in Edenderry, who wrote vehemently against the revival of 1859–60 in Ireland. Writing six years after the revival that began in the village of Kells, Hamilton's is a detailed and lengthy (250 pages) critique of revival generally, concluding that it is both 'unscriptural and anti-confessional'—by that he meant against the *Westminster Confession of Faith*. Hamilton is certainly trying to be faithful to Scripture, but he betrays an inflexible theology on non-vital issues. That there were excesses in 1859 few could doubt, but that does not justify a wholesale denial of any evidence of God at work. His was an undiscerning opposition; for example: 'It is certain that nothing is more liable to abuse than lay teaching; it's very nature is such.'[16] So wrote a Presbyterian who overlooked the army of

13 Evans, *Howell Harris, Evangelist*, p. 57.
14 Murray, *Revival and Revivalism*, p. 83.
15 As above, p. 88.
16 Hamilton, *An Inquiry*, p. 190.

ordained ministers who had led Presbyterian congregations into error. This bar against lay teaching effectively vetoed the establishment of the religious societies during the Awakening in the eighteenth century and during the Welsh revival in the next.[17] Hamilton's rigidity is illustrated by his dismissal of the word 'conversion' to refer to the work of the Holy Spirit in new birth and insisting that 'in Scripture conversion is said to be the work of man.' This conclusion is based on James 5:19,20.[18] For Hamilton, there could be only one of two agencies at work: God or Satan, and thus the entire work of 'revival' must be attributed to one or the other.[19] Fortunately Hamilton's published work came too late to upset those who had been so greatly transformed in the revival.

Even at Cambuslang in Scotland where, in 1742, God was so present to save hundreds, the Associate Presbytery found fault and issued a thirty-two-page booklet in which some of the mildest attacks accused Whitefield of being a member of the idolatrous Church of England which made him 'a limb of anti-Christ.'[20] James Robe, a minister involved in the revival at Cambuslang and Kilsyth, wrote of the 'lies, slanderous reports, and ridiculous stories' that were spread about to prejudice people against the work of God.[21]

Some who accepted Whitefield's gospel of the new birth, and who were convinced of his sincerity and honesty, nevertheless took issue with him on his style and forcefulness. Isaac Watts and Philip Doddridge were guilty of this, though it has to be said they modified their views as time progressed. Perhaps the maturing of Whitefield and the mellowing of Watts and Doddridge helped. Many of the Independents (or Congregationalists), who were themselves to experience great revival in the early part of the

---

17 Phillips, *The Welsh Revival*, pp. 119 on.
18 Hamilton, *An Inquiry*, p. 198.
19 As above pp. 207 on.
20 Dallimore, *George Whitefield*, vol. 2, pp. 131–132.
21 Robe, *When the Wind Blows*, pp. 137–138.

nineteenth century, strongly opposed Whitefield and the Awakening throughout his life.

But if the gospel was a stumbling-block to the Jews, it was utter foolishness to the Gentiles (1 Corinthians 1:23). There are always those who cannot understand what is happening and therefore oppose the work of God through blind ignorance. The apostles knew and expected vigorous opposition from the pagans. Often unbelievers will be forced to invent explanations for a work that defies normal understanding. Duncan Campbell was accused of hypnotizing people in the 1940s in the Scottish islands, and two hundred years earlier the cartoonist Hogarth viciously caricatured Whitefield in his powerful pictures of eighteenth century life.

Before his own conversion, Festo Kivengere despised the work of God in Uganda: 'We "enlightened" young people were angry. We maintained that church people ought to confine their singing to church buildings and not spread it out onto public roads and into market-places. Women going to draw water were praising Jesus—how unsuitable!'[22] Festo's uncle complained bitterly because the revival seemed to be a 'new kind of religion' that invaded personal privacy and broke with tribal taboos. As an important chief he gave orders that his men could beat up these Christians, but still it did not change them.

Violent opposition

Opposition to the gospel will often be greater in the time of revival. When the Spirit of God came in the sixteenth century, Christians were burnt at the stake. In the seventeenth century evangelical preachers were turned out of their churches. In the eighteenth century rioting mobs physically attacked the evangelists.

Whitefield reports often on the abuse of some in the crowds who were intent only to cause disorder and violence. At the fields of Mary Le Bone in

22 Kivengere, *Revolutionary Love*, p. 10.

London the rough opponents tried hard to push down the pulpit; another intended to stab Whitefield with a sword; others pelted the preacher with filth whilst trying to drown his voice with their own and yet another climbed a tree and 'shamefully exposed his nakedness' to the crowd. In the midst of scenes like this, when thousands of London's criminals and slum-dwellers mingled with the idle and rich, it is incredible that any heard the gospel at all. Clearly they did, and hundreds were converted. John Wesley suffered as much, if not more, from the rough handling of the mobs and both Wesley and Whitefield knew Paul's experience of being stoned and beaten by the crowds.

Howell Harris in Wales described how, during a journey of three months preaching in Wales, 'I was almost murdered once, and twice in danger of my life, besides once being before the Magistrates in a Quarter Sessions.' John Cennick, a companion of Harris, describes how, at Swindon in the 1740s, they took advantage of an ugly situation that must have been anything but amusing at the time:

> 'They then got the dust out of the highway and cover'd us all over, and then play'd an engine upon us which they fill'd out of the stinking ditches till we were just like men in the pillory, but as they play'd upon Brother Harris I spoke to the congregation, and when they turn'd their engine upon me, he preach'd and thus they continued till they had spoil'd the engine and then they threw whole buckets of water and mud over us.'[23]

In some villages across Moldova, fierce opposition to the work of God in revival was led by the local Orthodox priest, including a crowd wielding pitchforks led by the priest opposing open airs or the opening of a prayer house in the village.[24]

---

23 Evans, *Howell Harris*, p. 44.
24 Maureen Wise, the author of *Celestial Fire*, in personal correspondence.

Every revival will be ridiculed and dismissed. Arthur Wallis has written, 'If we find a revival that is not spoken against, we had better look again to ensure that it is a revival.'[25] If they scoffed at our Master and his great works, it is certain they will scoff again when he is at work. When we are confronted with a work that appears to have the stamp of God upon it, we will be wise to exercise great caution before we oppose it just because it does not come out of the correct denominational stable.

> 'If we find a revival that is not spoken against, we had better look again to ensure that it is a revival'

25 Wallis, *In the Day of Thy Power*, p.26.

6. After revival

Benefits of revival

A time of spiritual revival is always a time of benefit to the community. 'The LORD was with [Hezekiah]; he was successful in whatever he undertook. He rebelled against the king of Assyria and did not serve him. From watchtower to fortified city, he defeated the Philistines, as far as Gaza and its territory' (2 Kings 18:7–8).

The nation was sufficiently strong in the time of Hezekiah to throw off its subjection to Assyria; the revival gave the people of Judah moral and military fibre and it was this that led Hezekiah to make a bid to secure spiritual unity in the nation after two hundred years of warfare between the north and the south. This was Israel's last chance to come back to the covenant of David. The revival was also a time of Hezekiah's brilliant engineering—which is there to this day (2 Kings 20:20). Great stores of food were laid up and a strong armoury was built. In the time of Hezekiah Jerusalem was the strongest it had ever been since the time of Solomon. And when the Assyrians approached Jerusalem in the year 701 BC the city was secure. The key to all this is found in 2 Chronicles 31:21: 'In everything that he undertook in the service of God's temple and in obedience to the law and the commands, he sought his God and worked wholeheartedly. And so he prospered.'

Many revivals bring with them benefits that are enjoyed by Christians, often centuries later. Revival in the time of Wycliffe gave the people a hunger for Scripture in their own language that has never been lost. Who can question the lasting results of the sixteenth century revival-reformation? Other revivals, like that in Wales, spread across the world giving new life to the mission field far in excess of the story of revival soon lost in any particular Welsh town or village. The collective value of revivals in terms of lives changed for time and saved for eternity, communities 'cleaned up', missionaries sent out and God honoured in the worship of a myriad of new converts, cannot seriously be disputed. Stanley Griffin, whose father was converted in the Lowestoft revival in 1921 and who was himself converted a quarter of a century later, observed, 'Many of my generation agree with me that those post-war years were the most spiritually fruitful there have been in Lowestoft since the revival.'[1]

Under 'A passion for the lost', we have already seen the result of revival in the founding of, and strong support for, mission work. At the turn of the nineteenth century there were fourteen thousand Protestant missionaries around the world; by 1925, following the revivals of 1904–05, this figure had doubled. The greatest thrust behind world-wide evangelism in the nineteenth and early twentieth centuries was undoubtedly revival. But revival always brings huge improvements to society.

Before 1857 America was in a desperate condition. At Princeton, Dr Green knew of only two professing Christians among the students. The College of William and Mary in Virginia was a 'hot-bed of French politics and religion'. One writer describes the fortunes of the country before and after the revival in that year:

> 'Banks and business houses failed, factories and railways closed down, vast numbers were soon unemployed, and it needed the quietness of shut-out industry and transport in order for a nation to hear the still small voice of God! In 1857 God spoke to America ... Millions of converts were added to the churches of all denominations. And what proved the genuineness of the revival was the ethical result, for the social effects of the revival continued for almost half a century.'[2]

1 Griffin, *A Forgotten Revival*, p. 137.
2 Hayden, *Spurgeon on Revival*, p. 40.

A revival always has an effect upon the nation. In his doctorial study of English social history, J. Wesley Bready concluded that 'the democratic and cultural heritage of the modern English-speaking world is much more a spiritual than a political or economic achievement ... the Evangelical revival, which began with Wesley among the outcast masses, was the true nursing-mother of the spirit and character values that have created and sustained Free Institutions throughout the English-speaking world.' He called the Great Awakening 'a revival of vital, practical Christianity'.[3]

In the eighteenth and nineteenth centuries there were staggering benefits of revival in the social life of England, and some of the worst effects of the Industrial Revolution were avoided. It certainly saved England from the fate of the French Revolution. Revival gave the nation a social conscience and produced the men and women who campaigned for the abolition of slavery and brought the women and children up from the mines and the little boys down from the chimneys; revival contributed also to a greater concern for prisoners and the insane, a reduction in hours of work and a care for the living conditions of the poor. To claim that every benefit to society in these two centuries was directly the result of revival would be inaccurate, but revival was certainly one of the principal causes of social reform. The Victorian 'non-conformist conscience', that could unseat an erring politician, and the 'Reformation of Manners [morals]' in the previous century, both grew from revival.

The historian Dr John Stoughton, in *The History of Religion in England*, speaks of the Evangelical Awakening in the eighteenth century in this way: 'It laid hold upon multitudes of Englishmen with a firmer grasp and in a greater number of instances than ever before. It was exhibited under its most benevolent aspects ... as the helper of the poor, the friend of the prisoner, the liberator of the slave, the visitor of the sick, the comforter of the dying.'

3 J. Wesley Bready, *England Before and After Wesley*, pp. 11–12.

Similarly, the historian, Sir Robert Ensor, claims that it is impossible to understand the history of nineteenth century England without appreciating the Evangelical revival of the previous century.
He wrote:

'If one asks how 19th-century English merchants had the reputation of being the most honest in the world (a very real factor in the prominence of English trade), the answer is: because hell and heaven seemed as certain to them as tomorrow's sunrise; and the Last Judgement as real as the week's balance sheet … Evangelicalism made otherworldliness an everyday conviction, and induced a highly civilised people to put duty before pleasure to quite an amazing degree.'[4]

It is impossible to understand the history of nineteenth century England without appreciating the Evangelical revival of the previous century

The 'Forgotten Revival' in Cornwall which flowed on between 1790 and 1840 had a huge impact on the county: 'Cornish Methodists declared holy war on drink, hurling, wrestling, bull baiting, cockfighting, and folk superstitions … The Methodists stressed hard work, honesty, thrift, cleanliness, self-respect and mutual aid.'[5]

Captain Collins, the mine agent for lead mines near Aberystwyth, wrote at length on the value of the revival to his own workmen, the majority of whom were 'living in sin' of all kinds and especially drunkenness. Some would remain in the public houses for two or three days, and even a week, leaving their families destitute. Looking back over the previous two years in March 1860 he could write: 'The change which has taken place is beyond everything I have ever known … I believe there is not a drunkard,

4 Sir Robert Ensor, *England 1870–1914* (Clarendon Press 1968. First pub. 1936), p. 137.
5 Isaac, *A History of Evangelical Christianity In Cornwall*, p. 140.

or Sabbath-breaker, or openly immoral person to be found amongst our two hundred workmen.' He described the men working together who prayed in little groups and how delightful it was to hear the voice of prayer 'ascending to heaven from the very depths of the earth'. Even the children working on the surface prayed together: 'It is truly affecting to see fifty or sixty young people on their knees in the attitude of prayer.' Collins concluded, 'There is hardly a house in the whole neighbourhood without a family altar.'[6] Testimonies like that could be repeated a thousand times across Wales by 1860.

Revival in Romania in the 1970s led to massive benefits both during and after the Communist oppression. The Christians at Emmanuel Baptist Church in Oradea were only too aware of the tragic 'legacy of communist rule in the shape of broken lives, abandoned children and orphans, neglect of the disabled, and widespread crippling poverty'. Over the years they have established schools, Emmanuel Christian University (today, the finest university in the country), a Bible Institute, a Social Work Programme, a hospice which in the year 2011 provided palliative care for 214 adults and 40 children together with 7,000 home visits, a Medical Care Centre with up to 10,000 patients a year, providing general practitioner, dental, ophthalmic and gynaecological care and a pharmacy, and much more.[7]

The revival that swept across Moldova in Eastern Europe from 1988 has left a valuable Christian legacy to the present day, not only in the form of Bible distribution, theological training and a radio ministry, but a prison ministry, medical work, and care for street children, orphans and the disabled at a time when parents would hide children with disabilities.[8] After revival came to KwaZulu–Natal in 1966, the small Zulu church in Mapumulo has grown to a regular congregation of 4,500 and the

6 Phillips, *The Welsh Revival*, pp. 107–108.
7 Birnie, *'Just call me Paul'*, p. 62 and pp. 129 on.
8 Wise, *Celestial Fire*, pp. 135–141, 151–157.

centre at Kwasizabantu, meaning 'the place where people find help', has 140 'outstations' reaching out to the whole community and beyond. In addition to many education programmes, they have an agricultural project, bakery, jam factory, dairy industry and much more, including work among addicts.[9]

Drunkenness and profanity

Alcohol has always been a demon for society. It is no less so in our own day. Revival transforms the drinking habits of a significant number.

Jonathan Edwards wrote a letter to a minister in Boston dated 12 December 1743. He was describing some of the effects of the revival in Northampton, New England, between 1740 and 1742 and particularly noted what he called 'a great alteration, amongst both old and young, with regard to tavern-haunting'. Edwards continued: 'I suppose the town has been in no measure so free of vice in these respects … for sixty years, as it has been these nine years past.'[10]

The work of God at Cambuslang in 1742 'embraced all classes, all ages, and all moral conditions. Cursing, swearing and drunkenness were given up by those who came under its power.'[11] Similarly, the powerful work of the Spirit that swept across Kentucky in 1800 left the state entirely changed and, as one observer explained: 'I found Kentucky as remarkable for sobriety as they had formerly been for dissoluteness and immorality … A profane expression was hardly ever heard. A religious awe seemed to pervade the country.'[12]

Prior to the 1859 revival in Wales, drunkenness was a tragic and widespread curse destroying families and whole communities. The best attempts of the temperance movements were unable to stem the flow

9 Stegen, *Revival among the Zulus*, pp. 84–85.
10 Edwards, *A Narrative of Surprising Conversions*, p. 148.
11 Dallimore, *George Whitefield*, vol. 2, p. 136.
12 Orr, *The Eager Feet*, p. 63.

of drunkenness in Bala, North Wales; however, when revival came in 1858–59 the 'drink market' was so greatly affected that the revival in this town was known as the 'temperance revival'. Although it was not made a condition of membership, total abstinence was strongly recommended to the new converts, 'as a safeguard to themselves and as an example to others'.[13] This was typical right across Wales. It was reported from Aberystwyth that after David Morgan's preaching eight publicans had become Christians and had taken down their signs and become teetotal. In some areas they had little option since few patronised their bars.[14]

Local statistics were impressive. David Lloyd-George spoke of a tavern in his constituency which, at the time of the revival, took just fourpence-ha'penny (less than two and a half pence) on the drinking night of the week. R. B. Jones reports on the 1904 revival that it greatly affected the drink trade; breweries were worried by it all, and publicans went bankrupt. In some towns men who were never converted in the revival were nevertheless ashamed to go into the public houses.[15]

In March 1905 the Chief Constable of Glamorgan commented, 'The decrease in drunkenness has undoubtedly been most marked where the Revivalists have had the largest following.' Judge Gwilym Williams, reporting to the meeting of the Glamorgan County Council, specifically drew attention to the results of the work of Evan Roberts; the judge claimed he was not interested in the methods of Mr Roberts but 'the results were everything'.[16]

About the same time the Bishop of Dorking wrote of a recent visit to Wales; when he spoke to a police sergeant and asked for his opinion of the revival, the reply was: 'This is a pretty rough part; and [they] don't think much of kicking a policeman like a football; but there's been none

13 Evans, *When He is Come*, p.101.
14 Phillpot, *The Welsh Revival*, pp.19, 96.
15 Jones, *Rent Heavens*, p.64.
16 *Wrexham & North Wales Guardian*, 10 March 1905.

of that these two months. There are twenty-two licensed houses in my district and they are not drawing enough beer to pay the gas; the men are all in the chapels.'[17] It is not hard to imagine the effect of all this upon the families of men who normally spent their earnings on drink before they arrived home at the end of the week.

In some mines in Wales in 1904 the work came to a standstill because the pit ponies could no longer understand the orders that were given to them; the hauliers, classed as the worst group of men in the pits, proverbial for their profanity and cruelty, were no longer cursing their commands and the ponies were confused.[18] The ministry of James Caughey in Birmingham in the 1830s was said to have left many public houses 'vocal with lonely grumblers'.[19]

When God came among the Lun Bawang people of Borneo in 1938, he did so without the presence of the missionaries. When the missionaries later came to the villages they knew how to test the genuineness of the work: 'Where is your borak [rice beer] now?', they asked. The reply was instant: 'Oh, we've given that up long ago!' Among these people this change had another, unexpected effect. The whole village was clean and tidy; to the extent that one missionary wrote that the place was swept so clean that there was no place to put the discarded banana skins. The longhouse used to be the foulest in Sarawak but was now the cleanest and best kept. Nearly forty years later, in 1973, when the Spirit of God was at work in Borneo, even discipline in the school changed and honesty affected every part of the life of the communities. One Kelabit Indian described the change by simply observing, 'The oranges are still on the trees.' The children would no longer steal the fruit.[20]

---

17 As above.
18 Jones, *Rent Heavens*, p. 62.
19 Orr, *The Eager Feet*, p. 145.
20 Lees, *Drunk Before Dawn*, pp. 63–64, 190–193.

Restitution

In Korea during 1907 one Chinese business man was amazed when a Christian returned a large sum of money that he had received from the merchant in error.[21] God is light and people could not live in fellowship with him if they were unholy. David Davies, a missionary in the Congo during the revival in 1953, reported:

'The reformation that resulted from this revival was wonderful. Many had stolen from the state, and the Christians and converts wanted to make restitution. So many things were being returned to the Belgian Office that an embarrassed official wrote to me, "Mr Davies, I've no time to handle all this. Tell them to come to your mission and fill a truck and you bring a load down."'[22]

The same thing happened in Uganda in 1939 when at times so many people were waiting outside the District Commissioner's office to return or pay for things, that the official complained it was hard for him to get on with his work. Festo Kivengere illustrated the effect of this kind of restitution in Uganda. One chief, Festo's uncle, was confronted by a man driving eight fine cows. The man, known to be a pagan and a rich man in cattle, addressed the chief: 'Your honour, I have come for a purpose. These cows are yours; I have brought them back to you.' 'What do you mean, they are mine?' responded the chief.' Well sir, when I was looking after your cattle, I stole four of them when I told you we had been raided. These four are now eight. I have brought them to you.' 'Who discovered this theft?' demanded the chief. 'Jesus did, sir. He has given me peace and told me to bring them.' When revival touched children it had the same effect. One child owned up to his father that he had received too much

---

21 Morod, *The Korean Revival*, p. 19.

22 Personal correspondence with David Davies, a missionary in the Belgian Congo from 1937 to 1964. See *Praying for Revival*, ch. 9 'I was there: The Congo (Zaire) 1953'.

change from a shopkeeper eighteen months prior to the revival; the father promptly sent the change to the store.[23]

Revival always has this effect. It is the experience of Zacchaeus on a grand scale (Luke 19:8). Stories of property being restored and debts paid in revival come from all over the world. Early in 1905 the *North Wales Guardian* reported on a sermon by Dr Oliver, the Secretary of the North Wales Federation of Free Church Councils:

'Referring to the revival, Dr Oliver said a South Wales shopkeeper had told him that many of his customers whose debts he had written off his books as "bad" were now paying them, and he knew of one tradesman who had just received a sum of £37 which would never have been paid him but for this revival. Referring to those cold, callous, self-complacent people who derided the revival, he said it was part of the current cant of materialism to throw doubt on all forms of religious enthusiasm. He believed the present revival was from God, and he thanked God for it from his heart.'[24]

Giving

Spiritual slackness makes people selfish. Everywhere today we hear of missions and gospel causes that are hindered from advance, not only because of a shortage of workers, but through lack of funds. That will never happen in revival. William Sprague in his *Lectures on Revival* commented, 'It is amidst the effusions of the Spirit of God that men are trained to engage actively and efficiently in the great enterprise of Christian benevolence. Here they have their hearts and their hands opened on behalf of those who are sitting in the regions and the shadows of death.'[25] Giving

23 Kivengere, *Revolutionary Love*, p.13.
24 The North Wales Guardian, 20 January 1905.
25 Sprague, *Lectures on Revival*, p.273.

for the support of the gospel and care for the needs of people are further results of revival.

During the years of spiritual decline in Jerusalem, the support for the priests and the temple maintenance had virtually disappeared; the people were no longer giving their tithe. The priests and Levites were forced to give up their full devotion to the service of God in order to earn their living. When the Spirit began to move during the reign of Hezekiah, the king 'ordered the people living in Jerusalem to give the portion due to the priests and Levites so that they could devote themselves to the Law of the LORD' (2 Chronicles 31:4). Although this was a royal command which could not be disobeyed, the people responded immediately and generously (31:5) and the whole-hearted response of the nation is evident from the expressions: 'The Israelites generously gave ... they brought a great amount, a tithe of everything ... They piled them in heaps ... This great amount is left over.' They added to the tithe their first-fruits (31:5) and freewill offerings (31:14). When Hezekiah asked about the progress he received the encouraging reply from Azariah, the chief priest: 'Since the people began to bring their contributions to the temple of the LORD, we have had enough to eat and plenty to spare, because the LORD has blessed his people, and this great amount is left over' (31:10).

The Isle of Lewis has received a number of spiritual awakenings in its history and one such occasion was between 1824–1835 when Andrew McLeod was ministering on the island. Among the results of this revival, McLeod commented particularly on the generosity of the people, and how they would have given more if only their poverty had allowed them to do so:

'Considering the circumstances of the people, I bear testimony, that their liberality and zeal in this case have cause to provoke very many to similar duties. It was most delightful to see the hoary head, and the young scholar of eight or nine years, joining in this contribution. The will preponderates over our purse, so that we cannot do exactly what we would.'[26]

In the autumn of 1839, the church at St Peters in Dundee held a thanksgiving service, and M'Cheyne records, 'A thank-offering was made among us to God for his signal mercies. The times were hard, and my people are far from wealthy, yet the sum contributed was £71. This was devoted to Missionary purposes.'[27] That figure likely represented the equivalent of the annual stipend of the minister.

Twenty years later, when God saturated Ulster with his presence, the same spirit of giving came from the people. Writing half a century after the event, Thomas Sinclair listed some of the long-term advantages of the revival, which included: 'the creation of a new spirit of Christian liberality; a forward movement in philanthropic and missionary enterprise, of which the Sabbath School Auxiliary to Mission, the Orphan Society, and the China and Zenana Missions are lasting fruits; and, finally, a sense of generous loyalty to the church which enabled her to surmount successfully the financial perplexities.'[28]

Between 1906 and 1910 the church in Korea doubled its membership, adding eighty thousand new believers to the churches; three years later it almost doubled again. With this great work of God came a feature that one observer claimed never to have met elsewhere in the world:

'Another characteristic of Korean Christians is their readiness to make sacrifices ... Many of these devout people are rice farmers. In spite of the biblical rule that the labourer shall be the first to enjoy the fruits of his toil, Korean Christians do not take advantage of the latitude allowed them; they sell their rice and buy millet, which is half the price. They give their profits, that is to say, fifty per cent

26 *Narratives of Revivals of Religion*, ch. 8, p. 5.
27 Bonar, *Memoirs and Remains*, p. 500.
28 Paisley, *The Fifty-Nine Revival*, p. 187.

of their earnings, in aid of missionary work, to send missionaries to neighbouring countries and so spread the Gospel. They give not a tenth, but a half of all they earn.'[29]

The same commitment was found among the Ethiopian Wallamo Christians when missionaries discovered the results of a revival that broke out during their wartime absence from the country. At a conference in 1949 the churches gave to the support of forty evangelists and then promised that in future half of all the local church offerings would go to support evangelists. The following year these Wallamo Christians, who earned little enough to live on, made promises of what they would trust God to help them give over the next year. A missionary continues the story:

'The idea immediately caught fire. Christians stood by the score to make similar faith promises: a sheep, a donkey, a horse, a blanket, ten dollars, the produce of ten coffee trees. These promises were not made lightly but as serious obligations between the individual and the Lord ... During the following year each one worked hard to pay the promise in full, often in small instalments. By the next conference, a careful check showed that every penny promised had been paid.'[30]

Even the women, who had little to call their own, would make promises and gifts at their Bible classes. The same missionary tells of one old woman who rushed into the class just as they were taking the offering; she was out of breath but gasping, 'Oh, thank you Lord! Oh, thank you for bringing me here in time!' Later she explained that she had longed to make an offering to the work of the gospel but had almost nothing to give. With just a few pennies she bought some cotton and sat up late each night spinning it into thread. Finally, she walked for five hours to get to market, sold her thread,

---

29 Morod, *The Korean Revival*, p. 39.
30 Davies, *Fire on the Mountains*, p. 182.

and returned just in time to place the proceeds in the offering. That kind of longing and zeal shames us as rich Christians in the West today. When the Spirit came to the naturally generous Penan tribes people of Borneo in 1959 a missionary commented, 'Penans were always careful to share out everything, but the gospel had given them joy in much greater generosity.'[31]

One of the practical benefits of revival is that gospel work is not held up because of a lack of finance. Revival loosens our hold on this world and create such an awareness of eternity that we see investment in the gospel as the most profitable use of our money.

Revival loosens our hold on this world and create such an awareness of eternity that we see investment in the gospel as the most profitable use of our money

Christian love and unity

The benefit of revival for the church is vast: renewed love towards God, reality in worship, holiness of life and zeal for evangelism; it is inevitable therefore that the community around will notice that God is among his people. One of the marks of the first-century Christians was that they 'enjoyed the favour of all the people ... [and] were highly regarded by the people' (Acts 2:47; 5:13). The people could not help but notice the love and care that the Christians had for one another. Paul reminded the young converts at Corinth that they were the aroma of Christ both 'among those who are being saved, and those who are perishing' (2 Corinthians 2:15). That should be true always of the life of the Christian community, but it is especially so in revival. The greater the work of God, the greater the effect across the nation. From the Khassi Hills in India came the description of 'Christians becoming more holy, more forgiving, more loving...'[32] Murray M'Cheyne

31 Lees, *Drunk Before Dawn*, p. 154.
32 Jones, *India Awake*, p. 31.

reported of Dundee in 1839 that the revival 'spread a sweet influence over the place,'[33] and that was a parish of 60,000 inhabitants.

Festo Kivengere wrote at length of the deep Christian love that was evident even to the unbelieving world. Christians met daily in Uganda to care for and help each other. It was a new experience for many. Kivengere comments:

'I have seen many methods devised in attempting to produce a love-fellowship. But the only known power for keeping together a group of believers—in love, fruitful and not ingrown—is the presence of the Author in the midst who is listened to and obeyed. It is not a product of man's desire for socializing. It is a fruit of Christ's self-giving love ... When the Lord is in the midst, the Holy Spirit makes us alert and sensitive to each other's needs ... There were many in Uganda, and eventually in all East Africa, who echoed the words of the pagan Romans which Tertullian tells us about, "Behold these Christians, how they love one another!" A widow whose house is in disrepair may find the believers together building a new one for her. A hungry family may find a bag of grain at the door in the morning. A young person may find that his school fees have been paid...'[34]

One of the greatest benefits of revival lies in its effects upon human relationships. In society, those converted to Christ are reconciled not only to God but to neighbours, workmates and others. Family feuds are healed, gossiping and slanderous tongues are silenced, and class and social barriers are pulled down. The gospel that makes us 'all one in Christ Jesus' and the Saviour, in whom there is 'neither Jew nor Greek, slave nor free, male nor female' (Galatians 3:28), unite those who are unnecessarily divided.

Count Nikolaus Ludwig of Zinzendorf recounted the events of that incredible morning in the life of the Herrnhut community in Saxony

---

33 Bonar, *Memoirs and Remains*, p. 500.
34 Kivengere, *Revolutionary Love*, pp. 42–43.

on Wednesday, 13 August 1727. It was a day when God came down and left the members 'hardly knowing whether they belong to earth or had already gone to heaven'. What preceded it? Zinzendorf tells us that the congregation which had been bitterly divided and quarrelsome on such issues as baptism, church government and prophecy, 'were all dissatisfied with themselves. They had quit judging each other because they had become convinced, each one, of his lack of worth in the sight of God...'[35]

It was reported from Wales in 1904 that women who 'sued one another in the courts, [now] prayed side by side in the same meeting.' An old miner, speaking of the feuds between union and non-union members prior to the 1859 revival in Wales, claimed, 'I have seen neighbours refuse to speak to each other, although they had been great friends. I have seen some refuse to descend the mine in the same cage with men who did not belong to the Federation, or to speak to them below ground, except with an oath. The Revival has stopped all that, and colliers look upon each other, spite of all the differences, as friends and companions. Some of the Non-unionists were among the best of men, and, at the meeting I have just left, one of them was leading the prayers, and Unionists joining in!'[36]

Nowhere is this seen more obviously than in the life of the churches. One of the sad marks of the church in its normal life is that evangelical churches are often found uniting with those from whom they should separate and separating from those with whom they should unite. Denominational ties and traditions are far more important than loyalty to the truth. Revival is an evangelical experience and it highlights the vital issues that unite, rather than the secondary issues that divide. This is not always the case, but it stands as a general truth.

35 Davies, *The Moravian Revival of 1727*, p.7.
36 Jones, *Rent Heavens*, p.60.

It was Hezekiah's purpose in sending couriers to the northern territory of Israel to bring about a reconciliation from the centuries of north-south aggression. The invitation was 'return to the LORD ... submit to the LORD ... serve the LORD' (2 Chronicles 30:6–8). It was a gospel of uniting in absolute obedience to God and his word. In the life of the infant church Paul had a clear yardstick for assessing preaching: whatever a man's motives may be, the apostle was concerned to know whether Christ was preached or not (Philippians 1:15–18).

William Haslam who, as a proud, unconverted Anglican, once boasted he would be glad to bury every dissenter as a breed of 'no goods', found some of his greatest fellowship and support from these dissenters once he had been converted and experienced revival in his church. A report in Scotland in 1839 claimed: 'As the revival swept Kilsyth, the various denominations worked together in perfect harmony.'[37]

Similar reports came from the Welsh press in 1860 and 1905. The *Wrexham Advertiser* for 4 August 1860 commented upon a talk given by the Rev. J. Baillie of the Church of England. He was speaking of the revival in Ulster and reported, 'To ask what denomination a convert belonged to, would excite a smile of pity, and that it is considered there are but two sects in the world, the one for Christ and the other against him.'

A similar report was carried in the *North Wales Guardian* on 17 March 1905. It was of a meeting in Rhosllanerchrugog (Rhos) where the evangelical vicar was sympathetic to the revival, and the reporter continued,

'One of the most remarkable scenes witnessed since the inception of the revival was enacted here on Monday afternoon. The Vicar [Thomas Pritchard] has taken keen interest in the meetings from the commencement and has worked in co-operation with the Nonconformists throughout. The Welsh Church was

37 Orr, *The Eager Feet*, p. 148.

filled with a vast congregation, composed mainly of Nonconformists, and with a few exceptions all the ministers were present. The Vicar presided, and the meeting was opened by Rev. E. Williams, Baptist minister. Prayers, praise, and solos followed for about two and a half hours. The Rev. Robert Jones, Welsh Calvinistic Methodist minister, having taken part, the Vicar said he could not express in words the happiness he felt in seeing so many present; he had attended many meetings during his career but he never felt such a thrill of emotion as he had on that occasion. The walls and hedges of dis-union had been swept away, they were now united, and they knew no distinction.'

Thirty years after the Welsh revival, Rhys Jones commented on some of the benefits. In particular he noted that 'sectionalism and suspicion' were ended, and he continued: 'Denominational walls, as high perhaps in Wales as in most countries, fell down as did Jericho's walls.' This was perhaps one advance of the 1904 revival in Wales over that of 1859; during the earlier revival the established church in Wales largely resisted the work of the Spirit, whereas in 1904 the barriers between church and chapel were broken down. R. B. Jones noted, 'Not only did Nonconformists of all hues blend together, but the wider gulf between Nonconformist and Conformist was also wonderfully bridged. Anglican clergy, as well as Free Church ministers, recognized the work as of God. Anglicans were seen in Nonconformist pulpits, and un-ordained revivalists welcomed in Anglican pulpits. What agitation and legislation could never have effected, to the Spirit of God was but the work of a moment.' [38]

It must be re-emphasized that unity like this is always an evangelical unity, and never an ecumenical unity where the true gospel is lost among the baggage of error and pretence.

38 Jones, *Rent Heavens*, p. 61.

Family relationships

Families are transformed in revival. In eighteenth century America Jonathan Edwards wrote of the joy that had been brought to whole families as salvation came to each member.[39]

In a very different age and culture, Festo Kivengere who was known as the Billy Graham of Africa and was powerfully used in the Uganda revival, reported on the radical change to family life that revival in East Africa brought to a culture where the husband was dominant and many wives were little more than servants:

'It was an amazing thing to me to see what dignity and freedom of Spirit the Lord had brought to the women of God. African men are often polygamous and traditionally they like to be treated as chiefs in their homes, with their wives as mere slaves. But here I saw a husband giving a place of honour to his wife and watched her fill the place competently as a beloved equal in the sight of the Lord. I even saw a man kneel down before his wife and say, "I have been mean and hurtful to you, my dear. I am sorry. Please forgive me." ... Before dawn every morning, the families who loved Jesus would rise and wash, gather in a room and begin to sing praises to the Lord. Each morning, when I woke, I could hear the singing rise from one nearby home after another. Then I knew they were reading the Scripture Union portion for the day and meditating on it together.'[40]

A minister reported from Ulster in 1859 that in one congregation, out of 209 families only two were not regularly observing family worship.[41] The following year Thomas Phillips wrote from Wales that family worship was expected of all converts: 'The general establishment of family worship is another blessed result of the present awakening.' New Christians were told not to be content with public worship: they must worship God as

39 Edwards, *A Narrative of Surprising Conversions*, p. 14.
40 Kivengere, *Revolutionary Love*, p. 55.
41 Paisley, *The Fifty-Nine Revival*, p. 64.

families in their own homes. In some homes where fathers were slow to start family worship, the children demanded it. This act of worship in the home almost became a test of true conversion.[42] This is unquestionably a mark of revivals; Howell Harris is typical when he commented, 'Family worship was set up in many houses.'[43] Exactly the same has happened in KwaZulu–Natal.[44]

Inevitably such a new life and closeness in the families had other, more obvious results. One NSPCC inspector told a newspaper reporter how, in the mining valleys of Glamorgan, the revival of 1904 had such a great influence on the care of parents for their children that, because of the remarkable change in their homes, he now no longer needed even to watch several families whom he had previously expected to have to prosecute.[45] In Swansea it was reported that adults were taking their parents from the workhouse to care for them at home.

These are merely examples. When God comes by his Spirit in revival then society is always aware of it, not only in the changed lives of the Christians and the more radical change in the lives of the converts, but also in the effect that all this has upon the community. Crime is reduced and the magistrates and police are among the first to notice a difference. This must be the case, and if it is not, then it is doubtful whether a true revival has happened at all. Nothing less than revival can halt the relentless march of drunkenness and violence in our society today.

These examples do not demonstrate the larger value of revival in a national context. The great revivals in Britain of the eighteenth and nineteenth centuries radically altered our social and political history as we have seen. They gave back a conscience to the nation. The national

---

42 Phillips, *The Welsh Revival*, pp. 92–94. If a reader has time for only one book on the Welsh revival of 1859, this is the one.

43 Evans, *Howell Harris*, p. 13.

44 Stegen, *Revival among the Zulus*, p. 60.

45 Jones, *Rent Heavens*, p. 66.

It was not the 'Glorious Revolution' but the 'Great Awakening' that changed the nation in the eighteenth century

conscience had been lost by the restoration of Charles II in 1660 and a godless age of immorality had forfeited many of the benefits of the Reformation and the Commonwealth. Even the 'Glorious Revolution' of 1688, when William sailed from Holland and snatched the crown from James, only settled the political and religious scene; it did little for the soul of the nation. When the eighteenth century opened, it could be described simply by that phrase of Thomas Carlyle: "Soul extinct, stomach well alive.' That is exactly where we are today.

It was not the 'Glorious Revolution' but the 'Great Awakening' that changed the nation in the eighteenth century.

After revival

Does it last?

Most people think of revival as a time of phenomenal growth in the numbers attending church, when crowds flock to church in order to hear the gospel accompanied by a sudden and startling increase in church membership. This is not the most significant aspect of revival. Revival is not the conversion of thousands of unsaved, but the awakening of the church, making it holy and alive once again. Crowds and conversions may be the result of this, but God's purpose in revival is first and foremost the awakening of his own people. If we pray for revival only because we want to see many converts and full churches, we have missed God's purpose. God must begin with the church and sometimes, as in the Congo in 1953, it may be months before he turns his attention to the unconverted.

In the time of Hezekiah the revival started in Judah and Jerusalem, representing the people belonging to God. These were those who now longed to worship at the temple and hear what God had to say through his word. Only then did the message impact the northern tribes. The same happened in the early church, except that someone was prepared to record statistics: first there were 3,000 (Acts 2:41), and later the number grew to about 5,000 (4:4). As the work of the Spirit continued, 'More and more men and women were added to their number' (Acts 5:14). The rest of the story of the early church concerns its growth throughout the empire.

There is no doubt that revival does leave its mark in the numerical growth of the church. There cannot be a great outpouring of the Holy Spirit so that a whole community is saturated with God, without eternity being impressed onto the minds of men and women who before were careless and indifferent. One of the most remarkable occasions in revival, as we have seen, occurred on 21 June 1630 when John Livingstone preached in the churchyard at Shotts in Lanarkshire, Scotland and it is estimated five hundred people were converted as a result of this single sermon.

Writing from Northampton, New England, Jonathan Edwards, who was naturally cautious in giving numbers of those converted, allowed himself this conservative estimate: 'I hope that more than three hundred souls were savingly brought home to Christ, in this town, in the space of half a year, and about the same number of males as females.'[1] This was 1734 in just one town with a population of some twelve hundred; during one five-week period Edwards saw thirty people saved each week. This Great Awakening was continuing across New England and it is estimated that out of a total population of 340,000, between 25,000 and 30,000 were converted.[2] If we take the lowest figure this means that over seven per cent of the population was converted during the revival. However, forty years later at the time of the War of Independence it was estimated that less than five percent of the population attended church and twenty years after the war, at Yale, a 'Christian' college, only twelve students professed Christ. After a new time of revival, one third of the student body professed.[3] In fact, only nine years after the revival in Northampton, Edwards wrote, 'There has been a very lamentable decay of religious affections … and the engagedness of people's spirit in religion.' However, after the visit by Whitefield in 1740 a new wave of revival transformed the whole town and three years later they were still enjoying the fruit of it.[4]

In London, George Whitefield was preaching to probably the largest crowds ever to hear the gospel in England up to that time. There was no accurate way of counting the vast crowds that listened to Whitefield

1 Edwards, *A Narrative of Surprising Conversions*, p. 19.
2 Lacy, *Revivals in the Midst of the Years*, p. 42.
3 Armstrong, *When God Moves*, pp. 106–107.
4 Edwards, *A Narrative of Surprising Conversions*, pp. 148–160.

in the open air from the late 1730s onwards, but *The Gentleman's Magazine* for 1739 estimated at least 20,000 at Kingswood. Whitefield's biographer, Arnold Dallimore, suggests that even if we halve some of the figures given in his time, that great preacher occasionally addressed up to 40,000 listeners—this by a young man of twenty-four and without amplification.[5] In 1742 God worked in a powerful way in Cambuslang in Scotland, partly under the ministry of Whitefield. Nearly six months after the revival, a local minister estimated that more than five hundred had been converted and were still following Christ.[6]

When John Wesley died in 1791 the membership of his Wesleyan Methodists in Britain was around 72,000; sixty years later it had increased fivefold.[7] However, this is only part of the Methodist history. The growth of the Primitive Methodists from their formation in 1811 to their unfortunate reunion with mainline Methodism in 1932 is too little known. Beginning with just 200 members, by 1836 they numbered over 62,000 and by 1905 they had 92,000 members with over 4,000 Sunday Schools, 60,000 teachers and half a million children. Their growth was almost entirely among the poorly paid working people. Even these figures do not tell all because many of their converts worshipped in other independent churches.[8]

The camp meetings in Kentucky in 1799/1800, for all their outbursts of extreme enthusiasm, witnessed a significant growth especially among the Baptists. The six Baptist Associations in the county saw an increase from 4,766 to 13,569.[9] This revival period radically transformed the moral and spiritual life of the whole area for years to come. A Presbyterian report in 1803 recorded the deep and lasting work of the Spirit.[10] The increase of

5 Dallimore, *George Whitefield*, vol. 1, pp. 295–296. Here Dallimore refers to similar open-air preachers in history.
6 As above, vol. 2, pp. 122, 127.
7 Paul Cook in Westminster Conference papers *Preaching and Revival*, p. 87.
8 Kendall, *The Origin and History of the Primitive Methodist Church*, Vol. 2 pp. 512 on.
9 Murray, *Revival and Revivalism*, p. 155.
10 As above pp. 157–158.

the churches in America after 1857 has been recorded as up to one million. However, in 1860 Thomas Phillips had heard that 600,000 'within the last two years, had been led to make a profession of religion.'[11]

In 1851, the combined population of England and Wales was eighteen million. If we take only the morning congregation recorded in the 1851 census of religion in England and Wales on Sunday 30 March, almost ten percent of the entire population were either Baptist or Methodists. This is a minimum figure because if we add the afternoon and evening services it more than doubles; however, it is not possible to know how many would then be counted twice.[12] On that Sunday morning two and a half million were in the Church of England and two and a quarter million were in the 'free churches', excluding the Roman Catholic church. This was almost a decade before the 1859 revival and was due largely to the periodic revivals across the nation in the early years of that century.

Revivals across Cornwall between 1790 to 1840 saw a dramatic increase in church membership. The census in March 1851 showed that in Cornwall 49% of the population were attending church, of which 32% belonged to one or other of the Methodist groups and a little over 13% in the Church of England. The 51% non-attenders would include the aged and infirm; therefore, well over half the population of Cornwall would be committed to a local church.[13]

When God came to Wales in 1859 it is estimated that 110,000 were added to the churches, and only slightly fewer were added between 1904–1905.[14] In each case the Calvinistic Methodists received the largest influx of 36,000 and 24,000 respectively. Thomas Phillips visited Cardiganshire on behalf of the Bible Society soon after 1860. He made careful enquiries in forty churches, which he suggested was about two thirds of the county.

11 Phillips, *The Welsh Revival*, p. 4.
12 On-line British Religion in Numbers, the census of 1851 in England and Wales.
13 Isaac, *A History of Evangelical Christianity In Cornwall*, p. 141.
14 Evans, *When He is Come*, p. 97.

Around 7,000 had been added to those churches and only one in twenty had relapsed; in some places not one had reneged on their faith or given cause for discipline.[15]

On 27 January 1905 the *North Wales Guardian* reported 70,000 added to the churches in Wales; but a week later, on 3 February, it increased the figure to over 74,000. The paper went on to comment that in Anglesey, Professor Mavis Jones of the University College estimated the number of converts at 10% of the total population. He put this down to systematic house-to-house visitation inviting non-chapel goers to attend the revival meetings.[16] However, these figures were perhaps too previous as we will see in the next section 'Tested by Fire'.

The revival that swept Ulster in 1859 claimed another 100,000 for Christ, and some, reporting at the time, considered that estimate to be too conservative.[17]

The first missionaries arrived in Ethiopia in 1928 and at that time there were no known believers in the country. In July 1935, when they received orders from the American and British embassies to leave the country, the missionaries could count only seventeen Wallamo believers. They ignored the orders and stayed on. In April 1937, when they were forced to leave after nine years' work, there were still only forty-eight believers. In 1943, less than six years later and after the cruel occupation of Ethiopia by the Italians, the missionaries were able to return and were greeted by more than 100 church leaders, representing around 10,000 Christians. In one church alone 400 believers gathered. One Christian commented: 'When you missionaries left it was difficult to find a Christian in Wallamo country. Now it is difficult to find a man who is not a Christian.' By 1945 there were 15,000 believers.[18]

---

15 Phillips, *The Welsh Revival*, p. 136.
16 Harris, *Extracts from the Welsh Press*, p. 14.
17 Paisley, *The Fifty-Nine Revival*, p. 137.
18 Davies, *Fire on the Mountains*, p. 109.

Surveying the scene of revival across the world, Edwin Orr points out that in Korea between 1906 and 1910 the net gain of all the churches was nearly 80,000, which was more than the total number of Christians in Japan after half a century of Protestant effort.[19]

Similarly, what has happened to the church in China over the last century can only be understood in terms of revival. When the missionaries were expelled in 1949 after 140 years of missionary activity there were fewer than an estimated one million national believers. By 1980 Bishop Peter Hsieh of Fuzhou reported that in his city of one million there were 20,000 Christians. On one of his pastoral journeys he discovered 7,000 new Christians in seven remote mountain villages. In this same year Christians throughout the whole province were known to number at least 600,000, and in one area alone, in one year, 6,000 new converts were baptized. After the 'limited freedom' of 1979 every province saw massive growth. In some rural areas it is estimated that over 90% of the population is Christian and that as many as 27,000 have been converted each day in China between 1980 and 1983. One elderly pastor in China commented: 'Before the Communists came, I remember that shepherds were searching for sheep. But now, all over China, it is the sheep who are searching for shepherds.'[20] In Fuyang prefecture in the province on Anhui, the number of believers shrank to 5,000 on the eve of the 'cultural revolution'. Careful research revealed that in 1990 that number had risen to almost 213,000. 30% of this number were in unregistered churches.

Today, Purdue University's Center on Religion and Chinese Society, estimates that there are between 93 million and 115 million Protestants in China and the church is growing at 10% each year.[21] If the history of the church in China teaches us anything, the current renewed pressure

19 Orr, *Evangelical Awakenings*, p. 29.
20 Lyall, *God Reigns in China*, pp. 166–169, 178–179.
21 On line The Council of Foreign Relations, October 2018.

on Christians by the communist government announced in 2018, will not slow this growth.

However, revival is not limited to vast numbers over a wide area brought to Christ. The story of God's church reveals many more local, and sometimes very short, outpourings of the Spirit. In 1794 an awakening came to the north of England, and in Sheffield, under the preaching of John Moon and Alexander Mather, the presence of God was unusually felt. One chapel meeting began quite normally until God came down and it then continued until two in the morning. During this meeting as many as seventy found peace with God and the power of God was present for another three days until around 100 had been converted. In the same year revival broke out in West Yorkshire, and in the Leeds Methodist circuit 2,000 new members were added in that one year.[22]

1799 was a year of God's favour for Cornwall. At Penzance there were 100 new members; at Zennor the Methodist Society increased from seventeen to 100 and at Walls eighty were added in two months. In St Ives the Methodists grew from 160, a figure that had been static for many years, to 550. And so we could go on.[23] In 1814 God began a work in Redruth which spread throughout Cornwall and within a few weeks it was estimated that 5,000 were added to the Methodist churches. In the course of one week, 2,000 people were converted at Tuckingmill during the meeting that lasted from Sunday, 27 February, through to the following Friday, with people coming and going all the time.[24]

During the early 1830s the name of James Caughey was well known in the Midlands. Converted in revival in the United States, he returned to Britain and after a short time in Dublin he preached in Liverpool where over 12,000 were converted. The same success accompanied him in Nottingham, where William Booth was converted, and at Huddersfield,

22 Paul Cook in Westminster Conference papers *Preaching and Revival*, pp. 95–97.
23 As above, p. 97.
24 As above, p. 99.

Goole, Sheffield, York, Chesterfield and Birmingham. It was here in Birmingham in the Methodist church (which seats 2,000) that 600 were brought to Christ and the revival left the 'bar-rooms and beershops vocal with lonely grumblers'.[25] When the revival that started in Lowestoft on the east coast of England in 1921 spread to the Scottish fishing ports, whole communities were transformed. At Cairnbulg, with a population of only 1,500, over 600 professions were recorded in two weeks.[26]

When Joseph Kemp came as pastor to Charlotte Chapel in Edinburgh in 1902, only thirty-five of the one hundred members attended his induction. Three years later God began to work in the chapel in such a way that the building was soon outgrown by the congregation and by 1907 the membership stood at 609. Joseph Kemp records:

'Under these influences the crowds thronged the chapel, which only three years before maintained a "sombre vacuum". After the first year of this work we had personally dealt with no fewer than one thousand souls, who had been brought to God during the prayer meetings ... I have yet to witness a movement that has produced more permanent results, in the lives of men, women and children.'[27]

Duncan Campbell revisited many of the churches in the Scottish Islands two and a half years after the revival, and he could report in May 1952 that of the hundreds who had professed Christ, only four were known to have fallen away.[28] In the early 1970s hundreds were converted in Borneo and at one convention over 200 were baptized.[29] The same thing was happening in India at the turn of the century.[30] But whilst revival touches

25 Orr, *The Eager Feet*, pp. 144–145.
26 Ritchie, *Floods Upon the Dry Ground*, p. 56.
27 Kemp, *Joseph W. Kemp*, pp. 31, 30.
28 Peckham, *Sounds from Heaven*, p. 60.
29 Lees, *Drunk Before Dawn*, p. 182.
30 Jones, *India Awake*, p. 33.

whole towns, counties or provinces, it is in the local church that the effect is certainly felt.

Conviction is not conversion, neither does an awakening mean conviction

Do they continue?

Statistics are dangerous. At a distance of time we can never be sure how accurate they are; some are over-generous in counting heads, and others are too conservative. Some statistics we know are accurate because of the careful records kept; others are good (or bad) guesses; some may be wishful thinking. Keri Evans, in Wales in 1905, gave a valuable reminder that in revival many are convicted of sin who never come to salvation: 'Conviction is not conversion, neither does an awakening mean conviction. The real thing is the Holy Spirit passing through the imagination and feelings to the conscience—so creating conviction—then through conscience to the will—so leading to conversion.'[31] On the other hand, however we read the records, it is impossible to avoid the conclusion that revival always brings with it a new and vigorous growth in the numbers regularly attending the places of worship and claiming allegiance to Jesus Christ. But do they all stand the test of time?

We may assume there were those who went back on their commitment when Manasseh came to the throne after Hezekiah, just as some in the early church made false professions like Simon the sorcerer and Demas. Overall, however, the converts of the New Testament church stood the rigorous tests of time and persecution. In true revival the numbers professing Christ are so much greater than in the 'normal' life of the church, but it is a matter of debate whether the percentage of false professions is more or less. Honest men involved in revival have always been concerned with this question of whether the converts stand.

31 Jones, *The King's Champions*, p. 60.

Reporting on the work of the Spirit in Dundee in 1839, Robert Murray M'Cheyne noted that 'Not fewer than from six hundred to seven hundred came to converse with the ministers about their souls ... With regard to the consistency of those who are believed to have been converted, I may first of all remark, that it must be acknowledged, and should be clearly understood, that many who came under concern about their souls, and seemed, for a time, to be deeply convinced of sin, have gone back again to the world.' M'Cheyne explains this by the fact that very few who came to the meetings were completely untouched by the Word of God; therefore many came for counselling who were not converted. However, M'Cheyne continued, 'Confining our view to those who, as far as ministers could judge by the rules of God's Word, seemed to be savingly converted, I may with safety say, that I do not know of more than two who have openly given the lie to their profession. Other cases of this kind may have occurred, but they are unknown to me.'[32] Here is a cautious minister who distinguishes between those who make a profession and those whom the ministers judged to be converted, and four years later M'Cheyne concluded that the great majority of the latter were still continuing well.

Thomas Jones was deeply involved in the Welsh revival of 1859 and he faced this same question, concluding, 'I have gathered from enquiry that not one person in every fifty of those who have assumed a profession of religion within the last four or six months, has relapsed into the world.' One estimate, given as late as 1897, claimed that only one in twenty failed to continue their profession.[33]

One reason for this high level of continuing is that the churches were careful never to allow people to conclude that a mere profession was enough to guarantee true conversion. In 1860 Thomas Phillips recorded the way the churches guarded those who made a profession:

32 Bonar, *Memoirs and Remains*, p.499.
33 Evans, *When He is Come*, pp.97–99.

'On every occasion care is taken to instruct the people in the true and unchangeable principles of religion. They are cautioned against resting in a mere outward profession. They are told that excitement is not conversion, that an awakening of the conscience to a sense of guilt and danger does not always result in a change of heart. It is strongly and constantly urged that whatever hope or confidence they may have in their own minds as to their having "passed from death unto life", it is a mistake, a delusion, unless it is accompanied by hatred to sin, and a renunciation of it in every shape or form; love to holiness, and the practical discharge of every moral duty. They are told that the Bible is to be the standard of religious feeling, as it is of religious faith. In short, they are admonished to seek a thorough change of heart, and to furnish evidence thereof in holiness of life.'[34]

Much the same was true of the work of God in Ulster at the same time. One minister, writing of the results in his own locality could report: 'I do not yet know of a single backslider.'[35] Among the many scores of thousands who professed Christ during that eventful year, there were some who did go back on their commitment, but the proportion was small and no one could dismiss the value of the revival because of them.

Though the numbers involved were much smaller, David Brainerd was able to report that of the forty-seven Indians who were converted at the Forks of Delaware in the early 1740s, 'None of them as yet have been left to disgrace their profession of Christianity.'[36]

The ministers involved at Kilsyth and Cambuslang in 1742 were concerned and honest in their assessment of the numbers that slipped back after a profession of faith during the revival. They freely admitted that, like the seed that fell on unsuitable soil in the parable told by Christ, there were many whose profession lasted only a while. The ministers were alert to this possibility at the time and were not willing to accept a profession

34 As above, pp. 98–99.
35 Paisley, *The Fifty-Nine Revival*, p. 47.
36 Page, *David Brainerd*, p. 100.

merely by outward appearances, least of all by the bodily-trembling that some experienced. However, in a letter written by William McCulloch to James Robe, nine years after that memorable event, the incumbent at Cambuslang records: 'I have now before me, at the writing of this, April 27th 1751, a list of about four hundred persons awakened here at Cambuslang in 1742 who from that time to the time of their death, or to this, for these nine years past, have been all enabled to behave in a good measure as becometh the gospel...'[37]

The revival that had the most widespread influence also appears to have had the greatest percentage of losses. The 1904 revival that began in Wales spread throughout the world as missionaries returned to their fields of service and the stories spread across every continent. Yet it is estimated that during the five years following the revival something around twenty-percent slipped away from the churches. This figure needs explanation, because not all these fell away from following Christ; some simply changed their church allegiance. However, it is a high loss rate and is probably due as much to Evan Roberts' later indifference to preaching and the teaching of young converts as to anything else. In spite of this, it is reported that ten years later, in 1914, 80,000 of the converts were still in the membership of the churches 'in spite of leakage to mission halls and emigration overseas'.[38] That is hardly a statistic of failure.

37 Robe, *When the Wind Blows*, p. 175.
38 Orr, *The Flaming Tongue*, p. 17.

After revival

Tested by fire

Revival is always tested: 'After all that Hezekiah had so faithfully done, Sennacherib king of Assyria came and invaded Judah. He laid siege to all the fortified cities, thinking to conquer them for himself' (2 Chronicles 32:1). The officers of Sennacherib challenged the work of God at every level. In their tirade around the walls of Jerusalem they challenged the faith of the people (2 Chronicles 32:10), discredited the leaders (32:12), undermined popular morale (32:13), insulted God (32:17) and belittled his work (32:19). The challenge of the Assyrians (32:1–23), the king's illness (32:24) and the Babylonian envoys (32:31) were all sent to test the king and the people. Only in the matter of the envoys did Hezekiah fail. The arrival of the Assyrian army was a God-sent test of the reality of the revival. Or perhaps the God-sent revival was intended to prepare the people for the severe test that was soon to follow. It is doubtful whether the persecution that followed the outpouring of the Spirit at Pentecost was intended simply to test the reality of apostolic faith. The experience of Acts 2 strengthened these frightened men and women for the trial that was soon to follow.

Revivals are often followed by a period of great persecution or the suffering of those who have experienced the power of God

It is remarkable how revivals are often followed by a period of great persecution or the suffering of those who have experienced the power of God. It is as if God is preparing his people for what he knows is to follow. We may do well to keep this in mind when we so eagerly pray for revival. Revival is often a preparation for suffering, and the suffering itself becomes a test of the quality and reality of the revival.

The 'Prayer Revival' that swept across north America from 1857 to 1858 and brought an estimated one million into the Kingdom of God, was followed three years later by a Civil War that bitterly divided the nation and slaughtered over half a million men. Strangely, revival continued on both sides even during that time. It has been claimed that one fifth of confederate soldiers were converted in revival during the conflict.[1] Looking back on a revival in his church in Charleston, America in 1858, John Girardeau frequently referred to it as the mercy of God in gathering in his elect before the Civil War.[2]

Within ten years of the 1904 revival, which spread from Wales to all parts of the world, thousands of young men who had been converted in the revivals never returned to the Welsh valleys from the choking mud of the Great War battlefields. However, the testing fire in Wales was more far-reaching than the Great War. Within a decade of the Armistice many churches had become cold and formal. The inroads of liberal theology, the cults (especially the Watchtower Movement, Mormons, British Israelites and extreme Pentecostalism) and dispensational views from America, had a disastrous effect. As early as March 1913 a *Times* journalist wrote that in contrast to 'the wonderful religious revival': 'A strangely different spirit prevails today. The old theology and all it stood for is rapidly losing its hold on the mind of young Wales ... A fundamental change is proceeding, and no one can predict the issue....'

Within a few years, prediction was not needed: 'intellectual doubt and spiritual backsliding' was everywhere evident across Wales. In reality, it was only a return to the liberal onslaught that diminished the faith in Wales prior to 1904.[3] R. B. Jones and many other faithful leaders were

1 Duwel, *Revival Fire*, p. 136.
2 See evidence in Lacy, *Revivals in the Midst of the Years*, pp. 115–145.
3 See Evans, *The Welsh Revival of 1904*, pp. 35–48.

fighting a rear-guard action against the downgrade of Scripture until Jones became 'the most loved and hated preacher in Wales'. Conventions, village missions, even a Gospel Van purchased in 1909, and eventually the Bible Institute of Wales, maintained life and truth; but much had been lost through the 'new theology'.[4] For his part, Evan Roberts broke down in physical, mental and spiritual health, was cared for by friends in Leicester and for twenty years never visited Wales.

When God came down to the church in North Korea in 1907, especially in its capital Pyongyang, the quality of the work of the Spirit has been tested through three terrible waves of suffering: the first during the atrocities committed by the Japanese after the close of the Great War in 1919; the second in the persecutions following the government order compelling shrine worship in 1938, and more recently as a result of the Communist take-over of the north from 1948.

A revival that began in Japan during the late 1920s and early 1930s was effectively destroyed by the compromise of many church leaders who were prepared, for the sake of their lives and freedom, to accept the government order to worship at Shinto shrines. This, together with the fervent nationalism of many Christians during the Japanese war effort and the horrific suffering of the Japanese people as the war came to a devastating close, effectively dealt a death-blow to what had been a hopeful indication of God's presence.

Revival came among the Lun Bawang people in Borneo just two years before the Japanese occupation in 1941, and again in 1973 before a government clamp-down refused to renew the visas of many missionaries. Revival among students in China in 1946 proved to be a preparation for the harsh regime of Mao Zedong. Similarly, revival in East Africa in the 1930s prepared the church for the eight years of terror under Idi Amin

4 Jones, *The King's Champions*, pp. 135–139, 198, 91, 108–110 and pp. 214 on for the Bible Institute.

in the 1970s when more than half a million were brutally killed. Revival also prepared Kenya for the Mau Mau atrocities and the terrible inter-tribal wars in Rwanda and Burundi between the Hutus and Tutsis in 1994 during which the 'Saved Ones' took no part.[5] Revival came to the Congo in 1953, preparing the church for the cruel Simba rebellion ten years later when many leaders, members and missionaries were massacred.

The revival in Moldova during the 1980s and 1990s was challenged by a civil war, a harsh economic downturn and high unemployment which led to almost half the population of four million working abroad and the emigration of around 30,000 Christians. The churches were badly hurt by this—one church alone lost 1,000 adult members. Many pastors were the first to leave and this robbed the young Christians of the wise and experienced leaders who had stood firm during the half century of communist persecution.[6]

Revival sometimes flourishes *during* persecution and this was certainly the experience of the Christian church for the first three hundred years of its life. The revival in Ulster under the preaching of W. P. Nicholson in 1921 was at the height of some of the most vicious sectarian violence in the province. It was also the experience of the Baptist church in Oradea under the cruel persecution of Ceausescu in communist Romania where the most vile and malicious attempts of the secret police could neither dampen the revival nor destroy the church.[7]

During the years of severe persecution, revival came to the church in Ethiopia. The more the Italians attempted to destroy the Wallamo church, the more the church grew: 'At one point the fifty leaders had been arrested and put in prison when the Italians realized that their efforts to stamp out the church were only increasing its strength and size. Each of the leaders received one hundred lashes, and one was given four hundred. None of

5 Bewes, *Under the Thorn Tree*, p.85.
6 Wise, *Celestial Fire*, pp.93–102.
7 Birnie, *'Just call me Paul'*.

them were able to lie on their backs for months, and three died…'[8] The suffering of some leaders, particularly men like Wandaro, who was beaten all day by a team of men, was intense; but the Spirit of God caused more and more to be converted until, when the missionaries returned at the end of the war, there were 10,000 Wallamo Christians to greet them. This is the story of the Acts of the Apostles over again. The blood of the martyrs is the seed of the church.

The Waldensian revival, which spread across Europe during the twelfth and thirteenth centuries, was similar to that in Ethiopia 700 years later. The Roman Catholic inquisitors persecuted these Christians so rigorously that prisons could not be built fast enough to hold them, and the cost of feeding the prisoners became a heavy drain on resources. But in spite of all this, one estimate claims that by the year 1260 more than 800,000 had professed the evangelical faith of the Waldensians. A people of disciplined and holy lives, fervent in prayer and strongly attached to the preaching of the word of God, the Waldensians spread all over Europe in spite of the most cruel and unceasing persecution wherever they settled in Catholic countries.

8 Davies, *Fire on the Mountains*, p. 115.

7. Our response to revival

Revivals rarely outlast one generation. Manasseh, the son of King Hezekiah is known as one of the most evil kings in Judah. So, why and how do they fade? The work of God during the preaching of Wesley and Whitefield and many others in the eighteenth century, continued for half a century or more, others pass within a few weeks; in the case of Wheaton College in March 1995 it was little more than five days. Sometimes God withdraws his hand because too much attention is focused on the men involved or on the phenomena accompanying the revival.

> Revivals rarely outlast one generation

Manasseh was not born until the revival under the leadership of his father had passed its peak, but he must have known of the great work of God, and he must also have seen the benefits in the nation. But hearing stories of revival, or even living in the results of revival, is not the same as experiencing the power of revival. The tragedy of the story of Manasseh is that it took him only a few years to return the nation to the days of his grandfather, Ahaz—and almost half a century to realize his terrible mistake. A whole generation can grow up neglecting that which their parents experienced. Speaking with those who have been involved in revival, even fifty years after the event, you cannot help but realize something of the glory has never fully faded from their lives. As one confessed, 'When you have lived through revival you can never be the same again.'

Towards the end of a decade of local church revival in the 1830s, the Methodist Conference declared, 'Some churches regard revivals of religion as gracious singularities in their history; we regard them as essential to our existence.' For this reason, whenever they considered the gospel was losing its impact on society, the Methodists of the early nineteenth century went to prayer for revival. This not only explains the continual 'out-bursts' of revival across Britain, but also the steady growth of Wesleyan Methodism, and especially the Primitive Methodists, during the first half of the nineteenth century.

Whether we regard revivals as 'gracious singularities' or essential to our existence, or as something else, if we have read so far, we must be forming a response to the subject. It is an issue that generally draws a reaction; it is not easy to remain coldly indifferent to the possibility of God coming among his people in such spiritual power and reality that the whole community seems to be 'saturated with God'.

It is not easy to remain coldly indifferent to the possibility of God coming among his people in such spiritual power and reality that the whole community seems to be 'saturated with God'

Why do revivals cease?

A few revivals have ended tragically because when the test came, men failed. Some led astray by excitement and phenomena as we have seen with Humphrey Jones and others. Some ended when men took over the organization of events. Douglas Brown was greatly used by God in the Lowestoft revival of 1921 and the following year saw him on the platform of the Keswick Convention where an expectation of widespread revival was evident. Shortly after, a well-meaning committee organised Brown's itinerary and he himself also took on committee responsibilities. One astute observer commented at the time, 'This is the end'—and sadly it was.[1] A well-meaning church leader from England visited the revival in East Africa during the 1930s and failed

1 Griffin, *A Forgotten Revival*, pp. 86–88.

to appreciate the valuable work of the local evangelists. His message home was that more clergy from England were needed. Dr Joe Church, a lay leader on the field commented that some of the rules of the Church Missionary Society: 'missed a wonderful opportunity of further fanning the flame of revival—all it did was to dampen it down.'[2] Finney's 'method' for creating a revival allowed the Spirit's work to downgrade into a system of revival meetings that has plagued many churches ever since.[3]

However, we cannot always discover a reason why a particular revival came to an end, and it is wrong to assume that there must always be a reason other than the sovereign time-keeping of God. William Haslam admitted, 'As a fact, it is well known that revivals begin and continue for a time, and that they cease as mysteriously as they began.'[4]

By March 1905 in Wales the press reported some decrease in attendance here and there; and by June, Christian leaders were seriously asking, 'Where now?' and how they should be caring for the new converts.[5] A gradual slowing down in any revival is inevitable and is no necessary criticism of revival itself or those leaders involved. The full force of Pentecost did not last for ever. By 1908 the awakening in Denmark had run its course but the leaders were quick to comment, 'We are not going backwards; a gracious congregational life prevails in so many parts of our beloved land.'[6] People now had a great hunger for the word of God.

The brevity of some revivals is illustrated by the minutes of the Presbyterian Church Assembly in America during the 1830s. In 1832 the report glows with the benefits of revival; in one congregation alone 300 conversions were recorded. Everywhere the churches and societies were alive and growing. Sadly, controversy quenched the Spirit and by 1835

2 Osborn, *Revival—a precious Heritage*, pp. 86–92.
3 For an assessment of Finney's theology and method see the companion volume to this, *Praying for Revival*, ch. 1, and Murray, *Revival and Revivalism*, pp. 228–252.
4 Haslam, *From Death Into Life*, p. 71.
5 See Harris, *Extracts from the Welsh Press*.
6 Orr, *The Flaming Tongue*, p. 55.

one sad paragraph, bemoaning the lack of the Spirit contrasted to former times, was the only reference to revival.[7]

The point at which Hezekiah failed was that at which others who have been used in revival have also failed: 'Hezekiah's heart was proud and ... God left him to test him and to know everything that was in his heart' (2 Chronicles 32:25,31). In showing his armoury and storehouses to the Babylonian envoys, Hezekiah revealed his pride in his own achievements and his enjoyment of the praise and respect that he commanded in the world around. Hezekiah failed to remember that his deliverance from Assyria had nothing to do with his own military power or genius but was wholly the intervention of God. The greatest battle Hezekiah ever had was not with his people, or with his enemies, but with himself. And that was the battle he lost. Perhaps the greatest threat to revival lies within the hearts of its leaders.

It was pride that ended the ministry of Humphrey Jones in Wales in 1859. Having been greatly used by God in America in 1858, Jones returned to his native Wales with a great passion to see his country set alight by the Holy Spirit. His early ministry was fruitful and undoubtedly revival began through his preaching, although many had been praying for it for years. During the early months of 1859 Jones found himself at Aberystwyth, where the work was hard and little was accomplished. Driven almost to distraction, he claimed divine 'revelations' which resulted in 'prophecies' to the church. These were quickly exposed as false and Jones was full of remorse. However, the damage was done, and it was left to David Morgan to continue the work in Wales. Humphrey Jones never fully recovered, and although he preached again in Aberystwyth some four years later, he was often ill and in 1871 he returned to America, where he died in 1895.[8] Similarly, Hezekiah never fully recovered from that one great error of

7 Lacy, *Revival in the Midst of the Years*, pp. 102–104.
8 Evans, *When he Is Come*, pp. 61–62.

> Few leaders are on record as having given in to the sin of robbing God of his glory and setting themselves up as oracles of the divine

boasting to the foreign envoys; whilst the fruits of revival continued, the best was past.

Although we have seen earlier under 'Error and the Extreme' how easily ungodly personalities can infiltrate revival, God has chosen his men carefully, and few leaders are on record as having given in to the sin of robbing God of his glory and setting themselves up as oracles of the divine. Asahel Nettleton was considered as great as George Whitefield in the nineteenth century story of revival in America. Crowds followed him as a celebrity because of the power of his preaching, but he hated this and often took a strong stand against it. If ever he felt a congregation was relying upon him for the work of revival, Nettleton would simply disappear for a while and leave the people to themselves. This caused great concern on a number of occasions, but at least it drove home the importance of Nettleton's theology that revival belongs exclusively to God. Similarly, the saintly Robert Murray M'Cheyne, in Dundee, trembled at the thought that he might rob God of his glory, and wept over his own sins as much as over the sins of others.

That is how all Christian leaders should view their work.

Every generation for itself

There is perhaps one particular reason why revival rarely outlasts one generation: revival is not intended to be the normal life of the church. Preaching in 1929, Martyn Lloyd-Jones, a man who passionately longed for revival again in his time, emphasized, 'There are not only the great experiences but also the ordinary, everyday experiences, and a church that is always praying for a continual revival is a church that has not understood her mission. The church is not meant always to be in a state of revival but is also to do ordinary, everyday work.' He wisely added, 'But some remember this fact so well that they forget that the church is meant to have special occasions!'[9]

Revival is a 'great experience' and our churches urgently need it. Revival pulls the church out of its rut, awakens it from its sleep and sets inertia in motion. But if God did this always for his people, they would never learn to fight battles in the desert. Outlining the excellent social, political, and missionary work of the nineteenth century evangelicals, one commentator suggests: '[Jonathan] Edwards might have thought that the work of God was continued through frequent outpourings of the Holy Spirit; however, his evangelical progeny thought that whatever the role of the Spirit, it required organisation and sheer hard work.'[10] There is wisdom in this, because only in this way do we learn and grow. Revival is God's rescue of a church in danger, but when the rescue is over, we must stand and fight in the 'ordinary, everyday experiences'.

Revival pulls the church out of its rut, awakens it from its sleep and sets inertia in motion

Today we have two or three generations who know nothing of revival. We can never long and pray for that of which we know nothing. Rhys Bevan Jones looked back at the 1904 revival in Wales from the vantage-point of 1930, and he assessed its causes and results. Writing of its causes he came to this conclusion:

> 'If it be asked why the fire, when it came, fell on Wales? ... No fire can burn where fuel lacks. Let then the fuel be prepared. Never let a generation grow up without that knowledge of Divine things which may contain the germ of national revival in years to come'[11]

---

9 Murray, *The First Forty Years*, p.204.
10 Jones, *The Fire Divine*, p.136.
11 Jones, *Rent Heavens*, pp.87–88.

'No fire can burn where fuel lacks.' Is that part of the reason why we lack revival today? With all our excitement and activity, our programmes, conferences, and our sound theology, we have forgotten to read and talk about the 'special occasions'. And when we know what these special occasions have been, there is only one more action urgently required: strong, insistent and believing prayer.

> With all our excitement and activity, our programmes, conferences, and our sound theology, we have forgotten to read and talk about the 'special occasions'

The year following the great prayer revival in America in 1857, Samuel Prime reflected on the lesson to be learnt: 'Union in prayer for the sake of a world lying in wickedness should become the watchword of the entire church of God.'[12] At the close of a challenging chapter on 'Prayer and Revivals' Henry Fish, writing in 1873, concluded: 'I very much doubt whether, if we could see the connection between prayer and the glorious revivals that have blessed this land, we should find one that was not definitely prayed for by some earnest wrestlers, or wrestler, at the throne of grace ... The conclusion is patent and important. If there are to be more revivals, there must be more prayer.'[13] Writing in 1991, Erroll Hulse concluded his own book on revival with the challenge: 'During the last thirty years or so, the value of the Reformed faith has been rediscovered at the intellectual level. Do we not equally need to discover the power of God in prayer, preaching and revival?'

God expects every generation to seek him for itself. For this reason, revivals rarely continue beyond one generation. Revival is God graciously giving his people all that they want—for a while. He does this for his

12 Prime, *The Power of Prayer*, p. 196. Also see here pp. 203–205 for J. C. Ryle's stirring *Call to Prayer*.

13 Fish, *Handbook of Revivals*, p. 287.

own glory and, like any good father, to show the children how much he loves them. But he cannot do it too often or for too long without weakening his people's strength for battle.

God expects every generation to seek him for itself. For this reason, revivals rarely continue beyond one generation

Nothing must be allowed to hinder our work in the 'ordinary times'. Our life of prayer, our striving for holiness, and our wholehearted evangelism must all go on as if the future of the church of Christ depended upon them. At the same time, we should long for our community to be 'saturated with God', we ought often to be talking of the great acts of God in revival, and our prayers should continually remind God that we need a 'special occasion' for this generation.

The prophet Micah could find little to encourage him in the nation. An honest assessment convinced him that the forces of evil were gaining ground. Because of this, Micah set out his own position:

'As for me, I watch in hope for the LORD,
I wait for God my Saviour;
my God will hear me'
(Micah 7:7).

List of revivals

The following are the main revivals referred to in this book. The dates given are not necessarily either the beginning or the end of the revival; often the Spirit was moving the people before this date. A specific date indicates the commencement of the main outpouring of the Spirit. The Christian church has seen very many more revivals in her history than those listed here.

Date	Location	Christian leader/preacher
1150 on	Italy and Europe	Peter Waldo and Waldensians
1381 on	England and Scotland	Wycliffe's preachers
1500 on	England, Scotland, Wales, Czechoslovakia and Holland	Jan Hus and Gerhard Groote
	Spread of Tyndale's New Testament and the Reformation	
21.6.1630	Scotland: the churchyard of Shotts in Lanarkshire	John Livingstone
13.8.1727	Germany: Herrnhut in Saxony	Ludwig von Zinzendorf
1730s–40s	America: New England, Northampton etc	Jonathan Edwards and others
1730 on	England, Wales, Scotland and America	George Whitefield, Howell Harris, Daniel Rowland, John Wesley and others
16.5.1742	Scotland: Kilsyth	James Robe and others
15.8.1742	Scotland: Cambuslang	George Whitefield and others

1742	Scotland: Baldernock	
1743	America: Susquehanna Indians	David Brainerd
1790–1840	Cornwall	Many evangelists
1791	Wales: Bala	Thomas Charles
1794	England: Sheffield	John Moon and Alexander Mather
1798	America: Connecticut and Massachusetts	
1799	Cornwall; Penzance, Zennor, Walls, St Ives	
1800	America: Kentucky	
1805	Wales: Aberystwyth	
1807	Throughout the century Primitive Methodists	Hugh Bourne, 'Billy' Clowes and many others
1812–44	America	Asahel Nettleton
1820–70	America	Charles G Finney
1814	Cornwall: Redruth, Tuckingmill	
1824–35	Scotland: Isle of Lewis	Andrew McLeod
1828	America: Savannah	Daniel Baker
1830s	England: Midlands	James Caughey
1832	America: Rhode Island	
1832	China	
23.7.1839	Scotland: Kilsyth	William Chalmers Burns

1839	Scotland: Dundee	William Chalmers Burns and Robert Murray M'Cheyne
1851–4	Cornwall: Baldhu	William Haslam
1858	America: Charleston	John Girardeau
1859–60	Wales	David Morgan and many others
	Scotland	Brownlow North and others
	Ireland	James McQuilkin and others
	England	Charles H Spurgeon and others
1863–71	Norfolk: Buckenham	Willam Haslam
1880s	America	Dwight L Moody
1903–4	Denmark	
1904–5	Wales	Rhys Bevan Jones, Evan Roberts and others
1904	South Africa	Fransch Hoek
1905	India: Assam	
1905	Australia	
1905	Norway	Hans Hauge
1905	Edinburgh	Joseph Kemp
1906	India: Dohnavur	
1906 to the present	China	
1907	Korea: Pyongyang and across the country	

1910	Malawi	
1921	Norfolk: Lowestoft and Great Yarmouth	Douglas Brown
	Scotland: East coast fishing ports	Jock Troup
	Northern Ireland	William Nicholson (WP)
1930s on	East Africa, especially Uganda	
1930s on	Kenya	
1931	Wales: Aberavon	Martyn Lloyd-Jones
1934–9	Scotland: Isle of Lewis	
1937–43	Ethiopia: Wallamo tribes	
1938	Borneo: Lun Bawang people	
1939–50	India: Madras	Bakht Singh
1949	Scotland: Isle of Lewis	Duncan Campbell
1953	Borneo	
1953	Congo (Zaire)	
1960s–70s	Indonesia	Petrus Octavianus
1960s–80s	China	
1966 to present	KwaZulu	Erlo Stegen
1970	Asbury College, America	
1970 to mid 1980s	Romania	Liviu Olah and Paul Negrut
1973	Borneo	
1988–2000	Moldova	

Book list

Of the many books used in preparation, only those referenced in the footnotes are listed here.

Armstrong, John H, *When God Moves*, Harvest House Publishers 1998

Baird & Collins, *Protestantism in Italy & the Waldenses*, 1847

Beougher and Dorsett, *Tears of Revival*, Kingsway Publications 1995. The account of revival at Wheaton College and beyond in 1995.

Bewes, Richard, *Under the Thorn Tree*, Christian Focus, 2017

Birnie, John, *'Just call me Paul'—The story of God's grace in the life of Romanian leader Paul Negrut*, Slavic Gospel Association 2014

Blair & Hunt, *The Korean Pentecost*, Banner of Truth, 1977

Bonar, *Memoirs & Remains of R. M. M'Cheyne*, Middleton, 1854

Bready, J Wesley, *England: Before and After Wesley*, Hodder and Stoughton, 1939

Brown, *Revival Addresses*, Morgan and Scott, 1922

Campbell, *The Lewis Awakening 1949–53*, Faith Mission, 1954

Carvosso, *The Life of William Carvosso*, Jennings & Pye, 2nd ed., 1835

Lambert, Tony, *China's Christian Millions*, OMF Monarch Books 1999

Clowes, William, *The Journal of William Clowes*, Tentmaker Publications 2002, orig. Hallam and Holliday 1844

Culpepper, *The Shantung Revival*, Southern Baptist Home Mission Board, 1971

Davies, Andrew, *The Moravian Revival of 1727*, Evangelical Library, 1977

Davies, Eryl, *The Beddgelert Revival*, Bryntirion Press, 2004

Davies, Raymond E, *I Will Pour Out My Spirit*, Monarch Publications 1992. Perhaps the nearest we have to listing possible revivals from the earliest post-apostolic times to the 1990s. Also a brief survey of possible revivals in the Bible

Davies, Raymond J, *Fire on the Mountains*, Zondervan, 1966

Dallimore, *George Whitefield*, 2 vols, Banner of Truth, 1970

Diesen, *The Free Church Movement*, Norway, 1957

Duewell, Wesley, *Revival Fire*, Zondervan 1995. A useful survey of some of the revivals across history.

Edwards, Brian H, *Praying for Revival*, Day One Publications, 2019

Edwards, Jonathan, *A Narrative of Surprising Conversions*, Banner of Truth, 1965

Edwards, Jonathan, *Select Works of Jonathan Edwards*, Banner of Truth

Evans, *Howell Harris Evangelist*, University of Wales Press, 1974

Evans, *The Welsh Revival of 1904*, Evangelical Press, 1969

Evans, Eifion, *When He is Come*, SMW, 1959

Fish, Henry C, *Handbook of Revivals*, Passmore and Alabaster, London, 1873

Gillies, *Historical Collections of Accounts of Revival*, Banner of Truth, 1981 (first pub. 1754)

Glasgow Revival Tract Society, *Narratives of Revivals of Religion*, William Collins, 1839

Goforth, *By My Spirit*, Marshall, Morgan and Scott, 1929

Greenfield, *Power from on High*, World Wide Revival Prayer Movement, 1950

Griffin, Stanley C, *A Forgotten Revival*, Day One Publications 1992 and 2000

Hamilton, William, *An Inquiry into the Scriptural Character of the Revival of 1859*, The Reformed Book Outlet, Michigan, 1993 (orig. 1866 Belfast)

Harris, *Extracts from the Welsh Press*, published privately

Haslam, *From Death Into Life*, Morgan & Scott

Haslam, *Yet Not I*, Morgan & Scott

Hayden, *Spurgeon on Revival*, Zondervan, 1962

Houghton, *Amy Carmichael of Dohnavur*, 1955

Hulse, Erroll, *Give Him No Rest*, Evangelical Press ,1991

Isaac, Peter, *A History of Evangelical Christianity in Cornwall*, self-published 1999

Jones, *India Awake! Thy King has Come*, Sylhet, 1905

Jones, David Ceri, *The Fire Divine*, Inter-Varsity Press, 2015. A careful 'behind the scenes' analysis of the eighteenth century revivals. Penetrating, disturbing, challenging and provocative.

Jones, Rhys Bevan (R B), *Rent Heavens*, Pioneer Mission, 1931

Jones, B. P., *The King's Champions* (self-published) 1968. A detailed critique of the best, the worst and the aftermath of the 1904 revival in Wales

Kemp, Winnie, *Joseph W. Kemp*, Marshall, Morgan & Scott, 1936

Kendall, H. B., *The Origin and History of the Primitive Methodists*, Edwin Dalton, London 1899 two vols

Kivengere, *Revolutionary Love*, CLC & Kingsway, 1985

Koch, Kurt, *God among the Zulus*, Kwa Sizibantu, Natal, 1981

Koch, Kurt, *The Revival in Indonesia*, Evangelization Publishers, 1970

Lacy, *Revivals in the Midst of the Years*, John Knox Press, 1943

Lambert, Tony, *China's Christian Millions*, Monarch Books, 1999

Lees, Shirley, *Drunk Before Dawn*, OMF, 1979

Lloyd-Jones, *The Puritans: Their Origins and Successors*, Banner of Truth 1987. Addresses delivered at the Puritan and Westminster Conferences 1959–1978

Lloyd-Jones, *Revival—Can We Make it Happen?*, Marshall Pickering, 1986

Lyall, *God Reigns in China*, Hodder & Stoughton, 1985

Macaulay, *The Burning Bush in Carloway*, Carloway Free Church, Lewis

Morod, *The Korean Revival*, Hodder & Stoughton, 1969

Murray, Iain, *Jonathan Edwards—a new biography*, Banner of Truth, 1987

Murray, Iain, *The First Forty Years*, Banner of Truth, 1982

Murray, Iain, *Revival and Revivalism—the Making and Marring of American Evangelicalism 1750–1858*, Banner of Truth, 1994

Moody-Stuart, *Brownlow North*, Banner of Truth, 1961

Monod, *The Korean Revival*, Hodder & Stoughton, 1969

Moravian Publishing Office, *The Memorial Days of the Renewed Church of the Brethren*, 1895. Originally 1821 and translated and published in English 1822.

Orr, J Edwin, *Evangelical Awakenings in Eastern Asia*, Bethany Fell Inc., 1975

Orr, J Edwin, *The Eager Feet*, Moody Press, 1975

Orr, J Edwin, *The Flaming Tongue*, Moody Press, 1973

Orr, J Edwin, *The Second Evangelical Awakening*, Marshall, Morgan & Scott, 1949

Osborn H H, *Revival—A precious heritage*, Apologia Publications, 1995

Page, *David Brainerd*, Partridge & Co (modern—Edwards, *The life of David Brainerd*, Baker, 1978)

Paisley, *The Fifty-Nine Revival*, Martyrs' Memorial Free Presbyterian Church, 1958

Phillips,Thomas, *The Welsh Revival—its Origin and Development*, The Banner of Truth Trust 1989. First pub.1860. If a reader has time for only one book on the Welsh revival of 1859, this is the book to read.

Peckham, Colin & Mary, *Sounds from Heaven*, Christian Focus, 2003. One of the most heart-warming books on revival and written by those personally involved in the revival in the Western Isles of Scotland 1949 to 1953

Prime, Samuel, *The Power of Prayer—The New York Revival of 1858*, The Banner of Truth Trust (1991). Orig.1859.

Rajamani, R R & Kinnear, Angus, *Monsoon Daybreak*, Open Books, 1971

Ritchie, *Floods Upon the Dry Ground*, 1980(?)

Robe, *When the Wind Blows*, Ambassador Productions Ltd, 1985

Roberts, Richard Owen (ed), *Scotland Saw His Glory—A History of Revivals in Scotland*, Internationally Awakening Press, Wheaton 1995

Rosell, Garth and others, *The Memoirs of Charles G Finney*, Zondervan 1989

Sprague, *Lectures on Revivals of Religion*, Banner of Truth, 1959 (first pub. 1832)

Spurgeon, C H, *Sermons on Revival*, Kelvedon ed.

Spurgeon, C H, *Revival Year Sermons*, Banner of Truth, 1959

Stegen, Erlo, *Revival among the Zulus*, Kwa Sizibantu, Natal, 1998

Telford, John (ed), *The letters of the Rev. John Wesley, A.M.* vol. 1.The Epworth Press, London, 1931.

Thornbury, *God Sent Revival*, Evangelical Press, 1977

Told, Silas, *The Life of Silas Told*, Epworth, 1954

Visser, Theo, *Revival and Conviction of Sin*, Christian Liberty Books, 2014. Sub. A quest for God's working in times of spiritual awakening

Wallis, *In the Day of Thy Power*, CLC, 1956

Wesley, *Journal*

Westminster Conference, *Preaching & Revival*, 1984

Whitefield, George, *Whitefield's Journals*, Banner of Truth Trust, 1960

Williams, William, *The Experience Meeting*, Evangelical Press, 1973. Trans. Bethan Lloyd-Jones

Wise, Maureen, *Celestial Fire*, Bryntirion Press, 2018

Woolsey, *Duncan Campbell*, Hodder & Stoughton, 1974

Index—People

Index—Places and events

Index—Scripture

Praying for Revival

Brian H Edwards

200pp | ISBN 978-1-84625-647-9
REF REVPRAY6479 | £8.00

The present volume has answered the question: What is 'revival' in the history of the Christian church and how can we distinguish a genuine work of God's Spirit from the false claims that often distract us? The hallmarks of God's special occasions across the centuries and across the continents have been gathered together to present a thrilling account of God's great work in spiritual revival.

However, some questions remain:

- Is revival an experience taught throughout the Bible?
- If it is, can we confidently expect revival at any time?
- Will there be a final great revival of gospel success before Jesus returns?
- What hinders our prayer for revival?
- How can we maintain effective prayer for revival?

These are some of the issues discussed in the twin volume *Praying for Revival*. It steers us through the minefield of misunderstanding and provides a theological framework to support praying for revival.

Grace—amazing grace

Brian H Edwards

304pp | ISBN 978-1-84625-336-2
REF GRACE | £9.00

'Grace is the most beautiful word in our language and the supreme description of God.' With these opening words the author introduces his theme, and in seventeen chapters portrays the grace of God in its vast array. In a popular and penetrating style, the author compels us forward with theology for the heart. This book is firmly theological, warmly devotional and incisively practical.

Brian Edwards questions the commonly accepted positions in 'forgiving grace', provides a robust chapter on 'universal grace' and a moving chapter on 'incarnate grace'. In particular his approach to 'ultimate grace' is an intriguing and fitting conclusion to the whole subject. The questions at the close of each chapter make this an excellent book for small group discussion.

'As Brian Edwards tells us, "Grace encompasses all the great truths of Christianity, for without grace they would have no meaning." He then guides us on a delightful tour that takes us from God's common grace for all mankind to the ultimate grace of heaven for God's people. I have never read anything better on the subject than this superb and sure-footed treatment.'

DR JOHN BLANCHARD, *evangelist, author and Christian apologist*

BIBLE

THE BIBLE
Book 1:
can we trust it?
BRIAN H EDWARDS
THE BIBLE
Book 2:
big claims from a unique book
BRIAN H EDWARDS
THE BIBLE
Book 3:
have we got the right books?
BRIAN H EDWARDS
THE BIBLE
Book 4:
a journey from then to now
BRIAN H EDWARDS
THE BIBLE
Book 5:
sense as well as faith
BRIAN H EDWARDS
THE BIBLE
Book 6:
enjoy your Bible!
BRIAN H EDWARDS

EVIDENCE for the BIBLE

Clive Anderson and
Brian Edwards

LARGE FORMAT HARDBACK
FULL COLOUR THROUGHOUT
225mm × 275mm
260pp | ISBN 978-1-84625-416-1
REF EFB4161 | £25.00

Evidence will surprise and inform you as you turn over the soil of history with the pages of your Bible. The witness of the trowel authenticates and illuminates the people and events, lifting them from the pages of the Book and setting them in the context of time and place. Join us on an exciting journey with this evidence from the past.

Evidence for the Bible can be found in many places, from the Ancient Near East to museums and private collections. Whilst artefacts can never prove the authority of the Bible, they can and do show that the events described in the Bible occurred in time and history.

This book provides a selection of the many items that demonstrate the reliability of the Bible as a historical document.

'Clive Anderson and Brian Edwards have captured the essence of generations of middle-eastern archaeology, historical context and biblical landscape in a quite remarkable way. Their book is accessible, informative and enjoyable. The pictures beautifully complement the text. The Bible comes alive. I warmly and wholeheartedly commend it to everyone who wishes to be a little wiser and better informed about the Book which has formed our culture and is the source of the Christian Faith.'

THE VERY REVD JAMES ATWELL,
Dean of Winchester.

'This is a marvellous introduction to the finds of archaeology that illumine our understanding of the Bible. It helps the reader to see that the biblical events and writings took place within history. When the reader studies the Bible, this book will serve as a wonderful tool to help get at its depth and richness. I highly recommend it.'

DR JOHN D CURRID
Carl McMurray Professor of Old Testament at the Reformed Theological Seminary, Charlotte, USA.

Through the British Museum with the Bible

Clive Anderson and Brian Edwards

FULL COLOUR TRAVEL GUIDE
128pp | ISBN 978-1-90308-754-6
REF TWBM | £10.00

This guide centres on those items in the British Museum that are related to the history recorded in the Bible. You will be introduced to rulers, empires and cultures that, without the careful work of many scholars, would have been lost for ever. In this guide you have all that you need to make your tour both enjoyable and relevant. The past is brought to light in front of you.

'The British Museum is a great storehouse of treasures from the past; the Bible is the greatest treasure of all. This guide brings them together in a concise way that will help readers to understand more clearly what each has to offer.'

—ALAN MILLARD, *Rankin Professor Emeritus of Hebrew and Ancient Semitic Languages, The University of Liverpool. Formerly Assistant Keeper of Western Asiatic Antiquities at the British Museum.*

'I am delighted that this fine guide is available in a second and fully revised edition. The British Museum is unique worldwide for its collection of antiquities which illustrate Bible times and customs and this guide enables anyone, either alone or with a group, to identify them accurately. It is both reliable and easy to use.'

—DONALD J. WISEMAN, *Professor Emeritus of Assyriology in the University of London, formerly Assistant Keeper in the Egyptian and Western Asiatic Antiquities at the British Museum and President of the British School of Archaeology in Iraq.*

Footsteps of the past: The Old Testament in the British Museum

Kings, pharaohs and bandits

Brian Edwards and Clive Anderson

A4 | 32pp | ISBN 978-1-84625-035-4
REF FPBMOT358 | £3.00

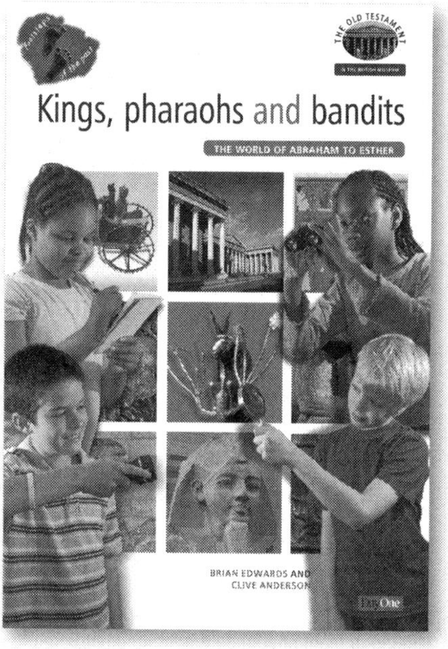

Treasure that is not jewels, bandits' gold, mysterious writing and dead bodies all wrapped up helps us to understand the world of the Old Testament. Here you can see the fantastic Pharaohs, the horrible pictures of the Assyrians, the elegant drinking vessels of the Persians, and the son of a king who conquered the world. With puzzles to solve, pictures to colour and items to find, this book will give you an understanding about a world that has passed but is living in front of your face!

'This book is a good twin to *Romans, Gladiators and Games*, by the same authors. It covers many Bible stories children will know well and points out where artifices mentioned in the Bible can be found in the Museum. It shows how to do hieroglyphics and how bodies were mummified in Egypt—little boys will love that bit. There are plenty of things to do and make at home as well as at the Museum, where there are many things to look for. At home you can make a model of a mummy and turn a box into a coffin to put it in to, among many other things. Included is a recipe for a Middle Eastern drink which looks tasty. I think that there is plenty in this book which would deepen the children's knowledge of Bible events and also keep them happily engaged for hours with the activities and crafts.'

BARBARA STONEHAM, *GoodBookStall Review*

Footsteps of the past: The New Testament in the British Museum

Romans, gladiators and games

Brian Edwards and Clive Anderson

A4 | 32pp | ISBN 978-1-84625-036-1
REF FPBMNT366 | £3.00

Gladiators fighting to the death, cruel emperors who control the lives of millions and marbles you cannot roll—all waiting for you to discover. Step into the exciting world of the first century, see how people lived, worked, played and died. Into this world a new religion was born. See what marks the Christian faith left on the lives of people, and wonder at the change it made to history. Colour in a centurion, find out the size of Diana, discover the lights that people used in the evenings and many more fascinating activities.

'This is a really interesting book. It is a guide book and also an activity book for children, which covers aspects of life in Ancient Rome, from gladiatorial battles to games the children played. It is a companion book to the adult version travel guide *Through the British Museum with the Bible*. It takes children around the various rooms at the Museum showing specific items of interest that children may like such as masks, swords etc. It also explains how some of our words came into being. It is especially good at including lots of activities for children such as how to make a copy of a mask that is in the Museum. But above all, it does this showing where in the Bible these things are mentioned and how the people of Jesus' time would have understood the use of the illustrations, for example lamps or swords. I think most children would learn a lot from the book yet most importantly enjoy while learning.'

BARBARA STONEHAM, *GoodBookStall Review*

Travel with William Tyndale

England's greatest Bible translator

Brian H Edwards

FULL COLOUR TRAVEL GUIDE
128pp | ISBN 978-1-84625-160-3
REF TWWT1603 | £10.00

Melvyn Bragg in 'The Adventure of English' claims that William Tyndale wrote 'the most influential book there has ever been in the history of language, English or any other.' That is not too extravagant to describe the significance of Tyndale's translation into English of the whole of the New Testament and much of the Old from the original Greek and Hebrew. Tyndale is undoubtedly one of the greatest Englishmen ever, and all who speak this language owe him a great debt.

'This is a guide not only to Tyndale's places in England and on the continent, but also to his time, his ideas and his spirit. It is based on meticulous research and profound scholarly insight, whilst remaining very readable and entertaining.'
GUIDO LATRÉ, *University of Louvain*

John Newton
Through many dangers

Brian H Edwards

COLOUR ILLUSTRATIONS THROUGHOUT

256pp | ISBN 978-1-84625-173-3
REF JN6103 | £12.00

Rejecting his mother's Christian faith, John became a reckless, blasphemous sailor and an evangelist for unbelief. Press-ganged onto a man-of-war, he faced death in naval battle, was flogged for deserting his ship, and eventually enslaved and starved in Africa. All because of his passion for 'Polly'—a girl beyond his reach.

Later, as a slave-ship captain, John's life was threatened by mutinous crews, callous traders, desperate slaves, Barbary pirates, tropical diseases and violent storms.

John's encounter with God in an Atlantic storm transformed him to become the caring Christian pastor of the most influential church in the country. Among his congregation, he could number a Lord Mayor, prominent politicians, wealthy bankers, a national poet, a leading playwright and hundreds of the labouring poor.

John's unfading love for his wife, his wise counsel, his hymns and correspondence and his fight against the slave-trade, influenced the lives of thousands in his day. More than two hundred years after his death his letters and example are as valuable as ever.

In this new and fully illustrated edition, the life of John Newton is seen against the colourful and cruel backcloth of the eighteenth-century.

The Ten Commandments
for today

Brian H Edwards

288pp | ISBN 978-1-90308-733-6
REF 10T | £9.00

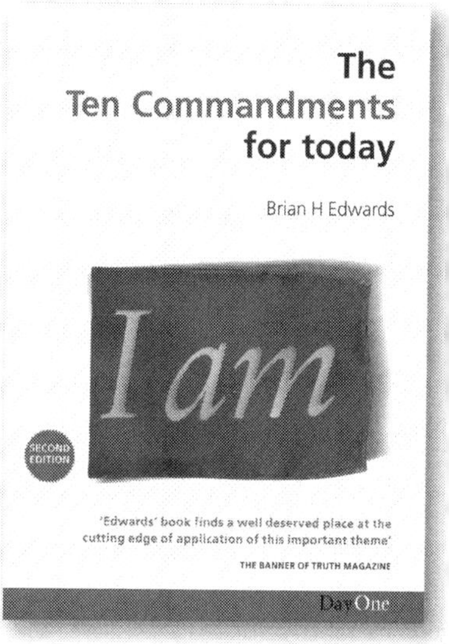

At a time when the nation's morality is in alarming decline, it is surprising that so little has been written on the Ten Commandments. This modern commentary carefully uncovers their true meaning and incisively applies them to our contemporary society. Probably never in the history of western civilisation have the Ten Commandments been more neglected and therefore more relevant than today.

This book is a superbly written modern commentary on God's changeless laws in today's changing and godless society.

'This book unpacks the crammed meaning of these terse commands, and applies them pointedly to life in a deregulated age.'

ANDREW ANDERSON

'This is a highly readable treatment of a vital subject and can be gratefully recommended."

EVANGELICAL TIMES

'Seldom have I appreciated a book more than this one…'

THE GOSPEL MAGAZINE

THE CELTIC SOURCES FOR THE ARTHURIAN LEGEND

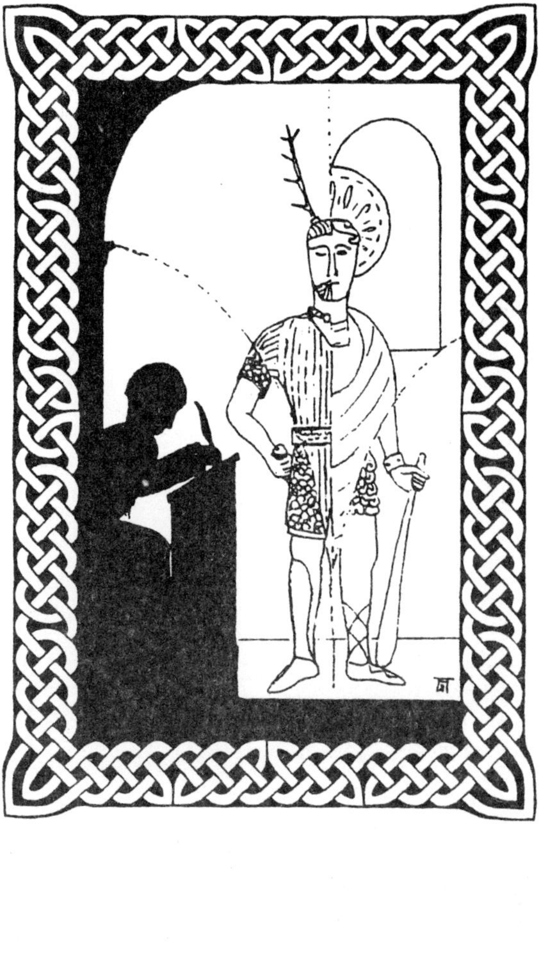

THE CELTIC SOURCES FOR THE ARTHURIAN LEGEND

JON B. COE
and
SIMON YOUNG

with drawings by
Lawrie Robertson

LLANERCH PUBLISHERS, FELINFACH.
ISBN 1 897853 83 1

Acknowledgements

The people who happily gave up their time to help us: Derek Bry
of Llanerch; Dr. David Dumville, Dr. Oliver Padel, Dr. Erich Popp
and Dr. Neil Wright of Cambridge University; Philip Round; Ar
Young; Jeremy Humphries; Rose Humphries; Stephen Lees; Edu Pri
(for the use of his room as well as his brain); UWP and (especiall
Rachel Bromwich for her generosity regarding the use of her wor

J.C. *S.Y.*

Preface

The popular image of King Arthur as a successful Dark Age leader of the British, fighting and — at least for a time — beating back the fifth and sixth-century Germanic invaders has proved a very resonant one. It has survived into the modern age with no sign of the energy behind it abating. The image as we have it, however, owes its existence not so much to the Celtic roots of the legend but to an obscure Anglo-French clerk, Geoffrey of Monmouth, who wrote his *Historia Regum Britanniae* or the *History of the Kings of Britain* in the year 1136. This Latin prose-epic, one of the most popular works of the high middle-ages and one which is still held in high esteem today, is absolutely crucial to our understanding of the Arthurian legend. Such was its success that earlier material was often obscured under the lengthening shadow of Geoffrey's masterpiece. Because of the incomplete record of writing prior to Geoffrey's *Historia,* it is very difficult to determine Geoffrey's relationship to this earlier material. He claimed to be very much a part of an existing tradition, indeed its mediator, for if we believe Geoffrey's words in the following extract he is merely a translator.

Whenever I have found myself speculating about the history of the kings of Britain, at these times when I have been thinking over a great many such things in my mind, it has seemed strange to me that apart from the comments which Bede and Gildas have each made in their wonderful books on the subject, I have not been able to find out anything about these kings who lived here before the Incarnation of Christ, or even about Arthur and all those who followed on after the Incarnation; yet their acts were such that they deserved to be celebrated for all time. And indeed these deeds were handed down happily in oral lore, so that they might as well have been committed to writing by a great number of folk who had only their memories to trust. At a moment when I was giving a great deal of thought to such things, Walter Archdeacon of Oxford, a man gifted in the skill of oratory and knowledgeable about the histories of foreign lands, entrusted me with a certain very old book written in the British language. This book which fortuitously set out to make a sequential and ordered history, gave all the acts of these men from Brutus the first king of the Britons down to Cadwaller the son of Cadwallo. At Walter's entreaty I have laboured to translate the book into Latin, although to be sure I have been happy with my own humble expressions and have taken no tawdry flowers of speech from other people's gardens. If perhaps I had decorated my page with contrived rhetorical devices I would have bored my readers, and they would have had to take more time to find the meaning of my language than in the story which follows.

Geoffrey's self-portrayal as a translator has generally been discarded by modern scholarship and it may be significant that many of Geoffrey's contemporaries condemned him as a liar. But Arthur was certainly not Geoffrey's creation; we have a considerable amount of evidence for his legend existing before 1136, and not just in Celtic Britain, Arthur's homeland, but even in continental Europe.

This book is primarily concerned with those works which present the evidence for the Arthurian legend among the Celtic peoples prior to Geoffrey, or at least (with texts later than 1136) independent of any obvious continental or Galfridian (that is, of Geoffrey's writings) influence. It is, as such, fairly complete. Material for this subject is not especially voluminous and the following sections are often just extracts, taken out of larger works which would need to be fully-digested prior to any in-depth study of Arthur. It is hoped that the most important records, tales and poems have been provided for the reader, and that the book can act as a resource for further study. There are a handful of works, listed in the appendix, which are not included in this book for reasons of space, Galfridian influence and copyright restrictions.

The study of Arthur has tended, in recent years, to move more and more towards an interest in Arthur's literary and ideological roles, and away from the search for an 'historical' character, which for all the academic pyrotechnics has tended to be a fairly barren quest. It has been the aim of this book to facilitate this kind of study by bringing the Celtic sources together.

***

The book has three sections: Latin, Welsh and Irish. Each item has a short introduction, text, facing translation, and limited bibliography. In the introduction the title is — if not English — given in translation. Much of the detailed material can only be found in periodicals which are often difficult to obtain; for this reason a general bibliography of some of the most useful (and more easily obtainable) books and articles treating the topic generally is given overleaf. Wherever possible we have used manuscript facsimiles to produce our texts, but in the cases when this has proved impossible an earlier edition has been used. Interested readers are referred to relevant books in the short-form bibliography for each section; full bibliographical details can be found in the main bibliography at the back of the book.

Names will not always correspond to the familiar romance appellations; Cai, Bedwyr, Gwenhwyfar and Drystan may be more familiar as Sir Kay, Sir Bedivere, Guinevere and Tristan respectively.

***

General Bibliography:

Barber, Richard *The Figure of Arthur*

Bromwich, Rachel 'Concepts of Arthur'

Arthur of the Welsh edd. Bromwich, Jarman & Roberts (Cardiff 1991

Chambers, E.K. *Arthur of Britain: the Story of King Arthur in History and Legend*

Dumville, David *Histories and Pseudo-Histories* [a collection of hi essays]

Jackson, Kenneth H. 'The Arthur of History'

Jones, Thomas 'The Early Evolution of the Legend of Arthur'

Loomis, Roger Sherman *Wales and the Arthurian Legend* [a collection of his essays]

Moorman, Charles 'Yet some men say...that kynge Arthure ys na ded.' [useful for a general account of the mutability of the Arthurian legend in later years]

Padel, Oliver 'The Nature of Arthur'

Contents

Gildas: De Excidio Britanniae

The *Ruin of Britain* is a tripartite pamphlet aimed at the moral reform of the British people and is almost certainly datable to the sixth century. Gildas, its author, blames present troubles and disasters, most particularly the Germanic invasions, on the sins of his compatriots, comparing them with, among others, the children of Israel. The extract below can be found in the first book at the end of a brief re-collection of British history which begins the work. Even here, where Gildas is describing events in a manner we would usually term historical and chronological it is uncertain how much his account of the recent centuries can be relied upon: first because we cannot be sure of the extent to which the text has been manipulated for the purpose of moral instruction; and second because of his lack of sure knowledge about the recent past. Yet the fact that Gildas is our only source for one of the darkest periods of the dark ages means historians have been tempted to take a great deal on trust.

The *Ruin of Britain* is unique in our collection in that it never mentions Arthur. The fact it is nearly contemporary with, and describes the period when Arthur was thought to have lived by Welsh scholars in the ninth century, means that those who favour an historical Arthur on a par with later legend have to explain his absence. It is particularly notable that Gildas does describe Badon, a battle later associated with Arthur, though arguably here linked to one Ambrosius. Gildas' description of British history prior to Ambrosius contains several identifiable fallacies (for example the dates of the Roman Walls) and it is questionable to what extent even the Badon material can be trusted although it is only forty years distant from the time of writing. As E.A. Thompson notes, 'the most frightening feature in the picture drawn by Gildas is not the destruction of city-life in Britain or the break-up of the Imperial system with its guarantee of peaceful life, but rather the destruction of knowledge itself. Knowledge of the outside world and knowledge of the past had been wiped out of men's minds.'

***

Bibliography:

Higham, N.J. *The English Conquest*
Lapidge, M. and D.N. Dumville *Gildas: New Approaches*
Padel, Oliver 'The Nature of Arthur', pp.16—19
Thompson, E.A. *St. Germanus of Auxerre*
Williams, H. *Gildae De Excido Britanniae*
Winterbottom, Michael *Gildas: The Ruin of Britain*

Itaque nonnulli miserarum reliquiarum in montibus deprehensi aceruatim iugulabantur. Alii fame confecti accedentes manus hostibus dabant in aeuum seruituri, si tamen non continuo trucidarentur, quod altissimae gratiae stabat loco. Alii transmarinas petebant regiones, cum ululatu magno ceu celeumatis uice hoc modo sub uelorum sinibus cantantes, dedisti nos tamquam oues escarum et in gentibus dispersisti nos. Alii montanis collibus minacibus praeruptis uallatis et densissimis saltibus marinisque rupibus uitam suspecta semper mente credentes in patria licet trepidi perstabant.

Tempore igitur interueniente aliquanto cum recessissent domum crudelissimi praedones, roborante Deo reliquiae, quibus confugiunt undique de diuersis locis miserrimi ciues tam auide quam apes aluearii procella imminente, simul deprecantes eum toto corde et, ut dicitur, innumeris onerantes aethera uotis, ne ad internicionem usque delerentur, duce Ambrosio Aureliano uiro modesto, qui solus forte Romanae gentis tantae tempestatis collisione occisis in eadem parentibus purpura nimirum indutis superfuerat, cuius nunc temporibus nostris suboles magnopere auita bonitate degenerauit, uires capessunt, uictores prouocantes ad proelium, quis uictoria domino annuente cessit. Ex eo tempore nunc ciues, nunc hostes, uincebant, ut in ista gente experiretur dominus solito more praesentem Israelem, utrum diligat eum an non; usque ad annum obsessionis Badonici montis, nouissimaeque ferme de furciferis non minimae stragis, quique quadragesimus quartus, ut noui, orditur annus, mense iam uno emenso, qui et meae natiuitatis est.

And so a number of forlorn survivors were caught in the mountains, crowded together and slain. Others, having been worn out by hunger, came and surrendered themselves to the enemy to be slaves forever; if that is they were not killed straight away — which stood in the place of the highest blessing. Others made for lands over the seas; under the folds of sails they loudly wailed singing a psalm in the place of a shanty: 'You have given us like sheep for the eating and scattered us among the heathen.' [Psalms xliv, 11] Others held out in their own land, — though not free of fear — with constant apprehension, trusting their lives to the high hills, precipitous, menacing and barricaded; to the densest forests, and to the cliffs of the sea coast.

After a time, when the cruel raiders returned to their home, God strengthened the survivors. Distraught citizens fled to them from different locations, as avidly as bees to the beehive when a storm is overhanging, and with all their hearts implored, 'burdening heaven with unnumbered prayers,' [Aeneid ix, 24] that they might not be destroyed to the point of extermination. Their leader was a gentleman, Ambrosius Aurelianus, who perhaps alone of the Romans had survived the impact of such a tempest; truly his parents, who had worn the purple, were overcome in it. In our times his stock have degenerated greatly from their excellent grandfather. With him our people regained their strength, challenged the victors to battle and with the lord acceding the victory fell to us. From then on now our citizens, and then the enemies conquered; so on this people, as the Lord is accustomed, he could make trial of his latter day Israel to see whether it loves him or not. This lasted up until the year of the siege of Badon Hill, almost the most recent defeat of the malefactors and certainly not the least. That was the year of my birth; and as I know since then forty-four years and one month have already passed.

Historia Brittonum

The *History of the Britons,* at one time attributed to Nennius, can be dated to 829-30. It is a typical synchronic history of the sort widely found in medieval Ireland. This type of record collects and then fuses different sources for its own political ends which, in the case of the *History of the Britons,* remain unfortunately obscure. As it is, with the *Annales Cambriae,* the earliest surviving British record since Gildas to include 'historical' information, the question of how far we can trust it historically is an especially pointed one. Most recent scholarship has tended to be pessimistic about its claim to accurately record the centuries prior to its own, seeing it instead as an invaluable source for the ninth century when it was written.

There are two pieces of strangely contrasting Arthurian material in the history. The first is a pseudo-historical account of a suspiciously formulaic list of twelve battles against the Germanic invaders. The rhyming of Celidon, Badon, Guinnion may mean there is an Old Welsh poem behind the Latin. The second is an account of various miraculous locations in and around south Wales, including the hot waters at Bath. 'The soldier Arthur' would seem to be a reference to the 'leader of battles' found in the aforementioned list, though it is just possible that the epithet points to more than one Arthur in early Welsh tradition. Interestingly the reference to a 'soldier Arthur' can also be found in a Scottish text of 1120 (i.e. pre-Geoffrey's history) written by Lambert of St. Omer: 'est palatium in Brittania in terra Pictorum Arturi militis, arte mirabili et uarietate fundatum in quo factorum bellorumque eius omnium gesta sculpta uidentur.' ['There is a palace of Arthur the soldier, in Britain, in the land of Picts, built with various and wondrous art, in which the deeds of all his acts and wars are seen to be sculpted.']

The Sawley Glosses, are marginal additions to the *History* taken from a late twelfth or early thirteenth-century manuscript. Although written in north Yorkshire, the author seems to have been someone who had an understanding of Welsh, and they probably represent different traditions (or learned fabrications?) of an Arthur who was by that time famous throughout Europe.

***

Bibliography:

Dumville, David N. 'The Liber Floridus of Lambert of Saint-Omer and the *Historia Brittonum*'

— 'Celtic-Latin texts in northern England, c.1150—c.1250' [for the Sawley Glosses]

— 'The Historical Value of the *Historia Brittonum*'

— '*Historia Brittonum*: an Insular history from the Carolingian Age'

Mommsen, Theodore *Monumenta Germanica Historica*, pp.199—201 & 217—18

Morris, John *Nennius*

Charles-Edwards, Thomas 'The Arthur of History'

In illo tempore Saxones inualescebant in multitudine et crescebant in Brittannia. Mortuo autem Hengisto, Octha filius eius, transiuit de sinistrali parte Brittanniae ad regnum Cantorum et de ipso orti sunt reges Cantorum. Tunc Arthur pugnabat contra illos in illis diebus cum regibus Brittonum sed ipse dux erat bellorum. Primum bellum fuit in ostium fluminis quod dicitur Glein. Secundum et tertium et quartum et quintum super aliud flumen quod ducitur Dubglas et est in regione Linnius. Sextum bellum super flumen quod uocatur Bassas. Septimum fuit bellum in silua Celidonis, id est Cat Coit Celidon. Octauum fuit bellum in castello Guinnion in quo Arthur portauit imaginem sanctae Mariae perpetuae uirginis super humeros suos et pagani uersi sunt in fugam in illo die caedes magna fuit super illos per uirtutem Domini nostri Jesu Christi et per uirtutem sanctae Mariae uirginis genetricis eius. Nonum bellum gestum est in urbe Legionis. Decimum gessit bellum in litore fluminis quod uocatur Tribruit. Undecimum factum est bellum in monte qui dicitur Agned. Duodecimum fuit bellum in monte Badonis in quo corruerunt in uno die nongenti sexaginta uiri de uno impetu Arthur, et nemo prostauit eos nisi ipse solus. Et in omnibus bellis uictor extitit. Et ipsi, dum in omnibus bellis prosternebantur, auxilium a Germania petebant et augebantur multipliciter sine intermissione et reges a Germania deducebant, ut regnarent super illos in Brittannia usque ad tempus quo Ida regnauit, qui fuit Eobba filius; ipse fuit primus rex in Beornica.

***

In that time the Saxons increased in numbers and grew strong in Britain. With the death of Hengest, Octha his son came from the northern part of Britain to the kingdom of Kentish, and from this one arose the kings of Kent. At that time Arthur fought against them with the kings of the Britons, for he was the leader of battles. The first battle was in the east at the river that is called Glein. The second, the third, the fourth and the fifth were by another river called Dubglas in the region of Linnius. The sixth battle was by the river that is named Bassas. The seventh battle was in the wood of Caledonia, that is Cat Coit Celidon. The eighth battle was in the stronghold of Guinnion, in which Arthur carried the image of holy Mary, the eternal virgin upon his shoulders and the pagans were turned around into a rout, and there was a great slaughter of them through the might of our Lord Jesus Christ and through the might of holy Mary, the virgin and his mother. The ninth battle was fought in the City of the Legion. He fought the tenth battle on the bank of the river which is called Tribruit. The eleventh battle was made on the mount that is called Agned. The twelfth battle was on Mount Badon, in which nine hundred and sixty men fell from one rally of Arthur's; and no-one brought them low except he; and he showed himself victor in all his battles. When they were laid low in all the battles, they sought reinforcements from Germany, and augmented themselves considerably without respite, and they brought kings from Germany so that they might reign over them in Britain up to the time when Ida reigned, who was the son of Eobba. That one was the first king in Bernicia.

***

Est aliud mirabile in regione quae dicitur Buelt. Est ibi cumulus lapidum et unus lapis superpositus super congestum cum uestigio canis in eo. Quando uenatus est porcum Troynt, impressit Cabal, qui erat canis Arthuri militis, uestigium in lapide et Arthur postea congregauit congestum lapidum sub lapide in quo erat uestigium canis sui et uocatur Carn Cabal. Et ueniunt homines et tollunt lapidem in manibus suis per spatium diei et noctis, et in crastino die inuenitur super congestum suum.

Est aliud miraculum in regione quae uocatur Ercing. Habetur ibi sepulcrum iuxta fontem qui cognominatur Licat Amr; et uiri nomen qui sepultus est in tumulo, sic uocabatur Amr, filius Arthuri militis erat et ipse occidit eum ibidem et sepeliuit. Et ueniunt homines ad mensurandum tumulum in longitudine aliquando sex pedes, aliquando nouem, aliquando duodecim, aliquando quindecim; in qua mensura metieris eum in ista uice, iterum non inuenies eum in una mensura et ego solus probaui.

***

The Sawley Glosses:

A: Mabutur id est filius horribilis quoniam a pueritia sua crudelis fuit. Artur latine translatum sonat ursum horribilem, uel malleum ferreum quo confringuntur mole leonum.

B: Nam Artur Ierosolimam perrexit. Et ibi crucem ad quantitatem salutifere crucis fecit; et ibi consecreta est. Et per tres continuos dies ieiunauit et uigilauit et orauit coram cruce dominica, ut ei Dominus uictoriam daret per hoc signum de paganis; quod et factum est. Atque secum imaginem sancte Marie detulit, cuius fracture adhuc apud Wedal seruantur in magna ueneratione.

There is another wonder in the region which is called Buellt. There is a mass of stones and one stone, placed on the top of the pile with the footprint of a dog on it. When Cabal, who was the dog of the soldier Arthur, hunted the pig Troynt, he pressed his footprint into a stone, after which Arthur gathered a pile of stones underneath the stone on which was the footprint of the dog, and it was called Carn Cabal. And men come, and carry the stone in their hands for a space of a day and a night, and on the next day the stone is found on the pile.

There is another wonder in the region which is called Erging. A grave is there next to a spring which is called Llygad Amr, and the name of the man who is buried there is Amr the son of Arthur the soldier, and this same one killed him and buried him there. And men come to measure the tomb and it is sometimes six feet long and sometimes nine feet, sometimes twelve, sometimes fifteen. At whatever length you measure it at one time, you will not find it again at the same length and I myself have tested this.

***

'Mab Utur' [i.e. 'son of Uthr'] that is 'son of the horrible' since from his youth he was cruel. 'Arthur' translated into Latin means 'horrible bear' or 'iron hammer' with which the jaws of lions were broken.

Then Arthur went to Jerusalem. And there he made a cross in the same dimensions as the Blessed Cross. And there it was consecrated. And for the space of three continuous days he fasted and kept vigil and prayed in the presence of the Lordly Cross, so that the Lord granted a victory to him over the pagans through this token, and that was done. And he himself carried the image of Holy Mary, the pieces of which were thus saved in great veneration at Wedale.

Annales Cambriae

The *Annals of Wales* is the oldest surviving chronicle of Welsh affairs. There are three recensions — A, B and C, of which the A text (that edited and translated here) is certainly the earliest. 'A' exists as an insertion into a manuscript of the *Historia Brittonum* (Brit. Mus. Harl. 3859), and must have been written soon after the date of its last annal, 954. The other two recensions belong to the thirteenth century, but all three are generally in agreement up to 954. Kenneth Jackson described the *Annals of Wales* as 'a sober historical document using good sources, not an annalized fiction'; however, he warns that some of the traditions drawn upon by the annalist were already only semi-historical, and, though closely connected with it, were already divergent from the material of the *Historia*.

***

Bibliography:

Charles-Edwards, Thomas 'The Arthur of History' pp.25—28
Hughes, K. 'The *Annales Cambriae* and Related Texts'
Jackson, Kenneth H. 'The Arthur of History' pp.4—5
Padel, Oliver 'The Nature of Arthur' p.15
Williams, John ab Ithel *Annales Cambriæ*

516. Bellum Badonis, in quo Arthur portavit crucem Domini nostri Jesu Christi tribus diebus et tribus noctibus in humeros suos, et Britones victores fuerunt.

The Battle of Badon, in which Arthur bore the Cross of our Lord Jesus Christ for three days and for three nights on his shoulders, and the Britons were the victors.

537. Gueith Camlann, in qua Arthur et Medraut corruere; et mortalitas in Brittania et in Hibernia fuit.

The Battle of Camlan, in which Arthur and Medrod fell; and there was death in Britain and in Ireland.

Note: One of the later manuscripts reads instead for the 537 annal: 'Bellum Camlan, in quo inclitus Arthurus rex Britonum et Modredus proditor suus, mutuis vulneribus corruerunt' ['the Battle of Camlan, in which the famous Arthur, king of the Britons, and Modred, his betrayer, fell by each other's wounds.']

Hagiography

Welsh and Breton saints' lives include several references to Arthur, collated below. Celtic hagiography has long been famous for its unusual perspective and especial interest in validating the ownership of church properties. Many lives resemble collections of title-deeds rather than holy biography and several of the stories below have an obvious 'agenda' often revealed when Arthur is said to have given land or privileges to a saint who in hagiographical terms represents a monastic grouping of some sort; St. Teilo, for example, was associated in tradition with the church of Llandaff and his life was used to validate their political claims. In the extracts below the references to property and asylum rights powerfully remind us of the way clerical needs can permeate secular tradition.

The (probable) pre-*Historia Regum Britanniae* dating (i.e. pre-1136) and their unusual perspective — tyrant Arthur etc. — makes these lives important studies of early Arthurian tradition. Whether as Brynley Roberts has suggested, 'the negative portrayal of Arthur may have been made easier if there existed an anti-heroic, or unfavourable, tradition of Arthur's character which clerical authors could use,' or, on the other hand, Arthur's villainy is simply an ecclesiastical inversion of heroic tradition, remains the central question arising from these texts. Compared with Maelgwn Gwynedd — another victim of hagiographical rebuke who is portrayed as an evil character — Arthur's wrong-doings are not irredeemable or truly malicious so Oliver Padel can note that Arthur is 'unruly or unpredictable, but open to negotiation,' while in the life of St. Illtud he is simply a 'celebrity' for the young saint to meet.

***

Bibliography:

De la Borderie, A. 'L'*Historia Britannica* avant Geoffroi de Monmouth et la vie inédite de S. Goueznou'
De la Borderie, A. 'St. Efflam. Texte inédit de la vie ancienne de ce saint'
Henken, Elissa R. *Traditions of the Welsh Saints*, pp. 301—306
Padel, Oliver 'The Nature of Arthur', pp.6—8
Roberts, Brynley F. '*Culhwch ac Olwen*, The Triads, Saints' Lives'
Wade-Evans, A.W. *Vitae Sanctorum Britanniae et Genealogiae*
Williams, Hugh *Two Lives of Gildas*

Uita Paterni:

Cum hec aguntur, celestis nuntius ad sanctum Dauid in Rosina Ualle Christo Deo seruientem uenit et ait illi, 'Surge et uade in Ierusalem, ut ibi ordineris. Adde tibi duos condignos comites, qui pariter ordinentur, id est, Paternum et Teliau.' Mox Dauid ad illos misit. Illi nec mora uenerunt. Perrexerunt pariter trans barbaras gentes, gratiam linguarum accipientes, nam essent uiri unius lingue unumquemque hominem propria lingua, in qua natus fuerat, alloquebantur. Peruenerunt tandem adusque Ierusalem. Ibique predicant nobilissima post apostolos predicatione. Postea per impositionem manus patriarche episcopi ordinati sunt illi tres sancti. Inde muneribus ditati sunt. Paternus quidem duplici munere ditatus est, baculo uidelicet, et tunica ex toto contexta. Reuersi sunt feliciter. Diuiserunt Brittaniam in tres episcopatus suos nisi postea malicia tirannorum turbaret.

Cum autem Paternus esset in ecclesia requiescens post tantum laborem marinam, deambulabat quidam tirannus regiones altrinsecus, Arthur nomine, qui quadam die uenit ad cellam sancti Paterni episcopi. Et dum Paternum alloqueretur, aspexit tunicam, quam, confossus zelo auaricie, petiuit ut sua fieret. Respondens sanctus ait, 'Non habitu cuiuslibet maligni hec tunica condigna est sed habitu clericatus.' Ille bacando monasterium exiuit. Iterumque indignando reuertitur ut tolleret tunicam contra comitum suorum consilia. Unus autem discipulorum Paterni, uidens illum in furore reuertentem cucurrit ad sanctum Paternum et ait, 'Tirannus, qui hinc antea exiuit, reuertitur. Insultans, subiciens, plantis terram planat.' Respondit Paternus, 'Immo absorbeat eum tellus.' Cum dicto statim terra aperit sinum suae profunditatis absorbetque Arthurum adusque mentum. Qui ilico agnoscens suum reatum

Life of Padarn: (12th or 13th century life of Welsh saint)

When these things were taking place, a heavenly messenger came to St. David who was serving Christ God in Rosina Vallis and said to him: 'Rise up and go to Jerusalem, so that there you may be ordained, and join to yourself two companions who may also be ordained there, namely, Padarn and Teilo.' Soon David sent for them, and they came without delay. Together they journeyed through barbaric peoples and they received the gift of tongues so though they were men of one language they greeted every man in the language with which he had been born. After a time they arrived, in Jerusalem, and there they pronounced, by preaching, the most noble things since the Apostles; after which, through the imposition of the Patriarch's hand, these three saints were ordained bishops. Then they were enriched with gifts. Padarn was enriched with a double gift; a staff and a completely woven tunic. Joyful they returned and divided Britain into their three episcopacies — unless afterwards the malice of tyrants might disorder them.

When Padarn was in his church recuperating after such maritime exertions, a certain tyrant, by the name of Arthur was passing through neighbouring regions, who, one particular day, came to the cell of St. Padarn the bishop, and while he was speaking to Padarn, noticed the tunic, which, he coveted for himself, pierced through by the zeal of avarice as he was. Responding the saint said, 'This tunic is not suitable for the habit of any man of baseness, but only for the habit of ecclesiastical office.' Arthur left the monastery in a fury; and in indignation, against the advice of his associates, he returned again, so that he might take the tunic. One of Padarn's disciples, seeing him returning in a fury, ran to St. Padarn and said, 'The tyrant who departed before returns here; insulting, stamping, he flattens the earth with his feet.' Padarn responded, 'Rather let the earth swallow him!' With these words, the earth immediately opened up the breast of its depths, and swallowed Arthur up to his chin. He then, incipit Deum pariter Paternumque laudare, donec ueniam petens terra illum sursum emitteret. Ab illo loco sanctum flexis genibus poposcit indulgentiam cui sanctus indulsit. Ille uero Paternum sibi sempiternum accepit patronum, ac sic discessit.

***

Uita prima sancti Carantoci:

Et postea uenit iterum ad suam propriam regionem Keredíciaun ad suam speluncam cum clericis multis et ibi multas uirtutes fecit, quas enumerare aliquis non potest. Et dedit illi Christus altare honorificabile de excelso, cuius nemo intelligebat colorem. Et postea ad Sabrinam (hoc est mare) amnem uenit ut nauigaret et misit altare in mare, quod et precedebat, ubi Deus uolebat illum uenire.

In istis temporibus Cato et Arthur regnabant in ista patria, habitantes in Dindraithou. Et uenit Arthur circuiens ut inueniret serpentem ualidissimum, ingentem, terribilem, qui uastauerat .xii. partes agri Carrum. Et uenit Carantocus et salutauit Arthurum, qui gaudens accepit benedictionem ab illo. Et interrogauit Carontocus Arthurum, utrum audisset ubi applicuisset altare suum, et Arthur respondit, 'Si habuero precium, nunciabo tibi.' Et ille dixit, 'Quid precium postulas?' Ille respondit, 'Ut deducas serpentem, qui inprope est tibi, si seruus Dei es, ut uideamus.' Tunc beatus Carantocus perrexit, et orauit ad Dominum, et ilico uenit serpens cum sonitu magno, quasi uitulus ad matrem currens. Inclinauitque caput suum ante seruum Dei, quasi seruus obediens domino suo humili corde et leuis oculis. Et dedit stolam suam circa collum eius, et deduxit illum quasi agnum, nec exaltauit pennas neque ungulas. Et erat collum ipsius quasi collum tauri septem annorum quod uix poterat stola circuire. Deinde perrexerunt una ad arcem et salutauerunt Catonem et bene suscepti sunt ab

admitting his guilt, began to praise God and St. Padarn equally, until, with him seeking forgiveness, the earth let him go. From that place, with bent knees, he implored the saint's indulgence and the saint forgave him. He then took Padarn as his eternal patron, and so left.

***

Life of Carannog: (Welsh life of the 12th or 13th century)

And afterwards, with many clerics, Carannog came again to his home district of Ceredigion and to his cave; and while there he performed many miracles which no one is able to enumerate. And Christ gave him a worthy altar from heaven, the colour of which no one could measure. Afterwards he came to the Severn estuary, so that he might sail; and he threw the alter into the sea, which preceded him wherever God wished him to go.

In those times Cadwy and Arthur reigned in that country, living in Dindraithov. And Arthur came wandering about in order that he might find a most powerful dragon, vast and terrible, which had been putting to waste the twelve portions of the territory of Carrum. And Carannog came and greeted Arthur, who rejoicing, received a blessing from him. And Carannog inquired of Arthur, whether he had heard where his altar had come to shore and Arthur replied, 'If I may have a reward, I will tell you.' And Carannog said, 'What reward do you ask for?' He answered, 'That if you are a servant of God, you will lead out the dragon, which is close to you, so that we may see it.' Then the blessed Carannog went away, praying to the Lord, and immediately the dragon came with a great sound like a calf running to its mother, and it bowed its head before the servant of God like a slave obeying his lord with shy glances and a meek heart. Carannog placed his stole about its neck and led it like a lamb — and it raised neither its wings nor claws. Its neck was as the neck of a bull of seven years which the stole was barely able to go around. They then went together to the stronghold and greeted Cadwy, and were

eo. Et duxit illum serpentem in media aula, et cibauit illum coram populo et conati sunt occidere illum. Non reliquit eum occidi, quia dixit quod ex uerbo Dei uenisset, ut deleret peccatores, qui in Carrum erant et ut ostenderet uirtutem Dei per illum. Et postea perrexit extra portam arcis, et Carantocus dissoluit illum et imperauit illi ut discedens nemini noceret, nec reuerteretur amplius. Et exiuit hesitque ante sicut dixit ordinatio Dei. Et accepit altare, quod cogitauerat Arthur in mensam facere, sed quicquit apponebatur super illam, iactabatur in longinquo. Et postulauit rex ab illo ut reciperet Carrum in sempiterno graphyo. Et postea edificauit ecclesiam ibi. Postea uenit uox illi de celo, ut mitteret altare in mare. Deinde misit Catonem et Arthurum, ut interrogarent de altari et nunciatum est illis, quod in ostium Guellit appulerat. Et dixit rex, 'Iterum date illi .xii. partes agri, ubi altare inuentum esset.' Postea uenit Carantocus, et edificauit ibi ecclesiam, et uocata est ciuitas Carrou.

***

Uita Sancti Iltuti:

Audiens interea, miles magnificus Arthurii regis sui consobrini magnificentiam cupiuit uisitare tanti uictoris curiam. Deseruit quam uocamus Ulteriorem Brittanniam, et peruenit nauigando ubi uidit maximam militum habundantiam, ibidem quoque receptus honorifice, et munificatus ad desiderium militare. Impleto autem desiderio capiendi munera, recessit gratissimus a regali curia.

***

welcomed favourably by him. Carannog led the dragon down the middle of the hall and fed it in front of the people. And they tried to kill it, but he did not allow it to be killed because he said that it had come at the word of God so that it might destroy the sinners who were in Carrum, and to show the power of God through him. And after this Carannog went outside the stronghold's gate and loosed it, ordering it, that departing it might neither hurt anyone nor return again. And it went away and stayed away as he had foretold, according to God's command. Padarn received the altar which Arthur had thought he might make a table; but whatever was placed upon it had been thrown a long way off. And the king required that he should receive Carrum eternally by a written deed. And afterwards he built a church there. Later a voice came to him from heaven requiring that he might put the altar into the sea. Then he sent Cadwy and Arthur so that they might ask about the altar, and it was told to them that it had come to shore at the mouth of the Guellit. And the king said 'Give him, once more, twelve portions of the land where the altar was discovered.' Afterwards Carannog came and built a church there, and the monastery was called the settlement of Carrov.

***

Life of Illtud: (12th or 13th century life of Welsh saint)

The great warrior [Illtud] meanwhile hearing of the magnificence of his cousin, King Arthur, desired to visit the household of such a champion. He left what we call Further Britain [Brittany] and arrived by sailing; there he saw a great company of warriors, being also honourably received in that place, and being rewarded as befitted their military status. With his desire to receive dividends being also satisfied, he withdrew most gratified from the royal household.

***

Uita Gildae:

Contemporaneus Gildas uir sanctissimus fuit Arturi regis totius maioris Britanniae, quem diligendum diligebat cui semper cupiebat obedire. Confratres tamen xxiii resistebant regi rebelli praedicto, nolentes pati dominum, sed crebro fugabant et expellebant a saltu et bello. Hueil maior natu belliger assiduus et miles famosissimus nulli regi obediuit, nec etiam Arthuro. Affligebat eundem commouebat inter utrumque maximum furorem. A Scotia ueniebat saepissime, incendia ponebat, praedas ducebat cum uictoria ac laude. Unde rex uniuersalis Britanniae audiens magnanimum iuuenem talia fecisse et aequalia facere persecutus est uictoriosissimum iuuenem et optimum, ut aiebant et sperabant indigenae, futurum regem. In persecutione autem hostili et in conuentu bellico in insula Minau interfecit iuuenem praedatorem. Post illam interfectionem Arthurus uictor remeauit, gaudens maxime quod superauerat suum fortissimum hostem. Gildas Britonum historiographus tunc remanens in Hibernia studium regens et praedicans in ciuitate Ardmaca audiuit fratrem ab Arthuro rege interfectum fuisse. Doluit ab auditu, fleuit cum gemitu, ut frater carissimus pro carissimo fratre; orauit pro spiritu fraterno cotidie, orabat insuper pro Arthuro fratris sui persecutore et interfectore complens apostolicum preceptum quod dicit: 'Orate pro persequentibus uos et bene facite his qui oderunt uos.'

Interea sanctissimus Gildas uenerabilis historiographus uenit ad Britanniam portans unam pulcherrimam et dulcissimam campanam, quam uouerat offerre apostolico Romanae ecclesiae in presentationem. Pernoctauit honorifice receptus a Cadaco uenerabili abbate in Carbana Ualle, qui monstrauit illi laudabilem campanam, monstratam accepit, acceptam emere

Life of Gildas by Caradoc of Llancarfan: (early 12th century life of Welsh saint)

The most holy Gildas was the contemporary of Arthur, the king of the whole of Britain, whom he loved attentively, and whom he always wished to obey. However his twenty three brothers constantly resisted the aforementioned war-like king, refusing to take him as their lord; and they frequently routed and chased him out of woodlands and off battlefields. Hueil, the elder brother, an energetic fighter and most distinguished warrior, submitted to no king, not even Arthur. He used to harass the latter, and to incite the greatest fury between them both. Very often he would swoop down from Scotland, start conflagrations, and carry off spoils with victory and fame. As a result, the king of all Britain, hearing that the mighty youth had done such things and was still doing similar things, pursued the very victorious and excellent youth, who, as the people used to affirm and hope, was destined to be king. During the hostile pursuit and in the military engagement, which took place on the Isle of Man, he killed the young raider. After that death the victorious Arthur returned extremely happy that he had overcome his most powerful enemy. Gildas, the historian of the Britons, who was staying in Ireland leading studies and preaching in the city of Armagh, heard that his brother had been slain by king Arthur. Pained by the news, he wept in lamentation, as a dearly loved brother for a dearly loved brother. He prayed daily for his brother's spirit; and, besides this, he used to pray for Arthur, the persecutor and murderer of his brother, complying with the apostolic commandment, which says: 'Pray for those who persecute you and do well by those who hate you.'

Meanwhile, the most holy Gildas, the venerable historian, came to Britain, carrying with him a most beautiful and sweet-sounding bell, which he had sworn to offer as a gift to the bishop of the Roman Church. He spent the night as a guest honourably received by the venerable abbot Cadog, in Nant Carban. Gildas showed the laudable bell to him; and after it was shown to him, Cadog handled it; and after handling it he

uoluit magno pretio, quam possessor uendere nolebat. Audito aduentu Gildae sapientis ab Arthuro rege et primatibus totius Britanniae episcopis et abbatibus conuenerunt innumerabiles ex clero et populo, ut Arthurum pacificarent ex supra dicto homicidio. At ille, sicut primitus fecerat, cognito rumore de obitu fratris indulsit inimico, ueniam postulanti osculum dedit et benignissimo animo benedixit osculanti. Hoc peracto rex Arthurus dolens et lacrimans accepit ab episcopis adstantibus paenitentiam et emendauit in quantum potuit, donec consummauit uitam.

***

Dum sic perseueraret sanctus Gildas intentus ieiuniis et orationibus, uenerunt piratae de insulis Orcadibus, qui afflixerunt illum raptis ab eo suis famulis seruientibus et ductis in exilium cum spoliis et omnibus suae habitationis supellectilibus. Unde afflictus nimium non potuit ibi amplius habitare, reliquit insulam, ascendit nauiculam et ingressus est Glastoniam cum magno dolore, Meluas rege regnante in aestiua regione. Susceptus uir suscipiendus a Glastoniense abbate docuit confratres et diuersas plebes seminans semen seminandum caelestis doctrinae. Ibi scripsit historias de regibus Britanniae. Glastonia, id est Urbs Uitrea, quae nomen sumsit a uitro, est urbs nomine primitus in Britannico sermone. Obsessa est itaque ab Arturo tyranno cum innumerabili multitudine propter Guennuuar uxorem suam uiolatam et raptam a praedicto iniquo rege et ibi ductam propter refugium inuiolati loci propter munitiones arundineti et fluminis ac paludis causa tutelae. Quaesiuerat rex rebellis reginam per

wished to purchase it at a great price; but its possessor would not sell it. With the announcement of the advent of Gildas the Wise, many of the people and clerics along with the foremost bishops and abbots gathered for Arthur's sake so that they might absolve him from the above-mentioned murder. But Gildas, as he had first done when he heard the news of his brother's death, was courteous to his enemy, embraced him as he prayed for his forgiveness, and with a most kind heart blessed him as the other embraced in return. With this done, king Arthur, lamenting and grieving, received his penance from the bishops who were present there, and corrected himself in what way he could, until his life was completed.

***

While St. Gildas was persisting in this manner, giving himself over to fasting and prayers, raiders came from the Orkneys, who plagued him by seizing his labouring servants from him, and carrying them off into exile, along with spoils and all the goods of their homes. Being extremely distressed he was not able to remain there and left the island; he climbed onto a small ship, and in great sorrow, came to Glastonbury, at the time when Melvas was reigning in the Summer Country [modern Somerset]. Received with a great welcome by the abbot of Glastonbury, he taught the brethren and the scattered people, sowing the precious seed of the heavenly doctrine. It was there that he wrote the history of Britain's kings. Glastonbury (that is the Glass City) took its name from glass — a city which originally had its name in the British tongue. It was besieged by the tyrant Arthur with an innumerable host because of his wife Gwenhwyfar, whom the aforesaid evil king Melvas had violated and carried off bringing her there for safety, because of the invulnerable position's protection, provided by the thicketed fortifications of reeds, rivers, and marshes. The war-like king had searched for the queen

unius anni circulum, audiuit tandem illam remanentem. Illico commouit exercitus totius Cornubiae et Dibneniae; paratum est bellum inter inimicos.

Hoc uiso abbas Glastoniae comitante clero et Gilda Sapiente intrauit medias acies, consuluit Meluas regi suo pacifice, ut redderet raptam. Reddita ergo fuit, quae reddenda fuerat, per pacem et beneuolentiam. His peractis duo reges largiti sunt abbati multa territoria, qui uenerunt ad templum sanctae Mariae uisitandum et orandum confirmante abbate fraternitatem dilectam pro pace habita et pro beneficiis quae fecerant et amplius quae facturi erant. Inde redierunt reges pacificati promittentes ueneranter obedire reuerentissimo abbati Glastoniensi et numquam uiolare sanctissimum locum nec etiam subiacentia loco principali.

***

Uita Sancti Cadoci:

Post multum uero temporis interuallum prefatus rex Gundleius, iam regno fretus quandam nobilissimis ortam natalibus puellam eleganti quidem specie sed et forma ualde decoram sericisque redimitam uestibus, cuius nomen Guladus, cuiusdam reguli filiam, qui uocabatur Brachanus, pro eius dulcissima fama flagranti affectu sibi legittimo copulari coniugio gestiuit. Exin quam plures ad patrem uirginis direxit legatos quo sibi eandem in coniugem despondi obnixius postularent. Pater uero puelle, accepta legatione indignatus furoreque repletus, filiam suam illi despondere renuit atque nuntios despexit, eosdemque sine honore dimisit, quod nimis

throughout the cycle of one year, and at last heard that she resided there. Thereupon he called up the armies of the whole of Cornwall and Devon and war was prepared between the enemies.

When the abbot of Glastonbury — attended by the clergy and Gildas the Wise — saw this, he stepped in between the contending armies, and peacefully advised his king Melvas, that he should restore the kidnapped lady. And so, she who was to be restored was restored in peace and good will. When these things had been done, the two kings gave to the abbot many territories; and they came to visit the church of St. Mary to pray; the abbot sanctioning the dear fraternity in return for the peace they enjoyed and the benefits which they had bestowed and which were about to bestow yet more plentifully. Then, reconciled, the kings left, swearing reverently to obey the most venerable abbot of Glastonbury, and not to violate the holiest part nor even the lands bordering on the land of its overseer.

***

Life of Saint Cadog: (early twelfth century life of Welsh saint)

After a long interval of time the aforementioned king Gwynllyw, supported now by his kingdom, desired with a burning affection — on account of the great sweetness of her renown — that a certain girl, born of the most noble lineage, of exquisite appearance, and what is more, very beautiful in form, and dressed in silk raiment, whose name was Gwladus, the daughter of a certain prince, who was called Brychan, should be joined to him in lawful wedlock. For that reason he sent very many messengers to the father of the maiden in order that they might more firmly demand that she be given to him as his wife. But the father of the girl, offended and full of anger because of the embassy received, refused to pledge his daughter, and offended the messengers, and sent them away without honour. Taking this very badly, they returned, and

egre ferentes, atque domino suo nuntiantes queque erga eos acta fuerant, redierunt. Quo audito, rex nimia debachans furia, trecentos quamtocius armauit uernulas, quo premissam puellam ui raperent. Deinde protinus iter arripientes ut ad prescripti reguli curiam uentum est, que uocatur Talgard, memoratam uirginem ante conclauis suae ianuam cum ipsius sororibus sedentem pudicisque sermonibus uacantem reperiunt, quam statim ui capientes festinato cursu regrediuntur. Quo accepto, genitor ipsius Brachanus dolore cordis tactus intrinsecus amissionem karissimae natae lugens, uocauit in auxilium sibi cunctos amicos et concessores suos ad eruendam natam suam. Conuenientibus autem uniuersis auxiliariis suis, citatis cursibus persequitur hostem suosque complices. Quos, cum conspexisset Gundleius, iussit sibi sepius dictam puellam afferi, illamque secum equitare fecit. Ipse quidem haut fugiendo, ceterum pedetentim secum gestans adolescentulam in equo, exercitum precessit, suos milites exspectando et ad bellum uiriliter hortando. Brachanus uero cum suis immitem regem suos quoque satellites audacter aggrediens, prostratis ducentis persecutus est eos usque ad collem, qui est in utriusque patriae confinio, qui Brittannica lingua Bochriucarn nuncupatur quod maxilla lapideae uiae interpretatur. At ubi Gundleius corpore incolumis cum prenotata uirgine, licet plurima strage mestus preliando cum aduersariis, terminos terrae suae attigisset, ecce, tres heroes strenui Arthurus cum duobus equitibus suis, Cei uidelicet, et Bedguir, super cacumen supradicti collis cum alea ludentes consedere. Illis enimuero cernentibus regem cum puella sibi apropinquantem, Arthurus ilico libidine in amorem adolescentule nimium succensus, ac iniqua cogitatione plenus consodalibus inquid, 'Scitote me uehementer in concupiscentiam puelle huius, quam ille miles equitando deuehit, accendi.' At illi prohibentes eum dixerunt, 'Absit a te

told their lord what had been done to them. When he had heard, the king, raging from a too great fury, armed with all possible speed three hundred of his young men so that they might seize the aforementioned girl by force. They immediately began their journey and when they reached the aforesaid princeling's household — which is called Talgarth — they found the said virgin sitting with her sisters, at rest, in modest conversation, before the door of her room. They straightaway took her by force, and retreated with hasty steps. When this was known, her father, Brychan — touched by pain of the heart and grieving inwardly at the loss of his beloved daughter — called to his aid all his friends and subjects so as to retrieve his daughter. With every one of his allies being assembled together, he chased after the enemy and his confederates, with quick steps. Gwynllyw, when he had seen them, ordered that the oft-mentioned girl must be brought up to him, and he made her ride with him. He, carrying the girl safely with him on horseback, preceded his troop, not indeed for flight, but to await his warriors and manfully incite them on to war. But Brychan, bravely attacking the fierce king and his household with his men, killed two hundred of them and chased them up to the hill, which is on the borders of either country, and in the Britannic tongue has the name Boch Rhiw Carn, meaning 'the Cheek of the Rocky Way'. But when Gwynllyw — his body safe with the aforementioned virgin — had arrived at the borders of his land, although pained at the very great slaughter in the fight with his opponents, behold he saw three powerful champions. Arthur and his two knights, namely Cai and Bedwyr, were sitting on top of the aforesaid hill playing at dice. And these saw the king and a girl approaching them. Arthur was straightaway greatly inflamed with lust in longing for this girl, so, filled with evil thoughts, he said to his companions, 'Know that I am greatly burning with passion for this girl, whom that warrior is carrying away on horseback.' But they, censuring him, said, 'Do not let it be

tantum scelus patrari, nos enim soliti sumus inopes anxiosque iuuare. Quocirca huic angustato prelio certaminis concurrentes cicius subueniamus.' At ille, 'Quum ambo mauultis ei succurrere quam puellam mihi ab eo uiolenter dirripere, pergite obuiam eis, ac quis illorum sit heres diligenter huius terrae sciscitamini.'

Illis autem confestim abeuntibus et pro regis precepto sciscitantibus, Gunduleius respondit, 'Testante Deo et omnibus Brittannorum peritissimis istius terrae heredem me esse profiteor.' Reuersisque nunciis ad dominum suum, retulerunt quae ab illo audierant. Tum, Arthuro sociisque eius armatis, in hostes Gundleii irruunt, eosque uersis tergis cum magna confusione ad patrium solum fugauerunt. Tunc Gundleius, per patrocinium Arthurii triumphans, ad suam palacium cum prescripta uirgine Gladusa perrexit, quod erat situm in illo colle, qui ab eius nomine deinceps uocabulum Brittannice Altgundliu, id est Collis Gundleii, accepit. Nam a Gundleio Gunliauc, a Brachano uero Brecheniauc uocatur.

***

In eodem igitur tempore dux quidam Brittannorum fortissimus, uocabulo Ligessauc, filius Eliman, cognomento quoque Lau hiir, id est, longa manus, tres milites Arthurii regis illustrissimi Britannie, trucidauit. Ceterum Arthurio quaquauersum eum persequente, nusquam tutum locum repperit nullusque ipsum tutari ob predigesti regis pauorem ausus fuit, donec tandem, creberrima fuga fatigatus, ad uirum Dei profugus peruenit. Qui ipsius miseratus labores, benignius illum suscepit, in Domino confidens, Arthurium uero nil metuens, secundum illud Dominicum, 'Nolite timere eos, qui corpus occidunt, animam autem non possunt occidere, sed potius eum timete, qui potest animam et corpus mittere in

that such a crime should be committed by you, for we are accustomed to aid the penniless and distressed. For that reason let us speed together with all haste and aid this violent fight so that it may cease.' And Arthur said, 'Since you both prefer to support him rather than snatch the girl violently off him for me, go towards them, and diligently inquire who is the holder of this land.'

They left immediately and in accordance with the king's wishes inquired. Gwynllyw replies, 'With God being witness and all those who are the most knowledgeable of the Britons, I swear that I am the holder of this land.' And the messengers having returned, reported to their lord, what they had heard from him. Then Arthur and his companions charged, armed, against Gwynllyw's opponents and made them retreat and fly in great bewilderment to their own land. Gwynllyw, — triumphal through Arthur's protection — with the aforementioned maiden Gwladus, came to his own home, which was situated on that hill which from then on took the British appellation of his name, Allt Wynllyw, that is, 'Gwynllyw's Hill', for it is from Gwynllyw that Gwynlliog is named, and Brycheiniog from Brychan.

***

In that same time a very powerful leader of the British, by the name of Lligessauc, the son of Eliman, also with the surname of Llaw Hir, that is 'Long Hand', killed three of Arthur's warriors, the most famous king of Britain. With Arthur hunting him everywhere, he nowhere found a safe place and no one dared to shelter him from fear of the aforementioned king; until fatigued by over-regular flights, he at last came — a fugitive — to the man of God. Cadog, sympathising with his troubles, welcomed him all the more kindly, trusting in the Lord, fearing Arthur not one bit, following that word of the Lord, 'Fear not those who kill the body but are not able to kill the soul, but rather fear him who

gehennam.' Mansit itaque cum eo in regione Guunliauc, Arthurio nesciente uii tem annis securus.

Quibus euolutis rursus prelibato regi proditus, idem demum placitandi causa, quod ui cum uiro Dei nullatenus auderet contendere, cum plurima militum copia ad amnem Oscam peruenit. Directis ergo legatis ad regem, uir Dei sciscitatur ab eo, si contrauersiam in sagacium iudicum arbitrio statueret. At ille adquieuit sanctus namque Cadocus, de diuersis eiusdem patrie partibus tribus ad se principalibus proceribus, Dauid, uidelicet, et Teliauuo, Iltuto et Dochou, Keneder et Maidoc accersitis, cum pluribus aliis clericis et senioribus totius Brittannie, iudicibus insimul coadunatis, usque ad ripam pregrandis fluminis Osce ipso precedente, pariter conuenerunt. Ibi quoque more hostium ex utraque fluuii parte causam amaris uerbis agitantes diutius utrinque litigauerunt. Post hanc autem altercationis intercapidinem, eruditiores ex iudicibus uiri decreuerunt Arthurium pro redemptione uniuscuiusque uirorum necatorum tres boues optimas debere suscipere. Alii uero c. uaccas illi in precium prescriptorum uirorum tribuendas sanxerunt a priscis enim temporibus apud Brittones huiusmodi iudicium ac istud precium de regum ducumque ministris constitutum erat. Hoc accepto Arthurius insultans uni coloris uaccas renuit, uerum discolores accipere libuit, scilicet, in anteriori parte rubei, in posteriori uero candidi coloris distinctas plurima tergiuersatione gestiuit. Illi quippe, quo huiuscemodi coloris peccora repperirentur penitus ignorantes, quid consilii super his caperent hesitabant. Quocirca uir Dei in trium Personarum nomine imperauit iuuenibus de concilio quatinus ix. siue uelut quidam fatentur c. iuuencas, ad se minare cuiuscunque coloris forent.

can throw soul and body down into Hell.' Therefore Lligessauc stayed with him securely in the land of Gwynlliog, without Arthur's knowledge, for seven years. These years being over and he once more betrayed to the aforesaid king, the same one [Arthur] soon came to the river Usk with a huge band of warriors, so he might set down a claim, for he did not dare to forcibly come to strife with the man of God. So messengers were directed to the king, and the man of God asked of him if he might submit the contention to the verdict of learned judges. He agreed for Saint Cadog had called to him the principal grandees from three different regions of the same nation, namely David, Teilo, Illtud and Dochau, Cynidr and Maeddog, with several other clerics and elders of the whole of Britain, judges being added to them there, to the bank of a very large river named the Usk; here they gathered together, Cadog himself walking before them. And there in the way of enemies, fighting out the matter with bitter words, they debated from either side of the river. Following a break in the dispute, the more knowledgeable of the judges ordered that Arthur ought to receive three of the best oxen in place of each one of his slain men, yet others judged that one hundred cows should be given to him in place of the aforesaid men, because from ancient times this kind of judgement and price, had been decided upon among the Britons by the learned-servants of kings and princes. This being accepted, Arthur insolently refused cows of one colour, taking only variegated cows, that is, with a great deal of indecision, he desired cows marked with a red colour in their front and a white colour on their rear. And they completely ignorant about where cattle of this sort of colouring were to be discovered, doubted what kind of approach they should take up to find these things. It was for this reason the man of God in the name of the Trinity instructed the young men of the council themselves to drive to him nine, or, as some claim, one hundred heifers of any colour.

Ut autem prenotata animalia pre occulis ipsius et aliorum Dei famulorum adducta fuerunt, diuino magnalio ex praua Arthurii cupidine, in prelibatis coloribus pro beniuolo iustorum precatu ac desiderio statim mutata fuere. Intuente autem totius cleri comitatu pluribusque aliis Dei fidelibus a beato uiro illo congregatis hoc miraculo gauisi sunt gaudio magno, Deum ualde glorificantes. Porro uir Dei consuluit quatenus iure prememoratas boues agere deberet. Et respondit ex altrinsecus iudicum cuneus, 'Ius quidem est te ipsas ad uadi medium gregatim compellere.' Compulit igitur illas eotenus occurreruntque eis Arthurius, Chei et Bedguur, ceteris in littore sedentibus. At Chei et Bedguur gliscentes eas manibus ad litus alterum per cornua trahere, sed extimplo inter ipsorum manus, cunctis uidentibus diuino nutu in filicis fascibus transfigurate sunt. Quod prodigium Arthurius aspectans ut sibi dimitteretur iniuria quam illi irrogauerat, beatum uirum humiliter flagitauit. Largitus est autem illi ueniam delicti iuxta illud Euangelicum, 'Dimittite et dimittetur uobis.' Inito igitur prelibatus rex cum agmine suo consilio, refugium eius per uii tem annos totidemque menses eiusdemque numeri dies protelauit. Si quis uero alienigena prefinito tempore de sancti Cadoci pago repatriare gestiens ad aliquam mundi plagam discesserit seu transfretauerit, si forte ualida ui procellarum ac sinistri flatus tempestate ingruente in illius portum, uidelicet Barren, appulsus fuerit atque ad pristinum refugii sui locum denuo remeauerit, secundum seniorum traditionem usque ad ultimum uitae suae terminum seruitio ipsius deputandus ac alacriter recipiendus est. Hoc Arthurius uniuersique duces eiusdem cum totius Brittannie senioribus corroborantes dixerunt, 'Nos quoque in omnium auditu uerba sanctionis huius contestamur et quicunque ea preuaricatus fuerit, addat super illum Deus omnes plagas in ueteri et noua lege scriptas, nomenque eius de libro uite deleatur. Qui uero hec custodierit, omnibus ueteris et noui testamenti benedictionibus repleatur,

When the aforesaid creatures were brought into presence of Cadog and the presence of the other servants of God, immediately, as Arthur had perversely wished, they were transformed by the divine power, into the aforesaid colours from the kindly prayer and desire of the just. The fellowship of all of the clergy and many others of God's faithful, seeing this miracle, came together by that blessed man and celebrating with a great joy, vigorously extolled God. Then the man of God asked what it was he should do with the aforementioned cattle. And the school of judges on both sides answered, 'The law is that you herd them to the middle of the ford.' For this reason he drove them as far as that place and Arthur, Cai and Bedwyr came to them, while the others sat on the bank. And Cai and Bedwyr gladly dragged them by their horns to the contrary bank with their hands; yet as soon as they came into their hands they — in the presence of all — were transformed by the divine intention into bunches of fern. When Arthur saw this wonder, meekly he asked the blessed man that the evil which he had done to him should be forgiven. He granted a pardon for the fault according to the Gospel which says, 'Forgive, and it shall be forgiven you.' At this the aforementioned king, after taking counsel with his army, increased the period of his refuge for seven years and the same number of months and the same number of days. If any stranger, desiring to go home from Cadog's property in the prescribed time, might depart or sail to any place in the world, if perchance he should be driven into Cadog's harbour (namely Barry) by the wild power of storms and with unfavourable windy conditions assailing him, and if he should return again to the original place of sanctuary, he is to be gladly received, and according to the tradition of the elders, to be given up to Cadog's service until the end of his life. Arthur, all his princes and the elders of the whole of Britain, agreeing with this, said, 'We also in the hearing of all bear witness to the words of this law, and whoever ignores them, may God put on him all the plagues written in the Old and New Testament, and may his

et super illum descendant et maneant nec non ipsius anima in requie consistat eterna.' Peracto uero concilio omnes uacce, que in filicum manipulis fuerunt, conuerse in suis bostaribus incolumes apud earundem possessores sunt reperte.

***

Uita Sancti Wohednouii:

Processu uero temporis Uortigernus rex usurpatiuus ad praestandum sibi pro defensione regni maioris Britaniae quod iniuste tenebat subsidium uiros bellicos de Saxoniae partibus euocauit et eos in regno socios sibi fecit. Qui cum essent pagani et uiri diabolici, humanum sanguinem ex sua propria natura effundere affectantes multa mala erogabant Britonibus. Quorum superbia postmodum per magnum Arturum Britonum regem fuit ad tempus repressa, eis pro parte maxima ab insula repulsis et seruire coactis. Sed eodem Arturo post multas uictorias quas in Britannicis et Gallicis partibus praeclare gessit, ab humanis tandem actibus euocato, uia iterum patuit Saxonibus, qua in insulam remearent et facta est maxima oppressio Britonum et ecclesiarum euersio persecutioque sanctorum.

***

name be rubbed out of the Book of Life. But as for the one who honours these, let him be enriched with all the boons found in the Old and New Testament, and let the boons descend upon him and remain with him, and also let his soul live in eternal rest.' With the council finished, all the cows which had been transformed into fern-bunches were found uninjured in their enclosures by their owners.

***

The Life of St. Goueznou: (life of Breton saint, dated tentatively to 1019)

[The writer has made reference to the *Historia Brittonum* from which he is elaborating]

...in the course of time, Vortigern the usurping king, summoned warriors from the lands of the Saxons to provide support for him in defending his kingdom of greater Britain [as opposed to Brittany] which he was holding unjustly, and he made them partners to himself in the kingdom. The Saxons, as they were pagans and demonic men, striving to shed human blood by their very nature, afflicted the Britons. Their pride was, afterwards, suppressed for a time by the great Arthur, king of the Britons so that they were repelled for the most part and compelled to serve. But when the same Arthur — after many victories which he famously won in Britain and parts of Gaul — was, at length, called forth from human affairs, the way was again open to the Saxons, by which they might return to the island, and there was a great oppression of the Britons and an overturning of the churches and a persecution of the saints.

***

Uita Euflami:

Arturi quoque fortissimi, qui eo tempore monstra in illis Britanniae partibus persequebatur, hoc modo multotiens deuitauerat occursum. Sed tandem, Deo uolente, belluae delusa est astucia pernitiosae. Nam forte Arturus, factis eius totum intendens animum, eam ubique uestigabat. Dumque circum latebrosa perquiteret saxa, sanctis in littore obuiait uiris; admiratur quod ausi essent in tam uastis et horribilibus habitare solitudinibus. Querit ab eis diligenter qui sint et unde: de quesito, illis docentibus, de spelunca etiam monstri, illis indicantibus, certificatur. Gratulatur Arturus de sanctorum aduentu et toto corde letatur de speluncae monstri demonstratione quoniam indignans sibi, tanquam a monstro uictus, tristis multotiens discesserat quod illud indignare non poterat. Armatur ergo claua trinodi, clipeo quem pellis tegebat leonis animosum defendit pectus; deinde publicum hostem, solus pro omnibus pugnans, uiriliter inuasit.

Contra, horribile monstrum se suis protegit armis. Ymo, primum in Arturum facit incursum, indignans quod ab uno impeteretur homine, cum saepe multos uictor populos superasset. Impetum ergo collecto robore faciens, Arturi ualidum ferit clipeum, quem leuiter unguibus perforat acutis. Quid mirum? Lapidis enim duricia, ut locus ille plagas in se gerens testimonium perhibet, illorum cederet acumini. Arturus reducto corpore, sine uulnere mansit; et magis commotus in iram acerrime percutit hostem. Moenia tanto dirrueret ictu, sed hostis, duricia pellis defensus, non letalem accipit ictum. Dolor tamen ictus ualidior descendit ad imum. Per totam hoc modo pugnauit diem: adhuc serpens sine letali manebat uulnere.

The Life of Saint Euflamm: (twelfth century life of Breton saint)

...it [the dragon] had constantly avoided an encounter with the most powerful Arthur who in that time used to seek out monsters in this part of Brittany. Nevertheless, after a while, with God granting, the cunning of the destructive beast was defeated, for it happened by chance that Arthur, giving all his attention to its deeds, sought it everywhere. While he searched around some concealing rocks, he met holy men on the seashore and wondered that they might dare to live in such vast and horrible solitudes. He inquired diligently from them who they might be and from where they had come. They answered his question, and he was also told about the cave of the monster with them showing him. Arthur was cheered by the advent of the holy men and he rejoiced with all his heart at the directions to the monster's cave, because he had so often departed sad because he had not been able to find the monster, angry with himself as though having been beaten by it. He armed himself with the triple-knotted club and defended his eager torso with the shield which a lion-skin covered, and then alone he vigorously attacked the public enemy, fighting for all.

Conversely the horrible monster defended itself with its arms. Indeed it made the first attack on Arthur, furious that it might be set upon by one man, when it had often, as the victor, overcome many people. Therefore making an attack with its gathered strength, it struck the great shield of Arthur, which it easily pierced with its sharpened claws. Is it surprising? For the hardness of stone would yield to the keenness of the monster's claw, as that place bears witness by showing the marks. Arthur, drawing back his body, remained without a wound but was all the more disturbed into anger so that he harshly attacked the enemy. Walls might have been destroyed by such a blow, but the enemy, defended by his hard pelt, did not receive a fatal stab. However a strong pain descended into its depths. He fought through all the day and yet this dragon remained without a mortal wound.

Arturus, ut noctem sensit adesse, certamen in crastinum differt. Ad sanctos uiros lassus labore et estu languidus reuertitur; fauces eius siti arebant ualida, querit aquam a uiris, Euflamus respondet pro omnibus unus: 'Domine, non habemus aquam, similiter et nos ea indigemus: superest ergo ut Dominum nostrum eam postulemus.' Laudat Arturus justum boni uiri consilium. Flexis genibus, omnes prosternuntur in terra. Euflamus a toto corpore prostratus, uox omnium sociorum, orat dicens: 'Deus, cuius potestas immutabilis cuncta sine prejacenti materia creauit et cui uniuersa res quaeque secundum suam proprietatem deseruit, ad cuius jussum omnia suam mutant qualitatem, ut quae dura sunt defluant mollia et quae sunt aspera fiant plana: declara uirtutem tuam super nos, et quemadmodum in deserto aquam manare de petra, sitiente populo, jussisti et famulo tuo Moyse orante, sic, Domine, in multitudine misericordiae tuae digneris aquam nobis infundere.' Oratione completa, rupem eminentem ascendit [per] quam, facto sanctae crucis signaculo, silice percussa, aqua copiose prorupit in aera. Quem laticem cum uir sitibundus gratias agens libasset, ante sancti Euflami pedes pronus corruit; supplicibus precibus expostulat ut manus imponendo ei dignetur benedicere et in orationibus pro eo ad Deum orare, utpote qui sepe pro gentis liberatione multa uitae discrimina dubius subire solebat. Euflamus, uir Dei, benedicens ei munus promittit orationum.

Discedit Arturus letabundus, siti fugata, uiribus haustu diuino reparatis, sancta benedictione munitus, confidensque de sancti uiri uirtute, certamen cum monstro eius reliquit arbitrio. Athleta igitur Christi, armis fidei munitus, monstrum immane jubet prodire, utque fidem sociorum confirmet, uoce sic affatur

When Arthur realised night was coming he postponed the struggle until the following day. Faint from his work and dulled by thirst he returned to the holy men. There he sought water from the men as his throat was parched by a powerful thirst: Euflamus responded, one voice for all of them 'O lord, we do not have water, yet now we too need it; therefore it remains to ask our Lord for it.' Arthur praised the just council of the good man. With bent knees all fell down on the earth. Euflamus, his whole body prostrate, the voice of all the group, prayed saying 'O God, whose immutable power created all material things without prior existence, and by whom absolutely every single thing serves according to its property; at the order of whom all things change their substance so those things which are hard flow into soft things and those things which are uneven are made level, O Lord, make your power manifest amongst us; and, in the way, with Moses your servant at prayer, you ordered water to flow from the rock in the desert for your thirsty people, so Lord, in the fullness of your mercy, may you see fit to pour upon us water.'

With the prayer completed, he climbed up onto on an outcropping boulder through which, when the rock was struck and the sign of the cross made, water erupted copiously into the air. While giving thanks the thirsty man had tasted the fluid; he tumbled down before the feet of Saint Euflamus begging with humble prayers that Euflamus might see fit to put a blessing on him by the laying on of hands and to speak for him in prayers to God seeing that he often used, in uncertainty, to undergo many mortal risks for the liberation of the people. Euflamus, the man of God, blessing him, promised the gift of prayer.

Rejoicing, Arthur departed with his thirst driven out and his strength replenished by the divine drinking, defended by heavenly benediction and confident of the might of the holy man, he freely left the fight with the monster to the authority of the saint. Therefore the champion of Christ, fortified with the arms of faith, ordered the terrible monster to come forth, and, so he might confirm the faith of the community, he spoke

aperta: 'Domine Jesu Christe, qui discipulis tuis tantam dedisti potentiam ut ligare atque soluere ualeant quaecumque uoluerint, de quibus etiam dixisti: Fugam demoniis imperabunt, serpentes tollent, huic serpenti impera discessum, ut hec regio a tam pestifera pernicie liberata et laudes tibi et gratias referre ualeat.' Et cum respondissent: 'Amen,' monstrum, supra silicem erectum, oculos partes circumtulit in omnes et clamorem magno gemitu miserabili permixtum emisit, cuius horrore etiam loca tremuerunt remota. Deinde, submisso capite, ore singultienti et naribus uomitum protulit sanguinem: illius loci saxa in testimonium huius miraculi adhuc tanquam recenti sanguine rubere uidentur.

thus in a clear voice: 'O Lord Jesus, you who have given such great power to your disciples that they might be able to tie and loose whatsoever they wish, about what you also said: "they will command the flight of demons, they will remove dragons." Command the banishment of this dragon from here, so that this kingdom, liberated from so deadly a danger may be able to give thanks and praise to you.'

And when they had responded 'Amen', the monster, rearing on the rock, rolled his eyes all around and let out a great clamour mingled with a pitiable groan, from whose horror even remote places trembled. Then with its head bowed, it coughed up bloody vomit from its nostrils and mouth with gaspings. The rock of that place still appears to be red, as if with fresh blood, a testimony of this miracle.

Herman: De Miraculis Sanctae Mariae Laudensis

The work, *The Miracles of St. Mary of Laon* was written by one Herman (possibly of Tournai) in 1145 after the visit of some canons from Laon to Britain for fund raising in 1113. It is a continental source, but bears on the British legend of Arthur, the pitch of interest in which, it quite unwittingly records. The account is important because it is the earliest indisputable evidence for belief in Arthur's messianic qualities whereby it is understood that he will return to help his country in its time of need (for earlier, less clear, documentation, see *Englynion y Beddau*). Herman describes how a fight was triggered by one Hangello, a visiting canon, who suggested that the erstwhile saviour of the British was very much dead and buried. This was obviously a matter of sensitivity with at least one local and it was only with some difficulty that a serious fight was avoided in the shrine itself.

The bibliography includes several references to Arthur's death-defying abilities in British tradition. It is possible that the concept was very localised or even a late development since in the prophetic text *Armes Prydein*, (a southern Welsh poem probably of the tenth century, in which ancient heroes are called upon to lead the British into battle against the English) Arthur is absent when any self-respecting hero of the people would most likely be present. Alternatively Oliver Padel has suggested that this might be because Arthur's return was known in early lore but was not necessarily connected with the defence of Britain. However we explain this, the extract is valuable because it shows us how one man, presumably a commoner, viewed Arthur in the early twelfth century.

***

Bibliography:

Bromwich, Rachel *Armes Prydein*
Bullock-Davies, Constance '"Exspectare Arthurum" Arthur and the Messianic Hope'
Loomis, R.S. *Wales and the Arthurian Legend*
Migne, J-P. *Patrologia Latina* 156, p.983
Padel, Oliver 'The Nature of Arthur', pp.8—12
Tatlock, J.S.P. 'The English Journey of the Laon Canons'

De puella caeca illuminata apud Danauexeriam:

Exinde uenimus in prouinciam quae uocatur Danauexeria, ubi ostenderunt nobis cathedram, et furnum illius famosi secundum fabulas Britannorum regis Arturi, ipsamque terram eiusdem Arturi esse dicebant. Ibi nos plurimum honorauit quidam clericus nomine Agardus, qui iam diu Lauduni manserat, quique postmodum in Northmannia factus est episcopus urbis Constantiniensis. Dum ergo ibi essemus, puella quaedam fere decennis, nomine Kenehellis, caeca a natiuitate, in uilla quae Bomine uocatur, ad feretrum uenit, et lota oculos ex aqua reliquiarum lumen recepit.

De surdo ibidem sanato:

Sed et juuenis quidam in eadem uilla surdus a natiuitate ad feretrum uenit, et lotus aures aqua reliquiarum protinus audiuit. Quidam etiam uir ibidem manum aridam habens, coram feretro pro sanitate recepienda uigilabat. Sed sicut britones solent jurgari cum Francis pro rege Arturo, idem uir coepit rixari cum uno ex famulis nostris, nomine Hangello, qui erat ex familia domni Guidonis Laudunensis archidiaconi, dicens adhuc Arturum uiuere. Unde non paruo tumultu exorto, cum armis ecclesiam irruunt plurimi, et nisi praefatus Algardus clericus obstitisset, pene usque ad sanguinis effusionem uentum fuisset. Quam rixam coram feretro suo factam credimus Dominae nostrae displicuisse, nam idem uir manum habens aridam, qui pro Arturo tumultum fecerat, sanitatem non recepit.

Concerning the blind girl cured in Devon:

Next we came into the province which is called Devon, where they showed to us the cathedral, and the oven which according to the tales of the Britons is that of the celebrated King Arthur and that same land they say was Arthur's. There a certain cleric by the name of Agardus who had already been in Laon a long time and who afterwards was in Normandy, welcomed us. He was later to be made the bishop of the City of Constantine. While we were there, a certain girl, nearly ten years old, by the name of Kenhelle, blind from birth in a town called Bodmin, came to the shrine, and with her eyes having been washed with the water of the reliquary, she gained her sight.

Concerning a deaf man cured in the same place:

A certain youth in the same town, deaf from birth, came to the shrine, and when his ears had been washed with the water of the reliquary he heard forthwith. Also a certain man having a withered hand kept a vigil at the shrine to recover his health. In just the same way as the Bretons are accustomed to arguing with the French about King Arthur, the same man began to bicker with one from our community by the name of Hangello of the community of Lord Guidon, Archdeacon of Laon, saying that Arthur still lived. Then there arose not a small tumult; many men rushed into the church with arms and if the aforementioned cleric Algardus had not prevented it, it would almost certainly have come to the spilling of blood. We believe the struggle at her shrine caused the displeasure of Our Lady, for the same man, having a withered hand, who made a fight about Arthur, did not receive a cure.

Brut y Brenhinedd

The *History of the Kings,* the Welsh translation of Geoffrey of Monmouth's *Historia Regum Britanniae,* survives in over seventy manuscripts. In places there are peculiar renderings of the Latin, at other points Geoffrey's purple passages have been ruthlessly cut out, but it is generally faithful to the 1136 work which mark the limits of this book's collection. Of interest here are the usually slight divergences from Geoffrey's history which may point to independent Welsh traditions, though in many cases the new material is less revealing than what was ultimately left out by the writer editing and translating this work. The passages below, can only act as an introduction, but hopefully one that will show the nature of the Welsh rendering. Each section has a reference by its side to a page number of Lewis Thorpe's English translation of Geoffrey's work for an easy cross reference. As a more immediate aid this translation is italicised to give an approximate idea of the differences as they are found in the Welsh Cotton Cleopatra manuscript.

The first passage is of interest for its tone. Some pious sentiments are introduced around the young boy Arthur who is associated with the nine men raised from Adam, a term that can be found in the Welsh Triads (Bromwich *Trioedd,* pp.122—128.)

The second passage gives the court list of the Whitsuntide feast. The additions and alterations are of great interest. Doris Edel has argued for the existence of such lists in Welsh tradition. It is possible that alterations to Geoffrey's work should be seen in this context.

The third passage is a description of Camlan; it is a normal rendering of Geoffrey up to the Latin poem which is known from an English source. The comment at the end, that 'the story does not tell about the death of Arthur more fully than that,' suggests some sense of incompletion.

***

Bibliography:

Edel, Doris 'The catalogues in *Culhwch ac Olwen*'
Parry, John Jay *Brut Y Brenhinedd*
Roberts, Brynley F. 'Geofrey of Monmouth, Historia Regum Britanniae and Brut y Brenhinedd'
Roberts, Brynley F. *Brut y Brehinedd,* pp.ix-lx
Thorpe, Lewis *Geoffrey of Monmouth: The History of the Kings of Britain*
Ward, Charlotte 'Arthur in the Welsh Bruts'

Ac yna y caussant yn eu kynghor urdaw Arthur yn vrenhyn, a hynny rac dirvawr govit, canis nyt oed o oedran y Arthur yna onyt pymtheng mlwyd. Nyt oed, hagen, hyt y klywit dyn vn gampeu ac ef; canys hael oed a doeth a dewr a digryf; allawen pan vei amser; a phrut pan vei reit idaw, ac ar vyrder yn wir, ac yn gryno. Ni oruc Duw, gwedy y naw nyn a wnaethpwyt o Adaf, vn dyn kyn gwpplet ac Arthur o gampeu da, a hynny a rodes Duw idaw yny aenedic dawn. Ac nyt yttoed Arthur yn gordiwes o da eluyd a rodei; canys ny adei ef neb yn llau wac y wrthaw, or adelei yervyn da attaw. A phwy bynnac ybo yndaw daeoni anyanawl: ny at Duw arnaw wastat anghenoctit.

***

Ac yna y perys Arthur darparu gwlet anveidraul y veynt y ssulgwyn; ac anvon kennadau y bop gwlat y wahawt y brenhinet, a'r ieirll, a'r barwnyeit, a'r marchogyon vrdolyon, a gwyr da ereill adwyn a'r ny ellit ev rif am law hynny. Y dyvot y Gaer Llion y rodi ydunt breiniev goreu a gausseint eriod val y dangossei ev boned ac ev delyhet ac ev gwaet. Ac yna y doeth o'r Alban Arawn vab Kynvarch Brenhin Yscotlont, ac Vrien vab Kynvarch Brenhin Reget, ac o Wyned Casswallawn Llaw Hir, a Meuric Brenhin Dyfet, a Chatwr Iarll Kernyw, a'r tri archescob o Ynys Brydein, a phennaf onadunt oed Archescop Caer Llion; canys breint legat a oed idaw, a gwr nefawl oed. A yno y doeth Morud iarll Caer Loew a Mor Iarll Caer Vrangon ac Anarawt o Amwithic a Marchud o Gaer Weir ac Ywein o Gaer Vallawc, nev Ssalysburi o ieith arall;

p.212:

And then they decided, as their counsel, to make Arthur king, because of their great affliction, although Arthur was only fifteen years of age. There was not, however, so far as had been heard, any man his equal in excellence, since he was generous, *and wise, and mighty, and agreeable, and joyful when it was suitable, and sober when there was need for it, and in short, truly and properly, God did not make — after the nine men who were made from Adam — a man as complete as Arthur in good deeds,* and God gave him that as an innate gift. And Arthur did not get as many goods as he gave away, since he would let no one of those who came to ask goods of him go away empty handed. *And whoever there is who has natural grace in him,* God will not let there be continual need on him.

***

p.225-228:

And then Arthur caused there to be made an immense feast for Whitsuntide, and he sent messengers to every country to invite the kings and earls and the barons and the upright knights, and countless other goodly nobles besides that, to come to Caerleon to be given the best honours they had ever obtained, as their good deeds and their descent and their blood might demand. And then there came from Albany *Arawn son of Cynfarch,* King of Scotland, and *Urien son of Cynfarch, King of Rheged,* and from Gwynedd Caswallon Long-Hand, and *Meurig,* King of Dyfed, and Cador, Earl of Cornwall, and the three Archbishops of the Isle of Britain. And the head of these was the Archbishop of Caerleon, for he had the honour of a legate and he was a blessed man. And then there came Morudd, Earl of Gloucester, and Mor, Earl of Worcester, and Anarawd of Shrewsbury, and *Marchudd of Durham,* and Owain of *Ballog's City — or* Salisbury *in the other language —*

Gwrssalem o Gaer Gynvarch, ac Urien o Gaer Vadon, a Jonathol o Dorcestyr, a Bosso o Ryt Ychen, a Dunawt vab Pabo post Prydein, Keneu vab Coel, Peredur vab Pruth, Grufud vab Nogoed, Regyn vab Klawd, Kynvarch, Gorbonyawn, Edelem vab Kolodawc, Kyngar vab Anghen, Maxwic Klof, Rvn vab Nwrthon, Gwrgant, Gweir, Catvan, ac y gyt a hynny llawer o wyrda ereill avydei ryvlin ev rifaw. O'r ynyssoed ereill y doeth Gillamwri brenhyn Iwerdon, a Gillamwri arall Brenhin Alont, a Doldaf Brenhin Gotlont, a Gwinwas Brenhin Orc, a Llew vab Kynvarch Brenhin Llychlyn ac Achel Vrenhin Denmarc. O'r tu draw yr mor y doeth Holdin Twyssawc Rwytwn, Burel Tywyssawc Conoman, Leodegar o Volwyn, Betwyr Tywyssawc Normandi, Kei Tywyssauc Angywf, Gwitard Tywyssauc Peitwf, a Deudec Gogyuurd Freinc, a Gereynt Carnwys yn eu blaen, a Howel vab Emyr llydaw, allawer y gyt a hynny a vydei ryhir menegi eu kymyrred pop vn arneill tu.

***

Ac yny erbyn ynteu y goruc Arthur naw mydin athywyssogeon kyfrwis kadarn yn eu blaen, a'r pedyt a rodet ar neilltu rwng deheu ac assw. Ac yna y dywat Arthur ha wyr da heb ef gobydwch chwi nac ymlad y bobil rackw vyth yn dvhun canys pobyl casgyl angkyfieith ysgymvn ynt. Ac nyt ynt vn galon a dynyon bydawl ereill canys ny ny yssyd gristionogeon a chyd ac iawn ac wyntav yn baganieit ysgymvn a chyt a'r [drwg]. A chan annoc y wyr ac ev dysgu ym gymyssgu ybydinoed ac ymlad yn chwere dost kreulon athrugar engiriawl. Ac velly y buant yn ymfust yny yttoed y rei byw yn dissynhwyraw y gwarandav disgrethin y rei a oed yn talu angheu o bop tu. A gwedy treulyaw onadunt llawer o'r dyd velly yn ymfust, mynet a oruc Arthur a'y vydin am ben bydin Medrawt a'y thyllu a'y gwasgaru megys llew diwal

Gwrsalem of Cynfarch's City, and *Urien* of Bath, and Jonathol of Dorchester, and Bosso from Oxford, and Dunod son of Pabo, *the support of Pictland,* Ceneu son of Coel, Peredur son of Pruth, Gruffydd son of Nogoed, Rhegin son of Clawd, Cynfarch, Gorbonion, Edlym son of Clydog, Cyngar son of Anghen, *Maxwig the Lame,* Rhun son of Nwrthon, *Gwrgant, Gweir, Cadfan,* and together with them many other men whom it would be tedious to number. From the other islands came Gillamwri, King of Ireland, and another Gillamwri, King of Alont, and Doldaf, King of Sweden, and Gwynwas, King of Orkney, and Lleu *son of Cynfarch,* King of Norway, and Achel, King of Denmark. From over the sea came Holdin, Prince of Rutenia, Burel, Prince of Conoman, Leodegar of Boulogne, Bedwyr, Prince of Normandy, Cai, Prince of Anjou, Gwitard, Prince of Poitou, and the twelve consorts of France with Geraint of Chartres as their leader and Hywel *son of Emyr* of Brittany, and many others together with them, to relate the fame of each one would be over-tedious.

***

pp.260-261:

And in opposition to him Arthur made nine divisions with strong and able princes in their vanguard, and the footmen he set apart to the right and left. And then Arthur spoke, 'Oh, nobles,' said he, 'know that those people there will never fight with a single mind, since they are a medley of accursed foreigners, and they do not have the same heart as other mortal men, *for we are Christians with right on our side, and they are pagans with wrong on theirs.*' And so he incited the men and instructed them to mix the divisions and to fight bitterly, sharply, savagely, terribly, and mightily. And so they fought until they were senseless with listening to the groaning of those who were giving up their lives all around. And after they had spent much of the day fighting in this way, Arthur, with his division went at Medrod's division, and broke it and

newynauc ymplith aniueilieit gwar. Ac yn y ruthyr hwnnw y llas Medrawt a milioed y gyt ac ef. Ac yr colli Medrawt ny orffwissaut adianghassei o'y lu o ymlad yny oed gymeynt yr aerua o bop tu a'r mwiaf o'r a uu erioed na chynt na gwedy. A [hynn] o dywyssogeon Medrawt a las, Eiaes, Ebrut, ac Eburiauc, a hynny oll o saesson. Gillamwri a Gillafadric a Gillassor a Gillarch, gwidyl oed y rei hynny. A chwybl o'r ffichtieit a'r ysgottieit a las ollyna. Oblegit Arthur y collet yna: Ebrit brenhin Llychlin; ac Achel brenhin Denmarc; a Chatwr Lemenic a Chasswallaun a llawer o vilioed o'r a dothoed o bop gwlat y gyt ac ef hyt yno. Ac yno y brathwyt Arthur yn angheuawl yn y benn, ac yducpwyt ef hyt yn Ynys Avallach y ev medegyn[iaythu]. Ac yna y gorchmynnws ef coron y dyrnas y Custennyn vab Kadwr ygar. Sef oed hynny dwy vlyned a deugeint a phymp cant gwedy geni mab Duw. Y gwersseu hynn.

[Quem morum probitas commendat laude] perhenni.
Hic iacet Arthurus [flos regum] gloria regni.
[Quae] meruit celos [uirtutum proli fecunda
Arthuri] iacet hec coniunx tumulata secunda.

Ac ny dyw[ot] yr ystoria hyspyssach am angheu Arthur no hynny.

scattered it like a ravenous, starving lion among domestic animals. And in this rush Medrod was killed, and thousands with him. And in spite of the loss of Medrod, those of his army who survived did not stop fighting until the slaughter was as great all around as the greatest slaughter that ever was, before or since. And of Medrod's princes: Eiaes, Ebrud and Eburiog, all Saxons; the Irish Gillamwri, and Gillafadrig, and Gillasor, and Gillarch, and all of the Picts and Scots were killed there.

There were lost from Arthur's household: Ebrut King of Norway, and Achel King of Denmark, and Cadwr the Bounding, and Caswallon, and many thousands others who had come from every country to that place with him. And there Arthur was mortally wounded in the head, and he was led off to the Isle of Afallach to be healed. And then he entrusted the crown of the kingdom to his cousin, Cystennin son of Cadwr. That was five hundred and forty-two years after the birth of God's son.

And there are these verses

Here lies Arthur the flower of kings, glory of the kingdom,
Who goodness commends with eternal honour;
Here lies the wife of Arthur entombed besides him,
Who deserves heaven with the fertile bearings of her virtues.

And the story does not tell about the death of Arthur more fully than that.

Culhwch ac Olwen

The tale of *Culhwch and Olwen* is of great importance to our understanding of the development of the Arthurian legend in Wales. The tale has long been recognised as a great treasury of Welsh tradition — the massive 'Court-List', in particular, preserves scraps of material otherwise lost. Part of its value, though, for the student of Arthuriana lies in its curious position somewhere between the early, heroic poetry and the later Romances.

Culhwch ac Olwen survives in two manuscripts, the White Book of Rhydderch (c. 1350) and the Red Book of Hergest (1385—1410). Both versions show a very close textual relationship and it is probable that they derive from a common original. Rachel Bromwich and D. Simon Evans put the date of the tale's earliest written redaction at around 1080—1100, though oral versions of the tale, or parts of it, must have been circulating long before that date. Unfortunately the White Book version is incomplete, giving only the first two-thirds of the story, so although that version is somewhat the earlier, the text given here is that of the Red Book.

As has often been noted, Culhwch belongs to the widespread 'Six Go Through the World' folktale-type (viz. 'Jason and the Golden Fleece'), Arthur was probably introduced later, and with him a mass of associated material. There is much to suggest that Arthur's role in early Welsh tradition was largely that of monster-slayer, and it may be that part of the reason for his introduction to the *Culhwch* folktale was due to the coincidence of an already existing tale of Arthur hunting the boar Twrch Trwyth, with an original boar-hunt integral to the folktale. The earliest association of Arthur with the Twrch Trwyth is in the *Mirabilia* attached to the *Historia Brittonum.* Arthur's portrayal here is quite definitely that of a great overlord, and he still appears as a monster-slayer (for example in his killing of the Very Black Witch). Sir Idris Foster remarked that 'unlike the Arthur of the French Romances, he is no *roi fainéant,* but takes an active part in perilous adventures', however, there is some indication that Arthur is on his way towards the Romance portrayal, in which his 'cotton-wool' treatment leaves him at risk of satire: he is twice advised by his men to stay out of trouble.

Given the vast hoard of material drawn on by *Culhwch ac Olwen* it is hardly surprising that parallels can be found throughout Welsh literature. The poems *Pa Gur* and *Preideu Annwfyn* are particularly notable for their similarities with the tale. The following text and translation excerpts are by no means the only references to Arthur in the tale, but it is hoped that they will convey some idea of the scope of his portrayal.

***

Bibliography:

Bromwich, R. & D. Simon Evans *Culhwch and Olwen*
Edel, Doris 'The Arthur of *Culhwch ac Olwen*'
Foster, Idris Llewelyn '*Culhwch and Olwen* and *Rhonabwy's Dream*'
Loomis, Richard M. 'The Tale of *Culhwch and Olwen*'
Roberts, Brynley F. '*Culhwch ac Olwen,* The Triads, Saints' Lives'
Sims-Williams, Patrick 'The Early Welsh Arthurian Poems'

Ac yna y doeth glewlwyt yr neuad. Ac y dywawt arthur wrthaw. Chwedleu porth gennyt. Ys ethyw gennyf deuparth vy oet. A deuparth y teu ditheu. Mi a uum gynt ygkaer se. ac asse. yn sach. a salach. yn lotor. a ffotor. Mi a uum gynt yn yr india uawr. ar india vechan. Mi A vum gynt yn ymlad deu ynyr. pan ducpwyt y deudec gwystyl o lychlyn. A mi a uum gynt yn yr egrop. A mi a uum yn yr affric. ac yn ynyssed corsica. Ac ygkaer brythwch. a brythach. A nerthach. Mi a uum gynt pan ledeist di deulu cleis mab merin. Pan ledeist mil du mab ducum. Mi a uum gynt pan oresgynneist roec wrth parth y dwyrein. Mi a uum gynt yg kaer oeth. ac anoeth. Ac ygkaer neuenhyr naw nawd teyrn. dynyon tec a welsam ni yno. ny weleis i eiryoet dyn kyuurd ar hwnn yssyd yn drws y porth yr awr honn. Ac y dywawt arthur. Os ar dy gam y doethost y mywn. dos ar dy redec allan. ar sawl a edrych y goleu. Ac a egyr y lygat. ac ae kae anghengaeth idaw. A gwassanaethet rei o vuelin goreureit. Ac ereill a golwython poeth pybreid hyt pan vo parawt bwyt a llynn idaw. Ys dyhed a beth gadu dan wynt a glaw y kyfryw dyn a dywedy di. Heb y kei. myn llaw vygkyueillt pei gwnelhit vygkyghor i ny thorrit kyfreitheu y llys yrdaw. Na wir kei wynn ydym wyrda hyt tra yn dygyrcher. yd yt uo mwyhaf y kyuarws a rodhom. Mwyvwy vyd yn gwrdaaeth ninneu ac an clot. ac an hetmic.

[Culhwch has journeyed to Arthur's court to request his aid in winning Olwen, his love. However, he has been stopped at the gate by the Gatekeeper, Glewlwyd Great-Grip. After some argument Glewlwyd has agreed to go and inform Arthur of his visitor.]

And then Glewlwyd came into the hall and Arthur said to him, 'Have you news from the gate?' 'Two-thirds of my time have gone, and two-thirds of yours. I was once in Caer Se and Asse, in Sach and Salach, in Lotor and Ffotor. I was once in the Greater India and the Lesser India. I was once in the battle of the two Ynyrs when the twelve hostages were brought from Scandinavia. And I was once in Europe, and I was in Africa, and in the Isles of Corsica, and in the Fort of Brythwch and Brythach and Nerthach. I was present once when you slew the war-band of Cleis son of Merin, when you slew Black-Beast son of Dugum. I was present once when you conquered Greece to the East. I was once in the Fort of Oeth and Anoeth, and in the Fort of Nefenhyr of the Nine Protections: fair, kingly men we saw there, I never saw a man of such rank as the one who is now at the entrance of the gate.' And Arthur said, 'If you came in at a stride, go out at a run! And such as looks at the light and opens his eye and closes it — an injunction against him. Let some serve him with a golden drinking-horn, and others with hot, peppered chops, until there be food and drink prepared for him. It is a disgraceful thing to leave such a man as you speak of under wind and rain.' Cai said, 'By the hand of my friend, if my counsel were taken, the customs of the court would not be broken for him.' 'Not true, fair Cai. We are noblemen as long as people seek us. Be it that we give the best of the gifts, all the greater will be our nobility and our fame and our praise.'

Heb y mab. ny deuthum i yma yr ffrawdunyaw bwyt a llynn. Namyn or kaffaf vygkyuarws y dalu ae uoli a wnaf. Onys kaffaf dwyn dy agclot ti a wnaf hyt y bu dy glot ym pedryual byt bellaf. Heb yr arthur yna. Kan ny thrigyy di yma unben. ti a geffy ykyfarws a notto dy benn ath dauawt. hyt y sych gwynt. hyt y gwlych glaw. hyt y treigyl heul. hyt yd amgyffret mor. hyt yd ydiw y dayar. eithyr vy llong. am llenn. a chaletuwlch uyg cledyf. a rongomyant uyg gwaew. Ac wyneb gwrthucher uyn taryan. a charnwenhan vyg kyllell. A gwenhwyuar vyg gwreic. Gwir duw ar hynny ti ae keffy yn llawen. Not a nottych. Diwyn vyg gwallt a uynnaf. Ti a geffy hynny. Kymryt crip eur o arthur. A gwelleu a doleu aryant idaw. A chribaw y benn a oruc.

Asswynaw y gyuarws ohonaw ar gei. a bedwyr. A greidawl galldouyd. A gwythyr uab greidawl...
A drustwrn hayarn. A glewlwyt gauaeluawr A lloch llawwynnyawc...
A theregut mab Iaen. A sulyen mab Iaen. A bratwen mab Iaen. A Moren mab Iaen. A siawn mab Iaen. A chràdawc mab Iaen. Gwyr kaer tathal oedynt kenedyl y arthur o bleit y dat...
A chalcas mab kaw. A hueil mab kaw. nyt asswynwys eiryoet yn llaw arglwyd...

[Culhwch has been admitted and has made a grand entrance.]

The boy [Culhwch] said, 'I did not come here to solicit food and drink. But if I get my boon, I shall repay it and praise it. If I do not get it I shall take your dishonour as far away as your fame was in the farthest four corners of the world.' Then Arthur said, 'Even if you do not stay here, chieftain, you shall get the boon that your head and your tongue name, as far as the wind dries, as far as the rain wets, as far as the sun wanders, as far as the sea stretches, as far as there is land; except for my ship and my mantle, and Caledfwlch [Hard-Cleft] my sword, and Rhongomyniad [Spear-Slayer] my spear, and Wyneb Gwrthucher [Evening-Face] my shield, and Carnwennan [Little White-Hilt] my knife, and Gwenhwyfar my wife.' 'The Truth of God on that?' 'You have it gladly. Name what you would name!' 'I want my hair trimmed.' 'You'll get that.' Arthur took up a comb of gold, and shears with handles of silver, and he combed his head.

[Here begins the great 'Court-List'.]

He invoked his boon from him in the names of Cai and Bedwyr, and Greidol Enemy-Subduer, and Gwythyr son of Greidol...

and Drust Iron-Fist, and Glewlwyd Great-Grip, and Llwch the Windy-Handed...

and Teregud son of Iaen, and Sulien son of Iaen, and Bradwen son of Iaen, and Moren son of Iaen, and Sion son of Iaen, and Caradog son of Iaen — men of the Fort of Dathal were they, kinsmen to Arthur on his father's side...

and Calcas son of Caw, and Huail son of Caw — he never sought patronage at the hand of a lord...

A gereint mab erbin. Ac erinit mab erbin. A dyuel mab erbin. A gwynn mab ermit. A chyndrwyn mab ermit. A hyueid unllenn. Ac eidon uawr urydic. A reidwn arwy. A gormant mab ricca. brawt y arthur o barth y uam. Pennhynef kernyw y tat. A llawnrodet uaruawc. A nodawl varyf twrch. a berth mab kado. A reidwn mab beli. Ac Iscouan hael. Ac Iscawin mab panon. A moruran eil tegit. ny dodes dyn y araf yndaw yg katgamlam rac y haccret. pawb a debygyt y uot yn gythreul canhorthwy. blew oed arnaw mal blew hyd. A sande bryt agel. ny dodes neb y waew yndaw yg kat gamlan. rac y decket. Pawb a debygynt y uot yn agel kanhorthwy. A chynnwyl sant. Y trydyd gwr a dienghis o gat kamlan. ef a ysgarwys diwethaf ac arthur y ar hengroen y uarch...
A charnedyr mab gouynyon hen. A gwenwynwyn mab naf gysseuin rysswr arthur. A llygatrud emys. A gwrbothu hen. ewythred arthur oedynt vrodyr y uam...
A llwydeu mab nwython. A gwydre mab llwydeu. o wennabwy merch kaw y uam. Hueil y ewythyr ae gwant. Ac am hynny y bu gas rwng hueil ac arthur am yr archoll. Drem vab Dremidyt. a welei o gelli wic ygkernyẇ. hyt ym penn blathaon ym prydein. pan dyrchauei y gwydbedyn y bore gan yr heul. Ac eidyol mab ner. A glwydyn saer. A wnaeth ehangwen neuad arthur. Kynyr keinuaruawc. Kei a dywedit y uot yn vab idaw. ef a dywawt wrth y wreic. o sit rann ymi oth uab di uorwyn oer vyth vyd y gallon. Ac ny byd gwres yn y dwylaw. kynnedyf arall arnaw. Os mab i mi uyd kyndynnyawc uyd. Kynnedyf arall a uyd arnaw. Pan dycko beich na mawr na bychan uo. ny welir vyth nac rac y wyneb na thraegeuyn.

and Geraint son of Erbin, and Ermid son of Erbin, and Dywel son of Erbin, and Gwyn son of Ermid, and Cyndrwyn son of Ermid, and Hyfaidd One-Mantle, and Eiddon the Magnanimous, and Rheiddwn Arwy, and Gormant son of Ricca — brother to Arthur on his mother's side; his father was Chief-Elder of Cornwall. And Llawfrodedd the Bearded, and Nodawl Boar-Beard, and Berth son of Cado, and Rheiddwn son of Beli, and Ysgofan the Generous, and Ysgafn son of Panon, and Morfran heir of Tegid — no man put his weapon into him at the Battle of Camlan because he was so ugly, everyone supposed that he was an attendant devil; there was hair on him like the hair of a stag. And Sandde Angel-Form — no-one put his spear into him at the Battle of Camlan because he was so fair, everyone supposed that he was an attendant angel. And Saint Cynwyl — one of the three men who escaped from the Battle of Camlan — he separated last from Arthur on Old-Skin, his horse...

and Carnedyr son of Gofynion the Old, and Gwenwynwyn son of Naf, Arthur's foremost warrior, and Llygadrudd the Stallion, and Gwrfoddw the Old— they were uncles of Arthur, brothers of his mother...

and Llwydeu son of Nwython, and Gwydre son of Llwydeu by Gwenabwy, daughter of Caw, his mother—Huail, his uncle, stabbed him, and from that, from the wound, there was enmity between Huail and Arthur. Look son of Looker, who could see, from Celliwig in Cornwall as far as Pen Blathaon in Scotland, whence a gnat was rising in the morning with the sun. And Eiddiol son of Ner, and Glwydyn the Builder who made Ehangwen, Arthur's hall. Cynyr the Fair-Bearded—Cai was said to be his son. He said to his wife, 'If there be a part of me in your son, maiden, his heart will ever be cold, and there will not be warmth in his hands. Another peculiarity about him: if he be my son, he will be steadfast. Another peculiarity will be about him: when he bear a burden, whether it be great or small, it will never be seen, neither before his face nor behind his back.

Kynnedyf arall heuyt a uyd arnaw. ny pheit neb a dwuyr ac a than yn gystal ac ef. Kynnedyf arall a uyd arnaw. ny byd gwassanaethwr na swydwr mal ef...

Gwydawc mab menestyr A ladawd kei. Ac Arthur a lladawd ynteu. ae urodyr yn dial kei. Garanwyn mab kei. Ac amren mab bedwyr. Ac ely a myr. A reu rwyd dyrys. A run rudwern. Ac eli. a thrachmyr penkynydyon arthur. A llwydeu mab kelcoet. A hunabwy mab gwryon. A gwynn gotyfron. A gweir dathar wennidawc. A gweir mab kadellin tal aryant. A gweir gwrhyt ennwir. A gweir baladyr hir. ewythred y arthur. vrodyr y uam. Meibon llwch llawwynnyawc or tu draw y uor terwyn. llenlleawc wydel. Ac arderchawc prydein. Cas mab saidi. Gwrvan gwallt auwyn. A gwyllennhin brenhin ffreinc. A gwittart mab oed brenhin Iwerdon. Garselit wydel. Panawr pen bagat. A fflendor mab naf. Gwynn hyuar maer Kernyw a dyfneint. y nawuet gwr a ystoues katgamlan...

Racymwri gwas arthur. dangossit yr yscubawr a uynnit idaw. kyt bei rwyf dec erydyr ar hugeint yndi. ef ae trawei a ffust hayarn hyt na bei well yr rethri ar trostreu. ar dulatheu. noc yr man geirch yng gwaelawt yr yscubawr yny ueiscawn...

Elidir gyfarwyd. Yskyrdaf. ac yscudyd. deu was y wenhwyuar oedynt. kynn ebrwydet oed eu traet wrth eu neges ac eu medwl...

Betwini escob a uendigei vwyt a llyn arthur. yr mwyn merchet eurdyrchogyon yr ynys honn. Y am wenhwyuar penn rianed yr ynys honn. a gwennhwyach y chwaer. A rathtyeu merch unic clememhill. A relemon merch kei. A thannwen merch weir dathar wenidawc. Gwennalarch merch kynnwyl canhwch. Eurneit merch clydno eidin. eneuawc merch uedwyr...

Arnadunt oll y hasswynwynwys kulhwch mab kilyd y gyuarws.

Another peculiarity will be about him also: no-one endures water and fire as well as he. Another peculiarity will be about him: there will not be a servant or an officer like him.'...

Gwyddog son of Mynystr, who killed Cai, and Arthur killed him and his brothers in revenge for Cai. Garanwyn son of Cai, and Amren son of Bedwyr, and Eli and Myr and Rheu Easy-Difficult, and Rhun Red-Alder, and Eli, and Trachmyr, Arthur's Chief-Huntsmen. And Llwydeu son of Celcoed, and Hunabwy son of Gwryon, and Gwyn Goddyfrion, and Gwair Servant of Birds, and Gwair son of Cadellin Silver-Brow, and Gwair Cruel-Courage, and Gwair Long-Spear — uncles to Arthur, brothers of his mother; Llwch the Windy-Handed from beyond the Tyrrhenian Sea. Llenlleog the Irishman, and Ardderchog of Britain, Cas son of Saidi, Gwrfan Gentle-Hair, Gwilenhyn King of France, Gwitard son of Aedd King of Ireland, Garselyd the Irishman, Panawr Chief-of-Host, and Fflewdwr son of Naf, Gwyn Bold-Anger Steward of Cornwall and Devon — one of the nine men who wove the Battle of Camlan...

Cacmwri, Arthur's servant, — were a chosen barn shown to him, though there were room for thirty ploughs in it, he would strike it with an iron flail until it were not better for the boards and the rafters and the side-beams than for the small oats at the bottom of the barn in the heap...

Elidir the Guide, Ysgyrdaf and Ysgudydd — they were two servants of Gwenhwyfar; their feet were as swift on their errand as their thought...

Bishop Bidwini, who would bless Arthur's food and drink for the gold-torqued daughters of this Island. As well as Gwenhwyfar, chief of the maidens of this Island, and Gwenhwyfach her sister, and Rhathtyeu daughter of Unig Clememhill, Celemon daughter of Cai, and Tanwen daughter of Gwair Servant of Birds, Gwenalarch daughter of Cynwyl Hundred-Swine, Eurneid daughter of Clydno of Edinburgh, Eneuog daughter of Bedwyr...

In all those names did Culhwch son of Cilydd invoke his boon.

Kyuodi a oruc arthur a milwyr ynys prydein gantaw y geissaw eidoel. A dyuot a orugant hyt yn rackaer glini yn y lle yd oed eidoel yg karchar. Seuyll a oruc glini ar vann y gaer. Ac y dywawt. Arthur, py holy di y mi pryt nam gedy yn y tarren honn. nyt da im yndi ac nyt digrif. nyt gwenith. nyt keirch im kyn ny cheissych ditheu wneuthur cam im. Arthur a dywawt. Nyt yr drwc ytti y deuthum i yma. namyn y geissaw y karcharawr yssyd gennyt. Mi a rodaf y carcharawr itti ac ny darparysswn y rodi y neb. Ac ygyt a hynny vy nerth am porth a geffy di. Y gwyr a dywawt wrth Arthur. Arglwyd dos di adref ny elly di uynet ath lu y geissaw peth mor uan ar rei hynn.

Ac odyna yd aethant ell deu hyt yg kelli wic yg kernyw. A chynllyuann o uaryf dillus uaruawc gantunt. Ae rodi a oruc kei yn llaw arthur. Ac yna y kanei arthur yr eglyn hwnn. Kynnllyuan a oruc kei. o uaryf dillus uab eurei. Pei Iach dy angheu uydei. Ac am hynny y sorres kei hyt pan uu abreid y uilwyr yr ynys honn tangneuedu y rwng kei ac arthur. Ac eissoes nac yr anghyfnerth ar arthur. nac yr llad y wyr. nyt ymyrrwys kei yn reit gyt ac ef o hynny allan.

[Culhwch has encountered Chief-Giant Ysbaddaden, Olwen's father, and has been given a great number of difficult tasks to fulfil. Finding Eiddoel son of Aer is a pre-requisite for one of these tasks.]

Arthur did arise, and the warriors of the Island of Britain with him, for the seeking of Eiddoel. And they came as far as Glywi's outer-wall where Eiddoel was in captivity. Glywi stood at the top of his fort and said, 'Arthur, what do you ask of me, as you will not spare me on this rock? I have no goods here and nothing pleasant, no wheat, no oats have I, though you may not be looking to do me harm.' Arthur said, 'Not for evil-doing against you have I come here, but for the seeking of the prisoner that you have.' 'I shall give the prisoner to you, but I had not intended to give him to anyone. And along with that, you will get my strength and my support.' [After that] the men said to Arthur, 'Lord, go home. You cannot go with your host to seek anything so petty as these.'

[Cai and Bedwyr have just obtained a certain leash, another of the tasks set by Ysbaddaden.]

And then both of them went to Celliwig in Cornwall, and the leash from the beard of Dillus the Bearded with them. And Cai gave it into Arthur's hand, and then Arthur sang this verse:

Cai made a leash
From the beard of Dillus son of Eurai.
Were he healthy, he would be your death.

And because of that Cai grew angry so that it was difficult for the warriors of this Island to make peace between Cai and Arthur. And nevertheless, neither due to an infirmity upon Arthur, nor due to the slaying of his men, thenceforth Cai would not concern himself with him in his need.

Gyrru o arthur gennat gwedy hynny ar odgar uab aed brenhin iwerdon. y erchi peir diwrnach wydel maer idaw. Erchi o otgar idaw y rodi. Y dywawt Diwrnach. duw a wyr pei hanffei well o welet un olwc arnaw nas kaffei. A dyuot o gennat arthur a nac genthi o Iwerdon. Kychwynnu a oruc arthur ac ysgawn niuer ganthaw A mynet ym prytwen y long. a dyuot y ywerdon. a dygyrchu ty diwrnach wydel a orugant. Gwelsant niuer otgar eu meint. A gwedy bwyta onadunt ac yuet eu dogyn. erchi y peir a oruc arthur. Y dywawt ynteu pei as rodei y neb. y rodei wrth eir odgar brenhin Iwerdon. Gwedy lleueryd nac udunt. Kyuodi a oruc bedwyr ac ymauael yn y peir. Ae dodi ar geuyn hygwyd gwas arthur. brawt oed hwnnw un uam y gachamwri gwas arthur. Sef oed y swyd ef yn wastat ymdwyn peir arthur a dodi tan y danaw. Meglyt o lenlleawc wydel yg kaletvwlch. ae ellwg ar y rot. a llad diwrnach wydel ae niuer achan. Dyuot lluoed Iwerdon ac ymlad ac wy. A gwedy ffo y lluoed achlan. mynet arthur ae wyr yn eu gwyd yn y llong. ar peir yn llawn o swllt iwerdon gantunt. A diskynnu yn ty llwydeu mab kel coet ym porth kerdin yndyuet. Ac yno y mae messur y peir.

Ac yna y kynnullwys arthur a oed o gynifywr yn teir ynys prydein. ae their rac ynys. Ac a oed yn freinc a llydaw. a normandi a gwlat yr haf. Ac a oed o gicwr·dethol. a march clotuawr. Ac yd aeth ar niueroed hynny oll hyt yn iwerdon. Ac y bu ouyn mawr ac ergryn racdaw yn Iwerdon.

[Two more of the difficult tasks: obtaining the Cauldron of Diwrnach, and hunting the boar, Twrch Trwyth.]

After that Arthur sent a representative to Odgar son of Aedd King of Ireland, to ask for the cauldron of Diwrnach the Irishman, his steward. Odgar asked him to give it up. Diwrnach said, 'God knows, if he could be better from one look at it, he would not get it.' And Arthur's representative came back with a "no" from Ireland. Arthur set out with a light force, and went in Prydwen his ship. He came to Ireland and made for the house of Diwrnach the Irishman. Odgar's forces saw their might, and after feasting because of them, and drinking their fill, Arthur asked for the cauldron. He said that if he could give it to anyone, he would give it at the word of Odgar King of Ireland. After they were refused Bedwyr rose up and got a grip on the cauldron, and set it on the back of Hygwydd, Arthur's servant (he was brother, by the same mother, to Cacmwri, Arthur's servant). This is what his permanent office was: to carry around Arthur's cauldron, and to kindle the fire beneath it. Llenlleog the Irishman seized Caledfwlch and swung it round, and killed Diwrnach the Irishman with his entire retinue. The hosts of Ireland came and fought with them. And after the flight of all the hosts, Arthur went in full view with his men to his ship, and the cauldron with them, full of the treasure of Ireland. And they disembarked at the house of Llwydeu son of Celcoed, at Porth Cerddin in Dyfed. And [now] 'The Measure of the Cauldron' is there.

And then Arthur gathered what there was of warriors in the Three Islands of Britain and her Three Adjacent Islands, and what there was in France, and Brittany, and Normandy, and Somerset, and what there was of select dogs, and celebrated horses. And all those forces went to Ireland, and there was a great fear and a trembling in Ireland because of him.

A gwedy disgynnu arthur yr tir. dyuot seint Iwerdon attaw y erchi nawd idaw. Ac y rodes ynteu nawd udunt hwy. ac y rodassant wynteu eu bendyth idaw ef. Dyuot a oruc gwyr iwerdon hyt att arthur a rodi bwyttal idaw. Dyuot a oruc Arthur hyt yn esgeir oeruel yn Iwerdon. yn y lle yd oed twrch trwyth. ae seithlydyn moch gantaw. gellwng kwn arnaw o bop parth. y dyd hwnnw educher yd ymladawd y gwydyl ac ef. Yr hynny pymhet ran y iwerdon a wnaeth yn diffeith. A thrannoeth ydym ladawd teulu arthur ac ef. namyn a gawssant o drwc y gantaw. ny chawssant dim o da. Y trydyd dyd yd ymladawd arthur ehun ac ef naw nos. a naw nieu. Ny ladawd namyn un parchell oe uoch. Gouynnwys y gwyr y arthur peth oed ystyr yr hwch hwnnw. Y dywawt ynteu. brenhin uu. ac am y bechawt y rithwys duw ef yn hwch.

Dywedut o arthur. a oes dim weithon or anoetheu heb gaffel. Y dywawt vn or gwyr. oes. gwaet y widon ordu, merch y widon orwen o penn nant gouut yg gwrthtir uffern. Kychwyn a oruc arthur parth ar gogled. A dyuot hyt lle yd oed gogof y wrach. A chynghori o wynn uab nud. a gwythÿr uab greidawl gellwng kacmwri. A hygwyd y urawt. y ymlad ar wrach. Ac ual y deuthant y mywn yr ogof y hachub a oruc y wrach. Ac ymauael yn hygwyd herwyd gwallt y benn. ae daraw yr llawr deni. Ac ymauel o gacmwri yndi hitheu. herwyd gwallt y phenn. Ae thynnu y ar hygwyd yr llawr. Ac ymchoelut a oruc hitheu ar kacmwri. ac eu dygaboli yll deu. ac eu diaruu. ae gyrru allan dan eu hub ac eu hob.

And after Arthur disembarked onto land the saints of Ireland came to him to ask for his protection. And he gave protection to them, and they gave their blessing to him. The men of Ireland came to Arthur and gave a food-tribute to him. Arthur came to the Ridge of Coldness in Ireland, where Twrch Trwyth was, and his seven young pigs with him. They set dogs on him from all sides. That day till evening the Irish fought with him. Despite that, he made waste a fifth part of Ireland. And the next day Arthur's retinue fought with him; except for what they got by way of evil from him, they got nothing good. On the third day Arthur fought with him himself, for nine nights and nine days. Of his pigs he killed nothing more than one piglet. The men asked Arthur what the story of that swine was. He said, 'He was a king, but because of his sins God transformed him into a swine.'

[The final task.]

Arthur said, 'Are any of the wonders still not obtained?' One of the men said, 'Yes, the blood of the Very Black Witch, daughter of the Very White Witch from the head of the Valley of Pain in the highlands of Hell.' Arthur set out towards the North, and came to where the hag's cave was. And Gwyn son of Nudd and Gwythyr son of Greidol advised sending Cacmwri and Hygwydd, his brother, to fight with the hag. And as they came into the cave the hag seized them, and she got a grip on Hygwydd by the hair of his head, and struck him to the ground beneath her. And Cacmwri got a grip on her by the hair of her head, and dragged her off Hygwydd to the ground. And she turned on Cacmwri, and battered them both and disarmed them. And they ran out with a bounding and a hopping.

A llidyaw a oruc arthur o welet y deu was hayachen. wedy eu llad a cheissaw achub yr ogof. Ac yna y dywedassant gwynn a gwythyr wrthaw. nyt dec ac nyt digrif genhym dy welet yn ymgribyaw a gwrach. gellwng hir amren a hir eidyl yr ogof. A mynet a orugant. Ac or bu drwc trafferth y deu gynt. gwaeth uu drafferth y deu hynny. hyt nas gwypei duw y vn ohonunt ell pedwar allu mynet or lle. namyn mal y dodet ell pedwar. ar lamrei kassec arthur. Ac yna achub a oruc arthur drws yr ogof. Ac y ar y drws a uyryei y wrach a charnwennan y gyllell. Ae tharaw am y hanner yny uu yn deu gelwrn hi. A chymryt a oruc kaw o brydein gwaet y widon ae gadw ganthaw.

And Arthur grew angry at seeing his two servants almost killed, and he tried to rush into the cave. But then Gwyn and Gwythyr said to him, 'It is not pleasant and not agreeable for us to see you wrestling with a hag. Send Eiddil the Tall and Amren the Tall into the cave.' And they did go. And if there was an evil predicament for the previous two, worse was the predicament of these two, so that God could not know how any one of those four would be able to go from the place, unless all four were set on Llamrei, Arthur's mare. And then Arthur did rush to the entrance of the cave, and from the entrance he could aim at the hag with Carnwenan, his knife. And he struck her down the middle until she was like two tubs. And Caw of Scotland took the witch's blood and kept it with him.

Trioedd Ynys Prydein

Much of Celtic literature shows a disposition to grouping ancestral knowledge, be it historical, gnomic or religious, in threes. The Welsh 'Triads of the Island of Britain' given here are presumed to have been mnemonic devices for bards who were expected to know 'tri pheth a beir y gerdawr vot yn amyl: kyfarwydyt ystoyaeu, a bardoniaeth, a hengerd.' [Three things that give amplitude to a poet: knowledge of histories, the poetic art, and old verse.]

Here follows a selection of Arthurian triads. As evinced elsewhere in Welsh tradition, the Arthurian complex is growing and absorbing other material: for example Llywarch Hen and Heledd who elsewhere appear as eponymous heroes of their own cycles of elegiac poems. Consequently Arthur's *Llys* ('court') replaces the *Ynys Prydein* formula (e.g. Triad 18W), and sometimes he becomes himself a fourth and greater character (e.g. Triad 2). The Triads date from the thirteenth century until well into the Early Modern period. The numbering system and the text itself derive from Rachel Bromwich's seminal work *Trioedd Ynys Prydein*. Interested readers will find therein textual variations, full glossaries, an important introduction to over ninety Welsh Triads, and an encyclopaedic series of notes to early Welsh tradition.

The 'Thirteen Treasures' and 'Twenty Four Knights', the earliest (surviving) redactions are fifteenth-century. They are related to the triadic tradition, and are to be found in Rachel Bromwich's work as appendices, fully annotated. The first includes the Hamper of Gwyddno, which can be found in *Culhwch ac Olwen*; it is possible other items have a similar antiquity. The northern provenance of much of this list is also worth noting. The 'Twenty Four Knights' owes much to Continental material which was quickly assimilated into Bardic lore, but some elements such as the Irresistible Knights belong to a milieu not known outside Britain.

***

Bibliography:

Bromwich, Rachel *Trioedd Ynys Prydein*
Roberts, Brynley F. '*Culhwch ac Olwen*, the Triads, Saints' Lives'
Barber, Richard *The Figure of Arthur*, pp.60—64

***

We would like to express our gratitude to Dr. Rachel Bromwich and to the University of Wales Press for very generously giving us permission to use the following extracts from *Trioedd Ynys Prydein*.

***

1) (Teir Lleithiclvyth Ynys Prydein:

Arthur yn Pen Teyrned ym Mynyv, a Dewi yn Pen Esgyb, a Maelgvn Gvyned yn Pen Hyneif;

Arthur yn Pen Teyrned yg Kelli Wic yg) Kernyw, a Bytwini Esgob yn Ben Esgyb, a Charadavc Vreichuras yn Ben Henyf;

Arthur yn Ben Teyrned ym Pen Ryonyd yn y Gogled, a Gerthmul Wledic yn Ben Hyneif; a Chyndeyrn Garthwys yn Ben Escyb.

2) Tri Hael Enys Prydein:
Nud Hael mab Senyllt,
Mordaf Hael mab Seruan,
Ryderch Hael mab Tudwal Tutclyt.
(Ac Arthur ehun oedd haelach no'r tri.)

4) Tri Deifnyawc Enys Prydein:
Gwalchmei mab Gwyar,
A Llacheu mab Arthur,
A Riwallawn Wallt Benhadlen.

9) Tri Vnben Llys Arthur:
(Gobrwy) mab Echel Vordwytwll,
A Chadr(i)eth mab Porthavr Gadw,
A Fleudur Flam.

12) Tri Overveird Enys Prydein:
Arthur,
A Chatwallan mab Catuan,
Rahaut eil Morgant.

1) Three Tribal Thrones of the Island of Britain:

Arthur as Chief Prince in Mynyw (=St. David's), and Dewi as Chief Bishop, and Maelgwn Gwynedd as Chief elder;

Arthur as Chief Prince in Celliwig in Cornwall, and Bishop Bytwini as Chief Bishop, and Caradawg Strong-Arm as Chief Elder;

Arthur as Chief Prince in Pen Rhionydd in the North, and Gerthmwl Wledig as Chief Elder, and Cyndeyrn Garthwys as Chief Bishop.

2) Three Generous Men of the Island of Britain:

Nudd the generous, son of Senyllt,
Mordaf the generous, son of Serwan,
Rhydderch the generous, son of Tudwal Tudglyd.
(And Arthur himself was more generous than the three.)

4) Three Well-Endowed Men of the Island of Britain:

Gwalchmai son of Gwyar,
and Llachau son of Arthur,
and Rhiwallawn Broom-hair.

9) Three Chieftains of Arthur's Court:

Gobrwy son of Echel Mighty-Thigh,
Cadr(i)eith ('Fine-Speech') son of Porthawr Gadw,
and Fleudur Fflam ('Flame').

12) Three Frivolous Bards of the Island of Britain:

Arthur,
and Cadwallawn son of Cadfan,
and Rahawd son of Morgant.

18 W.) Tri Annvyl Llys Arthur, a thri Chatwarchavc. Ac ny mynassant benteulu arnadunt eirioet. Ac y kant Arthur eglyn.

Sef yv uyn tri chat varchavc:
Mened, a Llud Llyurygavc,
A Cholouyn Kymry Karadavc.

20 W.) Tri Ruduoavc Ynys (Brydein):

Run ap Beli,
A Llew Llaw Gyffes,
A Morgan Mwynuawr,

Ac vn a oed ruduogach no'r tri. Arthur oed y henw; blvydyn ny doy na gvellt na llysseu y ford y kerdei yr vn o'r tri. a seith mlyned ny doy y ford y kerdei Arthur.

26W.)Tri Gvrueichiat Enys Brydein:

Pryderi vab Pvyll Pen Annwn, vrth voch Pendaran Dyuet y tatmeth. Ac y seth moch oedynt: y seithlydyn a duc Pvyll Pen Annvn, ac a'e rodes y Pendaran Dyuet y datmaeth. Ac y sef y lle y katwei, y Glyn Kuch yn Emlyn. A sef achavs y gelwit hvnnv yn wrueichiat: kany allei neb na thvyll na threis arnav;

A'r eil, Drystan ap Tallvch vrth voch March ap Meirchion, tra aeth y meichiat yn gennat ar Essyllt. Arthur, a March, a Chei, a Betvyr a vuant ell Petwar, ac ny chavsant kymint ac un banv, nac o dreis, nac o dvyll, nac o ledrat y ganthav;

18 W.) Three Favourites of Arthur's Court, and Three Battle-Horsemen: they would never endure a *penteulu* ['Head of Retinue'] over them. And Arthur sang an *englyn*.

These are my Three Battle-Horsemen:
Menedd, and Lludd of the Breastplate,
And the Pillar of the Cymry, Caradawg.

20 W.) Three Red Reapers of the Island of Britain:

Rhun son of Beli,
And Lle(u) Skilful Hand
And Morgan(t) the Wealthy.

But there was one who was a Red Reaper greater than all three: Arthur was his name. For a year neither grass nor plants used to spring up where one of the three would walk; but where Arthur went, not for seven years.

26 W.) Three Powerful Swineherds of the Island of Britain:

Pryderi son of Pwyll, Lord of Annwfn, tending the swine of Penndaran Dyfed his foster father. these swine were the seven animals which Pwyll Lord of Annwfn brought and gave them to Penndaran Dyfed his foster-father. And the place where he used to keep them was in Glyn Cuch in Emlyn. And this is why he was called a Powerful Swineherd: because no one was able either to deceive or to force him;

And the second, Drystan son of Tallwch, tending the swine of March son of Meirchyawn, while the swineherd went with a message to Essyllt. Arthur and March and Cai and Bedwyr were (there) all four, but they did not succeed in getting so much as one pigling — neither by force, nor by deception, nor by stealth;

A'(r) trydyd, Koll vab K(o)llurevy, vrth voch Dallwyr Dallben y Glyn Dallwyr yg Kerniv. Ac vn o'r moch a oed dorroc, Henwen oed y henv; a darogan oed yd hanuyde waeth ynys Brydein o'r torllwyth. Ac yna y kynullavd Arthur llu Ynys Brydein, ac yd aeth y geisso y diua. Ac yna yd aeth (hitheu) yn gordodv, ac ym Penryn Havstin yg Kerniv yd aeth yn y mor, a'r gvr(uei)chiat yn y hol. Ac y Maes Gvenith yg Went y dotwes ar wenithen a gvenynen, ac yr hynny hyt hediv y mae goreu lle gvenith a gvenyn Maes Gvenith yg Went. Ac yn Llonyon ym Phenvro y dotwes ar heiden a gvenithen. Am hynny y diharhebir o heid Llonyon. Ac yn Riw Gyuerthwch yn Aruon y dotwes a(r) geneu *cath* (=bleid) a chyv eryr. Ac y roet y bleid y Vergaed, ac y roet yr eryr y Vreat tywyssavc o'r Gogled, ac vynt a hanuuant waeth o nadunt. Ac yn Llanueir yn Aruon adan y Maen Du y dotwes ar geneu kath, ac y ar y Maen y bvryoed y gvrueichat yn y mor, a meibion Paluc yMon ae magassant, yr drvc vdunt.

A honno vu Gath Baluc. Ac a uu vn o Deir Prif Ormes Mon a uagvyt yndi. A'r eil oed Daronwy. A'r dryded, Edwin vrenhin Lloegyr.

37 R.) Tri Matkud Ynys Prydein:

Penn Bendigeituran uab Llyr, a guduwyt yn y Gvynuryn yn Llundein, a'e wyneb ar Ffreinc. A hyt tra uu yn yr ansavd y dodet yno, ny doei Ormes Saesson byth y'r Ynys honn;

Yr eil (M)atkud: y Dreigeu yn Ninas Emreis, a gudyavd Llud uab Beli;

A'r trydyd: Esgyrn Gvertheuyr Uendigeit, ym prif pyrth yr Ynys honn. A hyt tra vydynt yn y kud hvnnv, ny doei Ormes o Saesson byth y'r Ynys honn.

And the third, Coll son of C(o)llfrewy, tending the swine of Dallwyr Dallben in Glyn Dallwyr in Cornwall. And one of the swine was pregnant, Henwen was her name. And it was prophesied that the Island of Britain would be the worse for the womb-burden. Then Arthur assembled the army of the Island of Britain, and set out to seek to destroy her. And then she set off, about to farrow, and at Penrhyn Awstin in Cornwall she entered the sea, and the Powerful Swineherd after her. And in the Wheat Field in Gwent she brought forth a grain of wheat and a bee. And therefore from that day to this the Wheat Field in Gwent is the best place for wheat and bees. And at Llonion in Pembroke she brought forth a grain of barley and a grain of wheat. Therefore, the barley of Llonion is proverbial. At the hill of Cyferthwch in Arfon she brought forth a (wolf cub) and a young eagle. The wolf was given to (M)ergaed and the Eagle to Breat, a prince of the North: and they were both the worse for them. And at Llanfair in Arfon under the Black Rock she brought forth a kitten, and the Powerful Swineherd threw it from the Rock into the sea. And the sons of Palug fostered it in Môn, to their own harm: and that was Palug's Cat, and it was one of the Three Great Oppressions of Môn, nurtured therein. The second was Daronwy, and the third was Edwin, king of Lloegr.

37 R.) Three Fortunate Concealments of the Island of Britain:

The head of Brân the blessed, son of Llŷr, which was concealed in the White Hill in London, with its face towards France. And as long as it was in the position in which it was put there, no Saxon Oppression would ever come to this Island.

The second Fortunate Concealment: the Dragons in Dinas Emrys, which Lludd son of Beli concealed;

And the third: the Bones of Gwerthefyr the Blessed, in the Chief Ports of this Island. And as long as they remained in that concealment, no Saxon Oppression would ever come to this Island.

A llyna y Tri Anvat(dat)kud pan datgudwyt: A Gvrtheyrn Gvrtheneu a datkudyawd Esgyrn Gvertheuyr Uendigeit yr serch gvreic. Sef oed honno, Ronnwen baganes;

Ac ef a datkudyavd y Dreigeu;

Ac Arthur datkudyavd Penn Bendigeituran o'r Gvynnvrynn. Kan nyt oed dec gantav kadv yr Ynys honn o gedernit neb, namyn o'r eidav ehun.

52) Tri Goruchel Garcharavr Ynys Brydein:

Llyr Lledyeith a uu gan Euroswyd yg karchar,

A'r eil Mabon ap Modron,

A'r trydyd Gweir ap Geirioed.

Ac vn a oed goruchelach nor tri, a uu deirnos yg karchar yg Kaer Oeth ac Anoeth, ac a uu deir nos yg karchar gan Wen Bendragon, ac a uu deir nos yg karchar hut a dan Lech Echemeint. Ac y sef oed y Goruchel Garcharavr hvnnv, Arthur. A'r un gwas a'e gollygavd o'r tri charchar hynny. Ac y sef oed y gvas hvnnv, Goreu vab Kustenin y geuyderv.

53) (Teir Gvith Baluavt Ynys) Prydein:

Vn onadunt a drevis Matholvch Vydel ar Vranven verch Lyr;

A'r eil a drevis Gvenhyuach ar Wenhvyuar. Ac o achavs hynny y bu Weith Kat Gamlan gvedy hynny;

A'r dryded a drewis Golydan Vard ar Catwaladyr Vendigeit.

And they were the Three Unfortunate Disclosures when these were disclosed. And Gwrtheyrn the Thin disclosed the bones of Gwerthefyr the Blessed for the love of a woman: that was Ronnwen the pagan woman;

And it was he who disclosed the dragons;

And Arthur disclosed the Head of Brân the blessed from the White Hill, because it did not seem right to him that this Island should be defended by the strength of anyone, but by his own.

52) Three Exalted Prisoners of the Island of Britain:

Llŷr Half-Speech, who was imprisoned by Euroswydd,

and the second, Mabon son of Modron,

and third, Gwair son of Geirioedd.

And one (prisoner), who was more exalted than the three of them, was three nights in prison in Caer Oeth and Anoeth, and three nights imprisoned by Gwen Pendragon, and three nights in an enchanted prison under the stone of Echymeint. This Exalted Prisoner was Arthur. And it was the same lad who released him from each of these three prisons — Goreu, son of Custennin, his cousin.

53) Three Harmful Blows of the Island of Britain.

The first of them Matholwch the Irishman struck upon Branwen daughter of Llŷr;

The second Gwenhwyfach struck upon Gwenhwyfar: and for that cause there took place afterwards the Action of the Battle of Camlan;

And the third Golydan the Poet struck upon Cadwaladr the blessed.

54) Teir Drut Heirua Ynys Brydein:

Vn o nadunt, pan doeth Medravt y lys Arthur yg Kelliwig yg Kerniv; nyt edewis na bvyt na diavt yn y llys nys (treulei), a thynu Gvenhvyuar heuyt o'e chadeir vrenhiniaeth. Ac yna y trewis baluavt arnei;

Yr eil Drut Heirua, pan doeth Arthur y lys Vedravt. Nyt edevis yn y llys nac yn y kantref na bvyt na diavt;

(Ar trydydd Drut (Heirua), pan ddeuth Aydan Vradawc hyt yn Alclut y lys Rydderch Hael, ac nyt adewis na bvyt na llyn na llvdwn yn vyw.)

56) Teir Prif Riein Arthur:

Gvenhvyuar verch Gvryt Gvent,
A Gvenhyuar verch Vthyr ap Greidiavl,
A Gvenhyuar verch Ocuran Gavr.

57) A'e deir Karedicwreic oed y rei hynn:

Indec verch Arvy Hir,
A Garven verch Henin Hen,
A Gvyl verch Endavt.

65) Tri Trwydedavc Llys Arthur, a thri Anuodavc:

Llywarch Hen
a Llemenic,
a Heled.

73) Tri Gogyfurd Llys Arthur:

Ryhavt eil Morgant,
a Dalldaf eil Cvnyn Kof,
a Drystan eil March.

54) Three Unrestrained Ravagings of the Island of Britain:

One of them (occurred) when Medrawd came to Arthur's court at Celliwig in Cornwall; he left neither food nor drink in the court that he did not consume. And he dragged Gwenhwyfar from her royal chair, and then he struck a blow upon her;

The second Unrestrained Ravaging (occurred) when Arthur came to Medrawd's court. He left neither food nor drink in the court;

(And the third Unrestrained Ravaging (occurred) when Aeddan the Wily came to the court of Rhydderch the Generous at Alclud (=Dumbarton): he left neither food nor drink nor beast alive.)

56) Arthur's Three Great Queens:

Gwenhwyfar daughter of (Cywryd) Gwent,

and Gwenhwyfar daughter of (Gwythyr) son of Greidiawl,

and Gwenhwyfar daughter of (G)ogfran the Giant.

57) And his Three Mistresses were these:

Indeg daughter of Garwy the Tall,

and Garwen ('Fair Leg') daughter of Henin the Old

and Gwyl ('Modest') daughter of Gendawd ('Big Chin'?).

65) Three Unrestricted Guests of Arthur's Court, and Three Wanderers:

Llywarch the Old,

and Llemenig,

and Heledd.

73) Three Peers of Arthur's Court:

R(a)hawd son of Morgant,

and Dalldaf son of Cunyn Cof,

and Drystan son of March.

74) Tri An(heol) Llys Arthur:

Vchei mab Gvryon,
a Choledavc mab (Gwynn),
a Gerenhyr mab Gereinyavn Hen.

80) Teir Aniweir Wreic Ynys Prydein. Teir merchet Kulvanawyt Prydein:

Essyllt (F)yngwen, (godderch Trystan);
a Phenarwan, (gwreic Owein mab Urien);
A Bun, gwreic Flamdwyn.

Ac un oed aniweirach nor teir hynny: Gwenhwyvar gwreic Arthur, kanys gwell gwr y gwnai hi gyweilyd idaw no neb.

84) Tair (Ouergat) Ynys Prydein:

Vn onaddunt a vu Gat Godeu. Sef y gwnaethpvyt, o achavs yr Ast y ar ivrch fechvys a Chornvgil;

Yr eil a vu y Gweith Arderydd, a wnaethpvyt o achavs nyth yr Ychedydd;

A'(r) drydydd oed waethaf. Sef oedd honno, Camlan. A honno a wnaethpvyt o gywryssedd Gwenhwyuar a Gwenhvy(v)ach. Sef achaws y gelwit y rei hynny yn ouer: vrth y gwneuthur o achavs mor ddiffrvyth a hvnnv.

87) Tri Bardd Kaw oedd yn Llys Arthur:

Myrddyn vab Morvryn,
Myrddyn Embrys,
A Thaliessin.

88) Tair Rhiain Ardderchog Llys Arthur:

Dyfyr Wallt Eureit,
Enid verch i Niwl Iarll,
A Thegeu Eurfron.

74) Three who could not be expelled from Arthur's Court:
Uchei son of Gwryon,
and Coledawg son of (Gwynn),
and (C)erenhyr son of Gereinyawn the Old.

80) Three Faithless Wives of the Island of Britain. Three daughters of Culfanawyd of Britain:
Essyllt Fair-Hair (Trystan's mistress),
and Penarwan (wife of Owain son of Urien),
and Bun, wife of Fflamddwyn.

And one was more faithless than those three: Gwenhwyfar, Arthur's wife, since she shamed a better man than any (of the others).

84) Three Futile Battles of the Island of Britain:

One of them was the Battle of Goddeu: it was brought about by the cause of the bitch, together with the roebuck and the plover;

The second was the Action of Ar(f)derydd, which was brought about by the cause of the Lark's nest;

And the third was the worst: that was Camlan, which was brought about because of a quarrel between Gwenhwyfar and Gwennhwy(f)ach.

This is why those (Battles) were called Futile: because they were brought about by such a barren cause as that.

87) Three Skilful Bards were at Arthur's Court:
Myrddin son of Morfryn,
Myrddin Emrys,
And Taliesin.

88) Three Splendid Maidens of Arthur's Court:
Dyfyr Golden-Hair,
Enid daughter of Earl (Y)niwl,
and Tegau Gold-Breast.

Tri Thlws ar Ddeg Ynys Brydain

(Henwae y) Tri Thlws ar Ddeg Yn(y)s Brydain (a oedd yn y Gogledd):

1) Dyrnwyn, gleddyf Rhydderch Hael: os tynnai ddyn mwyn ef i hun, ef a ennyna(i) yn yn fflam o'i groes hyd i flaen; a ffawb a'r a'i harchai ef a'i kaei, ag o blygid y gyneddf honno, hwy a'i gwrthodynt; ag am hyn(n)y i gelwyd ef Rhydderch Hael.

2) Mwys Gwyddno Garanir: bwyd i un gwr a roid ynddo, a bwyd i ganwr a gaid ynddo pan agoryd.

3) Korn Bran Galed (o'r Gogledd): y ddiod a ddymunid i bod ynddo a gaid ynddo.

4) Kar Morgan Mwynfa(w)r: od ai ddyn ynddo, damuna(i) fod ll(e) mynai, ag ef a fyddai yn ebrwydd.

5) Kebystr Klydno Eidd(i)n, a oed mewn ystwffwl is draed i wely; a damunai y march a fynai yno, ef a'i kae(i) (yn y kebystr).

6) Kyllell Llawfroded(d) Farchog, yr honn a w(a)s(a)naethai i bedwar gwr ar higain i fwyta ar fwrdd.

7) Pair (Dyrnwch Gawr): pe rhoid ynddo gig i wr llwfwr i ferwi, ni ferwai fyth, o rhoid iddo gig i wr dewr, berwi a wnai yn ebrwydd (ag yno y caid gwahan rhwng y dewr a'r llwrf).

8) (H)ogalen Tudwal Tutklyd: o hogai wr dewr i gleddyf arni, od enwaedai ar wr, marw fyddai; ag os hogai wr llwfr, ni byddai waeth.

9) Pais Badarn Beisrydd: os gwisgai wr bonheddig, kymhessur fyddai iddo, ag os i iangwr, nid ai amdano.

10, 11) Gren a desgyl Rhygenydd Ysgolhaig: dymunyd ynddynt y bwyd a fynyd, ef a'i kaid.

(The Names of the) Thirteen treasures of the Island of Britain, (which were in the North):

1) Dyrnwyn ('White Hilt'), the Sword of Rhydderch the Generous: if a well-born man drew it himself, it burst into flame from its hilt to its tip. And everyone who used to ask for it would receive it; but because of this peculiarity everyone used to reject it. And therefore he was called Rhydderch the Generous.

2) The Hamper of Gwyddno Long-Shank: food for one man would be put in it, and when it was opened, food for a hundred men would be found in it.

3) The Horn of Brân the Niggard from the North: whatever drink might be wished for was found in it.

4) The Chariot of Morgan the Wealthy: if a man went in it, he might wish to be wherever he would, and he would be there quickly.

5) The Halter of Clydno Eiddyn, which was fixed to a staple at the foot of his bed: whatever horse he might wish for, he would find in the halter.

6) The Knife of Llawfrodedd the Horseman, which would serve for twenty-four men to eat at table.

7) The cauldron of Dyrnwych the Giant: if meat for a coward were put in it to boil, it would never boil; but if meat for a brave man were put in it, it would boil quickly (and thus the brave could be distinguished from the cowardly).

8) The Whetstone of Tudwal Tudglyd: if a brave man sharpened his sword on it, if it (then) drew blood from a man he would die. If a cowardly man (sharpened his sword on it), he (his opponent) would be no worse.

9) The coat of Padarn Red-Coat: if a well-born man put it on, it would be the right size for him; if a churl it would not go upon him.

10,11) The crock and the dish of Rhygenydd the Cleric: whatever food might be wished for in them, it would be found.

12) Gwyddbw(y)ll Gwenddoleu (ap Ceidio): o gosodid y werin, hwynt a chw(a)raen(t) i hunain; aur oedd y klawr, ag arian oedd y gwŷr.

13) Llen Arthyr (yng Nghernyw): a fai deni, nis gwelai neb ef, ag ef a welai bawb.

Pedwar marchog ar Hugain Llys Arthur

Pedwar Marchog ar hugeint o varchogion urddolion oedd yn Llys Arthur yn trigo yn wastadol, a chynneddf naturiol o orchest oedd ar bop un onaddunt, mwy noc ar ereill.

1) Tri Marchog Aurdavodiawc oedd yn Llys Arthur: Gwalchmai ap Llew ap Kenvarch, a Drudwas ap Tryffin, ac Eliwlod ap Mad(og) ap Uthur; ac nid oedd na brenhin nac arglwydd ar y delai y rhai hynny atto, na wrandawai arnunt; a pha ryw neges bynnac a geisynt, hwynt a'i mynynt (ac wynt a'i keffynt), y naill o vodd a'i o anvodd.

2) Tri Marchoc Gwyry oedd yn Llys Arthur: Bwrt ap Bwrt, brenhin G(w)asgwin, a Phredur ap Efroc Iarll, a Galath ap Lanslod Lak. Pa le bynnac y delai y rhai hynny, lle bai gawr na gwiddon na dyn anysbrydal, ni allai aros yr vn o'r Tri Marchog Gwyry hynny.

3) Tri Chadvarchoc oedd yn Llys Arthur: Cadwr Iarll Kernyw, a Lanslod Lak, ac Ywain ap Urien Rreget. Kynneddveu y rhai hynny: ni chilynt er ofn gwayw na chleddyf na saeth; ac ni chavas Arthur erioed gywilydd mewn brwdyr y dydd i gwelai eu hwynebeu yn y maes — ac am hynny i gelwid hwynt cad varchogion.

4) Tri Lledrithawc Varchoc oedd yn Llys Arthur: Menw ap Teirgwaedd, a Thrystan ap Tallwch, ac Eddili(g) Cor: cans ymrithiaw a wneynt yn y rith y mynnynt pan vai galed arnunt, ac am hynny ni allai neb eu gorvod.

12) The Chessboard of Gwenddolau son of Ceidio: if the pieces were set, they would play by themselves. The board was of gold, and the men of silver.

13) The mantle of Arthur in Cornwall: Whoever was under it could not be seen, and he could see everyone.

Twenty-four ordained Knights were in Arthur's Court dwelling continuously, and each one of them had an innate peculiarity of achievement beyond other people.

1) Three Golden-Tongued Knights were in Arthur's Court: Gwalchmai son of Llew son of Cynfarch, and Drudwas son of Tryfin, and Eliwlod son of Madog son of Uthur: and there was neither king nor lord to whom those came who did not listen to them; and whatever quest they sought, they wished for and obtained it, either willingly or unwillingly

2) Three Virgin Knights were in Arthur's Court: Bwrt son of Bwrt king of Gascony, and Peredur son of Earl Efrog, and Galath son of Lanslod Lak. Wherever those came, where there might be giant or witch or fiendish being — (such) could not withstand one of those Three Virgin Knights.

3) Three Knights of Battle were in Arthur's court: Cadwr Earl of Cornwall, and Lanslod Lak, and Ywain son of Urien Rheged. The peculiarities of those were that they did not flee for fear of spear or sword or arrow; and Arthur was never shamed in battle on the day that he saw their faces in the field. And therefore they were called Knights of Battle.

4) Three Enchanter Knights were in Arthur's Court: Menw son of Teirgwaedd, and Trystan son of Tallwch, and E(i)ddilig the Dwarf; since they changed themselves into the form they wished when they were hard-pressed, and therefore no one could overcome them.

5) Tri Brenhinawl Varchoc oedd yn Llys Arthur: Nasiens mab Brenhin Denmarck, a Medrod ap Llew ap Kenvarch, a Howel ap Emyr Llydaw. Kyneddveu y rhai hynny: nid oedd na brenhin nac emerodr o'r byd a allai balle uddynt rrac eu tecket a'u doethet mewn heddwch; mewn rryvel nis arhoi na milwr na rysswr, er daed i arveu. Ac am hynny i gelwid hwynt Brenhinawl Varchogion.

6) Tri Chyvion Varchoc oedd yn Llys Arthur: Blaes mab Iarll Llychlyn, a Chadawc ap Gwynlliw Varvoc, a Phetroc Baladrddellt ap Clement Tywyssawc Kernyw. Kyneddfeu y rhai hynny oedd: pwy bynnac a wnelai gam a(r) gwann, hwynt a ymleddynt yn erbyn a wnai gam ac ef, ynghweryl kyviawnder; a'r neb a wnelai gam hwynt a'(e) lleddynt er kydarnet vai. Cans ymroi a ddaroedd i'r tri hynny i gadw y kyfiawnder ymhob kyfreith: Blaes o gyfraith vyd, Cadawc o gyfraith eglwys, Pedroc o gyfraith arveu. A'(r) rain hynny i gelwid hwynt kyvion varchogion.

7) Tri Gwrthniviad Varchoc oedd yn Llys Arthur: Morvran ap Tegid, a Sandeff Bryd Angel, a Glewlwyd Gavaelvawr. Kyneddveu y rhai hynny: gwrthwynebawl oedd gan neb i nackau o ddim — Sanddef rac i decked, Morvran rac i hackred, Glewlwyd rac i vaint o'i gryved a'i greuloned. Ac am hynny i gelwid hwynt yn Wrthniviawc Varchogion.

8) Tri Chynghoriad Varchoc oedd yn Llys Arthur: Kynon ap Klydno Eidden, ac Aron ap Kenvarch, a Llywarch Hen ap Elidir Lydanwyn. A'r tri hynny a oedd gynghorwyr i Arthur, pa ryw galedi bynnac a ddelai arno, hwynt a'i kynghorynt ef val na allai neb orvod arno. Ac velly yr oedd Arthur yn gorvod ar bawb, ac ar bob gorchest, a phob kenedlaeth o'r byd — drwy gydernyd yr ysbryd kadarn, a'r ffydd a'r gobaith a oedd yn i galonn i'r gwyr hynny; a thrwy yr arveu kyssegredic a roessai Dduw iddo: Rongo(m)ian i waew, Caledvwlch i gleddyf, a Charnwennan i ddager.

5) Three Royal Knights were in Arthur's Court: Nasiens son of the King of Denmark, and Medrod son of Llew son of Cynfarch, and Howel son of Emyr Llydaw. The peculiarities of those were that there was neither king nor emperor in the world who could refuse them, on account of their beauty and wisdom in peace; while in war no warrior or champion could withstand them, despite the excellence of his arms. And therefore they were called the Royal Knights.

6) Three Just Knights were in Arthur's court: Blaes son of the Earl of Llychlyn, and Cadog son of Gwynlliw the bearded, and Pedrog Splintered-Spear, son of Clement Prince of Cornwall. The peculiarities of those were that whoever might do wrong to the weak, they contended against him who did him wrong in the cause of justice; and whoever might do wrong they slew, however strong he might be. For those three had dedicated themselves to preserve justice by every Law: Blaes by earthly Law, Cadog by the Law of the Church, and Pedrog by the Law of arms. And those were called the Just Knights.

7) Three Irresistible Knights were in Arthur's Court: Morfran son of Tegid, and Sanddef Angel-Face, and Glewlwyd Mighty-Grasp. The peculiarities of those were that it was repugnant to anyone to refuse them anything: Sandef because of his beauty, Morfran because of his ugliness and Glewlwyd because of his size and his strength and his ferocity. And therefore they were called irresistible knights.

8) Three Counsellor knights were in Arthur's Court: Cynon son of Clydno Eiddyn, and Aron son of Cynfarch, and Llywarch the Old son of Elidir Lydanwyn. And those three were Counsellors to Arthur: whatever hardship came upon him, they counselled him, so that nobody could overcome him. And thus Arthur triumphed over everyone, and in every feat, and over every nation in the world; through the strength of the powerful spirit and the faith and hope that were in his heart toward those men, and through the sacred weapons that God had given him: Rhongomiant his spear, Caledfwlch his sword, and Carnwennan his dagger.

Genealogies

'Oral transmission in the ages when writing was uncommon has been shown to be often remarkably accurate, and I believe that one may reasonably accept an apparently legendary pedigree (with reservations) unless it can be shown to wrong by chronological or other tests.' So wrote P.C. Bartrum, responding to cynicism about the historical accuracy of the Welsh genealogies. This cynicism has tended to see political motives inherent in the composition of aristocratic family-history. Dr. David Dumville has shown that past relationships are often projections of the present political fare. In Gwynedd, all sub-kingdoms expressed loyalty to the centre through ancestries claiming to go back to Cunedda the first king in Gwynedd after Maximus' death in 388 A.D. This is one illustration of the utility of genealogy; Arthur's role in Welsh pedigrees is another. By lodging Arthur in one's descent, prestige was reflected on one's line, or, patron in the case of the saints, who it was sometimes claimed were related to Arthur. One example would be St. David who is variably claimed to be Arthur's nephew or uncle depending on which genealogy is being used.

The selections below are from manuscripts dating from the thirteenth to fifteenth century. Arthur appears both as a family member and as a figure outside the bloodline, used as an historical marker for native scholars. Altogether he is present in several Welsh genealogies (of which those below are just a small sample), making this area potentially a very productive one for Arthurian studies; yet it is Arthur's relative absence from the greater proportion of the manuscripts — especially when his high status is borne in mind — which is perhaps most interesting.

***

Bibliography:

Bartum, P.C. *Early Welsh Genealogical Tracts*
Dumville, David 'Kingship, Genealogies and Regnal Lists'
Henken, Elissa R. *Traditions of the Welsh Saints,* p.32
Sims-Williams, Patrick P. 'Some Functions of Origin Stories'

Mostyn MS. 117:

Llywelyn ap Gruffyd mab Llywelyn mab Ioruerth mab Owein mab Gruffyd mab Kynan mab Iago mab Idwal voel mab Anarawt mab Rodri mab Meruyn vrych, gwr priawt Esylt verch Kynan Tindaethwy mab Rodri maelwynawc mab Idwal iwrch mab Katwaladyr vendigeit mab Katwallawn mab Katuan mab Iago mab Belli mab Run mab Maelgwn Gwyned, herwyd dull y beird. Namyn o herwyd yr Istoria Beli oed vab y Eynyan vab Maelgwn, y gwr uu petweryd brenhin ar Ynys Prydein gwedy Arthur.

Jesus College MS. 20:

Severus, Basian, Carancius, Alectus, Asclepiodotus, Coel, Llyr, Constans. Gwreic y Constans hwnnw oed Elen verch Coel. Constantinus, Constans vanach, Gwrtheyrn, Gwertheuyr vendigeit, Emrys wledic, Vthurpendreic, Arthur, Constantinus, Aurelius, Iuor, Maelgwn Gwyned, Caterius, Catuan, Catwallawn, Catwaladyr vendigeit.

Bonedd Y Saint in Peniarth MS. 27:

....Eda Glynuawr ap Gwybei drahavg ap Mwg Mawr Drefydd ap Offa kyllellvawr, vrenhin Lloegyr, y gwr y ymladdodd ac Arthvr yNgwaith Vadon.

...Llywelyn son of Gruffydd son of Llywelyn son of Iorwerth son of Owain son of Gruffydd son of Cynan son of Iago son of Idwal the Bald son of Anarod son of Rhodri son of Myrfyn the Speckled, the husband of Esyllt daughter of Cynan Tindaethwy son of Rhodri Maelwynog son of Idwal the Buck son of Cadwaladr the Blessed son of Cadwallon son of Cadfan son of Iago son of Beli son of Rhun son of Maelgwn of Gwynedd, according to the tradition of the bards, except that according to the *Historia* Beli was son of Eynyan son of Maelgwn, the man who was the fourth king of the Island of Britain after Arthur. Maelgwn was the son of Cadwallon Long-Hand...

...Severus father of Basian father of Carancius father of Alectus father of Asclepiodotus father of Coel father of Llyr father of Constans. The wife of that Constans was Elen daughter of Coel. Constantinus father of Constans the Monk father of Gwrtheyrn father of Gwrthefyr the Blessed father of Emrys the Sovereign father of Uthr Pendragon father of Arthur father of Constantinus father of Aurelius father of Ifor father of Maelgwn of Gwynedd, father of Caterius father of Cadfan father of Cadwallon father of Cadwaladr the Blessed.

71) ...Eda Glynfawr son of Gwynbai Trahog son of Mwg the Great Soldier son of Offa Big-Knife, King of England, the man who fought against Arthur at the Battle of Badon.

Englynion Y Beddau

Collected below are the Arthurian verses of the collection commonly known as the *Stanzas of the Graves* from the Black Book of Carmarthen (unfortunately they are impossible to date securely.) They record, as Patrick Sims-Williams noted, 'often with unexpected poetic power, the sites of the graves of once famous heroes, testifying to the close association between heroes and places in early Welsh literature.' Indeed this 'poetic power' coupled with their nostalgia for an heroic past (and no doubt their 'Celticness') was such that W.B.Yeats included Ernest Rhys' loose translation of them in the *Oxford Book of Modern Verse 1892-1935*. In the stanzas below translation is relatively easy except for the last *englyn*, to which all four items on the bibliography refer. It has been suggested that the sense could either convey that Arthur's grave is lost; or that there is no grave and that this may be the first surviving reference to the once and future king's messianic qualities; or indeed it may be a reference to the fact that Welsh tradition records a number of different graves.

***

Bibliography:

Jones, Thomas 'The Early Evolution of the Legend of Arthur', pp.17—18

— 'The Black Book of Carmarthen: Stanzas of the Graves', pp.97—137

Rowland, Jenny *Early Welsh Saga Poetry*, p.560

Sims-Williams, Patrick 'The Early Welsh Arthurian Poems', pp.49—51

Bet Gwalchmei ym peryton
Ir diliv y dyneton
In Llan Padarn bet Kinon.

Bet Owein ab Urien im Pedryal bid
Dan gverid llan morvael
In Aberech Riderch hael.

Bet mab Ossvran yg Camlan
Gyvdi llauer kywlavan
Bet Bedwir in alld Tryvan.

Bet y March, Bet y Guythur
Bet y Gugan Cledyfrut
Anoeth bid bet y Arthur.

The grave of Gwalchmai in Perydon
As a reproach to men:
In Llanbadarn the grave of Cynon.

The grave of Owain son of Urien is a square grave
Beneath the earth of Llanforfael
In Aberech Rhydderch the Generous.

The grave of Osfran's son at Camlann,
After many a slaughter:
The grave of Bedwyr is on Tryfan Hill.

A grave for March, a grave for Gwythur.
A grave for Gwgan Red-Sword.
The world's wonder a grave for Arthur.

Ymddiddan Arthur a'r Eryr

The *Dialogue of Arthur and the Eagle* is extant in numerous manuscripts of the fourteenth century and later, though Ifor Williams demonstrated that the poem may date originally to the twelfth century. The bulk of the text is essentially a fairly standard Christian catechism, so only its frame — where we find the specifically Arthurian material — is given here. At the very beginning of the dialogue Arthur refers to himself as a bard, and this comment should be compared with Triad 12 where Arthur is one of the *Tri Overveirdd* ('the Three Frivolous/Part-Time Bards'), and with his englyn in *Culhwch ac Olwen.* Also noteworthy is the fact that the scene appears to be set in Cornwall, and that Arthur is described as 'Chief of the Battalions of Cornwall' (in stanza 34, not edited here). Some aspects of his depiction are reminiscent of the saints' Lives, though, as an enlightenment-seeking pagan, he is perhaps viewed more sympathetically. The Arthur presented here is not 'King Arthur', but is shown, rather, as the great warrior of earlier literature.

***

Bibliography:

Haycock, Marged *Blodeugerdd Barddas,* pp.297—312
Rowland, Jenny *Early Welsh Saga Poetry,* pp.284—86 & 356
Sims-Williams, Patrick 'The Early Welsh Arthurian Poems', pp.57—58
Williams, Ifor 'Ymddiddan Arthur a'r Eryr'

1 Es ryfedaf kann wyf bard.
o vlaen dar ae vric yn hard.
py edrych eryr py chward.

2 Arthur bellglot ordiwes.
arth llu llewenyd achles.
yr eryr gynt ath weles.

3 Ys ryfedaf o tu myr
as gofynnaf yn vyuyr
py chward py edrych eryr.

4 Arthur bellglot engyhynt
arth llu llewenyd dremynt
yr eryr ath welas gynt.

5 Yr eryr a seif ymbric dar.
pe hanfut o ryw adar
ny bydud na dof na gwar.

6 Arthur glydyfawc aruthyr
ny seif dy alon rac dy ruthyr
mi yw mab madawc uab uthyr.

7 Yr eryr ny wn dy ryw
a dreigla glyngoet kernyw
mab madawc uab uthur nyt byw.

8 Arthur ieith ...
arth gwyr nyt gwaret lit
eliwlat gynt ym gelwit.

9 Yr eryr golwc diuei
ar dy barabyl nyt oes vei
ae ti eliwlat vy nei.

1 I am amazed for I am a bard;
from the top of the oak with its beautiful branches,
why does the eagle stare, why does he laugh?

2 Arthur of surpassing far-flung fame,
bear of the host, joy of shelter,
the eagle has seen you before.

3 I am amazed beside the seas.
I shall ask in contemplation
why he laughs, why the eagle stares.

4 Arthur, far-flung fame of the journey,
bear of the host, joy of sight,
the eagle has seen you before.

5 Oh eagle who stands in the branches of the oak,
if you were of a race of birds
you would not be either tame or civilised.

6 Arthur of the terrible sword,
your enemies stand not before your rush.
I am the son of Madog son of Uthr.

7 I know not your shape, oh eagle
who roams the valley-woods of Cornwall.
The son of Madog son of Uthr lives not.

8 Arthur ...,
bear of men, not a deliverance of wrath,
I was called Eliwlad before.

9 Oh eagle of blameless appearance
in your utterance is no fault:
is it you, Eliwlad my nephew?

10 Arthur dihafarch ffossawc.
diarwrein arllwybrawt
ys gwiw kystlwn o honawt.

11 Yr eryr barabyl eglur
a dywedy di wrth arthur
beth yssyd drwc y wneuthur.

12 Medylyaw drwc drwy aferdwl
a hir drigyaw yny medwl.
rygelwit pechawt ardwl.

etc.

10 Arthur, undaunted of battle,
path of the fallen,
kinship to you is fitting.

11 Oh eagle of clear utterance,
tell Arthur
what is wrong of his doing.

12 Thinking evil through misfortune
and staying long in thought
was called a very sad sin.

etc.

Ymddiddan Gwenhwyfar ac Arthur

The *Dialogue of Gwenhwyfar and Arthur* exists in two redactions, both of which are found below. They are poetic accounts of an encounter between Gwenhwyfar and Melwas with a third figure, possibly Arthur, also speaking. The poem's background is the Welsh tradition of Melwas's abduction of Gwenhwyfar, though it is unclear where in this cycle we should place the poems; it is even possible the two versions do not belong to the same points of the narrative which is presumed to lie behind the dialogue. Certainly there are differences between them, but whether these stem from variable oral tradition, or garbled and innovatory transmission from one ancestor manuscript, or perhaps calculated variation is an important though probably unanswerable question. The two manuscripts date from the sixteenth and seventeenth centuries. Character designations are not marked in the manuscripts, and those included next to the translation are purely speculative, as indeed is the possibly unsuitable title.

Patrick Sims-Williams has shown how Melwas (marked 'M' below) was known as a magician in Welsh tradition: the poet Dafydd ab Edmwnd (1450—1497) tells of 'the art of Melwas, the robber who by magic and enchantment took a girl to the end of the world; to the green wood the deceiver went, to the walls of branches of tree-tops.' References to the 'Isle of Glass' (see 2 Wynn. below) can be found in the twelfth-century *Vita Gildae* verifiably linking the poem with a tradition older than Chrétien's *Knight of the Cart* which also tells of Gwenhwyfar's abduction.

***

Bibliography:

Jones, Evans D. 'Melvas, Gwenhwyfar a Chai'
Sims-Williams, Patrick 'The Early Welsh Arthurian Poems', pp.57—61
Williams, Mary 'An Early Ritual Poem in Welsh'

[Wynnstay 1, 91:]

1 Pa eistedd gwr yn gyffredinrwydd gwledd
Eb eiddaw nai dechreu nai diwedd
Eiste obry islaw'r cyntedd.

2 Y Melwas o Ynys Wyrdin
Di aur vlyche goreurin
Ni lewais i ddim o'th win.

3 Aro ychydic snevin
Ni wallaf vi vyngwin
Ar wr ni ado ag ni safai mewn trin
Ni ddaliai Gai yn i vin.

4 Ni arveisiwn ryd
Ag a vo gemyn a gwryd
A lluric drom drai
Mi yw'r gwr a ddaliai Gai.

5 Taw was taw a'th salwet
Onit well na'th welet
Ni ddalut Gai ar d'wythvet.

6 Gwenhwyvar olwg hyddgan
Na'm dirmic cyd bwy bychan
Mi ddaliwn Gai vyhvunan.

7 Tydi was ar ben maint
Ai ben coch val ysgyvaint
Anhebic i Gai wyt o vaint.

[Key: A=Arthur or Cai (?); G=Gwenhwyfar; M (& X?)=Melwas]

1 A: What man is it who sits in the lower ranks of the feast
Without its beginning or ending for him,
Sat down beneath the hall?

2 M: Melwas from the Isle of Glass;
You of the golden, gilded barrels
I have drunk none of your wine.

3 A: Wait for one moment.
I do not pour out my wine
For a man who cannot resist, cannot hold out in battle;
He could not resist Cai, drunk on his wine.

4 M: I would wade a ford
Though it were a fathom deep
With mail upon the banks:
I am the man who will resist Cai.

5 G: Silence lad, silence with your banter.
If you might not be better than your appearance
You would not stand up to Cai although you were one of eight

6 M: Gwenhwyfar of the deer's glance,
Though I may be young, despise me not:
I would resist Cai alone.

7 G: You boy, greater than many
With a head, red like lungs,
You are unlike Cai in size.

8 Gnawd i veddw gwecry
Jawn a gadwn velly
Mi ywr Melwas gadwn ar hyny.

9 Canys dechreuasoch
Ymddiddenwch rhagoch
Ef a edwyn mab ai lloch.

10 Ymhle gynt yr ymdelsawch
Mewn llys vrddasol i braint
yn yvet gwin o Geraint
Lle dwir gwir ar dir Dyfnaint.

11 Cas gennyf wen gwrllwyd hen
ai gledde n waell dan i en
A chwenych eb allel amgen.

12 Casach genyf ine
Gwr balch llwrf ond geirie
Ni thaw ni thyn i gledde
Hwde di hwde dithe.

***

[Llanstephan 122, 426:]

1 Dv yw fy march a da dana
Ag er dwr nid arswyda
A rhag Vngwr ni chilia.

2 Glas yw fy march o liw y dail
Llwyr ddirmygid........
Nid gwr ond a gywiro ei air.

3 ....
........................ymlaen y drin
Nid deil gwr ond Cae Hir ap Sefin.

8 M: The flesh of the drunkard is weak
So let us keep order;
I am Melwas; leave it at that.

9 G: Since you have begun,
Continue your talking,
A boy knows who cherishes him.

10 M: In what place did you see me before?
G: Inside a court of honour and nobility,
Drinking the wine of Geraint.
The place, ..?.. and true in the land of Devon.

11 M: Hate is with me for the old grey-haired one's smile
With his sword, as a skewer, under his chin
Who desires but cannot attain.

12 A: Most hateful with me is
The arrogant man, frightened except in words
Who will not be silent nor draw his sword.
M: Perish!
A: You perish!

***

1 ?: My black steed is good beneath me
And he will not tremble because of water
And will turn aside before no man.

2 ?: The green of the tint of the leaves is my steed.
He is hated ..?..
He is no man who does not keep his word.

3 G?: ..?..
..?.. in the vanguard of battle
No man resists but Cai the Tall, son of Sefin.

4 Myfi a ferchyg ag a sai
Ag a gerdda yn drwm gan lan trai
Myfi yw'r gwr a ddalia Gai.

5 Dyd was, rhyfedd yw dy glowed
Onid wyd amgen noth weled
Nid ddalid Gai ar dy ganfed.

6 Gwenhwyfar olwg Eirian
Na ddifrawd fi cyd bwy bychan
Mi a ddaliwn gant fy hvnan.

7 Dyd was o ddv a melyn
Wrth hir edrych dy dremyn
Tybias dy weled cyn hyn.

8 Gwenhwyfar olwg wrthroch
Doedwch i mi os gwyddoch
Ymha le cyn hyn im gwelsoch.

9 Mi welais wr graddol o faint
Ar fwrdd hir ... Dyfnaint
Yn rhannv gwin iw geraint.

10 Gwenhwyfar barabl digri
Cnawd o ben gwraig air gwegi
Yno y gwelaist di fi.

4 X: It is I who will ride and will stand
And walk heavily at the ebb's limit
I am the man to resist Cai.

5 G: Nonsense lad, it is strange to hear you
Unless you be other than your appearance
You would not resist Cai as one of a hundred.

6 X: Gwenhwyfar of the silvery gaze,
Do not hate me although I may be small
I myself would resist a hundred.

7 G: Nonsense boy of black and yellow;
After gazing long at your appearance
I imagined I had seen you before.

8 X: Gwenhwyfar of the haughty gaze,
Tell me if you know
The place where you saw me before.

9 G: I saw a man of moderate size
on the long table ..?.. in Devon
Sharing the wine out to his loved ones.

10 X: Gwenhwyfar of the foolish speech,
Stupid words are to be expected from the mouth of a woman,
There indeed you saw me.

Gereint filius Erbin

The poem, *Geraint son of Erbin* is found in the Black Book of Carmarthen. Its importance for students of Arthurian literature is twofold: the hero, Geraint, is linked with the Geraint/Erec of later romance, and the poem also provides an early direct reference to Arthur himself. Another recension exists in the Red Book of Hergest, but as the Black Book version is undoubtedly earlier (dated precisely to 829/830 by Thomas Charles-Edwards, though usually more vaguely put at ninth to eleventh century) and there is no additional Arthurian material in the Red Book version, the Black Book text is that given here. (Perhaps it is noteworthy that the Red Book of Hergest also contains a version of the Romance of *Gereint*.) The poem takes the form of a eulogy to the Dumnonian (i.e. Devon and Cornwall) prince, Geraint son of Erbin, though Jenny Rowland has suggested that it may have belonged to an earlier 'Geraint saga'. Stanza 8 is the Arthur stanza, the equivalent lines in the Red Book recension begin:

Yn llongborth llas y arthur.
Gwyr dewr...

At Llongborth were slain Arthur's
brave men...

It is probable that in this case the Red Book reading is correct since this gives greater continuity with the accompanying stanza on the slaying of Geraint's men. It should be noted that the poem does not state that Arthur himself was present, though it may be intended that we infer that. *Gereint filius Erbin* is significant for its early connection of Arthur with the South-West and for providing the earliest use of the term 'emperor' to describe him (however *ameraudur* here may mean something more like 'general' or 'commander'.)

***

Bibliography:

Bollard, John K. 'Arthur in the Early Welsh Tradition', pp.16—18
Jarman, A.O.H. 'The Arthurian Allusions in the Black Book of Carmarthen', p.106
Roberts, Brynley F. 'Rhai o Gerddi Ymddiddan', pp.287—96
Rowland, Jenny *Early Welsh Saga Poetry*, pp.240—43, 273, 365, 457—61, & 504—05
Sims-Williams, Patrick 'The Early Welsh Arthurian Poems', pp. 46—49

1 Rac gereint gelin kystut.
y gueleise meirch can crimrut.
A gwidy gaur garv achlut.

2 Rac gereint gelin dihad.
gueleise meirch crimrut o kad.
A guydi gaur garu puyllad.

3 Rac gereint gelin ormes.
gueleis meirch can eu crees.
A guydi gaur garv achles.

4 En llogborth ygueleise vitheint.
a geloraur mvy nomeint.
aguir rut rac ruthir gereint.

5 Enllogborth ygueleise giminad.
guirigrid aguaed am iad.
rac gereint vaur mab y tad.

6 En llogporth gueleise gottoev.
a guir nygilint rac gvaev.
ac y ved gvin o guydir gloev.

7 En llogporth y gueleise arwev
guir. a guyar in dinev.
agvydi gaur garv atnev.

8 En llogporth y gueleise. y arthur
guir deur kymynint a dur.
ameraudur llywiaudir llawur.

9 En llogporth y llas y gereint.
guir. deur o odir diwneint.
a chin rillethid ve.llatysseint.

1 Before Geraint, enemy's affliction,
I saw white steeds, fetlocks reddened,
and after the battle-cry, a grim grave.

2 Before Geraint, enemy's lineage-breaker,
I saw steeds, fetlocks reddened from battle,
and after the battle-cry, grim deliberation.

3 Before Geraint, enemy's oppression,
I saw steeds, white their skin,
and after the battle-cry, grim silence.

4 At Llongborth I saw fury
and biers beyond number,
and reddened men before the rush of Geraint.

5 At Llongborth I saw hewing,
and men in battle with blood about the head,
before Geraint the Great, son of his father.

6 At Llongborth I saw spurs,
and men who would not flee before spears,
and drinking of wine from bright glass.

7 At Llongborth I saw the weapons
of men, and gushing blood,
and after the battle-cry, grim burial.

8 At Llongborth I saw Arthur's
brave men, they hewed with steel,
emperor, leader in toil.

9 At Llongborth were slain Geraint's
brave men from the lowlands of Devon,
and before they were slain, they slew.

10 Oet re rereint dan vortuid gereint
garhirion graun guenith.
Rution ruthir eririon blith.

11 Oet re rerent dan vortuid gereint.
garhirion graun aebv.
Rution ruthir eriron dv.

12 Oet re rereint dan mortuid gereint.
garhirion graun boloch.
Rution ruthir eriron coch.

13 Oet rerereint dan mortuid gereint
garhirion graun wehin.
Rution ruthir eririon gvinn.

14 Oet rerereint dan vortuid gereint.
garhirion grat hit.
turuf goteith ar diffeith mynit.

15 Oet re rereint. dan vortuid gereint
garhirion gran anchvant.
Blaur blaen euraun inariant.

16 Oet rerereint dan mortuid. gereint.
garhirion. graun adas.
Rution ruthir eryrion glas.

17 Oet re rereint dan mortuid gereint.
garhirion graun eu buyd.
Rution ruthir eririon llvid.

18 Ban aned gereint oet agored pirth new.
rotei crist aarched
prid mirein prydein wogoned.

10 It was swiftly that there ran under Geraint's thigh
long-shanked [horses], grains of wheat,
reddened, the rush of speckled eagles.

11 It was swiftly that there ran under Geraint's thigh
long-shanked [horses], grain was theirs,
reddened, the rush of black eagles.

12 It was swiftly that there ran under Geraint's thigh
long-shanked [horses], grain-scattering,
reddened, the rush of red eagles.

13 It was swiftly that there ran under Geraint's thigh
long-shanked [horses], grain-exhausting,
reddened, the rush of white eagles.

14 It was swiftly that there ran under Geraint's thigh
long-shanked [horses], leap of a stag,
thunder of a blaze on a mountain waste.

15 It was swiftly that there ran under Geraint's thigh
long-shanked [horses], grain-greedy,
grey the tips of their hair, as silver.

16 It was swiftly that there ran under Geraint's thigh
long-shanked [horses], grain-worthy,
reddened, the rush of blue eagles.

17 It was swiftly that there ran under Geraint's thigh
long-shanked [horses], grain their feed,
reddened, the rush of grey eagles.

18 When Geraint was born the gates of heaven were
open,
Christ gave what was asked for,
a noble form, the glory of Britain.

Mi a Wum

The poem known as *Mi a Wum* ('I have been'; *Mi a Fûm* in modern orthography), dated to the tenth or eleventh centuries, is found in the Black Book of Carmarthen. Immediately preceding it in the manuscript is a dialogue poem between Gwyddno Garanhir and Gwyn ap Nudd, and, in fact, we cannot be certain that these seven stanzas do not belong to that poem.

The Arthurian significance of the poem lies in its third stanza where Llachau son of Arthur is mentioned. It seems that Llachau may once have played an important part in the Arthurian legend, but was gradually forgotten. His name also crops up in *Pa Gur*, where he is described as 'fulfilling battles' with Cai, which leaves some doubt as to whether those battles were fought alongside or against Cai. The ambiguity of that phrase in *Pa Gur* is unfortunate as there are some indications of an early tradition of hostility between Cai and Llachau. There are two points of difficulty regarding the words *uthir ig kertev* in line 3b: the phrase is probably best translated 'awful in songs' (i.e. in songs he was said to be awful); but, more important, does the description apply to Arthur or to his son?

***

Bibliography:

Bromwich, Rachel *Trioedd Ynys Prydein*, p.416
Jarman, A.O.H. *Llyfr Du Caerfyrddin*, pp.lxiv, 72—73, & 115
Jarman, A.O.H. 'The Arthurian Allusions in the Black Book of Carmarthen', p.107
Roberts, Brynley F. 'Rhai o Gerddi Ymddiddan', pp.311—18
Rowland, Jenny *Early Welsh Saga Poetry*, pp.297, 299, 462—63, 507, 640
Sims-Williams, Patrick 'The Early Welsh Arthurian Poems', p.44

1 Mi awum iny lle llas guendolev.
Mab keidav colowin kertev.
Ban ryerhint brein ar crev.

2 Mi awum in lle llas bran.
Mab ywerit clod lydan.
Ban ryerint brein garthan.

3 Mi awum lle llas llachev.
Mab arthur uthir ig kertev.
Ban ryreint brein ar crev.

4 Mi awum lle las meuric.
Mab karreian clod edmic.
Ban ryreeint brein ar cic.

5 Ny buum lle llas gwallauc
Mab goholheth teithiauc.
Attwod lloegir mab lleynnac.

6 Mi awum lle llas milvir
Pridein. or duyrein ir goglet.
Mi. wi. wiw. vintev. y. bet.

7 Mi awum lle llas milguir
Bridein or duyrein ir dehev.
Mi. wi. wiv. vintev. y aghev.

1 I have been where Gwenddolau was slain,
the son of Ceido, a pillar of songs,
when ravens croaked over blood.

2 I have been where Brân was slain,
the son of Ywerydd, of widespread fame,
when rampart-ravens croaked.

3 I have been where Llachau was slain,
the son of Arthur, awful in songs,
when ravens croaked over blood.

4 I have been where Meurig was slain,
the son of Careian, of praiseworthy fame,
when ravens croaked over flesh.

5 I have not been where Gwallog was slain,
a boy of rightful lineage,
the affliction of England, the son of Llehynog.

6 I have been where were slain the warriors
of Britain, from the East to the North,
myself alive, they in their grave.

7 I have been where were slain the warriors
of Britain, from the East to the South,
myself alive, they in death.

Pa Gur

Poem 31 of the Black Book of Carmarthen (conventionally entitled *Pa Gur* from its opening line) is usually dated to the eleventh century. Unfortunately it is cut short at line 90 due to a missing leaf. The poem begins as a dialogue between Arthur and Glewlwyd, the porter or gate-keeper, but soon develops into a list of Arthur's men and their exploits, apparently recounted by Arthur himself for the most part. The use of similar names and of references to the same events demonstrates some relationship between *Pa Gur* and the prose tale *Culhwch ac Olwen*. Rachel Bromwich (in her *Trioedd Ynys Prydein*) has suggested that *Culhwch* is in part a burlesque of *Pa Gur*. The motif of the dialogue with a gate-keeper may once have been widespread: in an Arthurian context we find it in *Culhwch ac Olwen* and in the scene depicted on the Modena archivolt; it also occurs in Irish literature in *The Battle of Mag Tuired*. The poem marks the movement of Arthur's name away from the historical frame; despite occasional reference to 'genuine' events (such as the battle of Tryfrwyd, mentioned in the *Historia Brittonum*), Arthur is here presented as 'leader of a band of wonderful, monster-slaying heroes' (— Jackson). Cai's character, however, has not yet developed (or deteriorated) into that of the impetuous Sir Kay, here he is a simpler, heroic type.

***

Bibliography:

Bollard, John K. 'Arthur in the Early Welsh Tradition', pp.21—23

Haycock, Marged '"Preiddeu Annwn"'

Jackson, Kenneth H. 'Arthur in Early Welsh Verse', pp.15—18

Loomis, R.S. *Wales and the Arthurian Legend*, pp.131—78

Sims-Williams, Patrick 'The Early Welsh Arthurian Poems', pp.54—57

Pa gur yv y porthaur.
Gleuluid gauaeluaur.
Pa gur aegouin.
arthur.a chei guin.
Pa imda genhid.
Guir gorev im bid.
Ym ty ny doi.
onys guaredi.
Mi ae guardi.
athi ae gueli.
Vythneint elei.
Assivyon ell tri.
Mabon am mydron.
guas uthir pen dragon.
KysCaint . mab. Banon.
A guin godybrion.
Oet rinn vy gueisson
in amuin ev detvon.
Manawidan ab llyr.
oet duis y cusil.
Neustuc manauid
eis tull o trywruid.
a mabon am melld.
maglei guaed ar guelld.
Ac anguas edeinauc.
a lluch. llauynnauc.
Oetin diffreidauc
ar eidin cyminauc.
Argluit ae llochei
mynei ymtiwygei.
kei ae heiriolei.
trae llathei pop tri.
Pan colled kelli.
caffad cuelli.
Aseirolei kei
hid trae kymynhei.
Arthur ced huarhei.

'What man is the porter?'
'Glewlwyd Great-Grip.
— What man asks it?'
'Arthur and Cai the Fair.'
'What [retinue] travels with you?'
'The best men in the world.'
'Into my house you will not come,
unless you vouch for them.'
'I shall vouch for them,
and you will see them:
the vultures of Elei,
and wise ones those three;
Mabon son of Modron,
the servant of Uthr Pendragon;
Cyscaint son of Banon,
and Gwyn Goddyfrion.
My lads were brave,
defending their customs.
Manawydan son of Llŷr,
his counsel was solid.
Indeed Manawyd bore them —
pierced shields from Tryfrwyd;
and Mabon son of Mellt,
he would stain blood on grass;
and Anwas the Winged,
and Llwch the Windy-Handed,
they were defending
at Edinburgh on the border.
A lord would support them,
where he would make amends to them.
Cai would implore them,
while he slew them, three at a time.
When Celli [Wig] was lost,
fury was got.
Cai would implore them
while he cut them down.
Although Arthur was playing,

y guaed gouerei.
In neuat awarnach
in imlat ew a gurach.
Ew aguant pen palach.
in atodev. dissethach.
Ym minit eidin
Amuc .a. chinbin.
Pop cant id cuitin.
id cvitin. pop cant.
rac beduir bedrydant.
Ar traethev trywruid.
in amvin agarvluid.
Oet guychir y annuyd.
o cletyw ac yscuid.
Oet guaget bragat
vrth .kei ig kad.
Oet cletyw ighad.
oe lav diguistlad.
Oet hyneiw guastad
ar lleg ar lles gulad.
Beduir. A Bridlav.
Nau cant guarandau.
chuechant y eirthau.
a talei y ortinav.
Gueisson am buyint
oet guell ban uitint.
Rac riev emreis.
gueleise. Kei ar uris.
Preitev gorthowis.
oet gur hir in ewnis.
Oet trum y dial.
oet. tost y cynial.
Pan yuei o wual
yuei urth peduar.
yg kad pandelhei.
vrth cant idlathei.
Ny bei duv ae digonhei.

her blood flowed
in the hall of Afarnach —
fighting, he and the witch.
He pierced Pen Palach
in the dwellings of Disethach.
At the mount of Edinburgh
he fought against dog-heads.
A hundred at a time fell,
there fell a hundred at a time,
before Bedwyr Perfect-Sinew.
On the shores of Tryfrwyd
fighting against Garwlwyd,
his nature was ferocious
as regards sword and shield.
The host was vain
against Cai in battle.
He was a sword in battle,
from his hand pledges were given.
He was a strong leader
over a host for the land's profit.
Bedwyr and Bridlaw —
nine hundred listening,
six hundred to scatter
was his urging worth.
I had servants,
it was better when they were alive.
Before the lords of Emrys
I saw Cai at haste.
The prince of booty,
the man was long as an enemy,
his vengeance was heavy,
his anger was bitter.
When he drank from a horn
he would drink like four.
In battle, when he would come,
he would slay like a hundred.
If it were not God who managed it,

Oet diheit aghev kei.
Kei guin a llachev.
digonint we kadev.
kin gloes glas verev.
Y guarthaw ystaw in gun.
Kei a guant nav guiton.
Kei win a aeth von
y dilein lleuon.
Y iscuid oet mynud
erbin cath paluc.
Pan gogiueirch tud.
Puy guant cath paluc.
Nau ugein kinlluc.
a cuytei in y buyd.
Nau ugein kinran.
A.

Cai's death would be impossible.
Cai the Fair and Llachau,
they fulfilled battles
before the grey pain of spears.
At the peak of Ystafngwn
Cai pierced nine witches.
Cai the Fair went to Anglesey
to destroy lions.
His shield was polished
against the cat of Palug.
When people ask,
"Who pierced the cat of Palug?":
Nine-score soldiers
would fall as its food;
nine-score champions
...

Preideu Annwfyn

Preideu Annwfyn ('The Spoils of Annwn' — *Preiddiau Annwn* in modern orthography) is Poem 30 in the Book of Taliesin (NLW Peniarth 2). It was probably composed between the late ninth- and the early twelfth-century, and, like most of the poems in its manuscript, has no connection with the Taliesin of history. Rather it is part of a great body of mythological and mystical poetry which later gathered round his name as he passed into legend. The background to the poem is the story of an expedition by Arthur in his ship, Prydwen, to seize a magical cauldron from a fortress (referred to by various names throughout the text) in Annwn, the Celtic Otherworld. This story should be compared with that of the quest for Diwrnach's cauldron in *Culhwch ac Olwen;* strikingly similar tales (but not involving Arthur) are also found in the Second Branch of the *Mabinogi* and in the *Historia Brittonum.* This motif of the Otherworld expedition in search of a magical cauldron may well be the precursor of the Grail legend. Although the tale's basis must be in genuine tradition we cannot rely on all its details, some may be pure invention and others may be borrowed motifs from different areas of Welsh tradition.

***

Bibliography:

Bollard, John K. 'Arthur in the Early Welsh Tradition', pp.21—23
Budgey, Andrea "'Preiddeu Annwn"'
Haycock, Marged "'Preiddeu Annwn"'
Jackson, Kenneth H. 'Arthur in Early Welsh Verse', pp.15—18
Loomis, R.S. *Wales and the Arthurian Legend*, pp.131—78
Sims-Williams, Patrick 'The Early Welsh Arthurian Poems' pp.54—57

Golychaf wledic pendeuic gwlat ri.
Py ledas y pennaeth dros traeth mundi.
Bu kyweir karchar gweir ygkaer sidi.
Trwy ebostol pwyll a phryderi.
Neb kyn noc ef nyt aeth idi.
Yr gadwyn tromlas kywirwas ae ketwi.
A rac preideu annwfyn tost yt geni.
Ac yt urawt parahawt yn bard wedi.
Tri lloneit prytwen yt aetham ni idi.
Nam seith ny dyrreith o gaer sidi.
Neut wyf glot geinmyn cerd o chlywir.
Igkaer pedryuan pedyr y chwelyt.
Ygkynneir or peir pan leferit.
O anadyl naw morwyn gochyneuit.
Neu peir pen annwfyn pwy y vynut.
Gwrym am y oror a mererit.
Ny beirw bwyt llwfyr ny rytyghit.
Cledyf lluch lleawc idaw rydyrchit.
Ac yn llaw leminawc yd edewit.
A rac drws porth vffern llugyrn lloscit.
A phan aetham ni gan arthur trafferth lethrit.
Namyn seith ny dyrreith o gaer vedwit.
Neut wyf glot geinmyn kerd glywanawr.
Igkaer pedryfan ynys pybyrdor.
Echwyd a muchyd kymysgetor.
Gwin gloyw eu gwirawt rac eu gorgord.
Tri lloneit prytwen yd aetham ni ar vor.
Namyn seith ny dyrreith o gaer rigor.

I shall worship the lord — the prince, the land's king—
who spread his rule over the shore of the world.
Perfect was Gwair's prison in the Otherworld Fort
according to the tale of Pwyll and Pryderi.
No-one before him went there,
to the heavy grey chain — the loyal servant that held him;
and painfully before the spoils of Annwn he sang.
But our bard-prayer will last till Doomsday.
Three loads for Prydwen, we went there,
but for seven, none returned from the Otherworld Fort.
I am of honourable fame, [my] song is heard
in the Four-Cornered Fort — four its sides:
my first word — from the cauldron it was spoken.
From the breath of nine maidens it was kindled up.
The Chief of Annwn's cauldron, what of its liberality?
Blue about its edge with pearl,
it boils not a coward's food, that has not been destined.
Llwch Lleog's sword was raised for it,
and in a keen hand it was left.
And before the door of the gate of Hell lanterns burned.
And when we went with Arthur — famous toil —
but for seven, none returned from the Fort of Drunkenness.
I am of honourable fame, [my] song will be heard
in the Four-Cornered Fort, staunch door of the island.
Midday is confused with jet-blackness.
Bright wine their drink before their retinue.
Three loads for Prydwen, we went on the sea,
but for seven, none returned from the Fort of Numbness.

Ni obrynafi lawyr llen llywyadur
Tra chaer wydyr ny welsynt wrhyt arthur.
Tri vgeint canhwr a seui ar y mur.
Oed anhawd ymadrwad ae gwylyadur.
Tri lloneit prytwen yd aeth gan arthur.
Namyn seith ny dyrreith o gaer golud.
Ny obrynaf y lawyr llaes eu kylchwy.
Ny wdant wy py dyd peridyd pwy.
Py awr y meindyd y ganet cwy.
Pwy gwnaeth ar nyt aeth doleu defwy.
Ny wdant wy yr ych brych bras y penrwy.
Seith vgein kygwng yny aerwy.
A phan aetham ni gan arthir auyrdol gofwy.
Namyn seith ny dyrreith o gaer vandwy.
Ny obrynaf y lawyr llaes eu goheu.
Ny wdant py dyd peridyd pen.
Py awr y meindyd y ganet perchen.
Py vil a gatwant aryant y pen.
Pan aetham ni gan arthur afyrdwl gynhen.
Namyn seith ny dyrreith a gaer ochren.
Myneich dychnut val cunin cor.
O gyfranc udyd ae gwidan hor.
Ae vn hynt gwynt ae vn dwfyr mor.
Ae vn ufel tan twrwf diachor.
Myneych dychnut val bleidawr.
O gyfranc udyd ae gwydyanhawr
Ny wdant pan yscar deweint a gwawr.
Neu wynt pwy hynt pwy y rynnawd.
Py va diua py tir a plawd.
Bet sant yn diuant a bet allawr.
Golychaf y wledic pendefic mawr.
Na bwyf trist crist am gwadawl.

I, a governor of lore, do not merit the lowly.
Beyond the Glass Fort they could not see Arthur's valour,
the three-score hundred men who stood on the wall.
It was difficult talking with their watchman.
Three loads for Prydwen went with Arthur,
but for seven, none returned from the Fort of Obstruction.
I do not merit the lowly, loose their shield.
They know not who is created on what day,
at what hour of the middle of the day God[?] was born,
who made that which went not to Dolau Defwy.
They know not of the Speckled Ox, fat his head-ring,
seven-score links in his collar.
And when we went with Arthur — sad tribulation —
but for seven, none returned from Fandwy Fort.
I do not merit the lowly, loose their aim.
They know not what day the leader is created,
at what hour of the middle of the day the owner was born,
what beast they keep — silver its head.
When we went with Arthur — sad strife —
but for seven, none returned from Ochren Fort.
Monks howl like a dog-pack choir
from the meeting of lords who will be known.
Is the wind of one course? Is the sea of one water?
Is the fire — irresistible tumult — of one spark?
Monks howl like wolves
from the meeting of lords who will be known.
They know not when midnight and dawn divide;
or the wind: What is its course? What is its attack?
What place does it destroy? What land does it strike?
The lost grave of a saint, and the grave of an altar.
I shall worship the Lord — the great prince.
May I be not sad, Christ endows me.

Book of Taliesin

The scarcity of Arthurian material in the fourteenth-century Book of Taliesin is quite remarkable. In addition to *Preideu Annwfyn* there are only four other poems which refer to Arthur in the manuscript: *Kat Godeu, Kadeir Teyrnon, Kanu y Meirch* and *Marwnat Uthyr Pendragon*. As Arthur is not central to any of these poems only the relevant sections are given here.

Kat Godeu (*Cad Goddeu* in modern orthography) is one of the so-called transformational poems of the Book of Taliesin. The title is usually translated 'Battle of the Trees' (or 'Army of the Trees') though *Goddeu* also occurs as a proper noun, possibly to be identified with the vast *Coed Celyddon* ('Caledonian Forest') north of Hadrian's Wall. As it stands, the poem is certainly later than the sixth century (perhaps tenth century) but some aspects of it — such as its apparent exposition of metempsychosis and the possible survival of pagan tree-lore — may reflect much older sources. Arthur is mentioned explicitly only once (in line 238) when the druids of 'the wise one' are instructed to prophesy either of or to Arthur (the Welsh leaves this ambiguous). It seems more likely that they are to prophesy to Arthur since the following lines (referring to the Flood, to the Crucifixion, and to Doomsday) appear to be the prophecies they are asked to make. The 'wise one' here is possibly Arthur or the poet himself. In addition to this rather vague direct reference, it may be that the 'lord of Britain' mentioned earlier in line 27 should also be interpreted as Arthur. The bulk of the poem concerns a great battle fought between armies of trees (in which the prowess of each tree or plant is reckoned), and includes an account of the poet's magical birth and career. It should be noted that the Battle of Goddeu occurs in the Triads as one of the Three Futile Battles, together with the Battle of Camlann (where Arthur fell) and the Battle of Arfderydd (where Myrddin went mad).

Kadeir Teyrnon ('Teyrnon's Chair' or 'The Prince's Chair') is unfortunately clouded in obscurity; the poem seems to relate to Taliesin's releasing of his patron Elffin from captivity. Arthur is mentioned only in connection with the importance of preserving the old traditions, but the preceding reference to the raiding of Cawrnur's horses may be an allusion to a now lost Arthurian tale (particularly since Cawrnur's name also crops up in the *Marwnat Uthyr Pendragon*).

Kanu y Meirch ('Poem of the Horses') is the title generally given to poem 25 in the Book of Taliesin. Much of the poem is taken up with a list of heroes and their horses, with occasional lines of description. There are two points of interest for us in this text. First is the association of the names of Gwawrddur and Arthur, as occurs also in the *Gododdin*, and of Gwythur and Arthur, as in the *Englynion y Beddau*; but to what extent these reflect real tradition, rather than merely simple convenience of rhyme, is debatable. And second is the fact that although both Arthur and Llamrei (a horse) are mentioned here, there is no apparent association made between the two, despite the mass of tradition in which Llamrei is identified as Arthur's mare (e.g. *Culhwch ac Olwen*).

Marwnat Uthyr Pen[dragon] ('Uthr Pendragon's Elegy' — *Pendragon* is abbreviated in the manuscript) should probably be interpreted as being in Uthr's own voice, though it may be that the title is incorrect and that the speaker was supposed to be Taliesin (but, of course, in reality the poem is no more Uthr's composition than it is Taliesin's.) If we assume Uthr's voice, then the reference to Arthur takes on a more personal tone and should perhaps be read, as Professor Sims-Williams has suggested, as the proud boast of a father that he has passed on his kingdom or personal qualities to his son. This interpretation also explains the later remark that 'the world would not exist were it not for my offspring.'

***

Bibliography:

Bollard, John K. 'Arthur in the Early Welsh Tradition', pp.14—15 [for *Kanu y Meirch*]
Bromwich, Rachel *Trioedd Ynys Prydein*, pp.xcviii—cvii [for *Kanu y Meirch*]
Evans, J.G. *The Book of Taliesin*, pp.23—27 [*Kat Godeu*], pp.34—36 [*Kadeir Teyrnon*], pp.47—48 [*Kanu y Meirch*], & pp.71—72 [*Marwnat Uthyr P.*]
Ford, Patrick K. *The Mabinogi*, pp. 183—87 [for *Kat Godeu*]
Sims-Williams, Patrick 'The Early Welsh Arthurian Poems', pp.51—53
Williams, Ifor *Lectures on Early Welsh Poetry*, pp.49—65

Kat Godeu:

Bum yn lliaws rith
kyn bum disgyfrith.
Bum cledyf culurith.
credaf pan writh.
Bum deigyr yn awyr.
bum serwaw syr.
Bum geir yn llythyr.
bum llyfyr ym prifder.
Bum llugyrn lleufer
blwydyn a hanher.
Bum pont ar triger.
ar trugein aber.
Bum hynt bum eryr.
bum corwc ymyr.
Bum darwed yn llat.
bum das ygkawat.
Bum cledyf yn aghat.
bum yscwyt ygkat.
Bum tant yn telyn
lletrithawc naw blwydyn.
Yn dwfyr yn ewyn.
bum yspwg yn tan.
Bum gwyd yngwarthan.
Nyt mi wyf ny gan
Keint yr yn bychan.
keint ygkat godeu bric.
Rac prydein wledic.
gweint veirch canholic.
Llyghessoed meuedic.
gweint mil mawrein.
Arnaw yd oed canpen.
a chat er dygnawt.
Dan von y tauawt.
a chat arall yssyd
Yn y wegilyd.
llyffan du gaflaw.

Battle of the Trees:

I was in a host of shapes
before I was loosed.
I was a thin, mottled sword:
I believe that it was done.
I was drops in the air.
I was the beam of stars.
I was a word in letters.
I was a book in origin.
I was lamps of illumination
for a year and a half.
I was a bridge made to stay
over sixty estuaries.
I was a way. I was an eagle.
I was a coracle in seas.
I was a bubble in a drink.
I was a drop in a shower.
I was a sword in a hand.
I was a shield in battle.
I was a string in a harp,
spellbound for nine years.
In the water as foam.
I was a spark in a fire.
I was wood in a grove.
I am not one who sings not;
I have sung from when small.
I sang in the battle of branchy trees.
before the lord of Britain.
I pierced swift horses
and rich fleets.
I pierced a great scaly beast —
on him were a hundred heads,
and an army (for harshness)
under the root of his tongue,
and another army which was
on his necks.
A black, forked toad —

Cant ewin arnaw.
neidyr vreith gribawc.
Cant eneit trwy bechawt
aboenir yny chnawt.

...

ny ganet yn adwy.
A uu ym gowy
namyn goronwy
O doleu edrywy.
hir wynn vy myssawr.
Pell na bum heussawr.
treigleis y mywn llawr
Kyn bum lleenawr.
treigleis kylchyneis
Kysceis cant ynys.
cant caer a thrugys.
Derwydon doethur.
darogenwch y arthur.
Yssit yssyd gynt.
neur mi ergenhynt.
Ac vn aderyw
o ystyr dilyw.
A christ y croccaw.
a dyd brawt racllaw.
Eurein yn euryll.
mi hudwyf berthyll
Ac wydyf drythyll
o erymes fferyll.

on him a hundred claws.
A speckled, crested serpent,
a hundred souls through sin
are tormented in its skin.
...

The one wasn't born in Adwy
who attacked me,
except for Goronwy
from Doleu Edrywy.
Long and white my fingers—
long that I have not been a herdsman.
I wandered as a warrior
before I was a man of letters.
I wandered, I encircled.
I slept on a hundred islands.
In a hundred forts I dwelt.
O druids of the wise one,
prophesy to Arthur.
There is what is before;
they may have perceived me.
And one occurs
in the meaning of the Flood,
and Christ's Crucifixion,
and Doomsday after this.
Golden, with gold,
I may cover myself richly,
and I shall be luxuriant
due to Virgil's prophecy.

Kadeir Teyrnon:

...

Neus duc o gawr nur.
Meirch gwelw gostrodur.
Teyrnon henur.
Heilyn pacadur.
Treded dofyn doethur.
Y vendigaw arthur.
Arthur vendigan
Ar gerd gyfaenat.
Arwyneb ygkat.
Arnaw bystylat.
Pwy y tri chynweissat.
A werchetwis gwlat.
Pwy y tri chyfarwyd
A getwis arwyd.

...

Kanu y Meirch:

...

A march karadawc.
Kymrwy teithiawc.
A march gwythur.
A march gwardur.
A march arthur.
Ehofyn rodi cur.
A march taliessin.

...

A llamrei llawn elwic.
Affroenuoll gwyrenhic

...

Teyrnon's Chair:

...

He brought them from Cawrnur,
pale horses under saddle.
Teyrnon, old man,
cup-bearer, feeder.
The third deep matter for the wise one:
the blessing of Arthur
— Blessed Arthur —
with harmonious song,
— a defence in battle,
stamping on nine.
Who are the three foremost youths
who guarded the land?
Who are the three story-tellers
who preserved the portents?

...

Poem of the Horses:

...

And Caradog's horse,
lively and rightful;
And Gwythur's horse;
And Gwawrddur's horse;
And Arthur's horse,
boldly bestowing pain;
And Taliesin's horse;

...

And Llamrei, full valuable,
wide-nostrilled and powerful;

...

Marwnat Uthyr Pen[dragon]:

...

Cledyfal hydyr rac meibon cawrnur.
Neu vi araunwys vy echlessur.
Nawuetran yg gwrhyt arthur.
Neu vi a torreis cant kaer.
Neu vi aledeis cant maer.
Neu vi arodeis cant llen.
Neu vi aledeis cant pen.
Neu vi arodeis i henpen.
Cledyfawr goruawr gyghallen.
Neu vi oreu terenhyd
Hayarndor edeithor penmynyd.
Ym gweduit ym gofit. hydyr oed gyhir.
Nyt oed vyt ny bei fy eissillyd.

...

Uthr Pendragon's Elegy:

...

A victorious sword-stroke before the sons of Cawrnur.
I shared my shelter,
a ninth share in Arthur's valour.
I broke a hundred forts.
I slew a hundred stewards.
I bestowed a hundred mantles.
I cut a hundred heads.
I gave to an old chief
very great swords of protection.
[???]
An iron protection ...[???]... mountain-top.
To my deprivation, to my sorrow, ?[sinew was brave].
The world would not exist were it not for my offspring.

Y Gododdin

The early Welsh heroic poem 'The Gododdin' contains one reference to Arthur, which Kenneth Jackson described as 'one of the most convincing pieces of evidence for a historical Arthur' ('The Arthur of History', p.3). The poem describes the heroic defeat of a warband of the North British Gododdin tribe by a far larger Anglian army. The battle probably took place at Catterick (*Catraeth*) c. 600, and the work composed soon after. *Y Gododdin* survives in two versions in the late thirteenth century Book of Aneirin; the A version is longer and probably in better order, whereas the B version seems older (or, at least, uses older orthography). There is substantial agreement in terms of content between A and B, but each contains some stanzas not found in the other. The relevant stanza here (37th from the B text, and no. 99 in Jarman's conflated edition) is in praise of a certain Gwawrddur, and it is interesting that the names of Arthur and Gwawrddur are also linked in the poem *Kanu y Meirch* from the Book of Taliesin. Various objections have been raised concerning the reliability of this reference, the primary concern being that the line or the entire stanza may be a later interpolation. The case for the defence is not helped by the fact that these lines are found only in the B text, but then some variation in content would not be surprising in a long and popular poem, perhaps transmitted orally over centuries. The line, then, could have been added at any date between 600 and 1300 but if it is a later addition, post-dating the development of a legendary Arthur, it seems odd that this is the only instance of his name in the poem and that there is no elaboration here around it.

***

Bibliography:

—— Introduction to *The Arthur of the Welsh*, pp.4—5
Bollard, John K. 'Arthur in the Early Welsh Tradition', p.14
Bromwich, Rachel *Trioedd Ynys Prydein*, p.275
Jackson, Kenneth H. *The Gododdin*
Jarman, A.O.H. *Aneirin: Y Gododdin*
Jarman, A.O.H. 'The Arthurian Allusions in the Book of Aneirin', pp.17—20
Padel, Oliver 'The Nature of Arthur', pp.13—14

Ef guant tra trigant echassaf
Ef ladhei a [pher]uet ac eithaf
Oid guiu e mlaen llu llarahaf
Godolei o heit meirch e gayaf
Gochore brein du ar uur
Caer ceni bei ef arthur
Rug ciuin uerthi ig disur
Ig kynnor guernor guaur[dur].

He struck before the three hundred bravest,
He would slay both middle and flank,
He was suited to the forefront of a most generous host,
He would give gifts from a herd of horses in winter,
He would feed black ravens on the wall
of a fortress, though he were not Arthur,
?[Among the strong ones in battle,]
In the van, an alder-palisade was Gwawrddur.

The Gaelic Material

Any study of Arthur in Gaelic literature is a complex task. The post-Geoffrey Romances reached the Gaelic-speaking world at some time during the Early Modern period, and rapidly established themselves. However, some traces of a pre-Geoffrey, Gaelic Arthur survive in earlier literature, the problem is: how should we interpret them? Are such references totally independent of those in our British sources, and, if not, in what direction was the flow of influence? Richard Barber, for example, sees an Irish Artúr as the original, absorbed into a Brythonic milieu at a later date, he thus explains the relative absence of Arthur from certain genres such as saga-poetry. Fortunately it is not our task to analyse; instead we shall simply present four of the more significant texts, each from a different literary genre: the *Senchus Fer nAlban*, Adomnán's *Vita Columbae, De Causis Torche na nDéssi,* and the *Acallam na Senórach.*

The *Senchus Fer nAlban* ('History of the Men of Britain') comprises a dense mixture of genealogy and military survey. The 'Britain' of the title refers in fact only to Dál Riada (Argyll and the Southern Hebrides), the region of Scotland first settled by the Irish. The surviving recensions of the text probably derive from a tenth-century version, but we may be reasonably confident that the material dates from the latter half of the seventh century. Our interest concerns just one inconspicuous name, buried deep in the text, one 'Artúr' son of Conaing. From the known dates of Áedán mac Gabráin we should place the birth of this Artúr at somewhere between 570 and 620. His father Conaing bears a suspicious name (apparently derived from Old English *cyning* 'king'), however the Annals of Ulster provide some evidence for his mortality: they record his death, in 622, by drowning. Some have suggested that Artúr is the historical Arthur, but this would seem rather unlikely given the apparent insignificance of the character mentioned here (but see Chadwick 'The Lost Literature of Celtic Scotland'). Its importance, though, may lie instead in the possible implication that already at an early date Arthur's fame had reached Dál Riada, and children were being given his name. A.A.M. Duncan, though, suggests that the name 'Artúr' derives from the same Pictish milieu as does 'Gartnait', the name borne by one of Conaing's brothers (*Scotland: the Making of the Kingdom*, p.43). The extracts from the text given below trace Artúr's pedigree back to the ancestor-figure, Eochaid Munremar.

The following extract from the Life of St. Columba, written in the seventh century (and therefore nearly contemporaneous) by Adomnán, the saint's successor in the abbacy of Iona, should be compared with the *Senchus Fer nAlban*. Here Artúr is the son of King Áedán mac Gabráin, whereas there he is his grandson. The Battle of the Miathi where Artúr is said to have fallen seems to have been one of Áedán's hardest won victories; in it, according to this Life, he lost 303 men. The Miathi are generally assumed to have been a tribe of northern Pictland.

Variants of the Old Irish tale 'Of the Reasons for the Migration of the Déssi' (sometimes referred to as *Tucait Indarba na nDéssi* — 'The Reason for the Expulsion of the Déssi') are to be found in several manuscripts (most notably the Bodleian manuscripts Rawlinson B. 502 and Laud 610, the latter being the version edited here). The tale is essentially an account of how King Cormac mac Airt drove the Déssi tribe from their territory in Meath, but our interest centres on just one paragraph which tells of the Déssi settlement of Dyfed in Wales. Much of this paragraph is taken up with a genealogy of the principal Déssi family in Wales, and this pedigree agrees strikingly (but not in every respect) with the Welsh genealogy of the early rulers of Dyfed. The equivalent section of the Welsh genealogy refers to 'Nougoy son of Arthur son of Petr', but it should be noted that a variant reading of *maic Petuir* in the Irish texts is *maic Retheoir*. Richard Barber argues that the Artúr here would have been born around 580—620, but his argument rests on an assumption regarding the date of Déssi migration westwards. It has been demonstrated that the tale must first have been written down around 750 — about the time of the Taulodar at the head of the genealogy if Barber's dates for Artúr are correct.

The *Acallam na Senórach* ('The Colloquy with the Ancients') is one of the most prominent texts from the great mass of Fenian (i.e. relating to Finn and his band of warriors, the Fíanna) literature produced in twelfth- and thirteenth-century Ireland. The frame of the work is a conversation between St. Patrick and the old *fénnid,* Cáilte. This frame is simply a device whereby a number of tales are recounted through the voice of Cáilte in response to the saint's 'questions'. Of particular interest to us is the story of how the Fíanna came by their horses, in which an Artúr, son of the King of Britain, is humbled by Finn and his men. William Gillies described the *Acallam* as seeming to antedate the possibility, or at least the likelihood, of acquaintance with the work of Geoffrey and the Romances. Another Artúr is mentioned later on in the text as a member of Finn's 'first battalion', though this one plays a more minor role and drowns in Loch Lurgan.

***

Bibliography:

Anderson, A.O. & M.O. *Adomnán's Life of Columba*, pp.158 & 228—29

Bannerman, J. *Studies in the History of Dalriada* [for the *Senchus Fer nAlban*]

Barber, Richard *The Figure of Arthur*, pp.29—30 [for the *Vita Columbae*] & pp.35—36 [for *De Causis Torche na nDéisi*]

Chadwick, Nora K. 'The Lost Literature of Celtic Scotland' [for the *Vita Columbae*]

Gillies, William 'Arthur in Gaelic Tradition II', pp.70—71

Meyer, Kuno 'The Expulsion of the Déssi'

O'Grady, Standish H. *Silva Gadelica*, Vol.1 pp.97—100; Vol.2 pp.105—07

Senchus Fer nAlban:

Incipit míniugud senchasa fer n-alban Dá mac echdach munremair .i. erc ocus olcú. Dá mac deac immorra la erc .i. a sé díb gabsat albain .i. dá loarnd .i. loarnd bec ocus loarnd mór Dá mac nisse .i. mac nisse becc ocus mac nisse mór. Dá fergus .i. fergus bec ocus fergus mór...

Fergus mór mac eirc ainm aile do mac nisse mór unum filium habuit .i. Domangart Dá mac immorra la domangart .i. gabrán ocus comgell dá mac fedlimthe ingine briúin meic echach mugmedóin...

Cúic meic immorra la gabrán .i. áedán. éoganán. cuildach domnall. domangart. Sect meic la áedán .i. dá echduig .i. eocho budhe. ocus eochaid find tuathal bran. báithíne. conaing. gartnait..

hii sunt filii conaing meic áedáin .i. rígallán ferchar. artán. artúr. dondcad. domungart. nectan. ném. crumíne.

***

The History of the Men of Britain:

Here begins an explanation of the history of the men of Britain. Eochaid Munremar's two sons were Erc and Olchú. Erc, moreover, had twelve sons — six of them took Britain: two Loarnds (Little Loarnd and Great Loarnd), two Mac Nisses (Little Mac Nisse and Great Mac Nisse), and two Ferguses (Little Fergus and Great Fergus)...

Great Fergus (another name for Great Mac Nisse), son of Erc, had one son, Domangart. Domangart, moreover, had two sons: Gabrán and Comgell (the two were the children of Fedelm daughter of Brión son of Eocho Servant of the Ollamh)...

Gabrán, moreover, had five sons: Áedán, Éoganán, Cuildach, Domnall and Domangart. Áedán had seven sons: two Eochaids (Eocho the Yellow and Eochaid the Fair), Tuathal, Bran, Báithíne, Conaing and Gartnait...

These are the sons of Conaing son of Áedán: Rígallán, Ferchar, Artán, Artúr, Dondchad, Domungart, Nechtan, Ném and Crumíne.

***

Vita Columbae:

Alio in tempore ante supra dictum bellum Sanctus Aidanum regem interrogat de regni successore. Illo se respondente nescire, quis esset de tribus filiis suis regnaturus, Arturius an Echodius Find an Domingartus, Sanctus consequenter hoc profatur modo: Nullus ex his tribus erit regnator; nam in bellis cadent ab inimicis trucidandi: sed nunc si alios juniores habes ad me veniant, et quem ex eis elegerit Dominus regem, subito super meum irruet gremium. Quibus accitis, secundum verbum Sancti Echodius Buide adveniens in sinu ejus recubuit. Statimque Sanctus eum osculatus benedixit, et ad patrem ait: Hic est superstes, et rex post te regnaturus, et filii ejus post eum regnabunt. Sic omnia post, suis temporibus, plene adimpleta sunt. Nam Arturius et Echodius Find non longo post temporis intervallo, Miatorum superius memorato in bello, trucidati sunt. Domingartus vero in Saxonia bellica in strage interfectus est: Echodius autem Buide post patrem in regnum successit.

***

Life of Columba:

Another time, before the aforementioned battle [the Battle of the Miathi], the saint asks King Áedán about the kingdom's successor. When he answers that he knows not who of his three sons might be going to reign — Artúr, Eochaid the Fair, or Domungart — the saint now consequently prophesies this: 'None of these three will be a ruler for they will fall in battles by the butchering of enemies. But now if you have others, younger, may they come to me; and whomsoever of them the Lord has chosen as king will rush at once to my bosom.' When those had been summoned according to the saint's word, Eochaid the Yellow, on arriving, sank down into his bosom. And at once, having kissed, the saint blessed him and said to his father: 'This is the survivor, and the one to rule after you as king, and his sons will rule after him.' Thus everything afterwards in its time was completely fulfilled. For, after a short period of time, Artúr and Eochaid the Fair were butchered in the battle of the Miathi recounted above. Indeed Domungart was killed in England in a military overthrow. Eochaid the Yellow, moreover, succeeded to the kingship after his father.

***

De Causis Torche na nDéssi:

Luid Eochaid dar muir hi crich Demeth conid and robo marb ocus a maic ocus a hui. Conid dib cenel Crimthain alle, diata Taulodar mac Rigind maic Catien maic Clothienn maic Noé maic Artúir maic Petuir maic Congair maic Goirtiben maic Alcon maic Tresund maic Aeda maic Brosc maic Corach maic Echdach Allmair maic Airt Chuirp.

***

Acallam na Senórach:

In rabatar eich nó echrada acaib isin féinn. do batar imorro ar Cáilte: trí caoca serrach aenlára ocus aeineich. cánas ar fríth sin ar Pátraic. adér frit a fhírinne a anam ar Cáilte:—

Oclách do búi ac Fionn .i. Artúir mac benne brit ocus ba hedh a líon trí naenbair. ocus dorónadh selg beinne hEdair le Fionn. ocus ba tuillmech toirtech in tselg soin. ocus do scáilset dá conaib ocus do shuid Fionn i carn in fhéinnedha idir beinn Edair ocus muir. ocus ba maith lais a menma ag éisdecht re raibhcedaig na ndam ndíscir ndásachtach acá lúthmarbad do chonaib na féinne.

Of the Reasons for the Migration of the Déssi:

Eochaid went over the sea to the territory of Dyfed and it is there that he died, and his sons and his descendants. And from them [come] the kindred of Crimthan to this day, of which is Taulodar son of Rigin son of Catien son of Clothien son of Noé son of Artúr son of Petor son of Congar son of Goirtiben son of Alcon son of Tresun son of Áed son of Brosc son of Corach son of Eochaid the Foreigner son of Art Corp.

***

The Colloquy with the Ancients:

'Did you have horses, or cavalry, with you in the Fíanna?' 'We had indeed;' said Cáilte, 'thrice fifty foals from one mare and one stallion.' 'Whence were they procured?', said Patrick. 'I will tell you the truth of the matter.', said Cáilte:—

'There was a young man serving with Finn, Artúr son of Béine Brit, and his complement was thrice nine men. Finn set on foot the hunting of Ben-Edar (and that hunt was bountiful and fruitful.) They slipped their hounds while Finn took his seat on the Cairn of the Fian between Benn Edair and the sea; and his spirit was glad within him to listen to the bellowing of the maddened stags during their rapid killing by the hounds of the Fíanna.

Is ann dorala d'Artúir mac Béine brit beith ac coiméd in mara idir an [fi]adach ocus muir co nach snáimdís in [damhrad] uatha. ocus mar do bhí Artúir amuich i cionn in chuain atchonnaic trí coin do chonaib Finn .i. Bran ocus Sceolaing ocus Adhnuall. ocus is í comairle ar ar chinn Artúir .i. é féin ocus a trí nónbair do imthecht tar muir ocus na coin sin do breith leis ina tír féin. ocus do críchnaigedh in comairle sin. dóig ám do chuadarsom tar muinchionn mara ocus na trí coin sin leo. ocus ro gabsat cuan ocus calad ac innber mara gaimiach i crích Bretan. ocus tiagat a tír ocus lotar rompa co sliab Lodáin meic Lir ocus dorónad selg in tsléibe sin acu.

...

'Where Artúr son of Béine Brit was stationed was between the main body of the hunt and the sea, so that the deer might not take to the sea and elude them by swimming. But Artúr, being thus on the outside and close against the shore, marked three of Finn's hounds, Bran, Sceolaing and Adnuall, and he resolved on a plan: himself and his three nines to depart away across the sea, he carrying off with him into his own land those same three hounds. And that plot was put into action. For well I know that they went over the sea's surface, and the three hounds with them, and took harbour and haven at Inber Mara Gaimiach in the land of Britain. They landed there and proceeded to the mountain of Lodán son of Lir, and they hunted on that mountain.

...

[The Fíanna, meanwhile, brought their hunt to an end and, when they counted the hounds, discovered the shortfall. By means of his tooth of knowledge Finn found out that the three hounds had been stolen by 'the son of the King of Britain', and he resolved to choose nine men to bring them back. Those nine were Diarmaid mac Duinn, Goll mac Mórna, Caol Ciódha, Oisín mac Finn, Oscar mac Oisín, Ferdoman mac Buidhb Derg, Raighne mac Finn, Cuinche mac Finn, Glas mac Áincherda Bera (and a tenth, Cáilte). The chosen Fíanna came to Lodán's mountain and found Artúr and his men.]

Dála Artúir meic Béine brit do eisid ina dhuma shelga ann sin cona mhuintir. innsaigter linne iat co hathlamh ocus ro mharbsam muintir Artúir uile. ocus iadhus Oscar a dá láim um Artúir ocus ainicios é. ocus tucsam ár trí coin linn. ocus déchain ro dhéc Goll mac Mórna secha confaca in tech bocóidech dubghorm co srian co cumdach óir fria. ocus in décsain ro dhéc dá láimh clí confaca in nech ndonn ndóghabla ocus srian línaide láingel d'airget aith[legtha] fria co mbéilgib óir fris. ocus g[abus G]oll in tech sin ocus cuiris í i láim Oisín ocus cuiris Oisín illáim Diarmada í Dhuibne. ocus táncamar romainn iar mbuaid coscair ocus commáidme ocus cinn na trí naonbar linn. ocus ár coin ocus ár neich ocus Artúir féin i láim. co hairm ambúi Fionn co senmag nelta nEdair. ocus táncamar ar in pubaill arraibe in rígfeinnid ocus atbert Cáilte: do ratsamar Artúir linn. conderna a cura re Fionn comba óglách d'Fionn iar soin cusin laithe luid d'écaib. ocus tucsam in dá nech sin d'Fionn .i. in feirech ocus in bainech. ocus is dá síol sin do bí echrad na féinne uile. ór nír chlechtsat eich co sin.'

'As for Artúr son of Béine Brit, he was sitting there on his hunting-mound with his retinue. We charge them in lively fashion and kill all Artúr's retinue, but Oscar flings his arms about Artúr and gives him quarter. So we got our three hounds. Here Goll son of Mórna chancing to look about him saw an iron-grey horse, flecked with white spots, and wearing a bridle fitted with wrought ornament of gold. At another glance that he threw to his left he discerned a bay horse (one not easy to lay hold of) and having a reticulated bridle of twice refined silver fitted with a golden bit. Goll son of Mórna seized this horse also and put it into the hand of Oisín, who passed him on to Diarmaid ua Dhuibne. After successfully carrying it out and duly celebrating our slaughter we came away, and the heads of those three nines with us, and our hounds, our horses, and Artúr himself as a prisoner, to where Finn was at the old *magh nelta* of Edar. We reached his tent, that of the ruler of the Fíanna, and Cáilte said, 'We have brought Artúr.' This latter entered into bonds with Finn, and thereafter, up to the day that he died, was Finn's follower. We gave the two horses to Finn, the stallion and the mare, of whose seed were all the horses of the Fíanna, who hitherto had not used any such.'

Bibliography

Anderson, A.O. and M.O. *Adomnán's Life of Columba* (London 1961)

Bannerman, J. *Studies in the History of Dalriada* (Edinburgh 1974)

Barber, Richard *The Figure of Arthur* (London 1972)

Bartum, P.C. *Early Welsh Genealogical Tracts* (Cardiff 1966)

Bollard, John K. 'Arthur in the Early Welsh Tradition' pp.13—25 in *The Romance of Arthur* edd. Wilhelm & Gross (New York 1984)

de la Borderie, A. 'L'*Historia Britannica* avant Geoffroi de Monmouth et la vie inédite de S. Goueznou' pp.225—46 in *Bulletin de la Société Archéologique du Finistère* (1882)

—— 'St. Efflam. Texte inédit de la vie ancienne de ce saint avec notes et commentaire historique' pp.279—312 in *Annales de Bretagne* 7 (1891)

Bromwich, Rachel 'Concepts of Arthur' pp.163—81 in *Studia Celtica* 10/11 (1975—76)

—— *Trioedd Ynys Prydein* (Cardiff 1961; 2nd edn. 1978)

—— *Armes Prydein: The prophecy of Britain from the Book of Taliesin* (Dublin 1982) [Originally edited and annotated by Sir Ifor Williams in Welsh.]

—— 'Celtic Elements in Arthurian Romance: a General Survey' pp.41—55 in *The Legend of Arthur in the Middle Ages* edd. Grout, Lodge, Pickford & Varty (Cambridge 1983)

Bromwich, Rachel & D. Simon Evans *Culhwch and Olwen: a Study and Edition of the Oldest Arthurian Tale* (Cardiff 1992)

Budgey, Andrea '"Preiddeu Annwn" and the Welsh Tradition of Arthur' pp.391—404 in *Celtic Languages and Celtic Peoples: Proceedings of the Second North American Congress of Celtic Studies* edd. Byrne, Harry & Ó Siadhail

Bullock-Davies, Constance '"Exspectare Arthurum" Arthur and the Messianic Hope' pp.432—40 in *Bulletin of the Board of Celtic Studies* 29 (1981)

Chadwick, Nora K. 'The Lost Literature of Celtic Scotland: Caw of Pritdin and Arthur of Britain' pp.115—83 in *Scottish Gaelic Studies* 7 (1953)

Chambers, E.K. *Arthur of Britain: the Story of King Arthur in History and Legend* (London 1927)

Charles-Edwards, Thomas 'The Arthur of History' pp.15—32 in *The Arthur of the Welsh: the Arthurian Legend in Medieval Welsh Literature* edd. Bromwich, Jarman & Roberts (Cardiff 1991)

Dumville, David N. 'The Liber Floridus of Lambert of Saint-Omer and the *Historia Brittonum*' *Bulletin of the Board of Celtic Studies* 26 (1974—6) pp.103—122 [also to be found in *Histories and Pseudo-Histories of the Insular Middle Ages* (Great Yarmouth 1990)]

—— 'Celtic-Latin texts in northern England, c.1150—c.1250' in *Celtica* 12 (1977) [also to be found in *Histories and Pseudo-Histories of the Insular Middle Ages* (Great Yarmouth 1990)]

—— 'The Historical Value of the *Historia Brittonum*' pp.1—26 in *Arthurian Literature* 6 (Cambridge 1986) [also to be found in *Histories and Pseudo-Histories of the Insular Middle Ages* (Great Yarmouth 1990)]

—— 'Kingship, Genealogies and Regnal Lists' pp.72—104 in *Early Medieval Kingship* edd. P.H. Sawyer and I.N. Wood (Leeds 1987) [also to be found in *Histories and Pseudo-Histories of the Insular Middle Ages* (Great Yarmouth 1990)]

—— '*Historia Brittonum*: an Insular history from the Carolingian Age', in *Historiographie im frühen Mittelalter*, edd. A. Scharer and G. Scheibelreiter (Vienna 1994)

Edel, Doris 'The catalogues in *Culhwch ac Olwen* and Insular Celtic learning' pp.253—73 in *Bulletin of the Board of Celtic Studies* 30 (1983)

—— 'The Arthur of *Culhwch ac Olwen* as a Figure of Epic Heroic Tradition' pp.3—15 in *Reading Medieval Studies* 9 (1983)

Evans, J.G. *Report on Manuscripts in the Welsh Language* (London 1898—1910)

—— *The Book of Taliesin: Facsimile and Text* (Llanbedrog 1910)

Ford, Patrick K. *The Mabinogi and Other Medieval Welsh Tales* (Los Angeles 1977)

Foster, Idris L. '*Culhwch and Olwen* and *Rhonabwy's Dream*' pp.31—43 in *Arthurian Literature in the Middle Ages: a Collaborative History* ed. Loomis (Oxford 1959)

Gillies, William 'Arthur in Gaelic Tradition, Part II: Romances and Learned Lore' pp.41—75 in *Cambridge Medieval Celtic Studies* 3 (Summer 1982)

Haycock, Marged '"Preiddeu Annwn" and the Figure of Taliesin' pp.52—78 in *Studia Celtica* 18/19 (1983—84)

—— *Blodeugerdd Barddas o Ganu Crefyddol Cynnar* (Llandybïe 1994)

Henken, Elissa R. *Traditions of the Welsh Saints* (Cambridge N.H. 1987)

—— *The Welsh Saints: a Study in Patterned Lives* (Cambridge N.H. 1991)

Higham, N.J. *The English Conquest: Gildas and Britain in the Fifth Century* (Oxford 1994)

Hughes, K. 'The *Annales Cambriae* and Related Texts' pp.233—58 in *Proceedings of the British Academy* 59 (1973)

Jackson, Kenneth H. 'The Arthur of History' pp.1—11 in *Arthurian Literature in the Middle Ages: a Collaborative History* ed. Loomis (Oxford 1959)

—— 'Arthur in Early Welsh Verse' pp.12—19 in *Arthurian Literature in the Middle Ages: a Collaborative History* ed. Loomis (Oxford 1959)

—— *The Gododdin: the Earliest Scottish Poem* (Edinburgh 1969; 2nd edn. 1978)

Jarman, A.O.H. *Llyfr Du Caerfyrddin* (Cardiff 1982)

—— 'The Arthurian Allusions in the Black Book of Carmarthen' pp.99—112 in *The Legend of Arthur in the Middle Ages* edd. Grout, Lodge, Pickford & Varty (Cambridge 1983)

—— *Aneirin: Y Gododdin, Britain's Oldest Heroic Poem* (Llandysul 1988)

—— 'The Arthurian Allusions in the Book of Aneirin' pp.15—25 in *Studia Celtica* 24/5 (1989—90)

Jones, Evans D. 'Melvas, Gwenhwyfar a Chai' pp.203—08 in *Bulletin of the Board of Celtic Studies* 8 (1935—37)

Jones, Thomas 'The Early Evolution of the Legend of Arthur' in *Nottingham Medieval Studies* 8 (1964)

—— 'The Black Book of Carmarthen: Stanzas of the Graves' pp.97—137 in *Proceedings of the British Academy* 53 (1967)

Lapidge, M. & D.N. Dumville *Gildas: New Approaches* (Woodbridge 1984)

Loomis, R.S. *Wales and the Arthurian Legend* (Cardiff 1956)

—— 'The Tale of *Culhwch and Olwen*' pp.27—55 in *The Romance of Arthur* edd. Wilhem & Gross (New York 1984)

Meyer, Kuno 'The Expulsion of the Déssi' pp.135—42 in *Ériu* 3 (1907)

Migne, J.-P. *Patrologia Latina* 156 (Paris 1853)

Mommsen, Theodore *Monumenta Germanica Historica: Auctores Antiquissimi Chronicorum Minorum Saec. IV,V,VI,VII,* Vol.13 (1892)

Moorman, Charles '"Yet some men say...that kynge Arthure ys nat ded."' pp.188—99 in *The Arthurian Tradition* edd. Braswell and Bulee (Alabama 1988)

Morris, John *Nennius: British History and the Welsh Annals* (London 1980)

O'Grady, Standish H. *Silva Gadelica: a Collection of Tales in Irish* (2 vols.) (London 1892)

Padel, Oliver 'The Nature of Arthur', pp.1—31 in *Cambrian Medieval Celtic Studies* 27 (Summer 1994)

Parry, John Jay *Brut Y Brenhinedd: Cotton Cleopatra Version* (Cambridge MA 1937)

Philimore, E. [article on the Jesus MS.] pp.83—92 in *Y Cymmrodor* 8 (1887)

Roberts, Brynley F. *Brut y Brehinedd* (Dublin 1971)

—— 'Rhai o Gerddi Ymddiddan Llyfr Du Caerfyrddin' pp.281—325 in *Astudiaethau ar yr Hengerdd: Studies in Old Welsh Poetry* edd. Bromwich & Jones (Caerdydd 1978)

—— '*Culhwch ac Olwen*, The Triads, Saints' Lives' pp.73—95 in *The Arthur of the Welsh: the Arthurian Legend in Medieval Welsh Literature* edd. Bromwich, Jarman & Roberts (Cardiff 1991)

—— 'Geoffrey of Monmouth, *Historia Regum Britanniae* and *Brut y Brenhinedd*' pp.97—116 in *The Arthur of the Welsh: the Arthurian Legend in Medieval Welsh Literature* edd. Bromwich, Jarman & Roberts (Cardiff 1991)

Rowland, Jenny *Early Welsh Saga Poetry: a Study and Edition of the Englynion* (Cambridge 1990)

Sims-Williams, Patrick P. 'Some Functions of Origin Stories in Early Medieval Wales' pp.97—132 in *History and Heroic Tale: a Symposium* ed. Nyberg (Odense 1986)

—— 'The Early Welsh Arthurian Poems' pp.33—71 in *The Arthur of the Welsh: the Arthurian legend in Medieval Welsh Literature* edd. Bromwich, Jarman & Roberts (Cardiff 1991)

Skene, William F. *The Four Ancient Books of Wales Containing the Cymric Poems Attributed to the Bards of the Sixth Century* (2 vols.) (Edinburgh 1868)

Tatlock, J.S.P. 'The English Journey of the Laon Canons' pp.454—65 in *Speculum* 8 (1933)

Thompson, E.A. *St. Germanus of Auxerre and the Fall of Roman Britain* (Woodbridge 1984)

Thorpe, Lewis *Geoffrey of Monmouth: The History of the Kings of Britain* (London 1966)

Wade-Evans, A.W. [article on Peniarth MS. 27] pp.363—7 in *Revue Celtique* 50 (1933)

—— *Vitae Sanctorum Britanniae et Genealogiae* (Cardiff 1944)

Ward, Charlotte 'Arthur in the Welsh Bruts', pp.383—90 in *Celtic Languages and Celtic Peoples: Proceedings of the Second North American Congress of Celtic Studies edd. Byrne, Harry & Ó Siadhail*

Williams, Hugh *Two Lives of Gildas by a Monk of Ruys and Caradoc of Llancarfan* (Llanerch 1990; repr. of 1899 original)

Williams, H. *Gildae De Excido Britanniae,* Cymmrodorion Record Series III-IV (London 1899-1901)

Williams, Ifor 'Ymddiddan Arthur a'r Eryr' pp.269—86 in *The Bulletin of the Board of Celtic Studies* 2 (1925)

—— *Lectures on Early Welsh Poetry* (Dublin: DIAS 1944; repr. 1970)

Williams, John ab Ithel *Annales Cambriæ* (London 1860)

Williams, Mary 'An Early Ritual Poem in Welsh' pp.38—51 in *Speculum* 13 (1938)

Winterbottom, Michael *Gildas: The Ruin of Britain and Other Works* (London 1978)

Appendix

Unfortunately it has not proved possible to make this collection of the Celtic Arthurian sources entirely complete. Here below are references for additional material:

Chwedl Huail ap Caw ac Arthur

This Welsh tale accounts for the enmity between Arthur and Huail, referred to in *Culhwch ac Olwen*.

See:

Jones, Thomas 'Chwedl Huail ap Caw ac Arthur' pp.48—66 in *Astudiaethau Amrywiol a gyflwynir i Syr Thomas Parry-Williams* (Cardiff: UWP 1968)

Ymddiddan Arthur a'i Chwaer

This dialogue (some verse and some prose) is found in a late manuscript (NLW 1677), written by Walter Davies.

See:

Thomas, Graham C.J. 'Llen Arthur a Maen a Modrwy Luned' (University of Wales M.A., 1976)

The Trystan Englynion

There are many versions of the Tristan story in Welsh, all showing signs of influence from Welsh tradition. Arthur plays the role of peacemaker between Mark and Tristan.

See:

Cross, T.P. 'A Welsh Tristan Episode' pp.98—110 in *Studies in Philology* 17 (1920)

Jones, E.D. 'Trystan ac Esyllt' pp.25—27 in *Bulletin of the Board of Celtic Studies* 13 (1948)

Rowland, Jenny and Graham C.G. Thomas 'Additional Versions of the Trystan *Englynion* and Prose' pp.241—53 in *National Library of Wales Journal* 22 (1982)

Thomson, R.L. 'The Welsh Fragment of Tristan (Trystan ac Esyllt)' pp.1—5 in *The Tristan Legend* ed. Hill (Leeds 1977)

Williams, Ifor 'Trystan ac Esyllt' pp.115—29 in *Bulletin of the Board of Celtic Studies* 5 (1930)

The Three Romances and the Dream of Rhonabwy

The Welsh Romances *Owein, Peredur* and *Geraint* (corresponding to Chretien de Troyes's *Yvain, Perceval* and *Erec* respectively) hang under a cloud of suspicion regarding their relationship with the Continental Arthurian tales, so their usefulness in determining the nature of the 'Celtic Arthur' is dubious. *The Dream of Rhonabwy,* on the other hand, is more fully acknowledged as a native work, but does not seem to have been a traditional tale.

See:

Jones, Gwyn and Thomas Jones *The Mabinogion* (London: J.M. Dent 1949)

Santez Tryphina hag ar Roue Arzur

The late Breton tale of Saint Tryphina and King Arthur identifies the saint's husband, Arzur, as King Arthur; however, this identification is probably wrong.

See:

Luzel, F.-M. *Sainte Tryphine et le roi Arthur. Mystère Breton* (Quimperlé: Clairet 1863)

Gerald of Wales

In two of his works (*De Principis Instructione* and *Speculum Ecclesiae*) Gerald of Wales discusses the discovery of Arthur's body at Glastonbury.

See:

Thorpe, Lewis 'Gerald of Wales and King Arthur' in *The Journey Through Wales and the Description of Wales* (Harmondsworth: Penguin 1978), pp.281—88

Also published by Llanerch:

Symbolism of the Celtic Cross,
Derek Bryce.

Names from the Dawn of British Legend:
Merlin, Arthur, Taliesin, Aneirin,
Toby D. Griffen.

Sir Gawain at the Grail Castle,
translated by Jessie L. Weston.

Sir Gawain and the Lady of Lys,
translated by Jessie L. Weston.

Guingamor, Tyolet, Lanvel and the Were-wolf,
translated by Jessie L. Weston.

Arthurian Localities (in Scotland),
S. Stuart Glennie.

Taliesin Poems,
translated by Meirion Pennar.

The Black Book of Carmarthen,
selected translations by Meirion Pennar.

For a complete list, write to:
LLANERCH PUBLISHERS,
Felinfach, Lampeter, Dyfed,
Wales, SA48 8PJ.